ARMSTRONG'S ESSENTIAL

HUMAN RESOURCE MANAGEMENT PRACTICE

ARMSTRONG'S ESSENTIAL

HUMAN RESOURCE MANAGEMENT PRACTICE

A GUIDE TO PEOPLE MANAGEMENT

Michael Armstrong

KoganPage

LONDON PHILADELPHIA NEW DELHI

First published in Great Britain and the United States in 2010 by Kogan Page Limited

120 Pentonville Road	525 South 4th Street, #241	4737/23 Ansari Road
London N1 9JN	Philadelphia PA 19147	Daryaganj
United Kingdom	USA	New Delhi 110002
www.koganpage.com		India

© Michael Armstrong, 2010

The right of Michael Armstrong to be identified as the author of this work has been asserted by him in accordance with the Copyright, Designs and Patents Act 1988.

ISBN   978 0 7494 5989 5
E-ISBN   978 0 7494 5990 1

British Library Cataloguing-in-Publication Data

A CIP record for this book is available from the British Library.

Library of Congress Cataloging-in-Publication Data

Armstrong, Michael, 1928–
    Armstrong's essential human resource management practice : a guide to people management / Michael Armstrong.
        p. cm.
    ISBN 978-0-7494-5989-5 — ISBN 978-0-7494-5990-1 (ebook)   1. Personnel management—Handbooks, manuals, etc.   I. Title.   II. Title: Essential human resource management practice.
    HF5549.17.A758 2010
    658.3—dc22
                                                                                                                        2010000341

Typeset by Graphicraft Limited, Hong Kong
Printed and bound in India by Replika Press Pvt Ltd

Contents

This book is accompanied by additional online material. To access these resources go to
www.koganpage.com/resources and under 'Academic Resources' click on either 'Student
Resources' or 'Lecturer Resources' as appropriate.

Introduction

This book describes the essential features of human resource management (HRM). The aim is to provide practitioners and students with a succinct picture of the key processes and activities involved in managing people. The practical approaches to HRM described in the book are backed up with evidence from research. Critical evaluations are included for the following key HRM theories and concepts:

- HRM itself;
- the role of HR business partner;
- strategy;
- strategic HRM;
- the resource-based view;
- the choice between best practice and best fit;
- bundling;
- human capital measurement;
- motivation theory;
- emotional intelligence;
- the flexible firm;
- the learning organization;
- financial rewards.

Underpinning philosophy

The philosophy underpinning this book was well-expressed by Schneider (1987). He wrote that: 'Organizations are the people in them… people make the place.' His point was that:

Attraction to an organization, selection by it, and attrition from it yield particular kinds of persons in an organization. These people determine organizational behaviour... Positive job attitudes for workers in an organization can be expected when the natural inclinations of the persons there are allowed to be reflected in their behaviours by the kinds of processes and structures that have evolved there.

HRM has to serve the interests of the business but it must also be concerned with the interests of the people in the business. A stakeholder approach is adopted throughout the book. In accordance with the views of Freeman (1984), management, and this includes HR specialists, must satisfy a variety of constituents comprising employees, customers and the community at large as well as shareholders or, in the public or voluntary sectors, those who have the ultimate responsibility for what the organization does.

There is an important ethical dimension to HRM. As Boxall *et al* (2007) point out: 'While HRM does need to support commercial outcomes (often called "the business case"), it also exists to serve organizational needs for social legitimacy.' This means exercising social responsibility, or in other words being concerned for the interests (well-being) of employees and acting ethically with regard to the needs of people in the organization and the community.

Plan of the book

The book is dived into four Parts and an Appendix.

Part I   Human Resource Management

Part I deals with the fundamentals of HRM. It starts with a general review of the practice of HRM. It continues with a description of the processes that provide guidelines on the direction, scope and application of HRM, namely strategic HRM and HR policies and procedures. The need to base HRM decisions on data and information relating to the use and development of the organization's human capital is dealt with in Chapter 4, and the associated topic of knowledge management – increasing organizational capability by sharing the wisdom, understanding and expertise accumulated in a business about its processes, techniques and operations – is covered in Chapter 5. The requirement for organizations to conduct their business in an ethical way, taking account of the social, environmental and economic impact of how they operate, and going beyond compliance, is emphasized in Chapter 6. The final chapter of Part 1 recognizes that organizations operate in a global context, and explores the particular factors that affect international HRM.

Part II   Organizations and people

Part II recognizes that HRM takes place within the context of organizations, in which the way people behave and how the organizations of which they are members function will govern HRM policy and practice. It also deals with the concept of employee engagement, which is becoming increasingly prominent in people management, but which is often presented as a mantra without being properly understood. Chapter 9 examines the concept in detail by reference to recent research.

Part III   HRM practice

This is the heart of the book. It deals with:

- the basic HRM activities of competency-based HRM, job/role analysis and design;
- people resourcing;
- learning and development;
- managing performance;
- reward management;
- employee relations;
- providing for the well-being of employees.

Part IV   People management skills

The activities described in Part IV all require people management skills from line managers as well as HR specialists. The following skills are covered in this part:

- managing change;
- leadership;
- selection interviewing;
- performance management;
- learning and development;
- managing conflict;
- handling people problems.

Appendix   HRM research methods

This appendix describes the approaches and techniques used in conducting HRM research projects.

References

Boxall, P F, Purcell, J and Wright, P (2007) The goals of HRM, in *Oxford Handbook of Human Resource Management*, ed P Boxall, J Purcell and P Wright, Oxford University Press, Oxford

Freeman, R E (1984) *Strategic Management: A stakeholder perspective*, Prentice Hall, Englewood Cliffs, New Jersey

Schneider, B (1987) The people make the place, *Personnel Psychology*, **40** (2), pp 437–53

Part I
Human Resource Management

The Practice of
Human Resource Management

Key concepts and terms

- Business partner
- Centre of expertise
- Commitment
- Contingency theory
- Hard HRM
- HR philosophy
- HR policies
- HR practices
- HR processes
- HR programmes
- HR strategies
- HR system
- Human resource management
- Humanism
- Mutuality
- Organizational capability
- Shared service centre
- Soft HRM
- Strategic business partner
- Strategic integration

Learning outcomes

On completing this chapter you should be able to define these key concepts. You should also understand:

- The meaning and aims of human resource management (HRM)
- That HRM in practice is highly diverse
- How HRM functions as a system
- The ethical dimension of HRM
- The impact of HRM on performance
- The HRM role of line managers
- The role of the HR function

Introduction

The practice of Human Resource Management (HRM) is concerned with all aspects of how people are employed and managed in organizations. It covers activities such as:

- strategic HRM;
- human capital management;
- knowledge management;
- organization development;
- resourcing (human resource planning, recruitment and selection, and talent management);
- performance management;
- learning and development;
- reward management
- employee relations;
- employee well-being.

HRM can be described as a strategic, integrated and coherent approach to the employment, development and well-being of the people working in organizations. It has a strong conceptual basis drawn from the behavioural sciences and from strategic management, human capital and industrial relations theories. This foundation has been built with the help of a multitude of research projects.

The aims of this chapter are to provide a general introduction to the practice and underpinning concepts of HRM and to outline the HRM roles of line managers and the Human Resources (HR) function.

The philosophy of HRM

As originally conceived by the pioneers in the 1980s, the concept of HRM was based on a philosophy which was fundamentally different from the personnel management practices of the time. Beer *et al* (1984) believed that 'Today, many pressures are demanding a broader, more comprehensive and more strategic perspective with regard to the organization's human resources... These pressures have created a need for a longer-term perspective in managing people and consideration of people as potential assets rather than merely a variable cost.'

Beer and his colleagues (the Harvard school) were the first to underline the HRM tenet that it belongs to line managers. They suggested that HRM has two characteristic features, first, that line managers accept more responsibility for ensuring the alignment of competitive strategy and HR policies, and second, that HR has the mission of setting policies that govern how HR activities are developed and implemented in ways that make them more mutually reinforcing.

Fombrum *et al* (1984) held that HR systems and the organization structure should be managed in a way that is congruent with organizational strategy.

A full explanation of HRM philosophy by Legge (1989) stated that HRM consists of the following propositions:

> *That human resource policies should be integrated with strategic business planning and used to reinforce an appropriate (or change an inappropriate) organizational culture, that human resources are valuable and a source of competitive advantage, that they may be tapped most effectively by mutually consistent policies that promote commitment and which, as a consequence, foster a willingness in employees to act flexibly in the interests of the 'adaptive organization's' pursuit of excellence.*

The philosophy underpinning this notion of HRM provided a new vision which was strongly criticized by many commentators during the 1990s (see the critical evaluation of HRM at the end of this chapter). It was supposed to be substantially different from old-fashioned personnel management, a term which has virtually disappeared since then, although in some quarters the term 'people management' has been adopted, possibly by those who dislike the connotations of 'human resources' with its apparent emphasis on exploitation and treating people as factors of production. However, whether it is called human resource management or people management, the essential nature of the ways in which organizations manage and relate to their employees has not always changed significantly from that of personnel management, although new techniques may have been introduced. In 2000 I asked the question 'The name has changed but has the game remained the same?' and answered it with a broad affirmative.

A more recent and less philosophical reference to HRM was made by Boxall *et al* (2007), who defined it as 'The management of work and people towards desired ends.'

The purpose of HRM

The overall purpose of HRM (or people management) is to ensure that the organization is able to achieve success through people. HRM aims to increase organizational effectiveness and capability – the capacity of an organization to achieve its goals by making the best use of the resources available to it. Ulrich and Lake (1990) remarked that 'HRM systems can be the source of organizational capabilities that allow firms to learn and capitalize on new opportunities.' The following policy goals for HRM were suggested by David Guest.

Policy goals of HRM

1. Strategic integration: the ability of the organization to integrate HRM issues into its strategic plans, ensure that the various aspects of HRM cohere, and provide for line managers to incorporate an HRM perspective into their decision making.

2. High commitment: behavioural commitment to pursue agreed goals, and attitudinal commitment reflected in a strong identification with the enterprise.

3. High quality: this refers to all aspects of managerial behaviour which bear directly on the quality of goods and services provided, including the management of employees and investment in high-quality employees.

4. Flexibility: functional flexibility and the existence of an adaptable organization structure with the capacity to manage innovation.

Source: Guest (1991).

The policy goals for HRM identified by Caldwell (2001) included managing people as assets which are fundamental to the competitive advantage of the organization, aligning HRM policies with business policies and corporate strategy, and developing a close fit of HR policies, procedures and systems with one another.

HRM also has an ethical dimension, which means that it expresses its concern for the rights and needs of people in organizations through the exercise of social responsibility.

The diversity of HRM

There are no universal characteristics of HRM. Many models exist, and practices within different organizations are diverse, often only corresponding to the conceptual version of HRM in a few respects. Boxall *et al* (2007) remarked that 'Human resource management covers a vast array of activities and shows a huge range of variations across occupations, organizational levels, business units, firms, industries and societies.'

A distinction was made by Storey (1989) between the 'hard' and 'soft' versions of HRM. The hard version of HRM emphasizes that people are important resources through which organizations achieve competitive advantage. These resources have therefore to be acquired, developed and deployed in ways that will benefit the organization. The focus is on the quantitative, calculative and business-strategic aspects of managing human resources in as 'rational' a way as for any other economic factor.

The soft version of HRM has its roots in humanism – an approach devoted to human interests which views people as responsible and progressive beings. It also trace its origins to the human relations school, as founded by Elton Mayo (1933), which believed that productivity was directly related to job satisfaction and that the output of people will be high if they like their co-workers and are given pleasant supervision. But this is a fairly remote connection. Soft HRM as described by Storey (1989) involves 'treating employees as valued assets, a source of competitive advantage through their commitment, adaptability and high quality (of skills, performance and so on)'. The emphasis is on the need to gain the commitment – the 'hearts and minds' – of employees through involvement, communications, leadership and other methods of developing a high-commitment, high-trust organization. It was advocated by, among others, Walton (1985), who focused attention on his principle of 'mutuality' (a state that exists when management and employees are interdependent and both benefit from this interdependency) and the move from control to commitment. Attention is also drawn to the key role of organizational culture.

It has, however, been observed by Truss (1999) that 'even if the rhetoric of HRM is soft, the reality is often hard, with the interests of the organization prevailing over those of the individual'. And research carried out by Gratton et al (1999) found that in the eight organizations they studied, a mixture of hard and soft HRM approaches was identified. This suggested to the researchers that the distinction between hard and soft HRM was not as precise as some commentators have implied.

But as Dyer and Holder (1998) emphasized, 'HRM goals vary according to competitive choices, technologies or service tangibles, characteristics of their employees (eg could be different for managers), the state of the labour market and the societal regulations and national culture', and Boxall et al (2007) noted that 'The general motives of HRM are multiple.'

HRM as a system

In its traditional form, HRM, as pointed out by Boselie et al (2005), can be viewed as 'a collection of multiple discrete practices with no explicit or discernible link between them'. In contrast 'the more strategically minded systems approach views HRM as an integrated and coherent bundle of mutually reinforcing practices'. Kepes and Delery (2007) comment that a defining characteristic of HRM is that HRM systems and not individual HRM practices are the source of competitive advantage: 'Coherent and internally aligned systems form powerful connections that create positive synergistic effects on organizational outcomes.'

As illustrated in Figure 1.1, an HRM system brings together HR philosophies which describe the overarching values and guiding principles adopted in managing people, HR strategies which define the direction in which HRM intends to go, HR policies which provide guidelines defining how these values, principles and strategies should be applied and implemented in

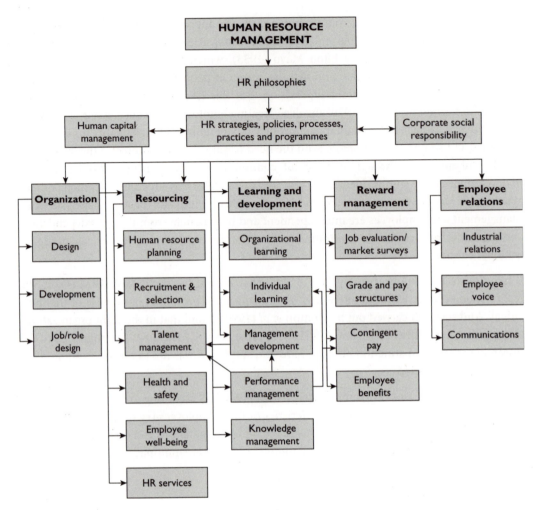

Figure 1.1   The HRM system

specific areas of HRM, HR processes which comprise the formal procedures and methods used to put HR strategic plans and policies into effect, linked HR practices which consist of the approaches used in managing people, and HR programmes which enable HR strategies, policies and practices to be implemented according to plan.

The context of HRM

HRM processes take place within the context of the internal and external environments of the organization. In line with contingency theory, these exert considerable influence on the decision over which HR practices are adopted.

The external environment

The external environment consists of social, political, legal and economic developments and competitive pressures. Global competition in mature production and service sectors is increasing. This is assisted by easily transferable technology and reductions in international trade barriers. Customers are demanding more as new standards are reached through international competition. Organizations are reacting to this competition by becoming 'customer focused', speeding up response times, emphasizing quality and continuous improvement, accelerating the introduction of new technology, operating more flexibly and 'losing cost'. The pressure has been for businesses to become 'lean and mean', downsizing and cutting out layers of management and supervision. They reduce permanent staff to a core of essential workers, increase the use of peripheral workers (subcontractors, temporary staff) and 'outsource' work to external service providers. These pressures can be considerable in an economic downturn such as the one beginning in 2008.

The internal environment

The following aspects of the internal environment will affect HR policy and practice:

- the type of business or organization – private, public or voluntary sector; manufacturing or service;
- the size of the organization;
- the age or maturity of the organization;
- the technology or key activities of the business will determine how work is organized, managed and carried out;
- the type of people employed, such as professional staff, knowledge workers, technicians, administrators, production workers, and sales and customer service staff;
- the financial circumstances of the organization, especially in economic downturns;
- the organization's culture – the established pattern of values, norms, beliefs, attitudes and assumptions which shape the ways in which people behave and things get done;
- the political and social climate.

Contingency theory

Contingency theory tells us that definitions of HR aims, policies and strategies, lists of activities, and analyses of the HRM roles of line managers and the role of the HR function are valid only if they are related to the situation of the organization in its environment. Karen Legge (1978) in her influential book *Power, Innovation and Problem Solving in Personnel Management* was the first commentator to insist that a contingent approach should be adopted: that is, 'the design and implementation of policy that matches, or is contingent upon specified organizational requirements and circumstances'.

As Paauwe (2004) explained, 'Contingency theory states that the relationship between the relevant independent variables (eg HRM policies and practices) and the dependent variable (performance) will vary according to the influences such as company size, age and technology, capital intensity, degree of unionization, industry/sector ownership and location.'

Contingency theory is associated with the concept of fit – the need to achieve congruence between an organization's HR strategies, policies and practices, and its business strategies, within the context of its external and internal environment.

The ethical dimension

As Boxall *et al* (2007) point out, 'While HRM does need to support commercial outcomes (often called "the business case"), it also exists to serve organizational needs for social legitimacy.' This means exercising social responsibility, or in other words being concerned for the interests (well-being) of employees and acting ethically with regard to the needs of people in the organization and the community.

Within the organization the requirement is to:

- Treat people equally in terms of the opportunities for employment, learning and development provided for them.

- Treat people according to the principle of procedural justice (Adams, 1965; Leventhal, 1980): that is, the ways in which people are managed are fair, consistent, transparent, and properly consider the views and needs of employees.

- Treat people according to the principles of distributive justice (Adams, 1965; Leventhal, 1980): in other words, rewards are distributed to them according to their contribution and they receive what was promised to them.

- Treat people according to the principles of natural justice: individuals should know the standards they are expected to achieve and the rules to which they are expected to conform, they should be given a clear indication of where they are failing or what rules have been broken, and except in cases of gross misconduct, they should be given a chance to improve before disciplinary action is taken.

- Treat people with respect.

- Avoid treating people as mere factors of production.

- Be concerned with the well-being of employees as well as the pursuit of commercial gain.

- Offer as much security of employment as possible.

- Provide a working environment that protects the health and safety of employees and minimizes stress.

- Act in the interests of providing a reasonable balance for employees between their life and their work.

- Protect employees against harmful practices at work, such as bullying, harassment and discrimination.

The impact of HRM on performance

As Guest (1997) argues, 'The distinctive feature of HRM is its assumption that improved performance is achieved through the people in the organization.' If, therefore, appropriate HR policies and processes are introduced, it can also be assumed that HRM will make a substantial impact on firm performance.

The Holy Grail sought by many HRM researchers is to establish that HRM practices demonstrably cause improvements in organizational performance. HR practitioners too would like to be able to justify their existence by saying to their bosses and their colleagues that this is the case. Much research has been carried out over the last decade or so, most of which at shows that there is a link between good HRM practice and firm performance. Examples are given in Table 1.1.

How HRM practices make an impact is summarized in Table 1.2.

The HRM role of line managers

On the basis of their research, Guest and King (2004) noted that 'better HR depended not so much on better procedures but better implementation and ownership of implementation by line managers'.

As pointed out by Purcell *et al* (2003), high levels of organizational performance are not achieved simply by having a range of well-conceived HR policies and practices in place. What makes the difference is how these policies and practices are implemented. That is, where the role of line managers in people management is crucial: 'The way line managers implement and enact policies, show leadership in dealing with employees and in exercising control come through as a major issue.' Purcell *et al* noted that dealing with people is perhaps the aspect of their work in which line managers can exercise the greatest amount of discretion, and they can misuse that discretion by not putting HR's ideas into practice. As they point out, it is line managers who bring HR policies to life.

Table 1.1   Research on the link between HRM and firm performance

Researcher(s)	Methodology	Outcomes
Huselid (1995)	Analysis of the responses of 968 US firms to a questionnaire exploring the use of high-performance work practices.	Productivity is influenced by employee motivation; financial performance is influenced by employee skills, motivation and organizational structures.
Patterson *et al* (1997)	The research examined the link between business performance and organizational culture and the use of a number of HR practices.	HR practices explained significant variations in profitability and productivity (19 per cent and 18 per cent respectively). Two HR practices were particularly significant: (1) the acquisition and development of employee skills and (2) job design including flexibility, responsibility and variety.
Appelbaum *et al* (2000)	Study of the impact of high-performance work systems (HPWSs) in 44 manufacturing facilities – over 4,000 employees were surveyed.	HPWSs produced strong positive effects on performance. They are associated with workshop practices that raise the levels of trust, increase workers' intrinsic reward from work and thereby enhance organizational commitment.
Guest *et al* (2000)	The Future of Work Survey covered 835 private sector organizations. Interviews were carried out with 610 HR professionals and 462 chief executives.	A greater use of HR practices is associated with higher levels of employee commitment and contribution and is in turn linked to higher levels of productivity and quality of services.
Thompson (2002)	A study of the impact of high-performance work practices such as team working, appraisal, job rotation, broad-banded grade structures and sharing of business information in UK aerospace establishments.	The number of HR practices and the proportion of the workforce covered appeared to be the key differentiating factor between more and less successful firms.

Table 1.1   *continued*

Researcher(s)	Methodology	Outcomes
West *et al* (2002)	Research conducted in 61 UK hospitals obtaining information on HR strategy, policy and procedures from chief executives and HR directors and mortality rates.	An association between certain HR practices and lower mortality rates was identified. As noted by Professor West, 'If you have HR practices that focus on effort and skill; develop people's skills; encourage co-operation, collaboration, innovation and synergy in teams for most, if not all employees, the whole system functions and performs better.'
Purcell *et al* (2003)	A University of Bath longitudinal study of 12 companies to establish how people management impacts on organizational performance.	Policy and practice implementation (not the number of HR practices adopted) is the vital ingredient in linking people management to business performance and this is primarily the task of line managers.

A further factor affecting the role of line managers is their ability to do the HR tasks assigned to them. People-centred activities such as defining roles, interviewing, reviewing performance, providing feedback, coaching, identifying learning and development needs, and dealing with capability and conduct problems all require special skills. Some managers have them: many do not.

Hutchinson and Purcell (2003) made the following recommendations on how to improve the quality of the contribution line managers make to people management.

- Provide them with time to carry out their people management duties which are often superseded by other management duties.

- Select them carefully with much more attention being paid to the behavioural competencies required.

- Support them with strong organizational values concerning leadership and people management.

- Encourage the development of a good working relationship with their own managers.

- Ensure they receive sufficient skills training to enable them to perform their people management activities such as performance management.

Table 1.2   The HR practices that impact on performance

HR practice area	How it impacts
Attract, develop and retain high-quality people	Match people to the strategic and operational needs of the organization. Provide for the acquisition, development and retention of talented employees, who can deliver superior performance, productivity, flexibility, innovation, and high levels of personal customer service, and who 'fit' the culture and the strategic requirements of the organization.
Talent management	Ensure that the talented and well-motivated people required by the organization are available to meet present and future needs.
Job and work design	Provide individuals with stimulating and interesting work, and give them the autonomy and flexibility to perform these jobs well. Enhance job satisfaction and flexibility to encourage high performance and productivity.
Learning and development	Enlarge the skill base and develops the levels of competence required in the workforce. Encourage discretionary learning which happens when individuals actively seek to acquire the knowledge and skills that promote the organization's objectives. Develop a climate of learning – a growth medium in which self-managed learning as well as coaching, mentoring and training flourish.
Manage knowledge and intellectual capital	Focus on organizational as well as individual learning, and provide learning opportunities and opportunities to share knowledge in a systematic way. Ensure that vital stocks of knowledge are retained and improve the flow of knowledge, information and learning within the organization.
Increase engagement, commitment and motivation	Encourage productive discretionary effort by ensuring that people are positive and interested in their jobs, that they are proud to work for the organization and want to go on working there, and that they take action to achieve organizational and individual goals.
Psychological contract	Develop a positive and balanced psychological contract which provides for a continuing, harmonious relationship between the employee and the organization.
High-performance management	Develop a performance culture which encourages high performance in such areas as productivity, quality, levels of customer service, growth, profits, and ultimately the delivery of increased shareholder value. Empower employees to exhibit the discretionary behaviours most closely associated with higher business performance, such as risk taking, innovation, and knowledge sharing of knowledge and establishing trust between managers and their team members.

Table 1.2   *continued*

HR practice area	How it impacts
Reward management	Develop motivation and job engagement by valuing people in accordance with their contribution.
Employee relations	Develop involvement practices and an employee relations climate which encourages commitment and cooperation.
Working environment – core values, leadership, work–life balance, managing diversity, secure employment	Develop 'the big idea' (Purcell *et al*, 2003): that is, a clear vision and a set of integrated values. Make the organization 'a great place to work'.

It can be added that better implementation and better ownership by line managers of HR practices is more likely to be achieved if:

- the practice demonstrably benefits them;

- they are involved in the development and, importantly, the testing of the practices;

- the practice is not too complicated, bureaucratic or time-consuming;

- their responsibilities are defined and communicated clearly;

- they are provided with the guidance, support and training required to implement the practice.

The role of the HR function

Overall role of the function

The role of the HR (human resources) function is to take initiatives and provide guidance, support and services on all matters relating to the organization's employees. Essentially, the HR function is in the delivery business – providing the advice and services that enable organizations to get things done through people.

The function ensures that HR strategies, policies and practices are introduced and maintained which enhance the employment relationship (how employers and employees work together and get on with one another), develop a positive psychological contract (the set of reciprocal but unwritten expectations which exist between individual employees and their employers) and cater for everything concerning the employment, development and well-being of people and the relationships that exist between management and the workforce. It plays a major part in the creation of an environment that enables people to make the best use of their capacities, to realize their potential to the benefit of both the organization and themselves, and by improving the quality of working life, to achieve satisfaction through their work.

Increasingly the role of the HR function is seen to be business-oriented – adding value and helping to achieve sustained competitive advantage. As such it contributes to the formulation of business strategy by ensuring that people issues affecting developments and performance are properly considered. This may involve bringing attention to the people issues related to new business development, expansion and takeovers, especially those concerning the availability of talent and making good use of it. The function contributes to the achievement of the business strategy by ensuring that the talented people required are available, and that high levels of performance are engaged and maintained.

This is the policy line taken by the Chartered Institute of Personnel and Development (CIPD), but one of the issues explored by Francis and Keegan (2006) is the tendency for a focus on business performance outcomes to obscure the importance of employee well-being in its own right. As Ulrich and Brockbank (2005a) point out, 'caring, listening to, and responding to employees remains a centrepiece of HR work'. Members of the HR function have to be aware of the ethical dimensions of their activities.

Organization of the HR function

The popular 'three-legged stool' model for the organization of the HR function as originated by Ulrich (1998) divided it into the following parts:

- Centres of expertise: these specialize in the provision of high-level advice and services on key HR activities. The CIPD survey on the changing HR function (CIPD, 2007) found that they existed in 28 per cent of respondents' organizations. The most common expertise areas were training and development (79 per cent), recruitment (67 per cent), reward (60 per cent) and employee relations (55 per cent).

- Strategic business partners: these work with line managers to help them reach their goals through effective strategy formulation and execution (Ulrich and Brockbank, 2005b). They are often 'embedded' in business units or departments.

- Shared service centres: these handle all the routine 'transactional' services across the business. These include such activities as recruitment, absence monitoring, and advice on dealing with employee issues such as discipline and absenteeism.

This Ulrich model has attracted a great deal of attention, but the CIPD 2007 survey found that only 18 per cent of respondents had implemented all three legs, although 47 per cent had implemented one or two elements, with business partners being the most common (29 per cent).

The role of HR practitioners

The roles of HR practitioners vary widely according to the extent to which they are generalist (with titles such as HR director, HR manager, business partner), or specialist (such as head of learning and development, head of talent management, head of reward), the level at which they work (strategic, executive or administrative) the needs of the organization, the view of senior management about their contribution, the context within which they work and their own capabilities. They can act as business partners, strategists, innovators, change agents, internal consultants, facilitators and coaches. Ulrich and Brockbank (2005a) listed five roles: employee advocates, human capital developers, financial experts, strategic partners and leaders. The competencies required by the role can be demanding.

The overall role

HR practitioners can play a proactive role, contributing to the formulation of corporate strategy, developing integrated HR strategies and volunteering guidance on matters related to upholding core values and ethical principles. They are involved in business issues and working with line managers to deliver performance targets, but they are also concerned with people issues. They help to improve organizational capability – the capacity of the organization to perform effectively and thus reach its goals. Research conducted by Hoque and Noon (2001) established that 'The growing number of specialists using the HR title are well qualified, are more likely to be involved in strategic decision-making processes and are most likely to be found in workplaces within which sophisticated methods and techniques have been adopted.'

However, in some situations they play a mainly reactive and transactional role. They spend much of their time doing what they are told or asked to do, responding to requests for services or advice. They provide the administrative systems required by management. This is what Storey (1992) refers to as the non-interventionary role, in which HR people merely provide a service to meet the demands of management and front-line managers.

For many HR practitioners their most important function is service delivery, which includes transactional activities such as recruitment, training and advisory services. The importance of this aspect of their work should not be underestimated by focusing on the more glamorous roles of business partner or strategist as described below.

The business partner role

The concept of HR practitioners as business partners has seized the imagination of HR people. In essence, the concept is that, as business partners, HR specialists share responsibility with their line management colleagues for the success of the enterprise, and get involved with them in implementing business strategy and running the business. They are often 'embedded' in business units or departments.

This concept was first mooted in 1985 by Shaun Tyson. He used the term 'business manager' rather than 'business partner', but it is much the same. He stated that personnel specialists carrying out this role integrate their activities closely with management and ensure that they serve a long-term strategic purpose. They have the capacity to identify business opportunities, to see the broad picture and to understand how their role can help to achieve the company's business objectives. They anticipate needs, act flexibly and are proactive. This is a clear case of a prophet being unhonoured in his own country. In 1998, 13 years later, Dave Ulrich seized the HR community's imagination with his similar concept of the HR executive as a 'strategic partner'.

In describing his strategic partner model, Ulrich maintained that as champions of competitiveness in creating value, HR executives can deliver excellence by becoming partners with senior and line managers in strategy execution, helping to improve planning from the conference room to the marketplace, and impelling and guiding serious discussion of how the company should be organized to carry out its strategy. He suggested that HR should join forces with operating managers in systematically assessing the importance of any new initiatives they propose, and obtaining answers to the following questions: Which ones are really aligned with strategy implementation? Which ones should receive immediate attention and which can wait? Which ones, in short, are truly linked to business results?

As business partners HR practitioners work closely with their line management colleagues. They are aware of business strategies, and the opportunities and threats facing the organization. They are capable of analysing organizational strengths and weaknesses, and diagnosing the issues facing the enterprise and their human resource implications. They know about the critical success factors that will create competitive advantage, and they adopt a 'value added' approach when making a convincing business case for innovations.

The term 'value added' looms large in the concept of the HR business partner. In accounting language, where the phrase originated, added value is defined as the value added to the cost of raw materials and bought-out parts by the process of production and distribution. In HR speak, a value-added approach means creating value through HR initiatives which make a significant contribution to organizational success.

Strictly speaking, added value is measured by the extent to which the value of that contribution exceeds its cost or generates a return on investment. But the term is often used more generally to signify the business-oriented approach HR professionals are expected to adopt, and how it contributes to the creation of value by the firm. Adding value is about improving performance and results – getting more out of an activity than was put into it. Francis and Keegan (2006) report the following comment from a recruitment consultant which illustrates how the term has become popular:

> *Most HR professionals will now have 'value added' stamped on their foreheads, because they are always being asked to think in terms of the business objectives and how what they do supports the business objectives and the business plan.*

Critical evaluation of the business partner concept

It can be argued that too much has been made of the business partner model. Perhaps it is preferable to emphasize that the role of HR professionals is to be part of the business rather than merely being partners. Tim Miller, group HR director of Standard Chartered Bank (as reported by Smethurst, 2005), dislikes the term: 'Give me a break!' he says. 'It's so demeaning. How many people in marketing or finance have to say they are a partner in the business? Why do we have to think that we're not an intimate part of the business, just like sales, manufacturing and engineering? I detest and loathe the term and I won't use it.' Another leading group HR director, Alex Wilson of BT (as reported by Pickard, 2005), is equally hostile. He says: 'The term worries me to death. HR has to be an integral and fundamental part of developing the strategy of the business. I don't even like the term close to the business because, like business partner it implies we are working alongside our line management colleagues but on a separate track, rather than people management being an integral part of the business.'

There is also the danger of over-emphasizing the seemingly glamorous role of business or strategic partner at the expense of the service delivery aspect of the HR practitioner's role. As an HR specialist commented to Raymond Caldwell (2004): 'My credibility depends on running an extremely efficient and cost effective administrative machine... If I don't get that right, and consistently, then you can forget about any big ideas.' Another person interviewed during Caldwell's research referred to personnel people as 'reactive pragmatists', a view which in many organizations is in accord with reality, and Syrett (2006) commented that 'Whatever strategic aspirations senior HR practitioners have, they will amount to nothing if the function they represent cannot deliver the essential transactional services their internal line clients require.'

The problem of the over-emphasis on the business partner role has been influenced by the erroneous belief that Ulrich was simply focusing on HR executives as business partners. This has had the unfortunate effect of implying that it was their only worthwhile function. However, Ulrich cannot be blamed for this. In 1998 he gave equal emphasis to the need for HR people to be administrative experts, employee champions and change agents, and this was confirmed in a revised model (Ulrich and Brockbank, 2005a).

The strategic role

The strategic role of HR specialists varies according to whether they are operating at strategic levels (as HR directors or heads of the HR function, heads of centres of expertise or key HR functions, and strategic business partners), or at a transactional level (as HR officers, advisors or assistants delivering basic HR services such as recruitment or training, or working in an HR shared service centre).

Strategic-level roles

The strategic roles of HR specialists are:

- To formulate and implement in conjunction with their management colleagues forward-looking HR strategies which are aligned to business objectives and integrated with one another. In doing so they adopt an 'outside-in' approach as described by Wright *et al* (2004), in which the starting point is the business, including the customer, competitor and business issues it faces. The HR strategy then derives directly from these challenges to create real solutions and add real value.

- To contribute to the development of business strategies. They do this by advising on how the business can achieve its strategic goals by making the best use of its human resources, and by demonstrating the particular contribution that can be made by the talented people it employs.

They work alongside their line management colleagues to provide on an everyday basis continuous support to the implementation of the business or operational strategy of the organization, function or unit.

To carry out these roles, they need to:

- understand the strategic goals of the organization or unit and appreciate the business imperatives and performance drivers relative to these goals;

- comprehend how sustainable competitive advantage can be obtained through the human capital of the organization or unit, and know how HR practices can contribute to the achievement of strategic goals;

- contribute to the development for the business of a clear vision and a set of integrated values;

- ensure that senior management understands the HR implications of its business strategy;

- be aware of the broader context (the competitive environment and the business, economic, social and legal factors that affect it) in which the organization operates;

- understand the kinds of employee behaviour required successfully to execute the business strategy;

- think in terms of the bigger and longer-term picture of where HR should go and how it should get there;

- be capable of making a powerful business case for any proposals on the development of HR strategies;

- act as a change agent in developing the organization and its culture, and as an internal consultant in advising on what needs to be done and how to do it;

- understand how the ethical dimensions of HR policy and practice fit into the present and future picture;

- believe in and practise evidence-based management (recommendations on strategy and its implementation are always backed up by hard data);

- intervene and innovate as required.

The strategic contribution of HR advisors or assistants

The role of HR advisors or assistants is primarily that of delivering effective HR services within their function or as a member of an HR service centre. While they will not be responsible for the formulation of HR strategies, they may contribute to them within their own speciality. They will need to understand the business goals of the departments or managers for whom they provide services, in order to ensure that these services support the achievement of those goals.

The innovation role

A strategic and therefore proactive approach to HRM will mean that HR specialists want to innovate – to introduce new processes and procedures which they believe will increase organizational effectiveness. The need for innovation should be established by processes of analysis and diagnosis which identify the business need and the issues to be addressed. 'Benchmarking' can take place to identify 'best practice' as adopted by other organizations. But 'best fit' is more important then 'best practice'. In other words, the innovation should meet the particular needs of the business, which are likely to differ from those of other 'best practice' organizations. It has to be demonstrable that the innovation is appropriate, beneficial, practical in the circumstances, and can be implemented without too much difficulty in the shape of opposition from those affected by it or the unjustifiable use of resources – financial and the time of those involved.

The danger, according to Marchington (1995), is that HR people may go in for 'impression management' – aiming to make an impact on senior managers and colleagues through publicizing high profile innovations. HR specialists who aim to draw attention to themselves simply by promoting the latest flavour of the month, irrespective of its relevance or practicality, are falling into the trap which Drucker (1955), anticipating Marchington by 40 years, described as follows:

> The constant worry of all HR administrators is their inability to prove that they are making a contribution to the enterprise. Their pre-occupation is with the search for a 'gimmick' which will impress their management colleagues.

As Marchington points out, the risk is that people believe 'all can be improved by a wave of the magic wand and the slaying of a few evil characters along the way'. This facile assumption means that people can too readily devise elegant solutions which do not solve the problem because of the hazards encountered during implementation – for example, indifference or open hostility. These have to be anticipated and catered for.

Guidelines for HR innovations

- Be clear on what has to be achieved and why.

- Ensure that what you do fits the strategy, culture and circumstances of the organization.

- Don't follow fashion – do your own thing as long as it is relevant and fits the organization's needs.

- Keep it simple – over-complexity is a common reason for failure.

- Don't rush – it will take longer than you think.

- Don't try to do much at once – an incremental approach is generally best.

- Assess resource requirements and costs.

- Pay close attention to project planning and management.

- Remember that the success of the innovation rests as much on the effectiveness of the process of implementation (line manager buy-in and skills are crucial) as it does on the quality of the concept, if not more so.

- Pay close attention to change management approaches – communicate, involve and train.

The change agent role

The implementation of strategy means that HR specialists have to act as change agents, facilitating change by providing advice and support on its introduction and management. Caldwell (2001) categorizes HR change agents in four dimensions.

- **Transformational change** – a major change that has a dramatic effect on HR policy and practice across the whole organization.

- **Incremental change** – gradual adjustments of HR policy and practices which affect single activities or multiple functions.

- **HR vision** – a set of values and beliefs that affirm the legitimacy of the HR function as a strategic business partner.

- **HR expertise** – the knowledge and skills that define the unique contribution the HR professional can make to effective people management.

The Ulrich model

In 1998 Dave Ulrich produced his model in which he suggested that as champions of competitiveness in creating and delivering value, HR professionals carry out the roles of strategic partners, administrative experts, employee champions and change agents. The response to this formulation concentrated on the business partner role. Ulrich in conjunction with Brockbank (2005a) reformulated the 1998 model, listing the following roles:

- **Employee advocate** – focuses on the needs of today's employees through listening, understanding and empathizing.

- **Human capital developer** – focuses on managing and developing human capital, preparing employees to be successful in the future.

- **Functional expert** – concerned with the HR practices which are central to HR value, acting with insight on the basis of the body of knowledge they possess. Some are delivered through administrative efficiency (such as technology or process design), and others through policies, menus and interventions.

- **Strategic partner** – consists of multiple dimensions: business expert, change agent, strategic HR planner, knowledge manager and consultant, combining them to align HR systems to help accomplish the organization's vision and mission, helping managers to get things done, and disseminating learning across the organization.

- **Leader** – leading the HR function, collaborating with other functions and providing leadership to them, setting and enhancing the standards for strategic thinking and ensuring corporate governance.

HR competency areas

As established by research conducted by Brockbank *et al* (1999), the key HR competency areas (domains) and their components are set out in Table 1.3.

HR behaviours

The CIPD's HR profession map as issued in June 2009 listed the following behaviours needed by HR professionals to carry out their activities:

- curious;
- decisive thinker;
- skilled influencer;
- driven to deliver;
- collaborative;

Table 1.3   Key HR specialist competency areas

Competency domain	Components
1. Personal credibility	Live the firm's values, maintain relationships founded on trust, act with an 'attitude' (a point of view about how the business can win, backing up opinion with evidence).
2. Ability to manage change	Drive change: ability to diagnose problems, build relationships with clients, articulate a vision, set a leadership agenda, solve problems, and implement goals.
3. Ability to manage culture	Act as 'keepers of the culture', identify the culture required to meet the firm's business strategy, frame culture in a way that excites employees, translates desired culture into specific behaviours, encourages executives to behave consistently with the desired culture.
4. Delivery of human resource practices	Expert in the speciality, able to deliver state-of-the-art innovative HR practices in such areas as recruitment, employee development, compensation and communication.
5. Understanding of the business	Strategy, organization, competitors, finance, marketing, sales, operations and IT.

- personally credible;
- courage to challenge;
- role model.

Critical evaluation of the concept of HRM

On the face of it, the concept of HRM has much to offer, at least to management. But reservations have been expressed about it, especially by academics. These can be summed up as follows:

- HRM is, in David Guest's (1991) words, an 'optimistic but ambiguous concept', it is all hype and hope.

- Even if HRM does exist as a distinct process, which many doubt, it is full of contradictions, manipulative, and, according to Blyton and Turnbull (1992) downright pernicious.

- HRM is simplistic. As Fowler (1987) wrote, 'The HRM message to top management tends to be beguilingly simple. Don't bother too much about the content or techniques of personnel management, it says. Just manage the context. Get out from behind your desk, bypass the hierarchy, and go and talk to people. That way you will unlock an enormous potential for improved performance.' The HRM rhetoric presents it as an all or nothing process which is ideal for any organization, despite the evidence that different business environments require different approaches.

● The managerialist approach to industrial relations implicit in HRM prompted Fowler (1987) to write 'At the heart of the concept is the complete identification of employees with the aims and values of the business – employee involvement but on the company's terms. Power in the HRM system, remains very firmly in the hands of the employer. Is it really possible to claim full mutuality when at the end of the day the employer can decide unilaterally to close the company or sell it to someone else?'

● There are problems with the concept of commitment: as Guest (1997) asked, 'commitment to what?'

● HRM appears torn between preaching the virtues of individualism (concentration on the individual) and collectivism in the shape of team work (Legge, 1989).

● There is a potential tension between the development of a strong corporate culture and employees' ability to respond flexibly and adaptively (Legge, 1989).

● HRM is manipulative. The forces of internal persuasion and propaganda may be deployed to get people to accept values with which they may not be in accord and which in any case may be against their interests. 'A wide and contradictory variety of regenerative initiatives have been introduced under the name of HRM and force-fed to a battered, bewildered and defensive workforce and a newly confident management' (Keenoy and Anthony, 1992).

● In its fullest sense HRM is difficult to apply. To put the concept of HRM into practice would involve strategic integration, developing a coherent and consistent set of employment policies, and gaining commitment. This requires high levels of determination and competence at all levels of management, and a strong and effective HR function staffed by business-orientated people.

However, concepts such as strategic integration, culture management, engagement, and investing in human capital, together with a unitary philosophy (the interests of management and employees coincide), are essential parts of the HRM model. And this model fits the way in which organizations have to do business and manage their resources in the environments in which they now exist. This is why, in spite of the reservations expressed by academics, the concept of HRM has become generally accepted even though it is not always realized in full. This is because the general opinion is that it is in tune with the realities of organizational life.

The practice of HRM: key learning points

The meaning and aims of human resource management (HRM)

- HRM is a strategic, integrated and coherent approach to the employment, development and well-being of the people working in organizations.

- The overall purpose of HRM is to ensure that the organization is able to achieve success through people.

The diversity of HRM

There are no universal characteristics of HRM. Many models exist, and practices within different organizations are diverse.

How HRM functions as a system

HRM should be viewed as an integrated and coherent bundle of mutually reinforcing practices.

The ethical dimension of HRM

HRM is not just concerned with supporting the business, it also has to exercise social responsibility: to be concerned about the interests (well-being) of employees and act ethically with regard to the needs of people in the organization and the community.

HRM and performance

Much research has been carried over the last decade or so, most of which shows that there is a link between good HRM practice and firm performance.

The HRM role of line managers

Line managers have the key role in HRM. In John Purcell's phrase, 'they bring HR policies to life'.

The role of the HR function

The role of the HR function is to take initiatives and provide guidance, support and services on all matters relating to the organization's employees.

The role of HR specialists

HR specialists develop integrated HR strategies, intervene, innovate, act as business partners operate as internal consultants, act as change agents, facilitators and coaches, and volunteer guidance on matters concerning upholding core values, ethical principles and the achievement of consistency. They focus on business issues and working with line managers to deliver performance targets.

Questions

1. At a meeting of trustees the chief executive of a medium-sized charity proposed that a director of human resources should be appointed. Two trustees protested that the term 'human resources' implied that employees would just be treated as factors of production, not as people. How would you respond?

2. John Storey wrote in 1995 that 'Human resource management is a distinctive approach to employment management which seeks to achieve competitive advantage through the strategic deployment of a highly committed and capable workforce, using an integrated array of cultural, structural and personnel techniques.' Examine the approach to HRM in your own organization or any other organization known to you, and analyse the extent to which Storey's description of HRM applies.

3. In 1998, Karen Legge defined the 'hard' model of HRM as a process emphasising 'the close integration of human resource policies with business strategy which regards employees as a resource to be managed in the same rational way as any other resource being exploited for maximum return'. To what extent do you agree with this comment?

4. Peter Reilly made these comments in 2006 on the three-legged Ulrich model: 'The model has many advantages, not least that it aims to centralize activities where there are scale advantages and also keep close to customers where decentralization is necessary. But it's not an easy structure to work with… Splitting the function into three distinct areas has created boundary disputes and sometimes left a hole at the very heart of HR operations… One consequence of this division of labour is that lines of accountability are not always clearly defined… The end result may be a remote service that does not that doesn't attend to the areas where managers need most assistance.' What can be done to avoid these problems?

References

Adams, J S (1965) Injustice in social exchange, in *Advances in Experimental Psychology*, ed L Berkowitz, Academic Press, New York

Appelbaum, E, Bailey, T, Berg, P and Kalleberg, A L (2000) *Manufacturing Advantage: Why high performance work systems pay off*, ILR Press, Ithaca, NY

Armstrong, M (2000) The name has changed but has the game remained the same? *Employee Relations*, **22** (6), pp 576–89

Beer, M, Spector, B, Lawrence, P, Quinn Mills, D and Walton, R (1984) *Managing Human Assets*, Free Press, New York

Blyton, P and Turnbull, P (eds) (1992) *Reassessing Human Resource Management*, Sage, London

Boselie, P, Dietz, G and Boon, C (2005) Commonalities and contradictions in HRM and performance research, *Human Resource Management Journal*, **15** (3), pp 67–94

Boxall, P F, Purcell, J and Wright, P (2007) The goals of HRM, in *Oxford Handbook of Human Resource Management*, ed P Boxall, J Purcell and P Wright, Oxford University Press, Oxford

Brockbank, W, Ulrich, D and Beatty, D (1999) HR professional development: creating the future creators at the University of Michigan Business School, *Human Resource Management*, **38** (Summer), pp 111–17

Caldwell, R (2001) Champions, adapters, consultants and synergists: the new change agents in HRM, *Human Resource Management Journal*, **11** (3), pp 39–52

Caldwell, R (2004) Rhetoric, facts and self-fulfilling prophesies: exploring practitioners' perceptions of progress in implementing HRM, *Industrial Relations Journal*, **35** (3), pp 196–215

Chartered Institute of Personnel and Development (CIPD) (2007) *The Changing HR Function*, CIPD, London

CIPD (2009) HR Profession Map, http://www.CIPD.co.uk/hr-profession-map

Drucker, P (1955) *The Practice of Management*, Heinemann, London

Dyer, L and Holder, G W (1998) Strategic human resource management and planning, in *Human Resource Management: Evolving roles and responsibilities*, ed L Dyer, Bureau of National Affairs, Washington, DC

Fombrun, C J, Tichy, N M, and Devanna, M A (1984) *Strategic Human Resource Management*, Wiley, New York

Fowler, A (1987) When chief executives discover HRM, *Personnel Management*, January, p 3

Francis, H and Keegan, A (2006) The changing face of HRM: in search of balance, *Human Resource Management Journal*, **16** (3), pp 231–49

Gratton, L A, Hailey, V H, Stiles, P and Truss, C (1999) *Strategic Human Resource Management*, Oxford University Press, Oxford

Guest, D E (1991) Personnel management: the end of orthodoxy, *British Journal of Industrial Relations*, **29** (2), pp 149–76

Guest, D E (1997) Human resource management and performance; a review of the research agenda, *International Journal of Human Resource Management*, **8** (3), 263–76

Guest, D E and King, Z (2004) Power, innovation and problem-solving: the personnel managers' three steps to heaven? *Journal of Management Studies*, **41** (3), pp 401–23

Guest, D E, Michie, J, Sheehan, M, Conway, N and Metochi, M (2000) *Effective People Management: Initial findings of future of work survey*, CIPD, London

Hoque, K and Noon, M (2001) Counting angels: a comparison of personnel and HR specialists, *Human Resource Management Journal*, **11** (3), pp 5–22

Huselid, M A (1995) The impact of human resource management practices on turnover, productivity and corporate financial performance, *Academy of Management Journal*, **38** (3), pp 635–72

Hutchinson, S and Purcell, J (2003) *Bringing Policies to Life: The vital role of front line managers in people management*, CIPD, London

Keenoy, T and Anthony, P (1992) HRM: metaphor, meaning and morality, in *Reassessing Human Resource Management*, ed P Blyton and P Turnbull, Sage, London

Kepes, S and Delery, J E (2007) HRM systems and the problem of internal fit, in *Oxford Handbook of Human Resource Management*, ed P Boxall, J Purcell and P Wright, Oxford University Press, Oxford

Legge, K (1978) *Power, Innovation and Problem Solving in Personnel Management*, McGraw-Hill, Maidenhead

Legge, K (1989) Human resource management: a critical analysis, in *New Perspectives in Human Resource Management*, ed J Storey, Routledge, London

Legge, K (1998) The morality of HRM, in *Experiencing Human Resource Management*, ed C Mabey, D Skinner and T Clark, Sage, London

Leventhal, G S (1980) What should be done with equity theory? in *Social Exchange: Advances in theory and research*, ed G K Gergen, M S Greenberg and R H Willis, Plenum, New York

Marchington, M (1995) Fairy tales and magic wands: new employment practices in perspective, *Employee Relations*, Spring, pp 51–66

Mayo, E (1933) *Human Problems of an Industrial Civilization*, Macmillan, London

Paauwe, J (2004) *HRM and Performance: Achieving long term viability*, Oxford University Press, Oxford

Patterson, M G, West, M A, Lawthom, R and Nickell, S (1997) *Impact of People Management Practices on Performance*, Institute of Personnel and Development, London

Pickard, J (2005) Part not partner, *People Management*, 27 October, pp 48–50

Purcell, J, Kinnie, K, Hutchinson, S, Rayton, B and Swart, J (2003) *People and Performance: How people management impacts on organizational performance*, CIPD, London

Reilly, P (2006) Falling between two stools, *People Management*, 23 November, p 36

Smethurst, S (2005) The long and winding road, *People Management*, 28 July, pp 25–29

Storey, J (1989) From personnel management to human resource management, in *New Perspectives on Human Resource Management*, ed J Storey, Routledge, London

Storey, J (1992) *New Developments in the Management of Human Resources*, Blackwell, Oxford

Storey, J (1995) Human resource management: still marching on or marching out? in *Human Resource Management: A critical text*, ed J Storey, Routledge, London

Syrett, M (2006) Four reflections on developing a human capital measurement capability, in *What's the Future for Human Capital?* CIPD, London

Thompson, M (2002) *High Performance Work Organization in UK Aerospace*, Society of British Aerospace Companies, London

Truss, C (1999) Soft and hard models of HRM, in *Strategic Human Resource Management*, ed L Gratton, V H Hailey, P Stiles, and C Truss, Oxford University Press, Oxford

Tyson, S (1985) Is this the very model of a modern personnel manager? *Personnel Management*, May, pp 22–25

Ulrich, D (1998) A new mandate for human resources, *Harvard Business Review*, January–February, pp 124–34

Ulrich, D and Brockbank, W (2005a) Role call, *People Management*, 16 June, pp 24–28

Ulrich, D and Brockbank, W (2005b) *The HR Value Proposition*, Harvard Business School Press, Cambridge, MA

Ulrich, D and Lake, D (1990) *Organizational Capability: Competing from the inside out*, Wiley, New York

Walton, R E (1985) From control to commitment in the workplace, *Harvard Business Review*, March–April, pp 77–84

West, M A, Borrill, C S, Dawson, C, Scully, J, Carter, M, Anclay, S, Patterson, M and Waring, J (2002) The link between the management of employees and patient mortality in acute hospitals, *International Journal of Human Resource Management*, 13 (8), pp 1299–1310

Wright, P M, Snell, S A and Jacobsen, H H (2004) Current approaches to HR strategies: inside-out versus outside-in, *Human Resource Planning*, 27 (4), pp 36–46

2

Strategic Human Resource Management

Key concepts and terms

- Best fit
- Best practice
- Bundling
- Competency framework
- Competitive advantage
- Configuration
- Contingent determinism
- Human resource advantage

- Life-cycle model
- Resource-based view
- Resource dependence theory
- Strategic configuration
- Strategic fit
- Strategic HRM
- Strategic management
- Strategy

Learning outcomes

On completing this chapter you should be able to define these key concepts. You should also understand:

- The conceptual basis of strategic HRM

- The fundamental characteristics of strategy

- How strategy is formulated

- The aims of strategic HRM

- The resource-based view and its implications

- The meaning of strategic fit

- The three HRM 'perspectives' of Delery and Doty

- The significance of the concepts of 'best practice' and 'best fit'

- The significance of bundling

- The significant features of strategic HRM

- The content and formulation of HR strategies

Introduction

Business objectives are accomplished when human resource practices, procedures and systems are developed and implemented based on organizational needs, that is, when a strategic perspective to human resource management is adopted.

(Baird and Meshoulam, 1988)

The aim of this chapter is to explore what this involves. It starts with an analysis of the meaning of strategic human resource management (strategic HRM) as provided by the concepts of HRM and strategic management. It then covers, first, a definition of strategic HRM and its aims; second, an analysis of its underpinning concepts – the resource-based view and strategic fit; and third, a description of how strategic HRM works, namely the universalistic, contingency and configurational perspectives defined by Delery and Doty (1996) and the three approaches associated with those perspectives – best practice, best fit and bundling. The chapter continues with a summary of the distinctive features of strategic HRM, and ends with an examination of the types of HR strategies that can be developed when a strategic HRM approach is adopted.

The conceptual basis of strategic HRM

Boxall (1996) explained that strategic HRM 'is the interface between HRM and strategic management'. It takes the notion of HRM as a strategic, integrated and coherent process and associates it with an approach to management which involves taking a broad and long-term view of where the business is going, and managing it in ways which ensure that this strategic thrust is maintained.

As defined by Pearce and Robinson (1988), 'Strategic management is the set of decisions and actions resulting in the formulation and implementation of strategies designed to achieve the objectives of an organization.' According to Rosabeth Moss Kanter (1984), its purpose is to 'elicit the present actions for the future' and become 'an action vehicle – integrating and institutionalizing mechanisms for change'. The concept of strategic management is built on the concept of strategy as considered below.

The concept of strategy

Strategy is the approach selected to achieve specified goals in the future. As defined by Chandler (1962), it is 'The determination of the long-term goals and objectives of an enterprise, and the adoption of courses of action and the allocation of resources necessary for carrying out those goals.' The formulation and implementation of corporate strategy can be described as a process for developing a sense of direction, making the best use of resources and ensuring strategic fit.

Strategy has three fundamental characteristics. First, it is forward looking. It is about deciding where you want to go and how you mean to get there. It is concerned with both ends and means. In this sense a strategy is a declaration of intent: 'This is what we want to do and this is how we intend to do it.' Strategies define longer-term goals but they also cover how those goals will be attained. They guide purposeful action to deliver the required result. A good strategy is one that works, one that, in Abell's (1993) phrase, enables organizations to adapt by 'mastering the present and pre-empting the future'. As Boxall (1996) explained, 'Strategy should be understood as a framework of critical ends and means.'

The second characteristic of strategy is that the organizational capability of a firm (its capacity to function effectively) depends on its resource capability (the quality and quantity of its resources and their potential to deliver results). This is the resource-based view as described later in this chapter.

The third characteristic of strategy is strategic fit – the need when developing functional strategies such as HR to achieve congruence between them and the organization's business strategies within the context of its external and internal environments.

Critical evaluation of the concept of strategy

The formulation of corporate strategy is often assumed to be a logical, step-by-step affair, the outcome of which is a formal written statement which provides a definitive guide to the organization's intentions. Many people still believe and act as if this were the case, but it is a misrepresentation of reality. In practice the formulation of strategy can never be as rational and linear a process as some writers describe it or as some managers attempt to make it. There are limitations to the totally logical model of management which underpins the concept of strategic HRM. In the words of Mabey *et al* (1998), this is 'a model of management which is more rational than is achievable in practice'.

The difficulty is that strategies are often based on the questionable assumption that the future will resemble the past. Some years ago, Robert Heller (1972) had a go at the cult of long-range planning. 'What goes wrong', he wrote, 'is that sensible anticipation gets converted into foolish numbers: and their validity always hinges on large loose assumptions.'

Strategy formulation is not necessarily a deterministic, rational and continuous process, as was pointed out by Mintzberg (1987). He believed that, rather than being consciously and systematically developed, strategy reorientation happens in what he calls brief 'quantum loops'. A strategy, according to Mintzberg, can be deliberate – it can realize the intentions of senior management, for example to attack and conquer a new market. But this is not always the case. In theory, he says, strategy is a systematic process: first we think, then we act; we formulate, then we implement. But we also 'act in order to think'. In practice, 'a realized strategy can emerge in response to an evolving situation' and strategic planners often manage a process in which strategies and visions can emerge as well as be deliberately conceived. They proceed by finding out what works well in practice for them. 'Sometimes strategies must be left as broad visions, not precisely articulated, to adapt to a changing environment.' This concept of 'emergent strategy' conveys the essence of how organizations develop their business and HR strategies.

Research conducted by Tyson (1997) confirmed that, realistically, strategy:

- has always been emergent and flexible – it is always 'about to be', it never exists at the present time;
- is not only realized by formal statements but also comes about by actions and reactions;
- is a description of a future-orientated action which is always directed towards change;
- is conditioned by the management process itself.

Strategic HRM defined

Strategic HRM is an approach that defines how the organization's goals will be achieved through people by means of HR strategies and integrated HR policies and practices. Strategic HRM can be regarded as a mindset underpinned by certain concepts rather than a set of techniques. It provides the foundation for strategic reviews in which analyses of the organizational context and existing HR practices lead to choices on strategic plans for the development of overall or specific HR strategies. Strategic HRM involves the exercise of strategic choice (which is always there) and the establishment of strategic priorities. It is essentially about the integration of business and HR strategies so that the latter contribute to the achievement of the former.

But strategic HRM is not just about strategic planning. It is also concerned with the implementation of strategy, and the strategic behaviour of HR specialists working with their line management colleagues on an everyday basis to ensure that the business goals of the organization are achieved and its values put into practice.

Aims of strategic HRM

The fundamental aim of strategic HRM is to generate organizational capability by ensuring that the organization has the skilled, engaged, committed and well-motivated employees it needs to achieve sustained competitive advantage. It has three main objectives: first, to achieve integration – the vertical alignment of HR strategies with business strategies and the horizontal integration of HR strategies. The second objective is to provide a sense of direction in an often turbulent environment so that the business needs of the organization and the individual and collective needs of its employees can be met by the development and implementation of coherent and practical HR policies and programmes. In accordance with the resource-based view, the strategic goal will be to 'create firms which are more intelligent and flexible than their competitors' (Boxall, 1996), by hiring and developing more talented staff and by extending their skills base. The third objective is to contribute to the formulation of business strategy by drawing attention to ways in which the business can capitalize on the advantages provided by the strengths of its human resources.

Schuler (1992) stated that:

> *Strategic human resource management is largely about integration and adaptation. Its concern is to ensure that: (1) human resources (HR) management is fully integrated with the strategy and strategic needs of the firm; (2) HR policies cohere both across policy areas and across hierarchies; and (3) HR practices are adjusted, accepted and used by line managers and employees as part of their everyday work.*

As Dyer and Holder (1998) remarked, strategic HRM provides 'unifying frameworks which are at once broad, contingency based and integrative'. The rationale for strategic HRM is the perceived advantage of having an agreed and understood basis for developing and implementing approaches to people management which take into account the changing context in which the firm operates and its longer-term requirements.

Strategic HRM is based on two key concepts: the resource-based view and strategic fit.

The resource-based view of strategic HRM

To a very large extent, the philosophy and approaches to strategic HRM are underpinned by the resource-based view. This states that it is the range of resources in an organization, including its human resources, that produces its unique character and creates competitive advantage. It is based originally on the ideas of Penrose (1959), who wrote that the firm is 'an administrative organization and a collection of productive resources'. It was expanded by Wernerfelt (1984), who coined the phrase and explained that strategy 'is a balance between the exploitation of existing resources and the development of new ones'.

Resource-based strategy theorists such as Barney (1991, 1995) argued that sustained competitive advantage stemmed from the acquisition and effective use of bundles of distinctive resources that competitors cannot imitate. Distinctive resources have four attributes: they must be valuable, rare, imperfectly imitable and non-substitutable. These resources include all the experience, knowledge, judgement, risk-taking propensity and wisdom of individuals associated with a firm.

Resource-based strategic HRM can produce what Boxall and Purcell (2003) referred to as human resource advantage. The aim is to develop strategic capability. This means strategic fit between resources and opportunities, obtaining added value from the effective deployment of resources, and developing managers who can think and plan strategically in the sense that they understand the key strategic issues and ensure that what they do enables the strategic goals of the business to be achieved. In line with human capital theory, the resource-based view emphasizes that investment in people increases their value to the firm. It proposes that sustainable competitive advantage is attained when the firm has a human resource pool that cannot be imitated or substituted by its rivals.

Boxall (1996, 1999) noted that human resource advantage is achieved by a combination of 'human capital advantage', which results from employing people with competitively valuable knowledge and skills, and 'human process advantage', which follows from the establishment of 'difficult to imitate, highly evolved processes within the firm, such as cross-departmental cooperation and executive development'. Accordingly, 'human resource advantage', the superiority of one firm's labour management over another's, can be thought of as the product of its human capital and human process advantages.

The strategic goal emerging from the resource-based view will be to 'create firms which are more intelligent and flexible than their competitors' (Boxall, 1996) by hiring and developing more talented staff and by extending their skills base. Resource-based strategy is therefore concerned with the enhancement of the human or intellectual capital of the firm. As Ulrich (1998) commented, 'Knowledge has become a direct competitive advantage for companies selling ideas and relationships. The challenge to organizations is to ensure that they have the capability to find, assimilate, compensate and retain the talented individuals they need.' Resource dependence theory (Pfeffer and Davis-Blake, 1992) suggests that some HR strategies in organizations such as those concerned with reward are strongly influenced by the need to attract, retain and energize high-quality people.

A concept map of the resource-based view is shown in Figure 2.1.

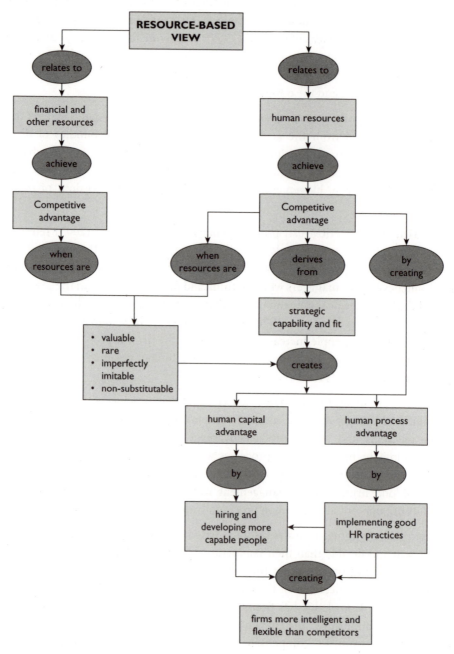

Figure 2.1 Concept map: resource-based view

Critical evaluation of the resource-based view concept

The resource-based view has had considerable influence on thinking about HRM. It provides a justification for attaching importance to resourcing activities, especially those concerned with talent management. It can also be used to enhance the value of the HR contribution in achieving competitive advantage. But it has the following limitations:

- It may be difficult to find resources which satisfy all the criteria.

- External factors such as product market pressures are ignored.

- It provides only generalized guidance on what resources are suitable.

- Different resource configurations can provide the same value for firms.

- As Priem and Butler (2001) point out, the theory is tautological because valuable resources and competitive advantage are defined in the same terms.

Strategic fit

Walker (1992) defines strategic HRM as 'the means of aligning the management of human resources with the strategic content of the business'. This is based on the concept of strategic fit, which means developing HR strategies that are integrated with the business strategy and support its achievement (vertical integration or fit), and also with the use of an integrated approach to the development of HR practices such as resourcing, employee development, reward and employee relations so that they complement and support one another (horizontal integration or fit).

Perspectives on strategic HRM

Taking into account the concepts of the resource-based view and strategic fit, Delery and Doty (1996) contended that 'organizations adopting a particular strategy require HR practices that are different from those required by organizations adopting different strategies,' and that organizations with 'greater congruence between their HR strategies and their (business) strategies should enjoy superior performance'. They identified three HRM perspectives:

- **The universalistic perspective** – some HR practices are better than others and all organizations should adopt these best practices. There is a universal relationship between individual 'best' practices and firm performance.

- **The contingency perspective** – in order to be effective, an organization's HR policies must be consistent with other aspects of the organization. The primary contingency factor is the organization's strategy. This can be described as 'vertical fit'.

- **The configurational perspective** – this is a holistic approach which emphasises the importance of the pattern of HR practices and is concerned with how this pattern of independent variables is related to the dependent variable of organizational performance.

This typology provided the basis for what has become the most commonly used classification of approaches, as advocated by Richardson and Thompson (1999), which was to adopt the terms 'best practice' and 'best fit' for the universalistic and contingency perspectives, and 'bundling' as the third approach. This followed the classification made by Guest (1997) of fit as an ideal set of practices, fit as contingency and fit as bundles.

The best practice approach

This approach is based on the assumption that there is a set of best HRM practices which are universal in the sense that they are best in any situation, and that adopting them will lead to superior organizational performance.

A number of lists of 'best practices' have been produced, the best known of which was produced by Pfeffer (1998):

- employment security;
- selective hiring;
- self-managed teams;
- high compensation contingent on performance;
- training to provide a skilled and motivated workforce;
- reduction of status differentials;
- sharing information.

The best fit approach

The best fit approach is in line with contingency theory. It emphasizes that HR strategies should be congruent with the context and circumstances of the organization. 'Best fit' can be perceived in terms of vertical integration or alignment between the organization's business and HR strategies. There are three models: life-cycle, competitive strategy, and strategic configuration.

The life-cycle model

The life-cycle model is based on the theory that the development of a firm takes place in four stages: start-up, growth, maturity and decline. This is in line with product life-cycle theory. The basic premise of this model was expressed by Baird and Meshoulam (1988):

Human resource management's effectiveness depends on its fit with the organization's stage of development. As the organization grows and develops, human resource management programmes, practices and procedures must change to meet its needs. Consistent with growth and development models it can be suggested that human resource management develops through a series of stages as the organization becomes more complex.

Best fit and competitive strategies

Three strategies aimed at achieving competitive advantage were identified by Porter (1985):

- innovation – being the unique producer;

- quality – delivering high-quality goods and services to customers;

- cost leadership – the planned result of policies aimed at 'managing away' expense.

It was contended by Schuler and Jackson (1987) that to achieve the maximum effect it is necessary to match the role characteristics of people in an organization with the preferred strategy.

Strategic configuration

Another approach to best fit is the proposition that organizations will be more effective if they adopt a policy of strategic configuration (Delery and Doty, 1996) by matching their strategy to one of the ideal types defined by theories such as those produced by Miles and Snow (1978). This increased effectiveness is attributed to the internal consistency or fit between the patterns of relevant contextual, structural and strategic factors. They identified the following four types of organizations, classifying the first three types as 'ideal' organizations.

- Prospectors: which operate in an environment characterized by rapid and unpredictable changes. Prospectors have low levels of formalization and specialization and high levels of decentralization. They have relatively few hierarchical levels.

- Defenders: which operate in a more stable and predictable environment than prospectors and engage in more long-term planning. They have more mechanistic or bureaucratic structures than prospectors, and obtain coordination through formalization, centralization, specialization and vertical differentiation.

- Analysers: which are a combination of the prospector and defender types. They operate in stable environments like defenders and also in markets where new products are constantly required like prospectors. They are usually not the initiators of change like prospectors, but they follow the changes more rapidly than defenders.

- Reactors: which are unstable organizations existing in what they believe to be an unpredictable environment. They lack consistent well-articulated strategies and do not undertake long-range planning.

Critical evaluation of the best practice and best fit models
The best practice model

The 'best practice' rubric has been attacked by a number of commentators. Cappelli and Crocker-Hefter (1996) comment that the notion of a single set of best practices has been overstated: 'There are examples in virtually every industry of firms that have very distinctive management practices... Distinctive human resource practices shape the core competencies that determine how firms compete.'

Purcell (1999) has also criticized the best practice or universalist view by pointing out the inconsistency between a belief in best practice and the resource-based view, which focuses on the intangible assets, including HR, that allow the firm to do better than its competitors. He asks how can 'the universalism of best practice be squared with the view that only some resources and routines are important and valuable by being rare and imperfectly imitable'?

In accordance with contingency theory, which emphasizes the importance of interactions between organizations and their environments so that what organizations do is dependent on the context in which they operate, it is difficult to accept that there is any such thing as universal best practice. What works well in one organization will not necessarily work well in another, because it may not fit its strategy, culture, management style, technology or working practices.

However, a knowledge of what is assumed to be best practice can be used to inform decisions on what practices are most likely to fit the needs of the organization, as long as it is understood why a particular practice should be regarded as a best practice and what needs to be done to ensure that it will work in the context of the organization. Becker and Gerhart (1996) argue that the idea of best practice might be more appropriate for identifying the principles underlying the choice of practices, as opposed to the practices themselves. It is best to think of 'good practice' rather than 'best practice'.

Best fit

The best fit model seems to be more realistic than the best practice model. As Dyer and Holder (1998) pointed out, 'The inescapable conclusion is that what is best depends.' But there are limitations to the concept. Paawue (2004) emphasized that 'It is necessary to avoid falling into the trap of "contingent determinism" (ie, claiming that the context absolutely determines the strategy). There is, or should be, room for making strategic choices.'

There is a danger of mechanistically matching HR polices and practices with strategy. It is not credible to claim that there are single contextual factors that determine HR strategy, and internal fit cannot therefore be complete. As Boxall *et al* (2007) asserted, 'It is clearly impossible to make all HR policies reflective of a chosen competitive or economic mission; they may have to fit with social legitimacy goals.' And Purcell (1999) commented that 'The search for a contingency or matching model of HRM is also limited by the impossibility of modelling all the contingent variables, the difficulty of showing their interconnection, and the way in which changes in one variable have an impact on others.'

Best fit models tend to be static and don't take account of the processes of change. They neglect the fact that institutional forces shape HRM – it cannot be assumed that employers are free agents able to make independent decisions. It is often said that best fit is better than best practice but this statement can only be accepted with reservations.

Bundling

As Richardson and Thompson (1999) commented, 'A strategy's success turns on combining vertical or external fit and horizontal or internal fit.' They concluded that a firm with bundles of associated HR practices should have a higher level of performance, providing it also achieves high levels of fit with its competitive strategy.

'Bundling' is the development and implementation of several HR practices together so that they are interrelated and therefore complement and reinforce each other. This is the process of horizontal integration which is also referred to as the use of 'complementarities'. MacDuffie (1995) explained the concept of bundling as 'Implicit in the notion of a "bundle" is the idea that practices within bundles are interrelated and internally consistent, and that "more is better" with respect to the impact on performance, because of the overlapping and mutually reinforcing effect of multiple practices.'

Dyer and Reeves (1995) note that 'The logic in favour of bundling is straightforward... Since employee performance is a function of both ability and motivation, it makes sense to have practices aimed at enhancing both.' Thus there are several ways in which employees can acquire needed skills (such as careful selection and training) and multiple incentives to enhance motivation (different forms of financial and non-financial rewards). Their study of various models listing HR practices which create a link between HRM and business performance found that the activities appearing in most of the models were involvement, careful selection, extensive training and contingent compensation.

The process of bundling HR strategies is an important aspect of the concept of strategic HRM. In a sense, strategic HRM is holistic; it is concerned with the organization as a total system or entity, and addresses what needs to be done across the organization as a whole. It is not interested in isolated programmes and techniques, or in the ad hoc development of HR practices.

Bundling can take place in a number of ways. For example, competency frameworks (a set of definitions of the competencies that describe the types of behaviour required for the successful performance of a role) can be devised which are used in assessment and development centres, to specify recruitment standards, to provide a framework for competency-based interviews, to identify learning and development needs, to indicate the standards of behaviour or performance required and to serve as the basis for human resource planning. They can also be incorporated into performance management processes in which the aims are primarily developmental and competencies are used as criteria for reviewing behaviour and assessing learning and development needs. Job evaluation could be based on levels of competency, and competency-based pay systems could be introduced. Job evaluation can also be used to clarify levels in an organization. Grade structures can define career ladders in terms of competency requirements (career family structures) and thus provide the basis for learning and development programmes. They can serve the dual purpose of defining career paths and pay progression opportunities. Total reward approaches 'bundle' financial and non-financial rewards together. High-performance systems are in effect based on the principle of bundling because they group a number of HR practices to produce synergy and thus increase their impact.

Critical evaluation of bundling

Bundling sounds like a good idea. The research by MacDuffie (1995) and others has shown that bundling can improve performance. But there are a number of inhibiting factors:

- deciding which bundles are likely to be best: there is no evidence that one bundle is generally better than another;

- actually linking practices together – it is always easier to deal with one practice at a time;

- managing the interdependencies between different parts of a bundle;

- convincing top management and line managers that bundling will benefit the organization and them.

These can be overcome by dedicated HR professionals but it is hard work. What can be done, with difficulty, is to look for ways in which different HR practices can support one another as in the examples given above.

The significant features of strategic HRM

- Creating sustained competitive advantage depends on the unique resources and capabilities that a firm brings to competition in its environment (Baron, 2001).

- Competitive advantage is achieved by ensuring that the firm has higher-quality people than its competitors (Purcell *et al*, 2003).

- The competitive advantage based on the effective management of people is hard to imitate (Barney, 1991, 1995).

- The challenge is to achieve organizational capability, ensuring that businesses are able to find, assimilate, reward and retain the talented individuals they need (Ulrich, 1998).

- It is unwise to pursue so-called 'best practice' (the 'universalistic' perspective of Delery and Doty, 1996) without being certain that what happens elsewhere would work in the context of the organization.

- 'Best fit' (the 'contingency' perspective of Delery and Doty, 1996) is preferable to 'best practice' as long as the organization avoids falling into the trap of 'contingent determinism' by allowing the context to determine the strategy (Paauwe, 2004).

- The search for best fit is limited by the impossibility of modelling all the contingent variables, the difficulty of showing their interconnection, and the way in which changes in one variable have an impact on others (Purcell, 1999).

- Best fit can be pursued in a number of ways, namely by fitting the HR strategy to its position in its life cycle of start-up, growth, maturity or decline (Baird and Meshoulam, 1988), or the competitive strategy of innovation, quality or cost leadership (Porter, 1985), or to the organization's 'strategic configuration' (Delery and Doty, 1996), such as the typology of organizations as prospectors, defenders and analysers defined by Miles and Snow (1978).

- Improved performance can be achieved by 'bundling', or the development and implementation of several HR practices together so that they are interrelated and therefore complement and reinforce each other (MacDuffie, 1995).

HR strategies

Strategic HRM involves the formulation and implantation of HR strategies which set out what the organization intends to do about its human resource management policies and practices, and how they should be integrated with the business strategy and each other. They aim to meet both the business and the human needs in the organization. HR strategies are described by

Dyer and Reeves (1995) as 'internally consistent bundles of human resource practices'. Richardson and Thompson (1999) suggest that 'A strategy, whether it is an HR strategy or any other kind of management strategy must have two key elements: there must be strategic objectives (ie things the strategy is supposed to achieve), and there must be a plan of action (ie the means by which it is proposed that the objectives will be met).' As Lynda Gratton (2000) commented, 'There is no great strategy, only great execution.' Strategies are forward-looking but as Fombrun *et al* (1984) remarked, businesses and managers should perform well in the present to succeed in the future.

Because all organizations are different, all HR strategies are different. There is no such thing as a standard strategy, and research into HR strategy conducted by Armstrong and Long (1994) and Armstrong and Baron (2002) revealed many variations. Some strategies are simply very general declarations of intent. Others go into much more detail. But two basic types of HR strategies can be identified: first, general strategies such as high-performance working, and second, specific strategies relating to the different aspects of human resource management such as learning and development and reward.

General HR strategies

General strategies describe the overall system or bundle of complementary HR practices that the organization proposes to adopt or puts into effect in order to improve organizational performance. The three main approaches are summarized below.

High-performance management

High-performance management or high-performance working aims to make an impact on the performance of the organization in such areas as productivity, quality, levels of customer service, growth and profits. High-performance management practices include rigorous recruitment and selection procedures, extensive and relevant training and management development activities, incentive pay systems and performance management processes.

High-commitment management

One of the defining characteristics of HRM is its emphasis on the importance of enhancing mutual commitment (Walton, 1985). High-commitment management has been described by Wood (1996) as 'A form of management which is aimed at eliciting a commitment so that behaviour is primarily self-regulated rather than controlled by sanctions and pressures external to the individual, and relations within the organization are based on high levels of trust.'

High-involvement management

As defined by Benson *et al* (2006), 'High-involvement work practices are a specific set of human resource practices that focus on employee decision making, power, access to information, training and incentives.' Camps and Luna-Arocas (2009) observe that 'High-involvement work practices aim to provide employees with the opportunity, skills and motivation to contribute to organizational success in environments demanding greater levels of commitment and involvement.' The term 'high-involvement' was used by Lawler (1986) to describe management systems based on commitment and involvement, as opposed to the old bureaucratic model based on control.

Specific HR strategies

Specific HR strategies set out what the organization intends to do in areas such as:

- Human capital management: obtaining, analysing and reporting on data that informs the direction of value-adding people management strategic, investment and operational decisions.

- Knowledge management: creating, acquiring, capturing, sharing and using knowledge to enhance learning and performance.

- Corporate social responsibility: a commitment to managing the business ethically in order to make a positive impact on society and the environment.

- Engagement: the development and implementation of policies designed to increase the level of employees' engagement with their work and the organization.

- Organization development: the planning and implementation of programmes designed to enhance the effectiveness with which an organization functions and responds to change.

- Resourcing: attracting and retaining high-quality people.

- Talent management: how the organization ensures that it has the talented people it needs to achieve success.

- Learning and development: providing an environment in which employees are encouraged to learn and develop.

- Reward: defining what the organization wants to do in the longer term to develop and implement reward policies, practices and processes which will further the achievement of its business goals and meet the needs of its stakeholders.

- Employee relations: defining the intentions of the organization about what needs to be done and what needs to be changed in the ways in which the organization manages its relationships with employees and their trade unions.

- Employee well-being: meeting the needs of employees for a healthy, safe and supportive work environment.

Criteria for an effective HR strategy

An effective HR strategy is one that works in the sense that it achieves what it sets out to achieve. Its criteria are:

- It will satisfy business needs.

- It is founded on detailed analysis and study, not just wishful thinking.

- It can be turned into actionable programmes which anticipate implementation requirements and problems.

- It is coherent and integrated, being composed of components which fit with and support each other.

- It takes account of the needs of line managers and employees generally as well as those of the organization and its other stakeholders. As Boxall and Purcell (2003) emphasized, 'HR planning should aim to meet the needs of the key stakeholder groups involved in people management in the firm.'

Formulating HR strategy

Research conducted by Wright *et al* (2004) identified two approaches that can be adopted by HR to strategy formulation. The *inside-out approach* begins with the status quo HR function (in terms of skills, processes, technologies and so on), then attempts (with varying degrees of success) to identify linkages to the business (usually through focusing on 'people issues'), making minor adjustments to HR activities along the way. In the *outside-in approach*, the starting point is the business and the customer, competitor and business issues it faces. The HR strategy then derives directly from these challenges to add real value.

Wright *et al* commented that HR strategies are more likely to flow from business strategies which will be dominated by product/market and financial considerations. But there is still room for HR to make an essential contribution at the stage when business strategies are conceived, for example, by focusing on resource issues. This contribution may be more significant if strategy formulation is an emergent or evolutionary process – HR strategic issues will then be dealt with as they arise during the course of formulating and implementing the corporate strategy. 'Remember that strategy is a process, not a document, intervention or event. Any strategy is a pattern in a stream of decisions, and as business and people issues change or obstacles appear, the patterns (strategy) will also have to change' (Wright *et al*, 2004).

Critical evaluation of the concept of strategic HRM

As an aspirational philosophy which emphasizes the importance of integrating business and HR strategies and the need to be forward-looking, the concept of strategic HRM has much to commend it. But there are problems.

First, the assumption behind the philosophy is that the formulation of strategy is a logical step-by-step process. But as explained earlier in this chapter, this is not the case.

Second, it is assumed that it is possible without undue difficulty to integrate business and HR strategy. When considering integration it should be remembered that business and HR issues influence each other, and in turn influence corporate and business unit strategies. It is also necessary to note that in establishing these links, account must be taken of the fact that strategies for change have also to be integrated with changes in the external and internal environments. Fit may exist at a point in time, but circumstances will change and fit no longer exists. An excessive pursuit of 'fit' with the status quo will inhibit the flexibility of approach that is essential in turbulent conditions.

Third, the following issues arise when attempting to achieve integration:

- The business strategy might not be clearly defined – it could be in an emergent or evolutionary state, which would mean that there is little or nothing with which to fit the HR strategy.

- Even if the business strategy is clear, it may be difficult to determine precisely how HR strategies could help in specific ways to support the achievement of particular business objectives. A good business case can only be made if it can be demonstrated that there will be a measurable link between the HR strategy and business performance in the area concerned.

- Even if there is a link, HR specialists do not always have the strategic capability to make the connection – they need to be able to see the big picture, understand the business drivers and appreciate how HR policies and practices can impact on them.

- Barriers exist between top management and HR – the former may not be receptive because they don't believe the strategy is necessary and HR is not capable of persuading them that they should listen, or HR lacks access to top management on strategic issues, or HR lacks credibility with top management as a function that knows anything about the business or should even have anything to do with the business.

Fourth, it is easy to say that you are going to do something; much harder to do it. The factors that contribute to creating this say / do gap between the strategy as designed and the strategy as implemented include:

- failure to understand the strategic needs of the business;

- inadequate assessment of the environmental, cultural, social and political factors which affect the content of the strategies;

- inadequate appreciation of the consequences of the strategy and the likely reaction of people affected by it;

- insufficient attention paid to practical implementation problems;

- failure to manage the change effectively;

- the development of ill-conceived and irrelevant initiatives, possibly because they are current fads or because there has been an poorly digested analysis of best practice which does not fit the organization's requirements;

- ignoring the important role of line managers and therefore neglecting to involve them in strategy formulation and in planning its implementation;

- overlooking the need to have established supporting processes for the initiative (such as performance management to support performance pay).

An implementation programme that overcomes these barriers needs to be based on a rigorous preliminary analysis of the strategic needs of the business and how the HR strategy will help to meet them. This should be followed by a communication programme that spells out what the strategy is, what it is expected to achieve and how it is to be introduced, and an involvement programme which ensures those concerned with the strategy, such as line managers, take part in formulating it, identify implementation problems and consider how they should be dealt with. Finally, action plans which indicate who does what and when need to be prepared as the basis for a project management programme.

Strategic HRM: key learning points

The conceptual basis of strategic HRM

Strategic HRM is 'the interface between HRM and strategic management'. It takes the notion of HRM as a strategic, integrated and coherent approach and develops that in line with the concept of strategic management (Boxall, 1996).

The fundamental characteristics of strategy are:

- forward looking – the organizational capability of a firm depends on its resource capability;

- strategic fit – the need when developing HR strategies to achieve congruence between them and the organization's business strategies within the context of its external and internal environment.

How strategy is formulated

An emergent and flexible process of developing a sense of direction, making the best use of resources and ensuring strategic fit.

The aim of strategic HRM

To generate organizational capability by ensuring that the organization has the skilled, engaged, committed and well-motivated employees it needs to achieve sustained competitive advantage.

Implications of the resource-based view

The resource-based view emphasizes the importance of creating firms that are 'more intelligent and flexible than their competitors' (Boxall, 1996) by hiring and developing more talented staff and by extending the skills base.

Implications of the concept of strategic fit

The concept of strategic fit means developing HR strategies that are integrated with the business strategy and support its achievement (vertical integration or fit), and the use of an integrated approach to the development of HR practices.

The three HRM 'perspectives' of Delery and Doty (1996)

- Universalistic perspective – some HR practices are better than others and all organizations should adopt these best practices.

- Contingency – in order to be effective, an organization's HR policies must be consistent with other aspects of the organization.

- Configurational – relating HRM to the 'configuration' of the organization in terms of its structures and processes.

The concepts of 'best practice' and 'best fit'

The concept of best practice is based on the assumption that there is a set of best HRM practices which are universal in the sense that they are best in any situation, and that adopting them will lead to superior organizational performance. This concept of universality is criticized because it takes no account of the local context.

The concept of best fit emphasizes that HR strategies should be congruent with the context and circumstances of the organization. 'Best fit' can be perceived in terms of vertical integration or alignment between the organization's business and HR strategies.

It is generally accepted that best fit is more important than best practice.

The significance of bundling

The process of bundling HR strategies is an important aspect of the concept of strategic HRM, which is concerned with the organization as a total system or entity, and addresses what needs to be done across the organization as a whole.

HR strategies

HR strategies set out what the organization intends to do about its human resource management policies and practices, and how they should be integrated with the business strategy and each other.

Questions

1. A junior colleague has sent you an e-mail saying 'During the course of my studies I have come across the phrase "best fit is more important than best practice". What does this mean exactly, and what is its significance to us?' Produce a reply.

2. Your chief executive has sent you the following e-mail. 'I have just returned from a one-day management conference in which an academic kept on referring to the "resource-based view" and its significance. What is it, and how relevant is it, if at all, to what we are doing here?' Produce a reply.

3. You are the recently appointed HR director of a medium-sized distribution company based in Dartford, with a staff of 350 including 130 drivers. After three months you have decided that the crucial HR issues facing the company are the high rate of turnover of drivers (35 per cent last year), an unacceptable level of road accidents, and an unsatisfactory climate of employee relations (there is a recognized union for drivers which is militant and hostile, and there are no formal procedures for employee communications or consultation). In spite of this the company is doing reasonably well, although it is felt by the board that is should do better, and there are plans for opening a new distribution centre in Essex. You have received an e-mail from the finance director who is preparing the company's business plan and asks for your proposals on what needs to be done in HR to support the forthcoming business plan. Formulate your response.

4. How would you distinguish between high-performance, high-commitment and high-involvement management?

5. Critically evaluate the concepts of best practice and best fit.

References

Abell, D F (1993) *Managing with Dual Strategies: Mastering the present, pre-empting the future*, Free Press, New York

Armstrong, M and Baron, A (2002) *Strategic HRM: The route to improved business performance*, CIPD, London

Armstrong, M and Long, P (1994) *The Reality of Strategic HRM*, Institute of Personnel and Development, London

Baird, L and Meshoulam, I (1988) Managing two fits of strategic human resource management, *Academy of Management Review*, **13** (1), pp 116–28

Barney, J B (1991) Firm resources and sustained competitive advantage, *Journal of Management Studies*, **17** (1), pp 99–120

Barney, J B (1995) Looking inside for competitive advantage, *Academy of Management Executive*, **9** (4), pp 49–61

Baron, D (2001) Private policies, corporate policies and integrated strategy, *Journal of Economics and Management Strategy*, **10** (7), pp 7–45

Becker, B E and Gerhart, S (1996) The impact of human resource management on organizational performance: progress and prospects, *Academy of Management Journal*, **39** (4), 779–801

Benson, G S, Young, S M and Lawler, E E (2006) High involvement work practices and analysts' forecasts of corporate performance, *Human Resource Management*, **45** (4), pp 519–27

Boxall, P F (1996) The strategic HRM debate and the resource-based view of the firm, *Human Resource Management Journal*, **6** (3), pp 59–75

Boxall, P F (1999) Human resource strategy and competitive advantage: a longitudinal study of engineering consultancies, *Journal of Management Studies*, **36** (4), pp 443–63

Boxall, P F and Purcell, J (2003) *Strategy and Human Resource Management*, Palgrave Macmillan, Basingstoke

Boxall, P F, Purcell, J and Wright, P (2007) The goals of HRM, in *Oxford Handbook of Human Resource Management*, ed P Boxall, J Purcell and P Wright, Oxford University Press, Oxford

Camps, J and Luna-Arocas, R (2009) High-involvement work practices and firm performance, *International Journal of Human Resource Management*, **20** (5), pp 1056–77

Cappelli, P and Crocker-Hefter, A (1996) Distinctive human resources are firms' core competencies, *Organizational Dynamics*, Winter, pp 7–22

Chandler, A D (1962) *Strategy and Structure*, MIT Press, Boston, MA

Delery, J E and Doty, H D (1996) Modes of theorizing in strategic human resource management: tests of universality, contingency and configurational performance predictions, *Academy of Management Journal*, **39** (4), pp 802–35

Dyer, L and Holder, G W (1998) Strategic human resource management and planning, in *Human Resource Management: Evolving roles and responsibilities*, ed L Dyer, Bureau of National Affairs, Washington, DC

Dyer, L and Reeves, T (1995) Human resource strategies and firm performance: what do we know and where do we need to go?, *International Journal of Human Resource Management*, **6** (3), pp 656–70

Fombrun, C J, Tichy, N M, and Devanna, M A (1984) *Strategic Human Resource Management*, Wiley, New York

Gratton, L A (2000) Real step change, *People Management*, 16 March, pp 27–30

Guest, D E (1997) Human resource management and performance; a review of the research agenda, *International Journal of Human Resource Management*, **8** (3), pp 263–76

Heller, R (1972) *The Naked Manager*, Barrie & Jenkins, London

Kanter, R M (1984) *The Change Masters*, Allen & Unwin, London

Lawler, E E (1986) *High Involvement Management*, Jossey-Bass, San Francisco

Mabey, C, Salaman, G and Storey, J (1998) *Human Resource Management: A strategic introduction*, 2nd edn, Blackwell, Oxford

MacDuffie, J P (1995) Human resource bundles and manufacturing performance, *Industrial Relations Review*, **48** (2), pp 199–221

Miles, R E and Snow, C C (1978) *Organizational Strategy: Structure and process*, McGraw-Hill, New York

Mintzberg, H (1987) Crafting strategy, *Harvard Business Review*, July–August, pp 66–74

Paauwe, J (2004) *HRM and Performance: Achieving long term viability*, Oxford University Press, Oxford

Pearce, J A and Robinson, R B (1988) *Strategic Management: Strategy formulation and implementation*, Irwin, Georgetown, Ontario

Penrose, E (1959) *The Theory of the Growth of the Firm*, Blackwell, Oxford

Pfeffer, J (1998) *The Human Equation*, Harvard Business School Press, Boston, MA

Pfeffer, J and Davis-Blake, A (1992) Understanding organizational wage structures: a resource dependence approach, *Academy of Management Journal*, **30**, pp 437–55

Porter, M E (1985) *Competitive Advantage: Creating and sustaining superior performance*, Free Press, New York

Priem, R L and Butler, J E (2001) Is the resource-based theory a useful perspective for strategic management research?, *Academy of Management Review*, **26** (1), pp 22–40

Purcell, J (1999) Best practice or best fit: chimera or cul-de-sac, *Human Resource Management Journal*, **9** (3), pp 26–41

Purcell, J, Kinnie, K, Hutchinson, S, Rayton, B and Swart, J (2003) *People and Performance: How people management impacts on organisational performance*, CIPD, London

Richardson, R and Thompson, M (1999) *The Impact of People Management Practices on Business Performance: A literature review*, Institute of Personnel and Development, London

Schuler, R S (1992) Strategic human resource management: linking people with the strategic needs of the business, *Organizational Dynamics*, **21** (1), pp 18–32

Schuler, R S and Jackson, S E (1987) Linking competitive strategies with human resource management practices, *Academy of Management Executive*, **9** (3), pp 207–19

Tyson, S (1997) Human resource strategy: a process for managing the contribution of HRM to organizational performance, *International Journal of Human Resource Management*, **8** (3), pp 277–90

Ulrich, D (1998) A new mandate for human resources, *Harvard Business Review*, January–February, pp 124–34

Walker, J W (1992) *Human Resource Strategy*, McGraw-Hill, New York

Walton, R E (1985) From control to commitment in the workplace, *Harvard Business Review*, March–April, pp 77–84

Wernerfelt, B (1984) A resource-based view of the firm, *Strategic Management Journal*, **5** (2), pp 171–80

Wood, S (1996) High commitment management and organization in the UK, *International Journal of Human Resource Management*, **7** (1), pp. 41–58

Wright, P M, Snell, S A and Jacobsen, H H (2004) Current approaches to HR strategies: inside-out versus outside-in, *Human Resource Planning*, **27** (4), pp 36–46

3

HR Policies and Procedures

Learning outcomes

On completing this chapter you should know about:

- The reasons for having HR policies and procedures
- The content of the main HR procedures
- Overall and specific HR policies

Introduction

HR policies and procedures are required to ensure that human resource management issues are dealt with consistently in line with the values of the organization on how people should be treated, and that legal requirements are met. HR policies should be distinguished from procedures. A policy provides continuing guidelines and generalized guidance on how HR issues should be dealt with to ensure that an appropriate approach is adopted throughout the organization. A procedure spells out precisely what steps should be taken to deal with major employment issues such as grievances, discipline, capability and redundancy.

HR policies

HR policies can be expressed formally as overall statements of the values of the organization or they can apply to specific areas of people management.

Overall HR policy

The overall HR policy defines how the organization fulfils its social responsibilities for its employees, Selznick (1957) emphasized the key role of values in organizations, when he wrote, 'The formation of an institution is marked by the making of value commitments, that is, choices which fix the assumptions of policy makers as to the nature of the enterprise, its distinctive aims, methods and roles.'

The values expressed in an overall statement of HR policies may explicitly or implicitly refer to the following requirements.

- Equity: treating employees fairly and justly by adopting an 'even-handed' approach. This includes protecting individuals from any unfair decisions made by their managers, providing equal opportunities for employment and promotion, and operating an equitable payment system.

- Consideration: taking account of individual circumstances when making decisions which affect the prospects, security or self-respect of employees.

- Respect: treating individuals with respect as human beings.

- Organizational learning: a belief in the need to promote the learning and development of all the members of the organization by providing the processes and support required.

- Performance through people: the importance attached to developing a performance culture and to continuous improvement; the significance of performance management as a means of defining and agreeing mutual expectations; the provision of fair feedback to people on how well they are performing.

- Quality of working life: consciously and continually aiming to improve the quality of working life. This involves increasing the sense of satisfaction people obtain from their work by, so far as possible, reducing monotony, increasing variety, autonomy and responsibility, avoiding placing people under too much stress and providing for an acceptable balance between work and life outside work.

- Working conditions: providing healthy, safe and, so far as practicable, pleasant working conditions.

Values such as these are espoused by many organizations in one form or another. But to what extent are they practised when making 'business-led' decisions, which can, of course be highly detrimental to employees if, for example, they lead to redundancy? A fundamental dilemma facing all those who formulate HR policies is 'How can we pursue policies that focus on business success and fulfil our obligations to employees in such terms as equity, consideration, respect, quality of working life and working conditions?' To argue, as some do, that HR strategies should be entirely oriented to supporting the achievement of business objectives implies that human considerations are unimportant. An over-emphasis on HRM as being about supporting the business strategy and on HR specialists as 'strategic business partners', which is a strong feature of current CIPD pronouncements, encourages businesses to ignore their responsibilities for the human rights of the people they employ. Organizations have obligations to all their stakeholders, not just their owners.

It may be difficult to express these policies in anything but generalized terms, but employers are increasingly having to recognize that they are subject to external as well as internal pressures which act as constraints on the extent to which they can disregard the higher standards of behaviour towards their employees that are expected of them.

Specific HR policies

HR policies typically cover the issues summarized below.

Age and employment

The policy on age and employment should take into account the UK legislation on age discrimination and the following facts:

- age is a poor predictor of job performance;
- it is misleading to equate physical and mental ability with age;
- more of the population are living active, healthy lives as they get older.

AIDS

An AIDS policy could include the following points:

- The risk through infection in the workplace is negligible.
- Where the occupation does involve blood contact as in hospitals, doctors' surgeries and laboratories, the special precautions advised by the Health and Safety Commission will be implemented.
- Employees who know that they are infected with AIDS will not be obliged to disclose the fact to the company, but if they do, the fact will remain completely confidential.
- There will be no discrimination against anyone with or at risk of acquiring AIDS.
- Employees infected by HIV or suffering from AIDS will be treated no differently from anyone else suffering a severe illness.

Bullying

An anti-bullying policy will state that bullying will not be tolerated by the organization and that those who persist in bullying their staff will be subject to disciplinary action, which could be severe in particularly bad cases. The policy will make it clear that individuals who are being bullied should have the right to discuss the problem with another person, a representative or a member of the HR function, and to make a complaint. The policy should emphasize that if a complaint is received it will be thoroughly investigated.

Discipline

The disciplinary policy should state that employees have the right to know what is expected of them and what could happen if they infringe the organization's rules. It would also make the point that, in handling disciplinary cases, the organization will treat employees in accordance with the principles of natural justice. It should be supported by a disciplinary procedure as described later in this chapter.

Diversity management

A policy on managing diversity recognizes that there are differences among employees and that these differences, if properly managed, will enable work to be done more efficiently and effectively. It does not focus exclusively on issues of discrimination, but instead concentrates on recognizing the differences between people. As Kandola and Fullerton (1994) express it, the concept of managing diversity 'is founded on the premise that harnessing these differences will create a productive environment in which everyone will feel valued, where their talents are fully utilized, and in which organizational goals are met'.

Managing diversity is a concept which recognizes the benefits to be gained from differences. It differs from equal opportunity, which aims to legislate against discrimination, assumes that people should be assimilated into the organization and, often, relies on affirmative action. This point was emphasized by Mulholland *et al* (2005):

> *The new diversity management thinking suggests that diversity management goes beyond the equal opportunities management considerations as described by the law, and promises to make a positive and strategic contribution to the successful operation of business. So diversity management is being hailed as a proactive, strategically relevant and results-focused approach and a welcome departure from the equal opportunities approach, which has been defined as reactive, operational and sometimes counterproductive.*

A management of diversity policy

The policy could:

- acknowledge cultural and individual differences in the workplace;

- state that the organization values the different qualities which people bring to their jobs;

- emphasize the need to eliminate bias in such areas as selection, promotion, performance assessment, pay and learning opportunities;

- focus attention on individual differences rather than group differences.

E-mails and use of the internet

The policy on e-mails could state that the sending or downloading of offensive e-mails is prohibited and that the senders or downloading of such messages are subject to disciplinary procedures. Any internet browsing or downloading of material not related to the business could also be prohibited, although this can be difficult to enforce. Some companies have always believed that reasonable use of the telephone is acceptable, and that policy may be extended to the internet.

If it is decided that employees' e-mails should be monitored to check on excessive or unacceptable use, then this should be included in an e-mail policy which would therefore be part of the contractual arrangements. A policy statement could be included to the effect that 'The company reserves the right to access and monitor all e-mail messages created, sent, received or stored on the company's system.'

Employee development

The employee development policy could express the organization's commitment to the continuous development of the skills and abilities of employees in order to maximize their contribution and to give them the opportunity to enhance their skills, realize their potential, advance their careers and increase their employability both within and outside the organization.

Employee relations

The employee relations policy will set out the organization's approach to the rights of employees to have their interests represented to management through trade unions, staff associations or some other form of representative system. It will also cover the basis upon which the organization works with trade unions, for example emphasizing that this should be regarded as a partnership.

Employee voice

The employee voice policy should spell out the organization's belief in giving employees an opportunity to have a say in matters that affect them. It should define the mechanisms for employee voice such as joint consultation and suggestion schemes.

Employment

Employment policies should be concerned with fundamental aspects of the employment relationship. They should take account of the requirements of relevant legislation. Recent UK Acts and EU Regulations which are important in the United Kingdom include those concerning age discrimination, the minimum wage, working time and part-time workers. The latter is especially significant because it requires that part-time workers should be entitled to the same terms and conditions as full-time workers, including pro rata pay. Note should also be taken of the UK Human Rights Act (1998), which gave further effect to rights and freedoms guaranteed under the European Convention on Human Rights. However, the rights are essentially civil and political rather than economic or social, and they only apply to a narrow range of employment. Moreover, they are not directly enforceable against an employer unless it is an 'obvious' public authority. It has, however, been held by the European Court of Human Rights that the statutory rights not to be unlawfully dismissed or discriminated against can be regarded as 'civil rights'. Provisions inserted into the Employment Rights Act must be interpreted by employment tribunals in a way that is compatible with the European Convention right to freedom of expression. This could apply to whistleblowing.

Equal opportunity

The equal opportunity policy should spell out the organization's determination to give equal opportunities to all, irrespective of sex, race, creed, disability, age or marital status. The policy should also deal with the extent to which the organization wants to take 'affirmative action' to redress imbalances between the numbers employed according to sex or race or to differences in the levels of qualifications and skills they have achieved.

An equal opportunity policy

- We are an equal opportunity employer. This means that we do not permit direct or indirect discrimination against any employee on the grounds of race, nationality, sex, sexual orientation, disability, religion, marital status or age.

- Direct discrimination takes place when a person is treated less favourably than others are, or would be, treated in similar circumstances.

- Indirect discrimination takes place when, whether intentional or not, a condition is applied which adversely affects a considerable proportion of people of one race, nationality, sex, sexual orientation, religion or marital status, or those with disabilities or older employees.

- The firm will ensure that equal opportunity principles are applied in all its HR policies, and in particular to the procedures relating to the recruitment, training, development and promotion of its employees.

- Where appropriate and where permissible under the relevant legislation and codes of practice, employees of under-represented groups will be given positive training and encouragement to achieve equal opportunity.

Grievances

The policy on grievances could state that employees have the right to raise their grievances with their manager, to be accompanied by a representative if they so wish, and to appeal to a higher level if they feel that their grievance has not been resolved satisfactorily. The policy should be supported by a grievance procedure (see later in this chapter).

Health and safety

Health and safety policies cover how the organization intends to provide healthy and safe places and systems of work.

New technology

A new technology policy statement could state that there will be consultation about the introduction of new technology and the steps that would be taken by the organization to minimize the risk of compulsory redundancy or adversely affecting other terms and conditions or working arrangements.

Promotion

A promotion policy could state the organization's intention to promote from within wherever this is appropriate as a means of satisfying its requirements for high-quality staff. The policy could, however, recognize that there will be occasions when the organization's present and future needs can only be met by recruitment from outside. The point could be made that a vigorous organization needs infusions of fresh blood from time to time if it is not to stagnate. In addition, the policy might state that employees will be encouraged to apply for internally advertised jobs and will not be held back from promotion by their managers, however reluctant the latter may be to lose them. The policy should define the approach the organization adopts to engaging, promoting and training older employees. It should emphasize that the only criterion for selection or promotion should be ability to do the job, and for training, the belief, irrespective of age, that the employee will benefit.

Redundancy

The redundancy policy should state that the aim of the organization is to provide for employment security. It is the organization's intention to use its best endeavours to avoid involuntary redundancy through its redeployment and retraining programmes and by allowing natural wastage to take place. However, if redundancy is unavoidable, those affected will be given fair and equitable treatment, the maximum amount of warning and every help that can be provided to obtain suitable alternative employment. The policy should be supported by a redundancy procedure (see later in this chapter).

Reward

The reward policy could cover such matters as:

- providing an equitable pay system;
- equal pay for work of equal value;
- paying for performance, competence, skill or contribution;
- sharing in the success of the organization (gain sharing or profit sharing);
- the relationship between levels of pay in the organization and market rates;
- the provision of employee benefits, including flexible benefits if appropriate;
- the importance attached to non-financial rewards resulting from recognition accomplishment, autonomy, and the opportunity to develop.

Sexual harassment

The sexual harassment policy should state that:

- Sexual harassment will not be tolerated.

- Employees subjected to sexual harassment will be given advice, support and counselling as required.

- Every attempt will be made to resolve the problem informally with the person complained against.

- Assistance will be given to the employee to complain formally if informal discussions fail.

- A special process will be available for hearing complaints about sexual harassment. This will provide for employees to bring their complaint to someone of their own sex if they so wish.

- Complaints will be handled sensitively and with due respect for the rights of both the complainant and the accused.

- Sexual harassment is regarded as gross industrial misconduct and, if proved, makes the individual liable for instant dismissal. Less severe penalties may be reserved for minor cases but there will always be a warning that repetition will result in dismissal.

Substance abuse

A substance abuse policy could include assurances that:

- Employees identified as having substance abuse problems will be offered advice and help.

- Any reasonable absence from work necessary to receive treatment will be granted under the organization's sickness scheme provided that there is full cooperation from the employee.

- An opportunity will be given to discuss the matter once it has become evident or suspected that work performance is being affected by substance-related problems.

- Employees have the right to be accompanied by a friend or employee representative in any such discussion.

- Agencies will be recommended to which the employee can go for help if necessary.

- Employment rights will be safeguarded during any reasonable period of treatment.

Work–life balance

Work–life balance policies define how the organization intends to allow employees greater flexibility in their working patterns so that they can balance what they do at work with the responsibilities and interests they have outside work. The policy will indicate how flexible work practices can be developed and implemented. It will emphasize that the numbers of hours worked must not be treated as a criterion for assessing performance. It will set out guidelines on the specific arrangements that can be made, such as flexible hours, compressed working week, term-time working contracts, working at home, special leave for parents and carers, career breaks and various kinds of child care.

HR procedures

HR procedures set out the ways in which certain actions concerning people should be carried out by the management or individual managers. In effect they constitute a formalized approach to dealing with specific issues arising in the employment relationship. Procedures are more exacting than policies. They state what must be done as well as spelling out how to do it.

The main areas where procedures are required are those concerned with handling disciplinary and capability problems, grievances, and redundancy.

Disciplinary procedure

The procedure should follow the principles set out in the ACAS Code of Practice, namely that:

- Employers and employees should raise and deal with issues promptly and should not unreasonably delay meetings, decisions or confirmation of those decisions.
- Employers and employees should act consistently.
- Employers should carry out any necessary investigations to establish the facts of the case.
- Employers should inform employees of the basis of the problem, and give them an opportunity to put their case in response before any decisions are made.
- Employers should allow employees to be accompanied at any formal disciplinary meeting.
- Employers should allow an employee to appeal against any formal decision made.

The procedure may indicate that that a verbal or informal warning will be given to the employee in the first instance or instances of minor offences. It will state that in the case of more serious offences or after repeated instances of minor offences, a formal disciplinary meeting will be held. The individual should be given a written notice of this meeting, which will give details of the alleged misconduct.

At the meeting the employer should explain the complaint against the employee and go through the evidence that has been gathered. The employee should be allowed to set out their case and answer any allegations that have been made. The employee should also be given a reasonable opportunity to ask questions, present evidence, call witnesses and raise points about any information provided by witnesses. The employee can be accompanied by a fellow worker or a union representative or official. If it is concluded that misconduct has taken place, the stages of the procedure are:

- A written formal warning which states the exact nature of the offence and indicates any future disciplinary action that will be taken if the offence is repeated within a specified time limit.

- A final written warning if the offence is repeated within the time limit.

Disciplinary action such as suspension, or in serious cases dismissal, can be carried out if, despite previous warnings, an employee still fails to reach the required standards in a reasonable period of time. The employee can appeal against this action.

Some acts, termed 'gross misconduct', are so serious in themselves or have such serious consequences that they may call for dismissal without notice for a first offence. But a fair disciplinary process should always be followed before dismissing for gross misconduct. Disciplinary rules should give examples of acts that constitute gross misconduct.

Capability procedure

Some organizations deal with matters of capability under a disciplinary procedure, but there is a good case to be made for dealing with poor performance issues separately, leaving the disciplinary procedure to be invoked for situations such as poor timekeeping. The main points covered by a capability procedure are summarized below.

If a manager/team leader believes that an employee's performance is not up to standard, an informal discussion should be held with the employee to try to establish the reason and to agree the actions required to improve performance by the employee and/or the manager/team leader.

Should the employee show no (or insufficient) improvement over a defined period (weeks or months), a formal interview should be arranged between the employee (together with a representative if so desired). The aims of this interview are to:

- explain the shortfall between the employee's performance and the required standard;

- identify the cause(s) of the unsatisfactory performance;

- determine what – if any – remedial treatment (such as training, retraining or support) can be given;

- obtain the employee's commitment to reaching that standard;

- set a reasonable period for the employee to reach the standard, and agree on a monitoring system during that period;

- tell the employee what will happen if that standard is not met.

The outcome of this interview should be recorded in writing, and a copy be given to the employee. At the end of the review period a further formal interview should held, at which time:

- If the required improvement has been made, the employee will be told of this and encouraged to maintain the improvement.

- If some improvement has been made but the standard has not yet been met, the review period will be extended.

- If there has been no discernible improvement and performance is still well below an acceptable standard, this will be indicated to the employee, and consideration will be given to whether there are alternative vacancies which the employee would be competent to fill. If there are, the employee will be given the options of accepting such a vacancy or being considered for dismissal.

- If such vacancies are available, the employee will be given full details of them in writing before being required to make a decision.

- In the absence of suitable alternative work, the employee will be informed and invited to give their views on this before the final decision is taken.

Employees may appeal against their dismissal.

Grievance procedure

A grievance procedure spells out the policy on handling grievances and the approach to dealing with them, as in the following example. The main stages through which a grievance may be raised are as follows:

- The employee raises the matter with his or her immediate team leader or manager, and may be accompanied by a fellow employee of their own choice.

- If the employee is not satisfied with the decision, the employee requests a meeting with a member of management who is more senior than the team leader or manager who initially heard the grievance.

- If the employee is still not satisfied with the decision, they may appeal to an appropriate higher authority. The decision made at this meeting is final.

Redundancy procedure

A redundancy procedure aims to meet statutory, ethical and practical considerations when dealing with this painful process. A procedure typically includes the following points.

Review of employee requirements

Management will continuously keep under review possible future developments which might affect the number of employees required, and will prepare overall plans for dealing with possible redundancies.

Measures to avoid redundancies

If the likelihood of redundancy is foreseen, the company will inform the union(s), explaining the reasons, and in consultation with the union(s) will give consideration to taking appropriate measures to prevent redundancy or alleviate the effects of redundancy.

Consultation on redundancies

If all measures to avoid redundancy fail, the company will consult the union(s) at the earliest opportunity in order to reach agreement.

Selection of redundant employees

In the event of impending redundancy, the individuals who might be surplus to requirements are selected in accordance with agreed principles. The union(s) will be informed of the numbers affected but not of individual names.

HR policies and procedures: key learning points

The reasons for having HR policies

HR policies provide guidelines on how key aspects of people management should be handled. The aim is to ensure that any HR issues are dealt with consistently in accordance with the values of the organization and in line with certain defined principles.

Overall HR policy

The overall HR policy defines how the organization fulfils its social responsibilities for its employees and sets out its attitudes towards them. It is an expression of its values or beliefs about how people should be treated.

Specific HR policies

Specific HR policies cover age and employment, AIDS, bullying, discipline, e-mails and the internet, employee development, employee relations, employee voice, employment, equal opportunity, grievances, health and safety, managing diversity, promotion, redundancy, reward, sexual harassment, substance abuse and work–life balance.

Procedures

The main procedures are concerned with discipline, capability, grievances and redundancy.

Questions

1. What is the distinction between HR policies and procedures?

2. What is the purpose of HR policies?

3. What principles should govern the operation of a disciplinary procedure?

References

Kandola, R and Fullerton, J (1994) *Managing the Mosaic: Diversity in action*, Institute of Personnel and Development, London

Mulholland, G, Ozbilgin, M and Worman, D (2005) *Managing Diversity: Linking theory and practice to business performance*, CIPD, London

Selznick, P (1957) *Leadership and Administration*, Row, Evanston, IL

4

Human Capital Management

Introduction

Human capital management (HCM) informs decisions on the issues critical to the organization's success by systematically analysing, measuring and evaluating how people policies and practices create value. This chapter first defines HCM in more detail and then examines the underpinning concept of human capital and the significance of HCM. The rest of the chapter focuses on human capital measurement.

Human capital management defined

As defined by Baron and Armstrong (2007), HCM is concerned with obtaining, analysing and reporting on data which informs the direction of value-adding people management strategic, investment and operational decisions at corporate level and at the level of front-line management. It is, as Paul Kearns (2005) emphasized, ultimately about value.

The defining characteristic of HCM is the use of measurements (metrics) to guide an approach to managing people which regards them as assets and emphasizes that competitive advantage is achieved by strategic investments in those assets through employee engagement and retention, talent management and learning and development programmes. HCM provides a bridge between HR and business strategy. It is based on the concept of human capital.

The concept of human capital

Individuals generate, retain and use knowledge and skill (human capital) and create intellectual capital. Their knowledge is enhanced by the interactions between them (social capital), and generates the institutionalized knowledge possessed by an organization (organizational capital).

Human capital consists of the knowledge, skills and abilities of the people employed in an organization. HCM is about generating and analysing the information needed to develop and manage these people.

The term 'human capital' was originated by Schultz (1961), who elaborated his notion in 1981 as follows:

> Consider all human abilities to be either innate or acquired. Attributes... which are valuable and can be augmented by appropriate investment will be human capital.

A more detailed definition was put forward by Bontis *et al* (1999):

> Human capital represents the human factor in the organization; the combined intelligence, skills and expertise that gives the organization its distinctive character. The

human elements of the organization are those that are capable of learning, changing, innovating and providing the creative thrust which if properly motivated can ensure the long-term survival of the organization.

Scarborough and Elias (2002) believe that 'The concept of human capital is most usefully viewed as a bridging concept – that is, it defines the link between HR practices and business performance in terms of assets rather than business processes.' They point out that human capital is to a large extent 'non-standardized, tacit, dynamic, context dependent and embodied in people'. These characteristics make it difficult to evaluate human capital, bearing in mind that the 'features of human capital that are so crucial to firm performance are the flexibility and creativity of individuals, their ability to develop skills over time and to respond in a motivated way to different contexts'.

Intellectual capital

The concept of human capital is associated with the overarching notion of intellectual capital. This is defined as the stocks and flows of knowledge available to an organization. These can be regarded as the intangible resources associated with people which, together with tangible resources (money and physical assets), comprise the market or total value of a business. Bontis (1998) defined intangible resources as the factors other than financial and physical assets that contribute to the value-generating processes of a firm and are under its control.

Social capital

Social capital is another element of intellectual capital. It consists of the knowledge derived from networks of relationships within and outside the organization. The concept of social capital was defined by Putnam (1996) as 'the features of social life – networks, norms and trust – that enable participants to act together more effectively to pursue shared objectives'. It is important to take into account social capital considerations, that is, the ways in which knowledge is developed through interaction between people. Bontis *et al* (1999) pointed out that it is flows as well as stocks that matter. Intellectual capital develops and changes over time, and a significant part is played in these processes by people acting together.

Organizational capital

Organizational capital is the institutionalized knowledge possessed by an organization which is stored in databases, manuals and so on (Youndt, 2000). It is often called structural capital (Edvinson and Malone, 1997), but the term organizational capital is preferred by Youndt because, he argues, it conveys more clearly that this is the knowledge that the organization actually owns.

The significance of human capital theory

The added value that people can contribute to an organization is emphasized by human capital theory. It regards people as assets, and stresses that investment by organizations in people will generate worthwhile returns. Human capital theory is associated with the resource-based view of the firm as described in Chapter 2 and also with knowledge management (see Chapter 5).

An approach to people management based on human capital theory involves obtaining answers to the following questions:

● What are the key performance drivers that create value?

● What skills have we got?

● What skills de we need now and in the future to meet our strategic aims?

● How are we going to attract, develop and retain these skills?

● How can we develop a culture and environment in which organizational and individual learning takes place which meets both our needs and the needs of our employees?

● How can we provide for both the explicit and tacit knowledge created in our organization to be captured, recorded and used effectively?

Human capital theory provides the conceptual framework for human capital management, which is based on human capital measurement as discussed below.

Human capital measurement

Human capital measurement has been defined by IDS (2004) as being 'about finding links, correlations and, ideally, causation, between different sets of (HR) data, using statistical techniques'.

As Becker *et al* (2001) emphasized, 'The most potent action HR managers can take to ensure their strategic contribution is to develop a measurement system that convincingly showcases HR's impact on business performance.' They must 'understand how the firm creates value and how to measure the value creation process'.

The primary aim of HCM is to assess the impact of human resource management practices and the contribution made by people to organizational performance. Methods of measuring impact and contribution based upon human capital data have therefore to be developed.

The need for human capital measurement

There is an overwhelming case for evolving methods of valuing human capital as an aid to people management decision making. This may mean identifying the key people management drivers and modelling the effect of varying them. The need is to develop a framework within which reliable information can be collected and analysed, such as added value per employee, productivity and measures of employee behaviour (attrition and absenteeism rates, the frequency/severity rate of accidents, and cost savings resulting from suggestion schemes).

Becker *et al* (2001) refer to the need to develop a 'high-performance perspective' in which HR and other executives view HR as a system embedded within the larger system of the firm's strategy implementation. They state that 'The firm manages and measures the relationship between these two systems and firm performance.'

Reasons for the interest in measurement

The recognized importance of achieving human capital advantage has led to an interest in the development of methods of measuring the value and impact of that capital:

- Human capital constitutes a key element of the market worth of a company. A research study conducted in 2003 (CFO Research Services) estimated that the value of human capital represented over 36 per cent of total revenue in a typical organization.

- People in organizations add value, and there is a case for assessing this value to provide a basis for HR planning and for monitoring the effectiveness and impact of HR policies and practices.

- The process of identifying measures and collecting and analysing information relating to them will focus the attention of the organization on what needs to be done to find, keep, develop and make the best use of its human capital.

- Measurements can be used to monitor progress in achieving strategic HR goals and generally to evaluate the effectiveness of HR practices.

- You cannot manage unless you measure.

Critical evaluation of human capital measurement

The case for human capital measurement seems to be overwhelming, but a number of voices have advised caution about measurement. Leadbeater (2000) observed: that measuring can 'result in cumbersome inventories which allow managers to manipulate perceptions of intangible values to the detriment of investors. The fact is that too few of these measures are focused on the way companies create value and make money.' The Institute for Employment Studies (Hartley, 2005) emphasized that reporting on human capital is not simply about measurement. Measures on their own such as those resulting from benchmarking are not enough; they must be clearly linked to business performance.

Research carried out by Scarborough and Elias (2002) found that it is not what organizations decide to measure that is important, but the process of measurement itself. As they noted:

In short, measures are less important that the activity of measuring – of continuously developing and refining our understanding of the productive role of human capital within particular settings, by embedding such activities in management practices, and linking them to the business strategy of the firm.

This sentiment was echoed by Richard Donkin (2005), when he wrote 'It is not the measuring itself that is the key to successful human capital management but the intentions behind the measuring and the resulting practices that emerge.'

In a lecture to commemorate the Institute for Employment Studies' 40th anniversary, Professor Mick Marchington (2008) commented that the HR function is 'obsessed with measuring its way to credibility'. His arguments were that HR measurement and benchmarking are often concerned with the most measurable rather than the most meaningful, and that we are in some cases in danger of abandoning 'the heart and the soul of people management'.

Notwithstanding these comments, the growing sophistication of HR information systems, particularly in larger organizations, means that a lot more data on employees and HR practices is now often available. A reasonable and balanced use of measurement provides the information required to guide HR decisions and to evaluate the effectiveness of HRM practices.

Approaches to measurement

Three approaches to measurement are described below.

The human capital index: Watson Wyatt

On the basis of a survey of companies that have linked together HR management practices and market value, Watson Wyatt (2002) identified four major categories of HR practice which could be linked to a 30 per cent increase in shareholder value creation. These are:

Practice	Percentage impact on market value
Total rewards and accountability	16.5
Collegial, flexible workforce	9.0
Recruiting and retention excellence	7.9
Communication integrity	7.1

The organizational performance model: Mercer HR Consulting

As described by Nalbantian *et al* (2004), the Organizational Performance Model developed by Mercer HR Consulting is based on the following elements:

- people;
- work processes;
- management structure;

- information and knowledge;
- decision making;
- rewards.

Each of the above elements plays out differently within the context of the organization to create a unique DNA. If these elements have been developed piecemeal, as often happens, the potential for misalignment is strong, and it is likely that human capital is not being optimized, creating opportunities for substantial improvement in returns. Identifying these opportunities requires disciplined measurement of the organization's human capital assets and the management practices that affect their performance. The statistical tool 'Internal Labour Market Analysis' used by Mercer draws on the running record of employee and labour market data to analyse the actual experience of employees rather than stated HR programmes and policies. Thus gaps can be identified between what is required in the workforce to support business goals and what is actually being delivered.

The human capital monitor: Andrew Mayo

Andrew Mayo (2001) has developed the 'human capital monitor' to identify the human value of the enterprise, or 'human asset worth', which is equal to 'employment cost × individual asset multiplier'. The latter is a weighted average assessment of capability, potential to grow, personal performance (contribution) and alignment to the organization's values set in the context of the workforce environment (that is, how leadership, culture, motivation and learning are driving success). The absolute figure is not important. What does matter is that the process of measurement leads you to consider whether human capital is sufficient, increasing or decreasing, and highlights issues to address. Mayo advises against using too many measures: instead, it is best to concentrate on a few organization-wide measures that are critical in creating shareholder value or achieving current and future organizational goals.

A number of other areas for measurement and methods of doing so have been identified by Mayo (1999, 2001). He believes that value added per person is a good measure of the effectiveness of human capital, especially for making inter-firm comparisons. But he considers that the most critical indicator for the value of human capital is the level of expertise possessed by an organization. He suggests that this could be analysed under the headings of identified organizational core competencies. The other criteria he mentions are measures of satisfaction derived from employee opinion surveys and levels of attrition and absenteeism.

Measurement data
Main HCM data used for measurement

- Basic workforce data: demographic data (numbers by job category, gender, race, age, disability, working arrangements, absence and sickness, turnover and pay).

- People development and performance data: learning and development programmes, performance management/potential assessments, skills and qualifications.

- Perceptual data: attitude/opinion surveys, focus groups, exit interviews.

- Performance data: financial, operational and customer.

A summary of human capital measures and their possible uses is given in Table 4.1.

Table 4.1   A summary of human capital measures and their possible uses

Measures	Possible use – analysis leading to action
Workforce composition – gender, race, age, full time, part time	• Analyse the extent of diversity. • Assess the implications of a preponderance of employees in different age groups, such as the extent of losses through retirement. • Assess the extent to which the organization is relying on part-time staff.
Length of service distribution	• Indicate level of success in retaining employees. • Indicate preponderance of long- or short-serving employees. • Enable performance of more experienced employees to be assessed.
Skills analysis/assessment – graduates, professionally/technically qualified, skilled workers	• Assess skill levels against requirements. • Indicate where steps have to be taken to deal with shortfalls.
Attrition – employee turnover rates for different categories of management and employees	• Indicate areas where steps have to be taken to increase retention rates. • Provide a basis for assessing levels of commitment.
Attrition – cost of	• Support business case for taking steps to reduce attrition.
Absenteeism/sickness rates	• Identify problems and need for more effective attendance management policies.
Average number of vacancies as a percentage of total workforce	• Identify potential shortfall problem areas.
Total payroll costs (pay and benefits)	• Provide data for productivity analysis.

Table 4.1   *continued*

Measures	Possible use – analysis leading to action
Compa-ratio – actual rates of pay as a percentage of policy rates	• Enable control to be exercised over management of pay structure.
Percentage of employees in different categories of contingent pay or payment-by-result schemes	• Demonstrate the extent to which the organization believes that pay should be related to contribution.
Total pay review increases for different categories of employees as a percentage of pay	• Compare actual with budgeted payroll increase costs. • Benchmark pay increases.
Average bonuses or contingent pay awards as a percentage of base pay for different categories of managers and employees	• Analyse cost of contingent pay. • Compare actual and budgeted increases. • Benchmark increases.
Outcome of equal pay reviews	• Reveal pay gap between male and female employees.
Personal development plans completed as a percentage of employees	• Indicate level of learning and development activity.
Training hours per employee	• Indicate actual amount of training activity (note that this does not reveal the quality of training achieved or its impact).
Percentage of managers taking part in formal management development programmes	• Indicate level of learning and development activity.
Internal promotion rate (percentage of promotions filled from within)	• Indicate extent to which talent management programmes are successful.
Succession planning coverage (percentage of managerial jobs for which successors have been identified)	• Indicate extent to which talent management programmes are successful.
Percentage of employees taking part in formal performance reviews	• Indicate level of performance management activity.
Distribution of performance ratings by category of staff and department	• Indicate inconsistencies, questionable distributions and trends in assessments.
Accident severity and frequency rates	• Assess health and safety programmes.
Cost savings/revenue increases resulting from employee suggestion schemes	• Measure the value created by employees.

Human capital reporting

Analysing and reporting human capital data to top management and line managers will lead to better-informed decision making about what kind of actions or practices will improve business results. The ability to recognize problems and take rapid action to deal with them will be increased, and the scope to demonstrate the effectiveness of HR solutions and thus support the business case for greater investment in HR practices will be enhanced.

The processes of reporting the data internally and obtaining inferences from them are therefore vital parts of HCM. It is necessary to be clear about what data is required, and how it will be communicated and used.

The factors affecting the choice of what should be reported in the form of metrics are:

- the type of organization – measures are context-dependent;
- the business goals of the organization;
- the business drivers of the organization, that is, the factors that contribute to the achievement of business;
- existing key performance indicators (KPIs) used in the organization;
- the use of a balanced scorecard which enables a comprehensive view of performance to be taken by reference to four perspectives: financial, customer, innovation, and learning and internal processes;
- the availability of data;
- the use of data – measures should only be selected that can be put to good use in guiding strategy and reporting on performance;
- the manageability of data – there may be a wide choice of metrics and it is essential to be selective in the light of the above analysis so that the burden of collecting, analysing and evaluating the data is not too great and people do not suffer from information overload (remember that the cost of perfection is prohibitive, the cost of sensible approximation is less).

Human capital information is usually reported internally in the form of management reports providing information for managers, often through the intranet and on dashboards. However this information will not be valued by managers unless:

- it is credible, accurate and trustworthy;
- they understand what it means for them personally and how it will help them to manage their team;
- it is accompanied by guidance as to what action can be taken;
- they have the skills and abilities to understand and act upon it.

It is not enough simply to give managers and other stakeholders information on human capital. It must be accompanied by effective analysis and explanation if they are going to understand and act upon it in the interests of maximizing organizational performance.

Human capital management: key learning points

The concept of human capital

Individuals generate, retain and use knowledge and skill (human capital) and create intellectual capital. Human capital 'defines the link between HR practices and business performance in terms of assets rather than business processes' (Scarborough and Elias, 2002).

Characteristics of human capital

Human capital is non-standardized, tacit, dynamic, context dependent and embodied in people (Scarborough and Elias, 2002).

Constituents of human capital

Human capital consists of intellectual capital, social capital and organizational capital.

Significance of human capital

Human capital theory regards people as assets and stresses that investment by organizations in people will generate worthwhile returns.

Importance of human capital measurement

Measuring and valuing human capital is an aid to people management decision making.

Reasons for interest in human capital measurement

- Human capital constitutes a key element of the market worth of a company.
- People in organizations add value.
- Focus attention on what needs to be done to make the best use of a company's human capital.
- Monitor progress in achieving strategic HR goals and evaluate HR practices.
- You cannot manage unless you measure.

Approaches to measurement

- The human capital index: Watson Wyatt.
- The organizational performance model: Mercer HR Consulting.
- The human capital monitor: Andrew Mayo.

Measurement elements

Workforce data, people development data, perceptual data and performance data.

Factors affecting choice of measurement

- Type of organization; its business goals and drivers.
- The existing key performance indicators (KPIs).
- Use of a balanced scorecard.
- The availability, use and manageability of data.

Human capital reporting

Analysing and reporting human capital data to top management and line managers will lead to better-informed decision making about what kind of actions or practices will improve business results.

Criteria for HCM data as a guide to managers

Data will only be useful for managers if:

- it is credible, accurate and trustworthy;
- they understand what it means for them;
- it is accompanied by guidance as to what action can be taken;
- they have the skills and abilities to understand and act upon it.

Questions

1. Your finance director has asked you 'What is the difference between human resource management and human capital management? And if they are different, why should we bother with the latter?' Formulate your response.

2. What is social capital and why is it significant?

3. You have given a presentation on human capital management at a local conference. At question time a member of the audience gets up and says 'This is all very well, but it sounds as if we will have to do an awful lot of work in getting a full programme of HCM off the ground (collecting, analysing and reporting on performance statistics). I don't think that we have the resources to do it and even if we had, that it would be a cost-effective use of people's time.' Respond.

References

Baron, A and Armstrong, M (2007) *Human Capital Management: Achieving added value through people*, Kogan Page, London

Becker, B E, Huselid, M A and Ulrich, D (2001) *The HR Scorecard: Linking people, strategy, and performance*, Harvard Business School Press, Boston, MA

Bontis, N (1998) Intellectual capital: an exploratory study that develops measures and models, *Management Decision*, **36** (2), pp 63–76

Bontis, N, Dragonetti, N C, Jacobsen, K and Roos, G (1999) The knowledge toolbox: a review of the tools available to measure and manage intangible resources, *European Management Journal*, **17** (4), pp 391–402

CFO Research Services (2003) *Human Capital Management: The CFO's perspective*, CFO Publishing, Boston, MA

Donkin, R (2005) *Human Capital Management: A management report*, Croner, London

Edvinson, L and Malone, M S (1997) *Intellectual Capital: Realizing your company's true value by finding its hidden brainpower*, Harper Business, New York

Hartley, V (2005) *Open for Business: HR and human capital reporting*, IES, Brighton

IDS (2004) *Searching for the magic bullet*, HR Study 783, IDS, London

Kearns, P (2005) *Evaluating the ROI from Learning*, CIPD, London

Leadbeater, C (2000) *Living on Thin Air: The new economy*, Viking, London

Marchington, M (2008) Where next for HRM? Rediscovering the heart and the soul of people management, IES Working Paper WP20, Falmer

Mayo, A (1999) Making human capital meaningful, *Knowledge Management Review*, January/February, pp 26–29

Mayo, A (2001) *The Human Value of the Enterprise: Valuing people as assets*, Nicholas Brealey, London

Nalbantian, R, Guzzo, R A, Kieffer, D and Doherty, J (2004), *Play to Your Strengths: Managing your internal labour markets for lasting competitive advantage*, McGraw-Hill, New York

Putnam, R (1996) Who killed civic America? *Prospect*, March, pp 66–72

Scarborough, H and Elias, J (2002) *Evaluating Human Capital*, CIPD, London

Schultz, T W (1961) Investment in human capital, *American Economic Review*, **51**, March, pp 1–17

Schultz, T W (1981) *Investing in People: The economics of population quality*, University of California, CA

Watson Wyatt Worldwide (2002) *Human Capital Index: Human Capital as a lead indicator of shareholder value*, Watson Wyatt Worldwide, Washington, DC

Youndt, M A (2000) Human resource considerations and value creation: the mediating role of intellectual capital, paper delivered at National Conference of U S Academy of Management, Toronto, August

5

Knowledge Management

Key concepts and terms

- Communities of practice
- Data
- Explicit knowledge
- Information
- Knowledge
- Knowledge management
- Tacit knowledge

Learning outcomes

On completing this chapter you should be able to define these key concepts. You should also know about:

- The purpose and significance of knowledge management
- Knowledge management strategies
- Knowledge management systems
- Knowledge management issues
- The contribution HR can make to knowledge management

Introduction

Knowledge management is concerned with storing and sharing the wisdom, understanding and expertise accumulated in an organization about its processes, techniques and operations. It treats knowledge as a key resource. As Ulrich (1998) pointed out, 'Knowledge has become a direct competitive advantage for companies selling ideas and relationships.'

There is nothing new about knowledge management. Hansen *et al* (1999) remark that 'For hundreds of years, owners of family businesses have passed on their commercial wisdom to children, master craftsmen have painstakingly taught their trades to apprentices, and workers have exchanged ideas and know-how on the job.' But they also comment that 'As the foundation of industrialized economies has shifted from natural resources to intellectual assets, executives have been compelled to examine the knowledge underlying their business and how that knowledge is used.'

Knowledge management is as much if not more concerned with people and how they acquire, exchange and disseminate knowledge as it is about information technology. That is why it has become an important area for HR practitioners, who are in a strong position to exert influence in this aspect of people management. Scarborough *et al* (1999) believe that they should have 'the ability to analyse the different types of knowledge deployed by the organization... [and] to relate such knowledge to issues of organizational design, career patterns and employment security'.

The concept of knowledge management is closely associated with human capital management (see Chapter 4) and organizational learning (see Chapter 13).

Knowledge management defined

Knowledge management is 'any process or practice of creating, acquiring, capturing, sharing and using knowledge, wherever it resides, to enhance learning and performance in organizations' (Scarborough *et al*, 1999). Scarborough *et al* suggested that it focuses on the development of firm-specific knowledge and skills that are the result of organizational learning processes. Knowledge management is concerned with both stocks and flows of knowledge. Stocks include expertise and encoded knowledge in computer systems. Flows represent the ways in which knowledge is transferred from people to people, or from people to a knowledge database.

Scarborough and Carter (2000) described knowledge management as 'the attempt by management to actively create, communicate and exploit knowledge as a resource for the organization'. They suggest that this attempt has the following components:

- In technical terms knowledge management involves centralizing knowledge that is currently scattered across the organization and codifying tacit forms of knowledge.

- In social and political terms, knowledge management involves collectivizing knowledge so that it is no longer the exclusive property of individuals or groups.

- In economic terms, knowledge management is a response by organizations to the need to intensify their creation and exploitation of knowledge.

Knowledge management involves transforming knowledge resources by identifying relevant information, and then disseminating it so that learning can take place. Knowledge management strategies promote the sharing of knowledge by linking people with people, and by linking them to information so that they learn from documented experiences.

Knowledge is possessed by organizations and the people in organizations. Organizational operational, technical and procedural knowledge can be stored in databanks and found in presentations, reports, libraries, policy documents and manuals. It can be moved around the organization through information systems and by traditional methods such as meetings, workshops, courses, 'master classes' and written publications. The intranet provides an additional and very effective medium for communicating knowledge. Another method is 'communities of practice', defined by Wenger and Snyder (2000) as 'groups of people informally bound together by shared expertise and a passion for joint enterprise'.

People in organizations have knowledge which will not necessarily be shared formally or even informally with their colleagues. This individual knowledge may be crucial to the interests of the business, and could be lost if it remains locked up in the minds of employees or is taken elsewhere by them if they leave the organization.

The concept of knowledge

Knowledge is defined as what people understand about things, concepts, ideas, theories, procedures, practices and 'the way we do things around here'. It can be described as 'know-how', or when it is specific, expertise. A distinction was made by Ryle (1949) between 'knowing how' and 'knowing that'. 'Knowing how' is the ability of a person to perform tasks, and 'knowing that' is holding pieces of knowledge in one's mind. Blackler (1995) noted that 'Knowledge is multifaceted and complex, being both situated and abstract, implicit and explicit, distributed and individual, physical and mental, developing and static, verbal and encoded.'

Nonaka (1991) suggested that knowledge is held either by individuals or collectively. In Blackler's (1995) terms, embodied or embraced knowledge is individual and embedded, and cultural knowledge is collective. It can be argued (Scarborough and Carter, 2000) that knowledge emerges from the collective experience of work and is shared between members of a particular group or community.

Explicit and tacit knowledge

Nonaka (1991) and Nonaka and Takeuchi (1995) stated that knowledge is either explicit or tacit. *Explicit knowledge* can be codified – it is recorded and available and is held in databases, in corporate intranets and intellectual property portfolios. *Tacit knowledge* exists in people's minds. It is difficult to articulate in writing, and is acquired through personal experience. As suggested by Hansen *et al* (1999), it includes scientific or technological expertise, operational know-how, insights about an industry, and business judgement. The main challenge in knowledge management is how to turn tacit knowledge into explicit knowledge.

The purpose of data, information and knowledge

Ultimately, the purpose of knowledge management evidence is to manage data and information which can be put to good use in evidence-based management. Data, information and knowledge can be distinguished as follows:

- *Data* consist of the basic facts – the building blocks – for information and knowledge.

- *Information* is data that have been processed in a way that is meaningful to individuals. It is available to anyone entitled to gain access to it. As Drucker (1988) wrote, 'information is data endowed with meaning and purpose'.

- *Knowledge* is information put to productive use. It is personal and often intangible, and it can be elusive – the task of tying it down, encoding it and distributing it is tricky.

The purpose and significance of knowledge management

As explained by Blake (1988), the purpose of knowledge management is to capture a company's collective expertise and distribute it to 'wherever it can achieve the biggest payoff'. This is in accordance with the resource-based view of the firm, which suggests that the source of competitive advantage lies within the firm (that is, in its people and their knowledge), not in how it positions itself in the market. Trussler (1998) commented that 'The capability to gather, lever, and use knowledge effectively will become a major source of competitive advantage in many businesses over the next few years.' A successful company is a knowledge-creating company.

Knowledge management is about getting knowledge from those who have it to those who need it in order to improve organizational effectiveness. In the information age, knowledge rather than physical assets or financial resources is the key to competitiveness. In essence, as pointed out by Mecklenberg *et al* (1999), 'Knowledge management allows companies to capture, apply and generate value from their employees' creativity and expertise.'

Knowledge management strategies

Two approaches to knowledge management strategy have been identified by Hansen *et al* (1999).

The codification strategy: Knowledge is carefully codified and stored in databases where it can be accessed and used easily by anyone in the organization. Knowledge is explicit and is codified using a 'people-to-document' approach. This strategy is therefore document-driven. Knowledge is extracted from the person who developed it, made independent of that person and re-used for various purposes. It will be stored in some form of electronic repository for people to use, which allows many people to search for and retrieve codified knowledge without having to contact the person who originally developed it. This strategy relies largely on information technology to manage databases, and also on the use of the intranet.

The personalization strategy: Knowledge is closely tied to the person who has developed it, and is shared mainly through direct person-to-person contacts. This person-to-person approach involves ensuring that tacit knowledge is passed on. The exchange is achieved by creating networks and encouraging face-to-face communication between individuals and teams by means of informal conferences, workshops, communities of practice, brainstorming and one-to-one sessions.

Hansen *et al* (1999) state that the choice of strategy should be contingent on the organization: what it does, how it does it, and its culture. Thus consultancies such as Ernst & Young, using knowledge to deal with recurring problems, may rely mainly on codification so that recorded solutions to similar problems are easily retrievable. Strategy consultancy firms such as McKinsey or Bains, however, will rely mainly on a personalization strategy to help them to tackle the high-level strategic problems they are presented with, which demand the provision of creative, analytically rigorous advice. They need to channel individual expertise, and they find and develop people who are able to use a person-to-person knowledge-sharing approach effectively. In this sort of firm, directors or experts can be established who can be approached by consultants by telephone, e-mail or personal contact.

The research conducted by Hansen *et al* (1999) established that companies that use knowledge effectively pursue one of these strategies predominantly and use the second strategy to support the first. Those who try to excel at both strategies risk failing at both.

Knowledge management systems

A survey of 431 US and European firms by Rugles (1998) found that the following systems were used:

- creating an intranet (47 per cent);

- creating 'data warehouses', large physical databases that hold information from a wide variety of sources (33 per cent);

- using decision support systems which combine data analysis and sophisticated models to support non-routine decision making (33 per cent);

- using 'groupware', that is, information communication technologies such as e-mail or Locus Notes as discussion bases, to encourage collaboration between people to share knowledge (33 per cent);

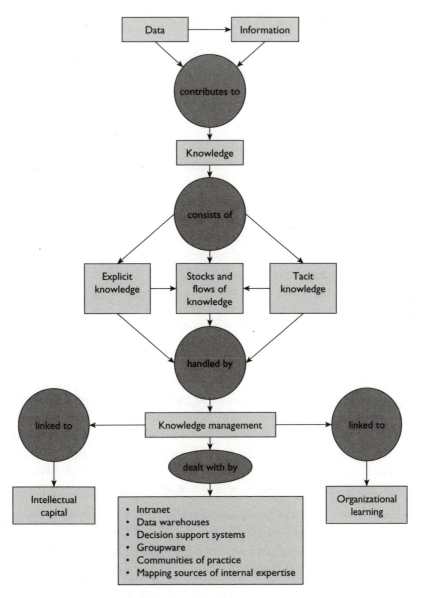

Figure 5.1   Concept map: knowledge management

- creating networks or communities of practice or interest of knowledge workers to share knowledge (24 per cent);

- mapping sources of internal expertise by, for example, producing 'expert yellow pages' and directories of communities (18 per cent).

Knowledge management issues

The various approaches referred to above do not provide easy answers. The issues that need to be addressed in developing knowledge management processes are discussed below.

The pace of change

One of the main issues in knowledge management is how to keep up with the pace of change and identify what knowledge needs to be captured and shared.

Relating knowledge management strategy to business strategy

As Hansen *et al* (1999) showed, it is not knowledge per se but the way it is applied to strategic objectives that is the critical ingredient in competitiveness. They point out that 'competitive strategy must drive knowledge management strategy', and that managements have to answer the question 'How does knowledge that resides in the company add value for customers?' Mecklenburg *et al* (1999) argued that organizations should 'start with the business value of what they gather. If it doesn't generate value, drop it?'

Technology and people

Technology may be central to companies adopting a codification strategy, but for those following a personalization strategy, IT is best used in a supportive role. As Hansen *et al* (1999) commented, 'In the codification model, managers need to implement a system that is much like a traditional library – it must contain a large cache of documents and include search engines that allow people to find and use the documents they need. In the personalization model, it's more important to have a system that allows people to find other people.'

Scarborough *et al* (1999) suggested that 'technology should be viewed more as a means of communication and less as a means of storing knowledge'. Knowledge management is more about people than technology. As research by Davenport (1996) established, managers get two-thirds of their information from face-to-face or telephone conversations.

There is a limit to how much tacit knowledge can be codified. In organizations relying more on tacit than explicit knowledge, a person-to-person approach works best, and IT can only support this process; it cannot replace it.

The significance of process and social capital and culture

Blackler (1995) emphasized that a preoccupation with technology may mean that too little attention is paid to the processes (social, technological and organizational) through which knowledge combines and interacts in different ways. The key processes are the interactions between people. This is the social capital of an organization, the 'network of relationships (that) constitute a valuable resource for the conduct of social affairs' (Nahpiet and Ghoshal, 1998). Social networks can be particularly important in ensuring that knowledge is shared. Trust is also required – people are not willing to share knowledge with those whom they do not trust.

The culture of the company may inhibit knowledge sharing. The norm may be for people to keep knowledge to themselves as much as they can because 'knowledge is power'. An open culture will encourage people to share their ideas and knowledge.

Knowledge workers

Knowledge workers were defined by Drucker (1993) as individuals who have high levels of education and specialist skills combined with the ability to apply these skills to identify and solve problems. As Argyris (1991) commented, 'The nuts and bolts of management... increasingly consists of guiding and integrating the autonomous but interconnected work of highly skilled people.' Knowledge management is about the management and motivation of knowledge workers who create knowledge and will be the key players in sharing it.

Knowledge management: key learning points

The purpose and significance of knowledge management

Knowledge management is about getting knowledge from those who have it to those who need it in order to improve organizational effectiveness.

Knowledge management strategies

The codification strategy: knowledge is carefully codified and stored in databases where it can be accessed and used easily by anyone in the organization. Knowledge is explicit and is codified using a 'people-to-document' approach.

The personalization strategy: knowledge is closely tied to the person who has developed it and is shared mainly through direct person-to-person contacts. This is a person-to-person approach which involves ensuring that tacit knowledge is passed on.

Knowledge management systems

- Creating an intranet.
- Creating 'data warehouses'.
- Using decision support systems.
- Using 'groupware', information communication technologies such as e-mail or Locus Notes discussion bases.
- Creating networks or communities of practice or interest of knowledge workers.

Knowledge management issues

- The pace of change.

- Relating knowledge management strategy to business strategy.

- IT is best used in a supportive role.

- Attention must be paid to the processes (social, technological and organizational) through which knowledge combines and interacts in different ways.

- The significance of knowledge workers must be appreciated.

The contribution HR can make to knowledge management

- Help to develop an open culture which emphasizes the importance of sharing knowledge.

- Promote a climate of commitment and trust.

- Advise on the design and development of organizations that facilitate knowledge sharing. Ensure that valued employees who can contribute to knowledge creation and sharing are attracted and retained.

- Advise on methods of motivating people to share.

- Help in the development of performance management processes that focus on the development and sharing of knowledge.

- Develop processes of organizational and individual learning that will generate and assist in disseminating knowledge.

- Set up and organize workshops, conferences and communities of practice and symposia that enable knowledge to be shared on a person-to-person basis.

- In conjunction with IT, develop systems for capturing and, as far as possible, codifying explicit and tacit knowledge.

- Generally, promote the cause of knowledge management with senior managers.

Questions

1. Many organizations are now introducing knowledge-sharing initiatives and processes. Outline one approach that you would like to see introduced in your organization, justifying how it would be of benefit to the business.

2. Your managing director has sent you the following e-mail: 'I have been hearing about the concept of communities of interest. What are they, would they be useful in our company, and if so, how should we introduce them?' Draft your reply.

3. The following questions were posed by Swart *et al* (2003) for the CIPD on knowledge-intensive firms:

   – What are the key characteristics of knowledge-intensive organizations?

   – What are the particular knowledge-intensive situations that are important for the success of organizations?

   – Which people management practices are particularly valuable in helping to manage these situations successfully?

   Drawing on Swart *et al* and other research, provide answers to these questions.

References

Argyris, C (1991) Teaching smart people how to learn, *Harvard Business Review*, May–June, pp 54–62

Blackler, F (1995) Knowledge, knowledge work and experience, *Organization Studies*, **16** (6), pp 16–36

Blake, P (1988) The knowledge management explosion, *Information Today*, **15** (1), pp 12–13

Davenport, T H (1996) Why re-engineering failed: the fad that forgot people, *Fast Company*, **1**, pp 70–74

Drucker, P (1988) The coming of the new organization, *Harvard Business Review*, January–February, pp 45–53

Drucker, P (1993) *Post-Capitalist Society*, Butterworth-Heinemann, Oxford

Hansen, M T, Nohria, N and Tierney, T (1999) What's your strategy for managing knowledge?' *Harvard Business Review*, March–April, pp 106–16

Mecklenberg, S, Deering, A and Sharp, D (1999) Knowledge management: a secret engine of corporate growth, *Executive Agenda*, **2**, pp 5–15

Nahpiet, J and Ghoshal, S (1998) Social capital, intellectual capital and the organizational advantage, *Academy of Management Review*, **23** (2), pp 242–66

Nonaka, I (1991) The knowledge creating company, *Harvard Business Review*, Nov–Dec, pp 96–104

Nonaka, I and Takeuchi, H (1995) *The Knowledge Creating Company*, Oxford University Press, New York

Rugles, R (1998) The state of the notion, *Californian Management Review*, **40** (3), pp 80–89

Ryle, G (1949) *The Concept of Mind*, Oxford University Press, Oxford

Scarborough, H and Carter, C (2000) *Investigating Knowledge Management*, CIPD, London

Scarborough, H, Swan, J and Preston, J (1999) *Knowledge Management: A literature review*, IPM, London

Swart, J, Kinnie, N and Purcell, J (2003) *People and Performance in Knowledge-Intensive Firms: A comparison of six research and technology organisations*, CIPD, London

Trussler, S (1998) The rules of the game, *Journal of Business Strategy*, **19** (1), pp 16–19

Ulrich, D (1998) A new mandate for human resources, *Harvard Business Review*, January–February, pp 124–34

Wenger, E and Snyder, W M (2000) Communities of practice: the organizational frontier, *Harvard Business Review*, January–February, pp 33–41

Corporate Social Responsibility

Introduction

Corporate social responsibility (CSR) is exercised by organizations when they conduct their business in an ethical way, taking account of the social, environmental and economic impact of how they operate and going beyond compliance. As defined by McWilliams *et al* (2006), CSR refers to the actions taken by businesses 'that further some social good beyond the interests of the firm and that which is required by law'.

CSR has also been described by Husted and Salazar (2006) as being concerned with 'the impact of business behaviour on society', and by Porter and Kramer (2006) as a process of integrating business and society. The latter argue that to advance CSR, 'We must root it in a broad under-standing of the interrelationship between a corporation and society while at the same time anchoring it in the strategies and activities of specific companies.'

Redington (2005) placed more emphasis on CSR in the workplace when he defined it as:

> *The continuing commitment by business to behave ethically and contribute to economic development while improving the quality of life of the workforce and their families as well as of the local community and society at large.*

Strategic CSR defined

Strategic CSR is about deciding initially the extent to which the firm should be involved in social issues and then creating a corporate social agenda – determining what social issues to focus on and to what extent. As Porter and Kramer (2006) emphasized, strategy is always about choice. They suggest that organizations that 'make the right choices and build focused, proactive and integrated social initiatives in concert with their core strategies will increasingly distance themselves from the pack'. They also believe that 'It is through strategic CSR that the company will make the greatest social impact and reap the greatest business benefits.' Baron (2001) pointed out that CSR is what a firm does when it provides 'a public good in conjunction with its business and marketing strategy'.

CSR strategy needs to be integrated with the business strategy, but it is also closely associated with HR strategy. This is because it is concerned with socially responsible behaviour both outside and within the firm – with society generally and with the internal community. In the latter case this means creating a working environment where personal and employment rights are upheld and HR policies and practices provide for the fair and ethical treatment of employees.

CSR activities

CSR activities as listed by McWilliams *et al* (2006) include incorporating social characteristics or features into products and manufacturing processes, adopting progressive human resource management practices, achieving higher levels of environmental performance through recycling and pollution abatement and advancing the goals of community organizations.

The CSR activities of 120 leading British companies

- Community – skills and education, employability and social exclusion were frequently identified as key risks and opportunities. Other major activities were support for local community initiatives and being a responsible and safe neighbour.

- Environment – most companies reported climate change and resource use as key issues for their business, and 85 per cent of them managed their impacts through an environmental management system.

- Marketplace – the issues most frequently mentioned by companies were research and development, procurement and supply chain, responsible selling, responsible marketing and product safety. There was a rising focus on fair treatment of customers, providing appropriate product information and labelling, and on the impacts of products on customer health.

- Workplace – this was the strongest management performing area as most companies have established employment management frameworks that can cater for workplace issues as they emerge. Companies recognized the crucial role of employees to achieve responsible business practices. Increasing emphasis was placed on internal communications and training to raise awareness and understanding of why CSR is relevant to them and valuable for the business. More attention was being paid to health and well-being issues as well as the traditional safety agenda. More work was being done on diversity, both to ensure the business attracts a diverse workforce and to communicate the business case for diversity internally.

Business in the Community also reported a growing emphasis on responsible business as a source of competitive advantage as firms move beyond minimizing risk to creating opportunities.

Source: Business in the Community (2007).

A survey conducted by Industrial Relations Services (Egan, 2006) found that:

- Most employers believe that employment practices designed to ensure the fair and ethical treatment of staff can boost recruitment and retention.

- Relatively few employers are strongly convinced of a positive link to business performance or productivity.

- The issue of ethics in employment is often viewed as part of a broader social responsibility package.

- Policies on ethical employment most commonly cover HR practice in the areas of recruitment, diversity, redundancy/dismissal proceedings and employee involvement.

The rationale for CSR

Stakeholder theory, which was first propounded by Freeman (1984), suggests that managers must satisfy a variety of constituents (such as workers, customers, suppliers and local community organizations) who can influence corporate outcomes. According to this view, it is not sufficient for managers to focus exclusively on the needs of stockholders or the owners of the corporation. Stakeholder theory implies that it can be beneficial for the firm to engage in certain CSR activities that non-financial stakeholders perceive to be important.

A different view was expressed by Theodore Levitt, the marketing expert. In his 1956 *Harvard Business Review* article 'The dangers of social responsibility', he warned that 'government's job is not business, and business's job is not government'. Milton Friedman (1970), the Chicago monetarist, expressed the same sentiment. His maxim was that the social responsibility of business is to maximize profits within the bounds of the law. He argued that the mere existence of CSR was an agency problem within the firm, in that it was a misuse of the resources entrusted to managers by owners which could be better used on value-added internal projects or returned to the shareholders.

Generally, however, academics at least have been in favour of CSR, and there is plenty of evidence in both the United Kingdom and the United States that many firms are pursuing CSR policies.

Arguments supporting CSR

- *The moral appeal* – the argument that companies have a duty to be good citizens. The US business association Business for Social Responsibility (2007) asks its members 'to achieve commercial success in ways that honor ethical values and respect people, communities and the natural environment'.

- *Sustainability* – an emphasis on environmental and community stewardship. As expressed by the World Business Council for Sustainable Social Development (2006) this involves 'meeting the needs of the present without compromising the ability of future generations to meet their own needs'.

- *Licence to operate* – every company needs tacit or explicit permission from government, communities and other stakeholders to do business.

- *Reputation* – CSR initiatives can be justified because they improve a company's image, strengthen its brand, enliven morale and even raise the value of its stock.

Source: Porter and Kramer (2006).

The rationale for CSR as defined by Hillman and Keim (2001) is based on two propositions. First, there is a moral imperative for businesses to 'do the right thing' without regard to how such decisions affect firm performance (the social responsibility argument), and second, firms can achieve competitive advantage by tying CSR activities to primary stakeholders (the stakeholders argument). Their research in 500 firms implied that investing in stakeholder management may be complementary to shareholder value creation, and could indeed provide a basis for competitive advantage, as important resources and capabilities are created that differentiate a firm from its competitors.

It can be argued, as did Moran and Ghoshal (1996), 'that what is good for society does not necessarily have to be bad for the firm, and what is good for the firm does not necessarily have to come at a cost to society'. It could also be argued, more cynically, that there is room for enlightened self-interest which involves doing well by doing good.

Much research has been conducted on the relationship between CSR and firm performance, with mixed results. For example, Russo and Fouts (1997) found that there was a positive relationship between environmental performance and financial performance. Hillman and Keim (2001) established that if the socially responsible activity was directly related to primary stakeholders, then investments may not only benefit stakeholders but also result in increased shareholder wealth. However, participation in social issues beyond the direct stakeholders may adversely affect a firm's ability to create shareholder wealth.

Developing a CSR strategy

The basis for developing a CSR strategy is provided by the following competency Framework of the CSR Academy (2006), which is made up of six characteristics:

- Understanding society: understanding how business operates in the broader context and knowing the social and environmental impact that the business has on society.

- Building capacity: building the capacity of others to help manage the business effectively. For example, suppliers understand the business's approach to the environment and employees can apply social and environmental concerns in their day-to-day roles.

- Questioning business as usual: individuals continually questioning the business in relation to a more sustainable future and being open to improving the quality of life and the environment.

- Stakeholder relations: understanding who the key stakeholders are and the risks and opportunities they present. Working with them through consultation and taking their views into account.

- Strategic view: ensuring that social and environmental views are included in the business strategy so that they are integral to the way the business operates.

- Harnessing diversity: respecting that people are different, which is reflected in fair and transparent business practices.

Corporate social responsibility: key learning points

- CSR refers to the actions taken by businesses that further some social good beyond the interests of the firm and what is required by law. It is concerned with the impact of business behaviour on society, and can be regarded as a process of integrating business and society.

- CSR strategy determines how socially responsible behaviour is exercised both outside and within the firm.

- CSR activities include incorporating social characteristics or features into products and manufacturing processes, adopting progressive human resource management practices, achieving higher levels of environmental performance through recycling and pollution abatement and advancing the goals of community organizations.

- There are two rationales for CSR (Hillman and Keim, 2001). First, there is a moral imperative for businesses to 'do the right thing' without regard to how such decisions affect firm performance (the social issues argument), and second, firms can achieve competitive advantage by tying CSR activities to primary stakeholders (the stakeholders argument).

Questions

1. What does the concept of CSR mean, and what are the main activities involved? Review the situation in your own organization, and identify what CSR activities are taking place and what more could be done.

2. Comment on the following remarks:

   - Porter and Kramer (2006): 'The most important thing a corporation can do for society, and for any community, is contribute to a prosperous economy.'

   - Matsushita (2000) 'Profits should be reflection not of corporate greed but a vote of confidence from society that what is offered by a firm is valued.'

3. You have been asked by your HR director to produce a memorandum setting out the business case on why the company should develop a more active corporate responsibility strategy. You looked at the research conducted by IRS (Egan, 2006) and came across the following information.

The main motivations for employers in engaging in community and charitable work seem to be varied and sometimes interlinked. The following factors were cited by 12 organizations each: to enhance corporate image/reputation, to promote the business, and to improve employee satisfaction and motivation. The desire to help others was mentioned by 10, with seven wishing to help employee development and four hoping to boost recruitment and retention. Two organizations each mentioned the aims of enhancing profitability, helping acquire public sector contracts and helping to acquire other contracts. Just one employer was motivated by a sense of moral obligation.

Taking into account these varied arguments, produce the business case.

References

Baron, D (2001) Private policies, corporate policies and integrated strategy, *Journal of Economics and Management Strategy*, **10** (7), pp 7–45

Business for Social Responsibility (2007) *Annual Report*, www.@BSR.org

Business in the Community (2007) *Benchmarking Responsible Business Practice*, bits.org.uk

CSR Academy (2006) *The CSR Competency Framework*, The Stationery Office, Norwich

Egan, J (2006) Doing the decent thing: CSR and ethics in employment, *IRS Employment Review*, 858 (3 November), pp 9–16

Freeman, R E (1984) *Strategic Management: A stakeholder perspective*, Prentice-Hall, Englewood Cliffs, NJ

Friedman, M (1970) The social responsibility of business is to increase its profits, *New York Times Magazine*, September, p 13

Hillman, A and Keim, G (2001) Shareholder value, stakeholder management and social issues: what's the bottom line? *Strategic Management Journal*, **22** (2), pp 125–39

Husted, B W and Salazar, J (2006) Taking Friedman seriously: maximizing profits and social performance, *Journal of Management Studies*, **43** (1), pp 75–91

Levitt, T (1956) The dangers of social responsibility, *Harvard Business Review*, September–October, pp 41–50

Matsushita, A (2000) Common sense talk, *Asian Productivity Organization News*, **30** (8), p 4

McWilliams, A, Siegal, D S and Wright, P M (2006) Corporate social responsibility: strategic implications, *Journal of Management Studies*, **43** (1), pp 1–12

Moran, P and Ghoshal, S (1996) Value creation by firms, in *Best Paper Proceedings*, Academy of Management Annual Meeting, Cincinnati, OH

Porter, M E and Kramer, M R (2006) Strategy and society: the link between competitive advantage and corporate social responsibility, *Harvard Business Review*, December, pp 78–92

Redington, I (2005) *Making CSR Happen: The contribution of people management*, CIPD, London

Russo, M V and Fouts, P A (1997) A resource-based perspective on corporate environmental performance and profitability, *Academy of Management Review*, **40** (3), pp 534–59

World Business Council for Sustainable Social Development (2006) *From Challenge to Opportunity: The role of business in tomorrow's society*, WBCSSD, Geneva

7

International HRM

Key concepts and terms

- Convergence
- Divergence
- Globalization
- Home-based pay
- Host-based pay

Learning outcomes

On completing this chapter you should be able to define these key concepts. You should also know about:

- The meaning of international HRM
- Issues in international HRM
- The impact of globalization
- International environmental and cultural differences
- Factors affecting the choice between convergence and divergence
- Global HR policies
- Managing expatriates

Introduction

It has been stated by Brewster *et al* (2005) that 'A critical challenge for organizations from both the public and private sectors in the twenty-first century is the need to operate across national boundaries.' In this chapter consideration is given to how organizations respond to this challenge through the practice of international human resource management (HRM). The chapter includes:

- a definition of international HRM;
- an examination of the issues involved in international HRM;
- the practice of global HRM;
- the management of expatriates.

International HRM defined

International HRM is the process of managing people across international boundaries by multinational companies. It involves the worldwide management of people, not just the management of expatriates. Companies that function globally comprise international and multinational firms. International firms are those where operations take place in subsidiaries overseas which rely on the business expertise or manufacturing capacity of the parent company; they may be highly centralized with tight controls. Multinational firms are ones in which a number of businesses in different countries are managed as a whole from the centre; the degree of autonomy they have will vary.

Dr Michael Dickman of the Cranfield School of Management (as reported by Welfare, 2006) believes that the main contrast between national and global HR practice is the need to see the bigger picture: 'The difference is the higher complexity and the need for sensitivity to different cultures and different business environments.' He stated that understanding the local context is key and an international HR person needs to be asking questions such as 'What is the business environment here? What is the role of the trade unions? What is the local labour law? Are these people different? Are their motivation patterns different?'

Issues in international HRM

There are a number of issues that specifically affect the practice of international as distinct from domestic HRM. These issues comprise the impact of globalization, the influence of environmental and cultural differences, the extent to which HRM policy and practice should vary in different countries (convergence or divergence), and the approaches used to employ and manage expatriates.

Globalization

Globalization is the process of international economic integration in worldwide markets. It involves the development of single international markets for goods or services accompanied by an accelerated growth in world trade.

Any company that has economic interests or activities extending across a number of international boundaries is a global company. This involves a number of issues not present when the activities of the firm are confined to one country. As Ulrich (1998) put it, 'Globalization requires organizations to move people, ideas, products and information around the world to meet local needs.'

The distinction between international and global HRM

Traditionally, international HR has been about managing an international workforce – the higher level organizational people working as expatriates, frequent commuters, cross-cultural team members and specialists involved in international knowledge transfer. Global HRM is not simply about these staff. It concerns managing all HRM activities, wherever they are, through the application of global rule sets.

Source: Brewster *et al* (2005).

Bartlett and Ghoshal (1991) argued that the main issue for multinational companies is the need to manage the challenges of global efficiency and multinational flexibility – 'the ability of an organization to manage the risks and exploit the opportunities that arise from the diversity and volatility of the global environment'.

Research conducted over a number of years by Brewster and Sparrow (2007) has shown that the nature of international HRM is changing fast. Among some of the larger international organizations, these changes have created a completely different approach to international HRM, one they dubbed 'globalized HRM'. Whereas international HRM has tended to operate in the same way as local HRM but on a wider scale, globalized HRM exploits the new technologies available in order to manage all the company's staff around the world in the same way that it has traditionally managed staff in the home country.

Environmental differences

Environmental differences between countries have to be taken into account in managing globally. Gerhart and Fang (2005) mention that these include 'differences in the centrality of markets, institutions, regulation, collective bargaining and labour-force characteristics'. For example, in Western Europe, collective bargaining coverage is much higher than in countries like the United States, Canada and Japan. Works councils are mandated by law in Western European countries like Germany, but not in Japan or America. In China, Eastern Europe and Mexico, labour costs are significantly lower than in Western Europe, Japan and the United States.

Cultural differences

Cultural differences must also be taken into account. Hiltrop (1995) noted the following HR areas which may be affected by national culture:

- decisions of what makes an effective manager;
- giving face-to-face feedback;
- readiness to accept international assignments;
- pay systems and different concepts of social justice;
- approaches to organizational structuring and strategic dynamics.

The significance of cultural differences was the influential message delivered by Hofstede (1980, 1991). He defined culture as 'the collective mental programming of people in an environment', referred to cultural values as broad tendencies 'to prefer certain states of affairs over others', and described organizations as 'culture-bound'. Using worldwide data on IBM employees he identified four national cultural dimensions: uncertainty avoidance, masculinity/femininity, power distance and individualism/collectivism.

One of the conclusions Hofstede reached was that the cultural values within a nation are substantially more similar than the values of individuals from different nations. This has been taken up by subsequent commentators such as Adler (2002), who claimed that Hofstede's study explained 50 per cent of the difference between countries in employees' attitudes and behaviours. But this view has been challenged by Gerhart and Fang (2005). They subjected Hofstede's findings to further analysis, and established that at the level of the individual as distinct from the country, only 2 to 4 per cent was explained by national differences, and that therefore 'Hofstede's study should not be interpreted as showing that national culture explains 50 per cent of behaviours.' They also established from Hofstede's data that culture varies more between organizations than countries. In their view, cross-country cultural differences, while real, have been overestimated and may well pale in importance compared with other unique country characteristics when it comes to explaining the effectiveness of HR practices. But they accepted that national culture differences can be critical, and that insensitivity to national culture differences can and does result in business failure (as well as failure and career consequences for individual managers).

On the basis of research conducted in 30 multinational companies by the Global HR Research Alliance, Stiles (2007) commented that 'while national cultural differences were less important than we had imagined, organizational culture actually had more influence on HR practice'. The conclusion from the research was that 'To think there is one best way to manage human resources is simplistic and wrong, but the variation and contextualization of HR, at least for the companies we studied, owes little to national culture.'

Convergence and divergence

According to Brewster *et al* (2005), the effectiveness of global HRM depends on 'the ability to judge the extent to which an organization should implement similar practices across the world (convergence) or adapt them to suit local conditions (divergence)'. The dilemma facing all multinational corporations is that of achieving a balance between international consistency and local autonomy. They have to decide on the extent to which their HR policies should either 'converge' worldwide to be basically the same in each location, or 'diverge' to be differentiated in response to local requirements.

Convergence and divergence issues

Strategic choices surrounding employment relationships may be influenced primarily by 'home country' values and practices. But those managing operations in one or a range of host country environments face the challenge of transplanting 'ethnocentric' principles, justifying the consequential policies and practices in their interactions with local managers, other employees and external representatives.

Source: Perkins and Shortland (2006).

There is a natural tendency for managerial traditions in the parent company to shape the nature of key decisions, but there are strong arguments for giving as much local autonomy as possible in order to ensure that local requirements are sufficiently taken into account. Hence the mantra 'Think globally but act nationally.' This leads to the fundamental assumption made by Bartlett and Ghoshal (1991), that 'Balancing the needs of co-ordination, control and autonomy and maintaining the appropriate balance are critical to the success of the multinational company.'

As Brewster *et al* (2005) pointed out, 'Where global integration and coordination are important, subsidiaries need to be globally integrated with other parts of the organization or/and strategically coordinated by the parent. In contrast, where local responsiveness is important, subsidiaries will have far greater autonomy and there is less need for integration.'

Brewster (2004) believes that convergence may be increasing as a result of the power of the markets, the importance of cost, quality and productivity pressures, the emergence of transaction cost economies, the development of like-minded international cadres, and benchmarking 'best practice'. Stiles (2007) noted that common practices across borders may be appropriate: 'Organizations seek what works and for HR in multinational companies, the range of options is limited to a few common practices that are believed to secure high performance.' Brewster *et al* (2005) think that it is quite possible for some parts of an HR system to converge while other parts may diverge. But there is choice, and Harris and Brewster (1999) listed the following factors affecting it:

- the extent to which there are well-defined local norms;

- the degree to which an operating unit is embedded in the local environment;

- the strength of the flow of resources – finance, information and people – between the parent and the subsidiary;

- the orientation of the parent to control;

- the nature of the industry – the extent to which it is primarily a domestic industry at local level;

- the specific organizational competencies, including HRM, that are critical for achieving competitive advantage in a global environment.

Dickmann, as reported by Welfare (2006), instanced organizations such as IBM and Oxfam that operate a model based on universal principles or values across the organization, which are then implemented differently at regional or national level. He suggested that the extent of integration or convergence depends on the business model of the organization: 'If the company is basically a McDonalds, where there are only limited local variations but the product is essentially the same all over the world, then the approach is likely to be different to a company like Unilever, whose products and processes tend to be much more responsive to the local market.'

The following comments were made by Farndale and Paauwe (2007) about the convergence or universality of global HR practices:

> The universality of HR practices within a company across the globe creates cross-border equity and comparability, and alignment of systems internationally to facilitate an internal labour market. However, this standardization can lead to conflict between company practices and local prevailing conditions in terms of national cultural phenomena, institutions and business systems. The extent of adaptation of HR practices required is thus largely related to the extent of difference that exists between the parent and host country in terms of national regulations, institutions and culture, as well as corporate strategic choice. There is thus a need to achieve legitimacy in all environments, but at the same time a requirement to remain competitive in these same markets.

But it is not necessarily a simple matter of convergence or divergence. International businesses may have to adopt either approach to varying degrees in different parts of the world. And as Makela et al (2009) commented, managers need to deal with the 'dual demands of global integration and local responsiveness'.

Global staffing

The term 'global staffing' was defined by Collings et al (2009) as 'the critical issues faced by multinational corporations when filling key positions in their headquarters and subsidiary operations'. The choice is from parent company nationals, host country nationals (employees from the subsidiary location) and third country nationals (employees from a country other than the home or host country). They go on to say that an appropriate mix of these 'can impact significantly on the multi-national enterprise's ability to achieve learning, innovation and corporate integration'.

Studies by Scullion (1994) and Schuler and Tarique (2007) have highlighted that shortages of leadership talent have emerged as major constraints on the successful implementation of global strategies and are increasingly recognized as a barrier to success in international business.

Tarique *et al* (2006) noted that 'Subsidiary staffing decisions should be based on national (cultural differences and similarities), organizational (top management orientation) and strategic (localization versus standardization) considerations.'

Global HR policies and practices

The research conducted by Brewster *et al* (2005) identified three processes that constitute global HRM: talent management/employee branding, international assignments management, and managing an international workforce. They found that organizations such as Rolls Royce had set up centres of excellence operating on a global basis. They observed that global HR professionals are acting as the guardians of culture, operating global values and systems.

It was established by the Global HR Research Alliance study (quoted by Stiles, 2007) that global HR policies and practices were widespread in the areas of maintaining global performance standards, the use of common evaluation processes, common approaches to rewards, the development of senior managers, the application of competency frameworks and the use of common performance management criteria.

Generally the research has indicated that while global HR policies in such areas as talent management, performance management and reward may be developed, communicated and supported by centres of excellence, often through global networking, a fair degree of freedom has frequently been allowed to local management to adopt their own practices in accordance with the local context as long as in principle these are consistent with global policies.

Managing expatriates

Expatriates are people working overseas on long- or short-term contracts, who can be nationals of the parent company or 'third country nationals' (TCNs).

The management of expatriates is a major factor determining success or failure in an international business. Expatriates are expensive; they can cost three or four times as much as the employment of the same individual at home. They can be difficult to manage because of the problems associated with adapting to and working in unfamiliar environments, concerns about their development and careers, difficulties encountered when they re-enter their parent company after an overseas assignment, and how they should be remunerated. Policies to address the issues are required as described below.

Resourcing policies

The challenge is to resource international operations with people of the right calibre. As Perkins (1997) observed, it is necessary for businesses to 'remain competitive with their employment offering in the market place, to attract and retain high quality staff with world-wide capabilities'. Meyskens *et al* (2009) noted that 'while international talent grows in value it is increasingly difficult to obtain, deploy and retain'. Policies are required on the employment of local nationals and the use of expatriates for long periods or shorter assignments. The advantages of employing local nationals are that they:

- are familiar with local markets, the local communities, the cultural setting and the local economy;
- speak the local language and are culturally assimilated;
- can take a long-term view and contribute for a long period (as distinct from expatriates who will are likely to take a short-term perspective);
- do not take the patronizing (neocolonial) attitude that expatriates sometimes adopt.

Expatriates may be required to provide the experience and expertise that local nationals lack, at least for the time being. But there is much to be said for a long-term resourcing policy which states that the aim is to fill all or the great majority of posts with local people. Welch *et al* (2009) observed that the need to reduce the cost of expatriation is often one of the major drivers of localization. Parent companies that staff their overseas subsidiaries with local nationals always have the scope to 'parachute in' specialist staff to deal with particular issues such as the start-up of a new product or service.

Recruitment and selection policies

Policies for recruitment and selection should deal with specifying requirements, providing realistic previews and preparation for overseas assignments.

Role specifications

Role specifications should take note of the behaviours required for those who work internationally. Leblanc (2001) suggested that they should be able to:

- recognize the diversity of overseas countries;

- accept differences between countries as a fact and adjust to these differences effectively;

- tolerate and adjust to local conditions;

- cope in the long term with a large variety of foreign contexts;

- manage local operations and personnel abroad effectively;

- gain acceptance as a representative of the company abroad;

- obtain and interpret information about foreign national contexts (institutions, legislations, practices, market specifics and so on);

- inform and communicate effectively with a foreign environment about the home company's policies;

- take into account the foreign environment when negotiating contracts and partnerships;

- identify and accept adjustments to basic product specifications in order to meet the needs of the foreign market;

- develop elements of a common framework for company strategies, policies and operations;

- accept that the practices that will operate best in an overseas environment will not necessarily be the same as the company's 'home' practices.

Realistic previews

At interviews for candidates from outside the organization, and when talking to internal staff about the possibility of an overseas assignment, it is advisable to have a policy of providing a realistic preview of the job. The preview should provide information on the overseas operation, any special features of the work, what will need to be done to adjust to local conditions, career progression overseas, re-entry policy on completion of the assignment, pay, and special benefits such as home leave and children's education.

Preparation policy

The preparation policy for overseas assignments should include the provision of cultural familiarization for the country(ies) in which the expatriate will work (sometimes called 'acculturization'), the preferred approach to leading and working in international teams, and the business and HR policies which will apply.

Training policy

Tarique and Caligiri (1995) proposed that the following steps should be taken to design a training programme for expatriates:

- Identify the type of global assignment, such as technical, functional, tactical, developmental or strategic/executive.

- Conduct a cross-cultural training needs analysis covering organizational analysis and requirements, assignment analysis of key tasks and individual analysis of skills.

- Establish training goals and measures – cognitive (such as understanding the role of cultural values and norms) and affective (modifying perception about culture and increasing confidence in dealing with individual behaviours to form adaptive behaviours such as interpersonal skills).

- Develop the programme – the content should cover both general and specific cultural orientation; a variety of methods should be used.

- Evaluate the training given.

Career management policy

Special attention has to be paid to managing the careers of expatriates either as part of their experience overseas or on return permanently or for a period to their home country.

Assimilation and review policies

Assimilation policies will provide for the adaptation of expatriates to overseas posts and their progress in them to be monitored and reviewed. This may take the form of conventional performance management processes but additional information may be provided on the potential and ability of individuals to cope with overseas conditions. Where a number of expatriates are employed it is customary for someone at headquarters to have the responsibility of looking after them.

Re-entry policies

Re-entry policies should be designed to minimize the problems that can arise when expatriates return to their parent company after an overseas posting. They want to be assured that they will be given positions appropriate to their qualifications, and they will be concerned about their careers, suspecting that their overseas experience will not be taken into account. Policies should allow time for expatriates to adjust. The provision of mentors or counsellors is desirable.

Pay and allowances policies

The factors that are likely to impact on the design of reward systems, as suggested by Bradley *et al* (1999), are the corporate culture of the multinational enterprise, expatriate and local labour markets, local cultural sensitivities, and legal and institutional factors. They refer to the choice that has to be made between seeking internal consistency by developing common reward policies in order to facilitate the movement of employees across borders and preserve internal equity, and responding to pressures to conform to local practices. But they point out that 'Studies of cultural differences suggest that reward system design and management needs to be tailored to local values to enhance the performance of overseas operations.' However, as Sparrow (1999) asserted, 'Differences in international reward are not just a consequence of cultural differences, but also of differences in international influences, national business systems and the role and competence of managers in the sphere of HRM.'

The policy of most organizations is to ensure that expatriates are no worse off because they have been posted abroad. In practice, various additional allowances or payments, such as hardship allowances, mean that they are usually better off financially than if they had stayed at home. The basic choice for expatriates is whether to adopt a home-based or host-based policy.

Home-based pay

The home-based pay approach aims to ensure that the value of the remuneration (pay, benefits and allowances) of expatriates is the same as in their home country. The home-base salary may be a notional one for long-term assignments (that is, the salary that it is assumed would be paid to expatriates were they employed in a job of equivalent level at the parent company). For shorter-term assignments it may be the actual salary of the individual. The notional or actual home-base salary is used as the foundation upon which the total remuneration package is built. This is sometimes called the 'build-up' or 'balance sheet' approach.

The salary 'build-up' starts with the actual or notional home-base salary. To it is added a cost of living adjustment which is applied to 'spendable income' – the portion of salary that would be used at home for everyday living. It usually excludes income tax, social security, pensions and insurance, and can exclude discretionary expenditure on major purchases or holidays on the grounds that these do not constitute day-to-day living expenses.

The expatriate's salary would then consist of the actual or notional home-base salary plus the cost of living adjustment. In addition, it may be necessary to adjust salaries to take account of the host country's tax regime in order to achieve tax equalization. Moves of less than a year which might give rise to double taxation require particular attention.

Some or all of the following allowances may be added to this salary:

- 'incentive to work abroad' premium;
- hardship and location;
- housing and utilities;
- school fees;
- 'rest and recuperation' leave.

Host-based pay

The host-based pay approach provides expatriates with salaries and benefits such as company cars and holidays which are in line with those given to nationals of the host country in similar jobs. This method ensures equity between expatriates and host country nationals. It is adopted by companies using the so-called 'market rate system', which ensures that the salaries of expatriates match the market levels of pay in the host country.

Companies using the host-based approach commonly pay additional allowances such as school fees, accommodation and medical insurance. They may also fund long-term benefits like social security, life assurance and pensions from home.

The host-based method is certainly equitable from the viewpoint of local nationals, and it can be less expensive than home-based pay. But it may be much less attractive as an inducement for employees to work abroad, especially in unpleasant locations, and it can be difficult to collect market rate data locally to provide a basis for setting pay levels.

The role of HR

HR managers should play a major part in all these activities, but Welch *et al* (2009) noted from their research that they were often separated from the important steps of defining the purpose of the assignment, setting realistic expectations, and post-assignment placement decisions. They tended to act as bureaucratic administrators during the assignment period.

International HRM: key learning points

The meaning of international HRM

International HRM is the process of managing people across international boundaries by multinational companies. It involves the worldwide management of people, not just the management of expatriates.

Issues in international HRM

International HRM issues comprise the impact of globalization, the influence of environmental and cultural differences, the extent to which HRM policy and practice should vary in different countries (convergence or divergence), and the approaches used to employ and manage expatriates.

The impact of globalization

Globalization requires organizations to move people, ideas, products and information around the world to meet local needs (Ulrich, 1998).

International environmental differences

Environmental differences between countries have to be taken into account in managing globally. These include markets, institutions, regulation, collective bargaining and labour-force characteristics.

International cultural differences

National culture differences can be critical, and insensitivity to them can result in business failure (as well as failure and career consequences for individual managers).

Factors affecting the choice between convergence and divergence (Harris and Brewster, 1999)

- The extent to which there are well-defined local norms.

- The degree to which an operating unit is embedded in the local environment.

- The strength of the flow of resources between the parent and the subsidiary.

- The orientation of the parent to control.

- The nature of the industry.

- The specific organizational competencies, including HRM, that are critical for achieving competitive advantage in a global environment.

Global HR policies

Three processes constitute global HRM: talent management/employee branding, international assignments management, and managing an international workforce (Brewster et al, 2005).

Managing expatriates

Expatriates can be difficult to manage because of the problems associated with adapting to and working in unfamiliar environments, concerns about their development and careers, difficulties encountered when they re-enter their parent company after an overseas assignment, and how they should be remunerated.

Questions

1. The conclusions reached by Brewster *et al* (2005) after their extensive research were that 'Our study has revealed an increasing emphasis on globalizing HR processes, with intense discussion around what needs to be global, regional or national. This new definition of global HR positions the global HR professional as the guardian of culture, operating global values and systems.' What do you think this means in practice for anyone involved in international HRM?

2. You are director of HRM (international) for an international firm operating mainly in Africa. The business strategy is to expand operations into the Far East, staring in Malaysia. A number of medium-sized firms based in Kuala Lumpur have been identified as possibilities for acquisition. It will, however, be necessary to place a number of expatriates in those firms to facilitate the acquisition and ensure that their operations fit into the strategic pattern envisaged for the company. Due diligence has established that these firms have a number of capable executives who are paid above the going rate locally. However, their pay is well below the level of remuneration that would be required to attract and retain expatriates to work there.

    You have been asked by the managing director, international operations to propose a remuneration policy for expatriates. What do you recommend, and why?

3. The chief executive officer of one of your company's overseas subsidiaries has e-mailed you as follows: 'I have come across the terms "convergence" and "divergence" in an *Economist* article about managing international businesses. Apparently they refer to the choice of how far either employment conditions should be standardized world-wide or local companies should adopt their policies. In these terms we are pretty convergent. Are there any arguments I could use to achieve a more divergent policy for us?' Draft your reply.

References

Adler, N J (2002) *International Dimensions of Organizational Behaviour*, South-Western, Cincinnati, OH

Bartlett, C A and Ghoshal, S (1991) *Managing Across Borders: The transnational solution*, London Business School, London

Bradley, P, Hendry, C and Perkins, P (1999) Global or multi-local? The significance of international values in reward strategy, in *International HRM: Contemporary issues in Europe*, ed C Brewster and H Harris, Routledge, London

Brewster, C (2004) European perspectives of human resource management, *Human Resource Management Review*, **14** (4), pp 365–82

Brewster, C and Sparrow, P (2007) Advances in technology inspire a fresh approach to international HRM, *People Management*, 8 February, p 48

Brewster, C, Harris, H and Sparrow, P (2002) *Globalizing HR*, CIPD, London

Brewster, C, Sparrow, P and Harris, H (2005) Towards a new model of globalizing HRM, *International Journal of Human Resource Management*, **16** (6), pp 949–70

Collings, D G, Scullion, H and Dowling, P J (2009) Global staffing: a review and thematic research agenda, *International Journal of Human Resource Management*, **20** (6), pp 1253–72

Farndale, E and Paauwe, J (2007) Uncovering competitive and institutional drivers of HRM practices in multinational corporations, *Human Resource Management Journal*, **17** (4), pp 355–75

Gerhart, B and Fang, M (2005) National culture and human resource management: assumptions and evidence, *International Journal of Human Resource Management*, **16** (6), pp 971–86

Harris, H and Brewster, C (1999) International human resource management: the European contribution, in *International HRM: Contemporary issues in Europe*, ed C Brewster and H Harris, Routledge, London

Hiltrop, J M (1995) The changing psychological contract: the human resource challenge of the 1990s, *European Management Journal*, **13** (3), pp 286–94

Hofstede, G (1980) *Cultural Consequences: International differences in work-related values*, Sage, Beverley Hills, CA

Hofstede, G (1991) *Culture and Organization: Software of the mind*, Sage, London

Leblanc, B (2001) European competitiveness – some guidelines for companies, in *International HRM*, ed M H Albrecht, Blackwell, Oxford

Makela, K, Bjorkmann, I and Ehrnrooth, M (2009) MNC subsidiary staffing architecture: building human and social capital within the organization, *International Journal of Human Resource Management*, **20** (6), pp 1273–90

Meyskens, M, Von Glinov, M A, Werther, W D and Clarke, L (2009) The paradox of international talent: alternative forms of international assignments, *International Journal of Human Resource Management*, **20** (6), pp 1139–50

Perkins, S J (1997) *Internationalization: The people dimension*, Kogan Page, London

Perkins, S J and Shortland, S M (2006) *Strategic International Human Resource Management*, Kogan Page, London

Schuler, R S and Tarique, I (2007) International human resource management: a North American perspective, a thematic update and suggestions for further research, *International Journal of Human Resource Management*, **18**, pp 717–44

Scullion, H (1994) Staffing policies and strategic control in multinationals, *International Studies of Management and Organization*, **3** (4), pp 86–104

Sparrow, P R (1999) *The IPD Guide on International Recruitment, Selection and Assessment*, IPD, London

Stiles, P (2007) A world of difference? *People Management*, 15 November, pp 36–41

Tarique, I and Caligiri, P (1995) Training and development of international staff, in *International Human Resource Management*, ed A-W Herzog and J V Ruyssevelde, Sage, London

Tarique, I, Schuler, R S and Gong, Y (2006) A model of multinational enterprise subsidiary staffing composition, *International Journal of Human Resource Management*, **17** (2), pp 207–24

Ulrich, D (1998) A new mandate for human resources, *Harvard Business Review*, January–February, pp 124–34

Welch, D, Steen, A and Tahvanainen, M (2009) All pain, little gain? Reframing the value of international assignments, *International Journal of Human Resource Management*, **20** (6), pp 1327–43

Welfare, S (2006) A whole world out there: managing global HR, *IRS Employment Review* 862 (29 December), pp 8–12

Part II

Organizations and People

8

Organizational Behaviour

Key concepts and terms

- Behavioural science
- Cognitive dissonance
- Emotional intelligence
- Equity theory
- Expectancy theory
- Extrinsic motivation
- Goal theory
- Intelligence

- Intrinsic motivation
- Motivation
- Organization
- Organizational behaviour
- Organizational culture
- Personality
- Psychological contract
- Self-efficacy

Learning outcomes

On completing this chapter you should be able to define these key concepts. You should also know about:

- What is meant by organizational behaviour
- The sources and applications of organizational behaviour theory
- How organizations function
- Organizational processes
- Organizational culture

- Organization design
- Motivation
- The psychological contract and its significance
- Job design
- Organizational development

Introduction

People perform their roles within complex systems called organizations. The study of organizational behaviour focuses on how organizations function and how people act within the context of their organizations – analysing and understanding what they do, how they do it, and the factors that affect their behaviour, which include their ability, intelligence, personality, attitudes, emotions and emotional intelligence.

An understanding of organizational processes and skills in the analysis and diagnosis of organizational behaviour is important to all managers. As Nadler and Tushman (1980) wrote:

> *The manager needs to understand the patterns of behaviour that are observed to predict in what direction behaviour will move (particularly in the light of managerial action), and to use this knowledge to control behaviour over the course of time. Effective management action requires that the manager be able to diagnose the system he or she is working in.*

Organizational behaviour defined

'Organizational behaviour' is the term used to describe how organizations function, with regard to their structure, processes and culture, and how people within their organizations behave individually or in groups. As defined by Ivancevich *et al* (2008), it involves the study of human behaviour, attitudes, and performance within an organizational setting; drawing on theory, methods and principles from such disciplines as psychology, sociology, political science and cultural anthropology to learn about individuals, groups, structure and processes.

The sources and applications of organizational behaviour theory

Figure 8.1 summarizes how each of the main behavioural science disciplines (defined as the fields of enquiry dedicated to the study of human behaviour through sophisticated and rigorous methods) contributes first to different aspects of organizational behaviour theory, which in turn influence HRM practices.

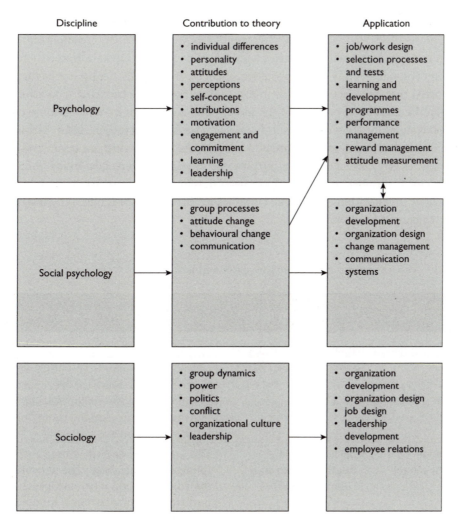

Discipline	Contribution to theory	Application
Psychology	• individual differences • personality • attitudes • perceptions • self-concept • attributions • motivation • engagement and commitment • learning • leadership	• job/work design • selection processes and tests • learning and development programmes • performance management • reward management • attitude measurement
Social psychology	• group processes • attitude change • behavioural change • communication	• organization development • organization design • change management • communication systems
Sociology	• group dynamics • power • politics • conflict • organizational culture • leadership	• organization development • organization design • job design • leadership development • employee relations

Figure 8.1   The sources and applications of organizational behaviour theory

How organizations function

An organization is an entity that exists to achieve a purpose through the collective efforts of the people who work in or for it. Organizing is the process of making arrangements in the form of defined or understood responsibilities and relationships to enable those people to work cooperatively together. Organizations can be described as systems which, as affected by their environment, have a structure which has both formal and informal elements.

Organization structures are frameworks for getting things done. Traditional formal structures were based on laid-down hierarchies (lines of command) represented in organization charts, and use was made of closely defined job descriptions. But to varying extents organizations operate informally as well as formally by means of a network of roles and relationships that cut across formal organizational boundaries and lines of command. Organization structures can evolve almost spontaneously as circumstances change and new activities have to be carried out. The processes that take place in organizations of interaction and networking, leadership, group behaviour, the exercise of power and the use of politics may well have much more effect on how organizations function than a well-defined organization chart supported by elaborate job descriptions and an organization manual. Moreover, the way in which an organization functions will be largely contingent on its purpose, technology, methods of working and external environment. A number of theories have been developed, as summarized in Table 8.1, to explain how organizations function, culminating in the contingency and post-modern schools which now predominate.

Table 8.1   Theories to explain how organizations function

School	Leading exponents	Summary of theory
The classical school	Taylor (1911), Fayol (1916), Urwick (1947)	Organizations need control, measurement, order and formality. To function well they need to minimize the opportunity for unfortunate and uncontrollable informal relations, leaving room only for the formal ones.
The human relations school	Barnard (1938), Roethlisberger and Dickson (1939)	Barnard emphasized the importance of the informal organization – the network of informal roles and relationships which, for better or worse, strongly influences the way the formal structure operates. In the Hawthorne studies Roethlisberger and Dickson stressed the importance of informal groups and decent, humane leadership.
The behavioural science school	Argyris (1957), Herzberg *et al* (1957), McGregor (1960), Likert (1961), Schein (1965)	A humanistic point of view is adopted which is concerned with what people can contribute and how they can best be motivated.

Table 8.1 *continued*

School	Leading exponents	Summary of theory
The bureaucratic model	Weber (translated in 1946)	Max Weber coined the term 'bureaucracy' as a label for a type of formal organization in which impersonality and rationality are developed to the highest degree. Bureaucracy, as he conceived it, was the most efficient form of organization because it is coldly logical and because personalized relationships and non-rational, emotional considerations do not get in its way.
The socio-technical model	Emery (1959), Trist *et al* (1963)	In any system of organization, technical or task aspects are interrelated with the human or social aspects. The emphasis is on interrelationships between, on the one hand, the technical processes of transformation carried out within the organization, and on the other hand, the organization of work groups and the management structures of the enterprise.
The systems school	Miller and Rice (1967)	Organizations should be treated as open systems which are continually dependent upon and influenced by their environments. The basic characteristic of the enterprise as an open system is that it transforms inputs into outputs within its environment.
The contingency school	Burns and Stalker (1961), Woodward (1965), Lawrence and Lorsch (1969)	Members of the contingency school analysed a variety of organizations and concluded that their structures and methods of operation are a function of the circumstances in which they exist. They do not subscribe to the view that there is one best way of designing an organization or that simplistic classifications of organizations as formal or informal, bureaucratic or non-bureaucratic are helpful.

Table 8.1   *continued*

School	Leading exponents	Summary of theory
The post-modern school	Pascale (1990), Ghoshal and Bartlett (1995)	Rather than seeing organizations as a hierarchy of static roles, members of the post-modern school think of them as a portfolio of dynamic processes which overlay and often dominate the vertical, authority-based processes of the hierarchical structure. The emphasis is on 'horizontal tasks', collaboration and networking across units rather than on 'vertical tasks' within functional units. Hence the concept of the 'boundaryless organization' popularized by Jack Welch.

Organizational processes

A number of processes take place in organizations which affect how they function: interaction and networking, communication, group behaviour, leadership, power, politics and conflict.

Interaction and networking

Interactions between people criss-cross the organization, creating networks for getting things done and exchanging information which are not catered for in the formal structure. 'Networking' is an increasingly important process in flexible and delayered organizations, where more fluid interactions across the structure are required between individuals and teams. Individuals can often get much more done by networking than by going through formal channels. This means that they can canvass opinion and enlist support to promote their projects or ideas.

People also get things done in organizations by creating alliances – getting agreement on a course of action with other people and joining forces to get things done.

Communication

The communications processes used in organizations have a marked effect on how they function, especially if they take place through the network, which can then turn into the 'grapevine'. E-mails encourage the instant flow of information (and sometimes produce information overload) but may inhibit the face-to-face interactions, which are often the best ways of getting things done.

Group behaviour

Organizations consist of groups or teams of people working together. They may be set up formally as part of the structure or they may be informal gatherings. They can be a permanent feature of the organization, or they might be set up, or form themselves, temporarily. Interactions take place within and between groups, and the degree to which these processes are formalized varies according to the organizational context.

Formal groups or teams are set up by organizations to achieve a defined purpose. People are brought together with the necessary skills to carry out the tasks and a system exists for directing, coordinating and controlling the group's activities. Informal groups are set up by people in organizations who have some affinity for one another. It could be said that formal groups satisfy the needs of the organization, while informal groups satisfy the needs of their members.

Groups develop an ideology which affects the attitudes and actions of their members and the degree of satisfaction they feel. If the group ideology is strong and individual members identify closely with the group, it will become increasingly cohesive. Group norms or implicit rules will evolve which define what is acceptable behaviour and what is not.

Leadership

Organizations largely function by means of managers and supervisors who get their teams into action and ensure that they achieve the results expected of them. Goleman (2000) reported that a study by Hay McBer of 3,871 executives, selected from a database of more than 20,000 executives worldwide, established that leadership has a direct impact on organizational climate, and that climate in turn accounts for nearly one-third of the financial results of organizations. The conclusion from research conduct by Higgs (2006) is that leadership behaviour accounts for almost 50 per cent of the difference between change success and failure. Research by Northouse (2006) into 167 US firms in 13 industries established that over a 20-year period, leadership accounted for more variations in performance than any other variable.

Power

Organizations exist to get things done, and in the process of doing this people or groups exercise power. Directly or indirectly, the use of power in influencing behaviour is a pervading feature of organizations, whether it is exercised by managers, specialists, informal groups or trade union officials. It is a way of achieving results but it can be misused.

Politics

Power and politics are inextricably mixed, and are a feature of all organizations. Kakabadse (1983) defines politics as 'a process, that of influencing individuals and groups of people to your point of view, where you cannot rely on authority'. Political behaviour can be harmful when it is underhand and devious, but it can sometimes help to enlist support and overcome obstacles to getting results. It is always necessary to be aware of the political situation when trying to get things done in organizations.

Conflict

Conflict is inevitable in organizations because they function by means of adjustments and compromises among competitive elements in their structure and membership. Conflict also arises when there is change, because it may be seen as a threat to be challenged or resisted, or when there is frustration. Conflict is not always deplorable. It is a result of progress and change and it can be used constructively.

Organizational culture

Organizational or corporate culture was described by Deal and Kennedy (1982) as 'the way we do things around here'. More specifically, it is the pattern of values, norms, beliefs, attitudes and assumptions which might not have been articulated but which shape the ways in which people in organizations behave and things get done. Values refer to what is believed to be important about how people and organizations behave. Norms are the unwritten rules of behaviour.

The characteristics of organizational culture

The characteristics of organizational culture as described by Furnham and Gunter (1993) are that:

- it is difficult to define (often a pointless exercise);
- it is multidimensional, with many different components at different levels;
- it is not particularly dynamic and ever-changing (being relatively stable over short periods of time);
- it takes time to establish and therefore time to change.

The significance of organizational culture

Organizational culture is significant because it strongly affects the way in which organizations function and people behave within them. Account has to be taken of the culture when considering any innovations in organization structures or processes.

Types of culture

The different types of culture were classified by Handy (1981):

- The *power culture* is one with a central power source which exercises control. There are few rules or procedures, and the atmosphere is competitive, power-oriented and political.

- The *role culture* in which work is controlled by procedures and rules and the role, or job description, is more important than the person who fills it. Power is associated with positions, not people.

- The *task culture* in which the aim is to bring together the right people and let them get on with it. Influence is based more on expert power than on position or personal power. The culture is adaptable and teamwork is important.

- The *person culture* in which the individual is the central point. The organization exists only to serve and assist the individuals in it.

Appropriate cultures

It is not possible to say that one culture is better than another, only that a culture is to a greater or lesser extent appropriate, in the sense of being relevant to the needs and circumstances of the organization and helping rather than hindering its performance. However, embedded cultures exert considerable influence on organizational behaviour and therefore performance. If there is an appropriate and effective culture it is therefore desirable to take steps to support or reinforce it. If the culture is inappropriate, attempts should be made to determine what needs to be changed, and to develop and implement plans for change.

Furnham and Gunter (1993) consider that a culture will be more effective if 'it is consistent in its components and shared amongst organizational members, and it makes the organization unique, thus differentiating it from other organizations'.

Organization design

Organization design is the process of deciding how organizations should be structured and function. Organizations are not static things. Changes are constantly taking place in the business itself, in the environment in which the business operates, and in the people who work in the business. There is no such thing as an 'ideal' organization. The most that can be done is to optimize the processes involved, remembering that whatever structure evolves will be contingent on the circumstances of the organization. An important point to bear in mind is that organizations consist of people working more or less cooperatively together. Inevitably, and especially at managerial levels, the organization may have to be adjusted to fit the particular strengths and attributes of the people available. The result may not conform to the ideal, but it is more likely to work than a structure that ignores the human element. It is always desirable to have an ideal structure in mind, but it is equally desirable to modify it to meet particular circumstances, as long as there is awareness of the potential problems that may arise.

In principle, organization design aims to:

- Clarify the overall purposes of the organization – the strategic goals which govern what it does and how it functions.

- Define how work should be organized to achieve that purpose, including the use of technology and other work processes.

- Define as precisely as possible the key activities involved in carrying out the work.

- Group these activities logically together to avoid unnecessary overlap or duplication.

- Provide for the integration of activities and the achievement of cooperative effort and teamwork.

- Build flexibility into the system so that organizational arrangements can adapt quickly to new situations and challenges.

- Clarify individual roles, accountabilities and authorities.

In practice, however, organization design is seldom as considered an affair as this list of aims suggests. This is partly because organizations are run by people – the 'dominant coalition' – who do not necessarily react logically to new demands, and are influenced by political pressures and power plays. It also arises from the dynamic nature of organizations as they adapt to ever-changing environmental conditions. This is why organizations often evolve rather than being designed. The aims stated above will not always be achieved. This is why some organizations are ineffective. However, others seem to muddle though, primarily through the informal processes which have the greatest influence on how they function.

Characteristics of people

To manage people effectively, it is necessary to take into account the factors that affect how they behave at work. The development of HR processes and the design of organizations are often predicated on the beliefs that everyone is the same and will behave rationally when faced with change or other demands. But the behaviour of people differs because of their characteristics and individual differences, and it is not always rational.

The management of people would be much easier if everyone were the same, but they are not. As discussed below, they are, of course, different because of variations in personal characteristics and the influence of their background (the culture in which they were brought up). Gender, race or disability are also considered to be factors by some people, although holding this view readily leads to discrimination. In addition, there will be differences in ability, intelligence and personality.

Variations in personal characteristics

The headings under which personal characteristics can vary have been classified by Mischel (1968) as:

- competencies: abilities and skills;
- constructs: the conceptual framework which governs how people perceive their environment;
- expectations: what people have learnt to expect about their own and others' behaviour;
- values: what people believe to be important;
- self-regulatory plans: the goals people set themselves and the plans they make to achieve them.

These are affected by environmental or situational variables, which include the type of work individuals carry out, the culture, climate and management style in the organization, the social group within which they work, and the 'reference groups' that individuals use for comparative purposes (such as comparing conditions of work or pay between one category of employee and another).

The personal characteristics that affect people's behaviour at work are discussed below: their ability, intelligence, personality, attitudes, emotions and emotional intelligence.

Abilities

Ability is the quality possessed by people that makes an action possible. Abilities have been analysed by Burt (1954) and Vernon (1961). They classified them into two major groups:

- V:ed – standing for verbal, numerical, memory and reasoning abilities.
- K:m – standing for spatial and mechanical abilities, as well as perceptual (memory) and motor skills relating to physical operations such as eye/hand coordination and mental dexterity.

They also suggested that overriding these abilities there is GMA, or general mental ability, which accounts for most variations in performance. It is interesting to note that, as established by Schmidt and Hunter (1998) following a meta-analysis of 85 years of research findings, the most valid predictor of future performance and learning for selecting people without previous experience is GMA.

Intelligence

Intelligence has been variously defined as:

- 'The capacity to solve problems, apply principles, make inferences and perceive relationships' (Argyle, 1989).

- 'The capacity for abstract thinking and reasoning with a range of different contents and media' (Toplis *et al*, 2004).

- 'The capacity to process information' (Makin *et al*, 1996).

- 'What is measured by intelligence tests' (Wright and Taylor, 1970).

The last, tautological definition is not facetious. As an operational definition, it can be related to the specific aspects of reasoning, inference, cognition (that is, knowing and conceiving) and perception (that is, understanding and recognition) which intelligence tests attempt to measure.

General intelligence in this sense consists of a number of mental abilities which enable a person to succeed at a wide variety of intellectual tasks that use the faculties of knowing and reasoning. It is measured by an intelligence test, and is sometimes expressed as an intelligence quotient (IQ), which is the ratio of an individual's mental age as measured by an intelligence test to the individual's actual age.

The concept of emotional intelligence, described later in this chapter, stresses that emotional maturity in the sense of the ability to identify, assess and manage your own and other people's emotions is also important.

Personality

Personality has been defined by Huczynski and Buchanan (2007) as 'The psychological qualities that influence an individual's characteristic behaviour patterns in a stable and distinctive manner.' As noted by Ivancevich *et al* (2008), personality appears to be organized into patterns which are to some degree observable and measurable. It involves both common and unique characteristics – every person is different from every other person in some respects, but similar to other persons in other respects. Personality is a product of both nature (hereditary) and nurture (the pattern of life experience). Personality can be described in terms of traits or types.

Traits are predispositions to behave in certain ways in a variety of different situations. A 'big five' have been classified (Costa and McRae, 1992):

- openness;
- conscientiousness;
- extraversion;
- agreeableness;
- neuroticism.

The assumption that people are consistent in the ways they express these traits is the basis for making predictions about their future behaviour. We all attribute traits to people in an attempt to understand why they behave in the way they do. But people do not necessarily express the same trait across different situations, or even the same trait in the same situation. Different people may exhibit consistency in some traits and considerable variability in others.

Type theories of personality identify a number of types of personality, which can be used to categorize people and may form the basis of a personality test. The types may be linked to descriptions of various traits. One of the most widely used type theories is that of Jung (1923). He identified four major preferences of people:

- relating to other people – extraversion or introversion;

- gathering information – sensing (dealing with facts that can be objectively verified), or intuitive (generating information through insight);

- using information – thinking (emphasizing logical analysis as the basis for decision making), or feeling (making decisions based on internal values and beliefs);

- making decisions – perceiving (collecting all the relevant information before making a decision), or judging (resolving an issue without waiting for a large quantity of data).

This theory of personality forms the basis of personality tests such as the Myers–Briggs Types Indicator.

A concept map explaining personality is shown in Figure 8.2.

Attitudes

An attitude can broadly be defined as a settled mode of thinking. Attitudes are evaluative. Makin *et al* (1996) commented 'Any attitude contains an assessment of whether the object to which it refers is liked or disliked.' Attitudes are developed through experience, but they are less stable than traits, and can change as new experiences are gained or influences absorbed. Within organizations they are affected by cultural factors (values and norms), the behaviour of management (management style), policies such as those concerned with pay, recognition, promotion and the quality of working life, and the influence of the 'reference group' (the group with whom people identify). Sometimes there may be a discrepancy between attitudes and behaviour: that is, someone might believe in one thing, such as being fair to people, but act differently. This is called 'cognitive dissonance'.

Emotions

Emotions are feelings such as anger, fear, sadness, joy, anticipation and acceptance, which arouse people and therefore influence their behaviour. The mildest forms of emotions are called moods, which are low-intensity, long-lasting emotional states.

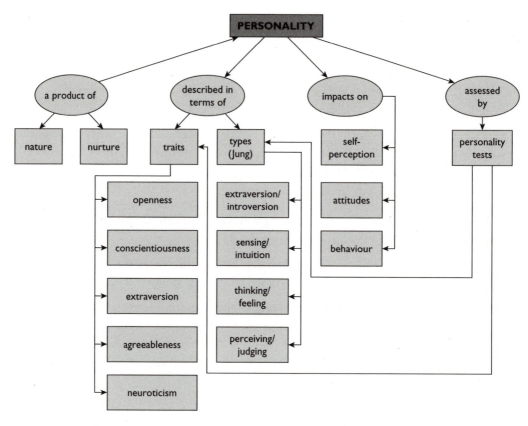

Figure 8.2   Concept map: personality

Emotional intelligence

Emotional intelligence is the capacity to understand the emotional make-up of yourself and others in order to relate to them more effectively. The notion of emotional intelligence was defined by Salovey and Mayer (1990) as the capacity to perceive emotion, integrate emotion in thought, understand emotion and manage emotion. This has been described as the ability-based model. An alternative 'trait model' has been developed. As described by Petrides and Furnham (2000, 2001) it refers to the following traits:

Adaptability   Self-esteem
Assertiveness   Self-motivation
Emotion appraisal   Social competence
Emotion expression   Stress management
Emotion management (others)   Trait empathy
Emotion regulation   Trait happiness
Impulsiveness   Trait optimism
Relationship skills

Goleman (1995, 2001) popularized the concept by producing a so-called mixed model. He defined emotional intelligence as 'The capacity for recognising our own feelings and that of others, for motivating ourselves, for managing emotions well in ourselves as well as others.' He suggested that its components are:

- Self-awareness: recognize and understand your moods, emotions and drives as well as their effect on others.

- Self-regulation: the ability to control or redirect disruptive impulses and moods and regulate your own behaviour, coupled with a propensity to suspend judgement – to think before acting.

- Motivation: a passion to work for reasons that go beyond money or status. A propensity to pursue goals with energy and persistence.

- Empathy: the ability to understand the emotional make-up of other people, Skill in treating people according to their emotional reactions.

- Social skill: proficiency in managing relationships and building networks. An ability to find common ground and build rapport.

These components encompass many of the areas covered by typical competency frameworks (see Chapter 10) such as interpersonal skills.

Critical evaluation of the concept of emotional intelligence

The notion that there is more to being effective as a manger or anyone working with people than having a high IQ is persuasive. What matters is how that intelligence is used, especially when relating to people. The term 'emotional intelligence' has become a convenient and recognizable label for this requirement. Someone who is poor at dealing with people is described as lacking in emotional intelligence.

There are instruments available for measuring emotional intelligence, such as the Trait Emotional Intelligence Questionnaire (Petrides and Furnham, 2000). On the basis of such questionnaires, learning and development programmes can be created for individuals or groups which focus on any weaknesses revealed.

But doubts have been expressed about it. Locke (2005), a well-respected occupational psychologist who with Gary Latham (1979) developed the concept of goal setting, asked 'What is the common or integrating element in a concept that includes: introspection about emotions self-regulation, planning, creative thinking and the direction of attention?' His answer was 'None.' Commenting on the multiple factors contained in definitions of emotional intelligence, he asked, 'What does emotional intelligence not include?' He suggested that emotional intelligence should be renamed as a skill. Goleman's mixed model of emotional intelligence, although the most popular, has been heavily criticized. Mayer *et al* (2008) described it as mere 'pop psychology'.

There is also the question of whether the concept of emotional intelligence adds anything significant to that of behavioural competencies. Dulewicz and Higgs (1999) have produced a detailed analysis of how the emotional intelligence elements of self-awareness, emotional management, empathy, relationships, communication and personal style correspond to competencies such as sensitivity, flexibility, adaptability, resilience, impact, listening, leadership, persuasiveness, motivating others, energy, decisiveness and achievement motivation. They conclude that there are distinct associations between competency modes and elements of emotional intelligence. There is a danger of confusion if emotional intelligence notions and competency frameworks overlap.

Motivation

Motivation is the force that energizes, directs and sustains behaviour. It provides the personal and dynamic element in the concept of engagement (discussed in Chapter 9). High performance is achieved by well-motivated people who are prepared to exercise discretionary effort. Even in fairly basic roles, Hunter *et al* (1990) found that the difference in value-added discretionary performance between 'superior' and 'standard' performers was 19 per cent. For highly complex jobs it was 48 per cent.

Motivation defined

A motive is a reason for doing something. Motivation is concerned with the strength and direction of behaviour and the factors that influence people to behave in certain ways. The term 'motivation' can refer variously to the goals individuals have, the ways in which individuals choose their goals, and the ways in which others try to change their behaviour. A distinction is made between extrinsic and intrinsic motivation. Extrinsic motivation occurs when things are done to or for people to motivate them, which include rewards such as incentives, increased pay, praise or promotion, and punishments such as disciplinary action, withholding pay or criticism. Intrinsic motivation is provided by the work itself.

Motivation theories

A number of theories have been produced to explain the process of motivation. The main ones are summarized in Table 8.2.

Critical evaluation of motivation theories

Instrumentality

This theory emerged in the second half of the 19th century, with its emphasis on the need to rationalize work and on economic outcomes. It assumes that people will be motivated to work if rewards and penalties are tied directly to their performance; thus the awards are contingent upon effective performance. Instrumentality theory has its roots in the scientific management methods of Taylor (1911), who wrote, 'It is impossible, through any long period of time, to get workmen to work much harder than the average men around them unless they are assured a large and permanent increase in their pay.' It has been suggested that behavioural theories based on the principle of reinforcement or the law of effect are limited because they imply, in Allport's (1954) phrase, a 'hedonism of the past'. They assume that the explanation of the present choices of individuals is to be found in an examination of the consequences of their past choices. Insufficient attention is paid in the theories to the influence of expectations, and no indication is given of any means of distinguishing in advance the classes of outcomes that would strengthen responses and that would weaken them.

This theory provides a rationale for incentive pay, albeit a dubious one. It is based on the principle of reinforcement. Motivation using this approach has been and still is widely adopted, and can be successful in some circumstances. But it relies exclusively on a system of external controls and fails to recognize a number of other human needs. It also fails to appreciate the fact that the formal control system can be seriously affected by the informal relationship existing between workers.

Reinforcement

It has been suggested that behavioural theories based on the principle of reinforcement or the law of effect are limited because they imply, in Allport's (1954) phrase, a 'hedonism of the past'. They assume that the explanation of the present choices of individuals is to be found in an examination of the consequences of their past choices. Insufficient attention is paid in the theory to the influence of expectations, and no indication is given of any means of distinguishing in advance the classes of outcomes that would strengthen responses and that would weaken them.

Maslow's hierarchy of needs

Maslow's needs hierarchy has an intuitive appeal and has been very popular, but it has not been verified by empirical research such as that conducted by Wahba and Bridwell (1979). It has been criticized first, for its apparent rigidity (different people may have different priorities); second, because it is difficult to accept that needs progress steadily up the hierarchy; and third, for the misleading simplicity of Maslow's conceptual language. In fact, Maslow himself expressed doubts about the validity of a strictly ordered hierarchy.

Table 8.2 Theories to explain the process of motivation

Category	Type	Theorist(s)	Summary of theory	Implications
Instrumentality	Taylorism	Taylor (1911)	If we do one thing it leads to another. People will be motivated to work if rewards and punishments are directly related to their performance.	Basis of crude attempts to motivate people by incentives. Often used as the implied rationale for performance-related pay although this is seldom an effective motivator.
Reinforcement	The motivation process	Hull (1951)	As experience is gained in satisfying needs people perceive that certain actions help to achieve goals while others are unsuccessful. The successful actions are repeated when a similar need arises.	Provide feedback which positively reinforces effective behaviour.
Content (needs) theory	Hierarchy of needs	Maslow (1954)	A hierarchy of five needs exists: physiological, safety, social, esteem, self-fulfilment. Needs at a higher level only emerge when a lower need is satisfied.	Focuses attention on the various needs that motivate people and the notion that a satisfied need is no longer a motivator. The concept of a hierarchy has no practical significance.

Two-factor model	Related to needs theory	Herzberg et al (1957)	Two groups of factors affect job satisfaction: (1) factors intrinsic to the work itself; (2) factors extrinsic to the job (extrinsic motivators or hygiene factors), such as pay and working conditions.	Identifies a number of fundamental needs: achievement, recognition, advancement, autonomy and the work itself. The research methodology has been strongly criticized and the underpinning assumption that everyone has the same needs is invalid. But it has influenced approaches to job design (job enrichment) and it supports the proposition that reward systems should provide for both financial and non-financial rewards.
Process/cognitive theory	Expectancy theory	Vroom (1964), Porter and Lawler (1968)	Effort (motivation) depends on the likelihood that reward will follow effort and that the reward is worthwhile.	The key theory informing approaches to rewards: that there must be a link between effort and reward (line of sight), and the reward should be achievable and worthwhile.
	Goal theory	Latham and Locke (1979)	Motivation will improve if people have demanding but agreed goals and receive feedback.	
	Equity theory	Adams (1965)	People are better motivated if treated equitably.	

Herzberg's two-factor model

Herzberg's two-factor theory has been attacked by, for example, Opsahl and Dunnette (1966). The research method has been criticized because no attempt was made to measure the relationship between satisfaction and performance. It has been suggested that the two-factor nature of the theory is an inevitable result of the questioning method used by the interviewers. It has also been suggested that wide and unwarranted inferences have been drawn from small and specialized samples, and that there is no evidence to suggest that the satisfiers do improve productivity. The underpinning assumption that everyone has the same needs is invalid. Denise Rousseau (2006) summed up the views of academics about Herzberg: 'Herzberg's long discredited two-factor theory is typically included in the motivation section of management textbooks, despite the fact that it was discredited over thirty years ago' (House and Wigdor, 1967).

In spite of these criticisms the Herzberg two-factor theory continues to thrive, partly because it is easy to understand and seems to be based on 'real life' rather than academic abstractions, and partly because it convincingly emphasizes the positive value of the intrinsic motivating factors. It is also in accord with a fundamental belief in the dignity of labour and the Protestant ethic – that work is good in itself. As a result, Herzberg had immense influence on the job enrichment movement, which sought to design jobs in a way that would maximize the opportunities to obtain intrinsic satisfaction from work and thus improve the quality of working life.

Expectancy theory

Expectancy theory has become a significant basis for explaining what motivates people to work. It is probably the leading theory of motivation, and is used to inform decisions on the design and management of contingent pay schemes and to measure the effectiveness of such schemes. It underpins the path–goal theory of leadership developed by House (1971).

The theory was developed by Vroom (1964) but has its origins in the ancient Greek principle of hedonism, which assumes that behaviour is directed towards pleasure and away from pain. Individuals will choose from alternative courses of action the one they think will maximize their pleasure or minimize their pain.

But research has not provided unequivocal backing for the theory. Connolly (1976) noted that 'The expectancy model appears to have enjoyed substantial if uneven support.' House *et al* (1974) commented that 'Evidence for the validity of the theory is very mixed.'

House *et al* (1974) established that there are a number of variables affecting expectations which make it difficult to predict how they function. These are:

- leadership behaviour – the function of the leader in clarifying expectations, guiding, supporting and rewarding subordinates;
- individual characteristics – the subjects' perception of their ability to perform the required task;

- nature of the task – whether accomplishing the task provides the necessary reinforcements and rewards;

- the practices of the organization – its reward and control systems and how it functions.

Research conducted by Behling and Starke (1973) established that individuals:

- make crucial personal decisions without clearly understanding the consequences;

- do not in practice consistently evaluate their order of preference for alternative actions;

- have to assign two values when making a decision, its desirability and its achievability, but they tend to be influenced mainly by desirability – 'they let their tastes influence their beliefs';

- may be able to evaluate the extrinsic rewards they expect but may find it difficult to evaluate the possibility of achieving intrinsic rewards;

- may find it difficult to distinguish the benefits of one possible outcome from another.

They concluded that 'Expectancy theory can account for some of the variations in work effort but far less than normally attributed to it.'

The findings of research by Reinharth and Wahba (1975) based on a survey of the sales forces of four industrial companies showed no support for either the Vroom expectancy model or its components. They concluded:

> The findings of the study point to the theory's ability to explain at best a very limited portion of human behavior. It may be that the theory, founded on considerations of rationality, can serve as a useful predictor in situations where contingencies between acts and outcomes and between first-level and second-level outcomes are clearly perceived by the individual, whereas ambiguous situations force the individual to develop a choice mechanism not based on the expectancy variables. In short, the earlier optimism for the universality of the theory appears to have been dashed.

Overall, the outcome of research suggests that while expectancy theory offers what appears to be a convincing explanation of the factors affecting the motivation to work, it does not provide a universal explanation because of individual differences in the approach to decision making, the circumstances in which the scheme operates and the impact of social forces on individuals.

However, when designing an incentive scheme and assessing its effectiveness, expectancy theory has considerable face-validity as a common-sense explanation of the factors affecting motivation and what makes incentive schemes work. It provides the theoretical basis for the concept of 'line of sight' developed by Lawler (1988), which states that for a scheme to be effective there has to be a clear and easily perceived link between effort and reward.

Goal theory

Goal theory provides the rationale for performance management, goal setting and feedback, but its universality too has been questioned. For example, Pintrich (2000) noted that people have different goals in different circumstances, and that it is hard to justify the assumption that goals are always accessible and conscious. Harackiewicz *et al* (2002) warned that goals are only effective when they are 'consistent with and match the general context in which they are pursued'. But support for goal theory was provided by Bandura and Cervone (1983), who emphasized the importance of self-evaluation and self-efficacy (a belief in one's ability to accomplish goals).

Goal theory is in line with the 1960s concept of management by objectives (MBO), a process of managing, motivating and appraising people by setting objectives or goals, and measuring performance against those objectives. But MBO fell into disrepute because it was tackled bureaucratically without gaining the real support of those involved, and importantly, without ensuring that managers were aware of the significance of the processes of agreement, reinforcement and feedback, and were skilled in practising them. Goal theory does however play a key part in performance management.

Equity theory

Equity theory has been criticized because it is over-simplified and is based on laboratory rather than real-life research (Huseman *et al*, 1982). It has also been suggested by Carrell and Dittrich (1978) that equity can be perceived not only on a person-to-person basis as the theory posits, but also by reference to the fairness of processes in the organization as a whole. The need to have equitable reward and employment practices which are supported by equity theory cannot be questioned; the problem is how to achieve equity.

Conclusions

In a sense, all the theories referred to above make a contribution to an understanding of the processes that affect motivation. But some, such as reinforcement and instrumentality, have considerable limitations, as do the needs hierarchy and two-factor theories of Maslow and Herzberg. Gerhart and Rynes (2003) pointed out that 'Although Maslow's and Herzberg's theories were intuitively appealing to many people, research has not supported either theory to any great extent.' In fact, people are far more varied and complex than these theories suggest. To state that there are strong similarities between people leads to the conclusion that there is 'one best way' to motivate and reward them, which is simply not true.

Process theories concerned with expectancy, goal setting and equity are based on more realistic ideas and are much more relevant than the theories of Maslow and Herzberg. Expectancy theory is particularly relevant when dealing with contingent pay (incentive schemes), but it is still dangerous to generalize that everyone is motivated in the same way by the same pattern of expectations.

The lessons learnt from motivation theory in the shape of the factors that affect motivation and how HR can apply them are summarized in Table 8.3.

Table 8.3   Lessons learnt from motivation theory

Factors affecting motivation strategies	The HR contribution
• The complexity of the process of motivation means that simplistic approaches based on instrumentality theory are unlikely to be successful.	• Avoid the trap of developing or supporting strategies that offer prescriptions for motivation based on a simplistic view of the process or that fail to recognize individual differences.
• People are more likely to be motivated if they work in an environment in which they are valued for what they are and what they do. This means paying attention to the basic need for recognition.	• Encourage the development of performance management processes which provide opportunities to agree expectations and give positive feedback on accomplishments. • Develop reward systems which provide opportunities for both financial and non-financial rewards to recognize achievements. Bear in mind, however, that financial reward systems are not necessarily appropriate, and the lessons of expectancy, goal and equity theory need to be taken into account in designing and operating them.
• The need for work which provides people with the means to achieve their goals, a reasonable degree of autonomy, and scope for the use of skills and competences should be recognized.	• Advise on processes for the design of jobs which take account of the factors affecting the motivation to work, providing for job enrichment in the shape of variety, decision-making responsibility and as much control as possible in carrying out the work.
• The need for the opportunity to grow by developing abilities and careers.	• Provide facilities and opportunities for learning through such means as personal development planning processes as well as more formal training. • Develop career planning processes.
• The cultural environment of the organization in the shape of its values and norms will influence the impact of any attempts to motivate people by direct or indirect means.	• Advise on the development of a culture which supports processes of valuing and rewarding employees.

Table 8.3   *continued*

Factors affecting motivation strategies	The HR contribution
• Motivation will be enhanced by leadership which sets the direction, encourages and stimulates achievement, and provides support to employees in their efforts to reach goals and improve their performance generally.	• Devise competence frameworks which focus on leadership qualities and the behaviours expected of managers and team leaders. • Ensure that leadership potential is identified through performance management and assessment centers. • Provide guidance and training to develop leadership qualities.

The psychological contract

A psychological contract is a set of unwritten expectations which exist between individual employees and their employers. As Guest (2007) noted, it is concerned with 'The perceptions of both parties to the employment relationship, organization and individual, of the reciprocal promises and obligations implied in that relationship.' A psychological contract is a system of beliefs which encompasses the actions employees believe are expected of them and what response they expect in return from their employer, and reciprocally, the actions employers believe are expected of them and what response they expect in return from their employees.

The psychological contract as defined by Guest et al (1996)

The psychological contract is concerned with assumptions, expectations, promises and mutual obligations. It creates attitudes and emotions which form and govern behaviour. A psychological contract is implicit. It is also dynamic – it develops over time as experience accumulates, employment conditions change and employees re-evaluate their expectations.

The concept of the psychological contract is commonly traced back to the early work of Argyris (1957) and to social exchange theory (Blau, 1964). The latter explains social change and stability as a process of negotiated exchanges between parties.

However, the key developments leading to its current use as an analytical framework were provided mainly by Schein (1965), who explained that 'The notion of a psychological contract implies that there is an unwritten set of expectations operating at all times between every member of an organization and the various managers and others in that organization.' This definition was amplified by Rousseau and Wade-Benzoni (1994):

Psychological contracts refer to beliefs that individuals hold regarding promises made, accepted and relied upon between themselves and another. (In the case of organizations, these parties include an employee, client, manager, and/or organization as a whole.) Because psychological contracts represent how people interpret promises and commitments, both parties in the same employment relationship (employer and employee) can have different views regarding specific terms.

Within organizations, as Katz and Kahn (1966) pointed out, every role is basically a set of behavioural expectations. These expectations are often implicit – they are not defined in the employment contract. Basic models of motivation such as expectancy theory (Vroom, 1964) maintain that employees behave in ways they expect will produce positive outcomes, but they do not necessarily know what to expect.

Employees may expect to be treated fairly as human beings, to be provided with work which uses their abilities, to be rewarded equitably in accordance with their contribution, to be able to display competence, to have opportunities for further growth, to know what is expected of them and to be given feedback (preferably positive) on how they are doing. Employers may expect employees to do their best on behalf of the organization – 'to put themselves out for the company' – to be fully committed to its values, to be compliant and loyal, and to enhance the image of the organization with its customers and suppliers. Sometimes these assumptions are justified – often they are not. Mutual misunderstandings can cause friction and stress and lead to recriminations.

The significance of the psychological contract

As suggested by Spindler (1994), 'A psychological contract creates emotions and attitudes which form and control behaviour.' The concept highlights the fact that employee/employer expectations take the form of unarticulated assumptions. Disappointments on the part of management as well as employees may therefore be inevitable. These disappointments can, however, be alleviated if managements appreciate that one of their key roles is to manage expectations, which means clarifying what they believe employees should achieve, the competencies they should possess and the values they should uphold. This is a matter not just of articulating and stipulating these requirements but of discussing and agreeing them with individuals and teams.

The research conducted by Guest and Conway (2002) led to the conclusion that 'The management of the psychological contract is a core task of management and acknowledged as such by many senior HR and employment relations managers, and shows that it has a positive association with a range of outcomes within the employment relationship and is a useful way of conceptualising that relationship.'

Developing and maintaining a positive psychological contract

As Guest *et al* (1996) pointed out, 'A positive psychological contract is worth taking seriously because it is strongly linked to higher commitment to the organization, higher employee satisfaction and better employment relations. Again this reinforces the benefits of pursuing a set of progressive HRM practices.' They also emphasize the importance of a high-involvement climate, and suggest in particular that HRM practices such as the provision of opportunities for learning, training and development, focus on job security, promotion and careers, minimising status differentials, fair reward systems and comprehensive communication and involvement processes will all contribute to a positive psychological contract. The steps required to develop a positive psychological contract are:

- Define expectations during recruitment and induction programmes.

- Communicate and agree expectations as part of the continuing dialogue which is implicit in good performance management practices.

- Adopt a policy of transparency on company policies and procedures and on management's proposals and decisions as they affect people.

- Generally treat people as stakeholders, relying on consensus and cooperation rather than control and coercion.

Organization development

Organization development (OD) is about taking systematic steps to improve organizational capability. It is concerned with process – how things get done. Organization development aims to help people work more effectively together, improve organizational processes such as the formulation and implementation of strategy and facilitate the transformation of the organization and the management of change. As expressed by Beer (1980), OD operates as 'A system wide process of data collection.'

The assumptions and values of OD programmes

- Most individuals are driven by the need for personal growth and development as long as their environment is both supportive and challenging.

- The work team, especially at the informal level, has great significance for feelings of satisfaction, and the dynamics of such teams have a powerful effect on the behaviour of their members.

- OD programmes aim to improve the quality of working life of all members of the organization.

- Organizations can be more effective if they learn to diagnose their own strengths and weaknesses.

- Managers often do not know what is wrong and may need special help in diagnosing problems, although an outside 'process consultant' ensures that decision making remains in the hands of the client.

- The implementation of strategy involves paying close attention to the people processes involved and the management of change.

Organization development programmes

OD programmes are concerned with system-wide change, and have the following features:

- They are managed, or at least strongly supported, from the top, but may make use of third parties or 'change agents' to diagnose problems and to manage change by various kinds of planned activity or 'intervention'.

- The plans for organization development are based upon a systematic analysis and diagnosis of the strategies and circumstances of the organization and the changes and problems affecting it.

- They use behavioural science knowledge and aim to improve the way the organization copes in times of change through such processes as interaction, communications, participation, planning and conflict management.

- They focus on ways of ensuring that business and HR strategies are implemented and change is managed effectively.

Organizational behaviour: key learning points

Organizational behaviour defined

The study of organizational behaviour focuses on how organizations function and how people act within the context of their organizations.

How organizations function

- An organization is an entity which exists to achieve a purpose through the collective efforts of the people who work in or for it. Organizing is the process of making arrangements in the form of defined or understood responsibilities and relationships to enable those people to work cooperatively.

- Organizations can be described as systems which, as affected by their environment, have a structure which has both formal and informal elements.

Organizational processes

A number of processes take place in organizations which affect how they function: interaction and networking, communication, group behaviour, leadership, power, politics and conflict.

Organizational culture

- Organizational culture is the pattern of values, norms, beliefs, attitudes and assumptions which may not have been articulated but which shape the ways in which people in organizations behave and things get done.

- Organizational culture is significant because it strongly affects the way in which organizations function and people behave within them.

Organization design

Organization design is the process of deciding how organizations should be structured and function.

Individual differences

The development of HR processes and the design of organizations are often based on the beliefs that everyone is the same and will behave rationally when faced with change or other demands. But the behaviour of people differs because of their characteristics and individual differences, and it is not always rational.

Personality

Personality is a product of both nature (so it is hereditary) and nurture (the pattern of life experience). Personality can be described in terms of traits or types.

Emotional intelligence

Emotional intelligence is a combination of skills and abilities such as self-awareness, self-control, empathy and sensitivity to the feelings of others.

Motivation

- Motivation is concerned with the strength and direction of behaviour and the factors that influence people to behave in certain ways.

- A distinction can be made between extrinsic motivation provided by the employer and intrinsic motivation provided by the work.

- Expectancy, equity and goal theory are the significant motivation theories.

The psychological contract

A psychological contract is a set of unwritten expectations which exist between individual employees and their employers.

Organization development

- Organization development (OD) is about taking systematic steps to improve organizational capability. It is concerned with process – how things get done.

- Organization development aims to help people work more effectively together, improve organizational processes such as the formulation and implementation of strategy, and facilitate the transformation of the organization and the management of change.

Questions

1. What does contingency theory tell us about organizations?

2. Charles Handy (1981) produced the following remarks on culture:

    In organizations there are deep-set beliefs about the way work should be organized, people rewarded, people controlled. What are the degrees of formalization required? How much planning and how far ahead? What combination of obedience and initiative is looked for in subordinates? Do work hours matter, or dress, or personal eccentricities? What about expense accounts, and secretaries, stock options and incentives? Do committees control or individuals? Are there rules and procedures or only results?

    Can you explain the culture of your own organization in these terms, or any other?

3. You have been asked to facilitate a group of employee representatives in a discussion on what should be the core values of your company. How would you set about doing it?

4. Jack Welch when CEO of General Electric was quoted by Krames (2004) as saying:

    The way to harness the power of these people is not to protect them… but to turn them loose, and get the management layers off their backs, the bureaucratic shackles off their feet and the functional barriers out of their way.

    Critically evaluate this statement from the viewpoint of its practicality in your own or any organization.

References

Adams, J S (1965) Injustice in social exchange, in *Advances in Experimental Psychology*, ed L Berkowitz, Academic Press, New York

Allport, G (1954) The historical background of modern social psychology, in *Theoretical Models and Personality*, ed G Lindzey, Addison-Wesley, Cambridge, MA

Argyle, M (1989) *The Social Psychology of Work*, Penguin, Harmondsworth

Argyris, C (1957) *Personality and Organization*, Harper & Row, New York

Bandura, A and Cervone, D (1983) Self-evaluation and self-efficacy mechanisms governing the motivational effects of goal systems, *Journal of Personality and Social Psychology*, **45** (5), pp 1017–28

Barnard, C (1938) *The Functions of an Executive*, Harvard University Press, Boston, MA

Beer, M (1980) *Organization Change and Development: A systems view*, Goodyear, Santa Monica, CA

Behling, O and Starke, F A (1973) The postulates of expectancy theory, *Academy of Management Journal*, **16** (3), pp 375–88

Blau, P (1964) *Exchange and Power in Social Life*, Wiley, New York

Burns, T and Stalker, G (1961) *The Management of Innovation*, Tavistock, London

Burt, C (1954) The differentiation of intellectual ability, *British Journal of Educational Psychology*, **24**, pp 45–67

Carrell, M R and Dittrich, J E (1978) Equity theory: the recent literature, methodological considerations and new directions, *Academy of Management Review*, **3** (2), pp 202–10

Connolly, T (1976) Some contested and methodological issues in expectancy models of work performance motivation, *Academy of Management Review*, **1** (4), pp 32–47

Costa, P and McRae, R R (1992) *NEO PI-R: Professional manual*, Psychological Assessment Resources, Odessa, FL

Deal, T and Kennedy, A (1982) *Corporate Cultures*, Addison-Wesley, Reading, MA

Dulewicz, V and Higgs, M (1999) The seven dimensions of emotional intelligence, *People Management*, 28 October, p 53

Emery, F E (1959) *Characteristics of Socio-Technical Systems*, Tavistock, London

Fayol, H (1916) *Administration Industrielle et General*, trans C Storrs (1949) as *General and Industrial Management*, Pitman, London

Furnham, A and Gunter, B (1993) *Corporate Assessment*, Routledge, London

Gerhart, B and Rynes, S L (2003) *Compensation: Theory, evidence and strategic implications*, Sage, Thousand Oaks, CA

Ghoshal, S and Bartlett, C A (1995) Changing the role of top management: beyond structure to process, *Harvard Business Review*, January–February, pp 86–96.

Goleman, D (1995) *Emotional Intelligence*, Bantam, New York

Goleman, D (2000) Leadership that gets results, *Harvard Business Review*, March–April, pp 78–90

Goleman, D (2001) What makes a leader? in *What Makes a Leader*, Harvard Business School Press, Boston, MA

Guest, D (2007) HRM: Towards a new psychological contract, in *Oxford Handbook of Human Resource Management*, ed P Boxall, J Purcell and P Wright, Oxford University Press, Oxford

Guest, D E and Conway, N (2002) Communicating the psychological contract: an employee perspective, *Human Resource Management Journal*, **12** (2), pp 22–39

Guest, D E, Conway, N and Briner, T (1996) *The State of the Psychological Contract in Employment*, IPD, London

Handy, C (1981) *Understanding Organizations*, Penguin, Harmondsworth

Harackiewicz, J M, Barron, P R, Pintrich, P R, Elliot, A J and Thrash, T M (2002) Revision of goal theory: necessary and illuminating, *Journal of Educational Psychology*, **94** (3), pp 638–45

Herzberg, F (1968) One more time: how do you motivate employees? *Harvard Business Review*, January–February, pp 109–20

Herzberg, F, Mausner, B and Snyderman, B (1957) *The Motivation to Work*, Wiley, New York

Higgs, M (2006) *Change and its Leadership*, Rowland, Fisher, Lennox Consulting, New York

House, R J (1971) A path-goal theory of leader effectiveness, *Administrative Science Quarterly*, **16**, pp 321–34

House, R J and Wigdor, L A (1967) Herzberg's dual-factor theory of job satisfaction and motivation, *Personnel Psychology*, **23**, pp 369–89

House, R J, Shapiro, H J and Wahba, M A (1974) Expectancy theory as a predictor of work behaviour and attitude: a re-evaluation of empirical evidence, *Decision Science*, **5** (3), pp 481–506

Huczynski, A A and Buchanan, D A (2007) *Organizational Behaviour*, 6th edn, FT Prentice Hall, Harlow

Hull, C (1951) *Essentials of Behaviour*, Yale University Press, New Haven, CT

Hunter, J E, Schmidt, F L and Judiesch, M K (1990) Individual differences in output variability as a function of job complexity, *Journal of Applied Psychology*, **75** (1), pp 28–42

Huseman, R C, Hatfield, J D and Milis, E W (1982) A new perception on equity theory: the equity sensitivity constant, *Academy of Management Review*, **12** (2), pp 222–34

Ivancevich, J M, Konopaske, R and Matteson, M T (2008) *Organizational Behaviour and Management*, 8th edn, McGraw-Hill/Irwin, New York

Jung, C (1923) *Psychological Types*, Routledge & Kegan Paul, London

Kakabadse, A (1983) *The Politics of Management*, Gower, Aldershot

Katz, D and Kahn, R (1966) *The Social Psychology of Organizations*, Wiley, New York

Krames, J A (2004) *The Welch Way*, McGraw-Hill, New York

Latham, G and Locke, E A (1979) Goal setting – a motivational technique that works, *Organizational Dynamics*, Autumn, pp 68–80

Lawler, E E (1988) Pay for performance: making it work, *Personnel*, October, pp 25–29

Lawrence, P R and Lorsch, J W (1969) *Developing Organizations*, Addison-Wesley, Reading, MA

Likert, R (1961) *New Patterns of Management*, Harper & Row, New York

Locke, E A (2005) Why emotional intelligence is an invalid concept, *Journal of Organizational Behavior*, **26**, pp 425–31

Makin, P, Cooper, C and Cox, C (1996) *Organizations and the Psychological Contract*, BPS Books, Leicester

Maslow, A (1954) *Motivation and Personality*, Harper & Row, New York

Mayer, J D, Salovey, P and Caruso, D R (2008) Emotional intelligence: new ability or eclectic traits? *American Psychologist*, **63** (6), pp 503–17

McGregor, D (1960) *The Human Side of Enterprise*, McGraw-Hill, New York

Miller, E and Rice, A (1967) *Systems of Organization*, Tavistock, London

Mischel, W (1968) *Personality and Assessment*, Wiley, New York

Nadler, D A and Tushman, M L (1980) A congruence model for diagnosing organizational behaviour, in *Resource Book in Macro-Organizational Behaviour*, ed R H Miles, Goodyear Publishing, Santa Monica, CA

Northouse, P G (2006) *Leadership: Theory and Practice*, 4th edn, Sage, Thousand Oaks, CA

Opsahl, R C and Dunnette, M D (1966) The role of financial compensation in individual motivation, *Psychological Bulletin*, **56**, pp 94–118

Pascale, R (1990) *Managing on the Edge*, Viking, London

Petrides, K V and Furnham, A (2000) On the dimensional structure of emotional intelligence, *Personality and Individual Differences*, **29**, pp 313–20

Petrides, K V and Furnham, A (2001) Trait emotional intelligence: psychometric investigation with reference to established trait taxonomies, *European Journal of Personality*, **15**, pp 425–48

Pintrich, P R (2000) An achievement goal perspective on issues in motivation technology, theory and research, *Contemporary Educational Psychology*, **25**, pp 92–104

Porter, L W and Lawler, E E (1968) *Managerial Attitudes and Performance*, Irwin-Dorsey, Homewood, IL

Reinharth, L and Wahba, M A (1975) Expectancy theory as a predictor of work motivation, effort expenditure and job performance, *Academy of Management Journal*, **18** (3), pp 520–37

Roethlisberger, F and Dickson, W (1939) *Management and the Worker*, Harvard University Press, Cambridge, MA

Rousseau, D M (2006) Is there such a thing as evidence-based management? *Academy of Management Review*, **31** (2), pp 256–69

Rousseau, D M and Wade-Benzoni, K A (1994) Linking strategy and human resource practices: how employee and customer contracts are created, *Human Resource Management*, **33** (3), pp 463–89

Salovey, P and Mayer, J D (1990) Emotional intelligence, *Imagination, Cognition and Personality*, **9**, pp 185–211

Schein, E H (1965) *Organizational Psychology*, Prentice-Hall, Englewood Cliffs, NJ

Schmidt, F L and Hunter, J E (1998) The validity and utility of selection methods in personnel psychology: practical and theoretical implications of 85 years of research findings, *Psychological Bulletin*, **124** (2), pp 262–74

Spindler, G S (1994) Psychological contracts in the workplace: a lawyer's view, *Human Resource Management*, **33** (3), pp 325–33

Taylor, F W (1911) *Principles of Scientific Management*, Harper, New York

Toplis, J, Dulewicz, V, and Fletcher, C (2004) *Psychological Testing*, Institute of Personnel Management, London

Trist, E L, Higgin, G W, Murray, H and Pollock, A B (1963) *Organizational Choice*, Tavistock, London

Urwick, L F (1947) *Dynamic Administration*, Pitman, London

Vernon, P E (1961) *The Structure of Human Abilities*, Methuen, London

Vroom, V (1964) *Work and Motivation*, Wiley, New York

Wahba, M A and Bridwell, L G (1979) Maslow reconsidered: a review of research on the need hierarchy theory, in *Motivation and Work Behaviour*, ed R M Sters and L W Porter, McGraw-Hill, New York

Weber, M (1946) *From Max Weber*, ed H H Gerth and C W Mills, Oxford University Press, Oxford

Woodward, J (1965) *Industrial Organization*, Oxford University Press, Oxford

Wright, D S and Taylor, A (1970) *Introducing Psychology*, Penguin, Harmondsworth

Employee Engagement

Introduction

The concept of employee engagement has attracted a lot of attention recently. Reilly and Brown (2008) noted that the terms 'job satisfaction', 'motivation' and 'commitment' are generally being replaced now in business by 'engagement' because it appears to have more descriptive force and face validity. As Emmott (2006) commented, 'Employee engagement has become a new management mantra – and it's not difficult to see why. Engaged employees – those who feel positive about their jobs – perform better for their employers and can promote their organization as "an employer of choice".'

Everyone believes that engagement is a good thing, but many are vague about what it really is. Perhaps this is because all sorts of different meanings are attached to it. It is often used loosely as a notion which embraces pretty well everything the organization is seeking with regard to the contribution and behaviour of its employees in terms of job performance, discretionary effort, motivation, commitment to the organization and organizational citizenship. Some definitions refer to engagement as a condition that is solely related to the jobs people do. Others define it as, in effect, commitment to the purposes and values of the organization. Yet others mix up job and organizational engagement in a way which makes it impossible to disentangle which is which (and therefore difficult to develop programmes for enhancing engagement that distinguish between what is needed to deal with the job aspects of engagement as distinct from the organizational aspects). Only Balain and Sparrow (2009) make a clear distinction between the two. It is difficult not to agree with the comment by Guest (2009) that 'the concept of employee engagement needs to be more clearly defined… or it needs to be abandoned'.

But the term 'employee engagement' seems to be here to stay, and this chapter therefore begins with an attempt to clarify its meaning and define its significance. This leads to an assessment of the drivers of engagement, and a discussion of one of the key notions associated with it – that of discretionary effort. The chapter ends with a review of approaches to engaging employees.

The meaning of employee engagement

In their comprehensive study of employee engagement, MacLeod and Clarke (2009) concluded that 'The way employee engagement operates can take many forms.' So can descriptions of what it means. There are four approaches to definition, described below.

Job engagement

The term 'engagement' can be used in a specific job-related way to describe what takes place when people are interested in and positive, even excited, about their jobs, exercise discretionary behaviour and are motivated to achieve high levels of performance.

Gallup (2009) defined engagement as 'The individual's involvement and satisfaction with as well as enthusiasm for work.' Balain and Sparrow (2009) noted that a number of other well-known applied research and consultancy organizations have defined engagement on similar lines, often emphasizing the importance of discretionary behaviour as the key outcome or distinguishing feature of an engaged employee. An academic definition based on research by Maslach *et al* (2001) referred to engagement as 'A positive, fulfilling, work-related state of mind that is characterized by vigour, dedication, and absorption.'

An engaged employee was defined by Bevan *et al* (1997) as someone 'who is aware of business context, and works closely with colleagues to improve performance within the job for the benefit of the organization'. Murlis and Watson (2001) defined 'engaged performance' as 'A result that is achieved by stimulating employees' enthusiasm for their work and directing it towards organizational success. This result can only be achieved when employers offer an implied contract to their employees that elicits specific positive behaviours aligned with the organization's goals'. Towers Perrin (2008) adopted a similar approach when it defined employee engagement as 'the extent to which employees put discretionary effort into their work, beyond the minimum to get the job done, in the form of extra time, brainpower or energy'.

Organizational engagement

Organizational engagement focuses on attachment to the organization as a whole. The Conference Board in the United States (2006) defined employee engagement as 'a heightened connection that an employee feels for his or her organization'. Robinson *et al* (2004) emphasized the organizational aspect of engagement when they defined employee engagement as 'a positive attitude held by the employee towards the organization and its values'.

This definition of engagement makes it more or less indistinguishable from the traditional notion of commitment. Porter *et al* (1974) defined this as the relative strength of the individual's identification with, and involvement in, a particular organization. The three characteristics of commitment identified by Mowday *et al* (1982) are:

- a strong desire to remain a member of the organization;
- a strong belief in and acceptance of the values and goals of the organization;
- a readiness to exert considerable effort on behalf of the organization.

Organizational engagement is associated with the notion of organizational citizenship behaviour, which Katz and Kahn (1966) defined as 'innovative and spontaneous activity directed toward achievement of organizational objectives, but which goes beyond role requirements'.

General definitions

General definitions of engagement tend to describe what it does rather than what it is. A good example is this one by Truss *et al* (2006):

> *Engagement is about creating opportunities for employees to connect with their colleagues, managers and wider organization. It is also about creating an environment where employees are motivated to want to connect with their work and really care about doing a good job... It is a concept that places flexibility, change and continuous improvement at the heart of what it means to be an employee and an employer in a twenty-first century workplace.*

Another example is provided by Robinson (2008), who stated that 'An engaged employee experiences a blend of job satisfaction, organizational commitment, job involvement and feelings of empowerment. It is a concept that is greater than the sum of its parts.'

MacLeod and Clarke (2009) also defined engagement generally as 'a workplace approach designed to ensure that employees are committed to their organization's goals and values, motivated to contribute to organizational success, and are able at the same time to enhance their own sense of well-being'.

Analytical definitions

Perhaps the most illuminating and helpful approach to definition is to analyse the concept specifically in terms of job and organizational engagement. A good example of this is the explanation by Balain and Sparrow (2009), based on the work of Saks (2006), of the antecedents, types and consequences of engagement. It is shown in Table 9.1.

Table 9.1   Antecedents, types and consequences of engagement

Antecedents of engagement	Types of employee engagement	Consequences
• Enriched and challenging jobs (job characteristics). • Quality of the employee– organization relationship (perceived organizational support). • Quality of the employee– supervisor relationship (perceived supervisor support). • Rewards and recognition. • Fairness in the processes that allocate resources or resolve disputes (procedural justice). • What is considered just or right in the allocation of goods in a society (distributive justice).	• Job engagement. • Organizational engagement.	• Job satisfaction. • Organizational commitment. • Level of intention to quit. • Organizational citizenship behaviour.

Source: Balain and Sparrow (2009).

Engagement defined

On the basis of the Balain and Sparrow analysis, engagement can be defined as:

Engagement happens when people are committed to their work and the organization and motivated to achieve high levels of performance. It has two interrelated aspects: first, job engagement, which takes place when employees exercise discretionary effort because they find their job interesting, challenging and rewarding; and second, organizational engagement, when they identify with the values and purpose of their organization and believe that it is a great place in which to work.

Discretionary behaviour

There is a close link between high levels of employee engagement and positive discretionary behaviour or effort. Purcell *et al* (2003) described discretionary behaviour as referring to the choices that people at work often have on the way they do the job and the amount of effort, care, innovation and productive behaviour they display. It can be positive when people 'go the extra mile' to achieve high levels of performance. It can be negative when they exercise their discretion to slack at their work. Discretionary behaviour is hard for the employer to define, monitor and control, but positive discretionary behaviour can happen when people are engaged with their work. On the basis of their longitudinal research Purcell *et al* suggested that the following conditions are required for discretionary behaviour to take place.

- It is more likely to occur when individuals are committed to their organization and/or when they feel motivated to do so and/or when they gain high levels of job satisfaction.

- Commitment, motivation and job satisfaction, either together or separately, will be higher when people positively experience the application of HR policies concerned with creating an able workforce, motivating valued behaviours and providing opportunities to participate.

- This positive experience will be higher if the wide range of HR policies necessary to develop ability, motivation and opportunity are both in place and are mutually reinforcing.

- The way HR and reward policies and practices are implemented by front-line managers and the way top-level espoused values and organizational cultures are enacted by them will enhance or weaken the effect of HR policies in triggering discretionary behaviour by influencing attitudes.

- The experience of success seen in performance outcomes helps reinforce positive attitudes.

Why engagement is important

David Guest (2009) suggested that:

> *Employee engagement will be manifested in positive attitudes (for example job satis-*
> *faction, organizational commitment and identification with the organization) and*
> *behaviour (low labour turnover and absence and high citizenship behaviour) on the*
> *part of employees; and evidence of perceptions of trust, fairness and a positive*
> *exchange within a psychological contract where two-way promises and commit-*
> *ments are fulfilled.*

Employee engagement is important to employers because a considerable amount of research indicates that high levels of engagement result in behaviours such as maximizing discretionary effort, taking initiative, wanting to develop, or aligning actions with organizational needs. These deliver a range of organizational benefits, for example:

- higher productivity/performance – engaged employees perform 20 per cent better than the average (Conference Board, 2006);

- lower staff turnover – engaged employees are 87 per cent less likely to leave (Corporate Leadership Council, 2004);

- improved safety (Vance, 2006).

Gallup (2006a) examined 23,910 business units and compared top quartile and bottom quartile financial performance with engagement scores. They found that:

- Those with engagement scores in the bottom quartile averaged 31–51 per cent more employee turnover, 51 per cent more inventory shrinkage and 62 per cent more accidents.

- Those with engagement scores in the top quartile averaged 12 per cent higher customer advocacy, 18 per cent higher productivity and 12 per cent higher profitability.

A second Gallup study in 2006(b) of earnings per share (EPS) growth in 89 organizations found that the EPS growth rate of organizations with engagement scores in the top quartile was 2.6 times that of organizations with below-average engagement scores.

Drivers of engagement

The following drivers of engagement were listed by MacLeod and Clarke (2009):

- leadership which ensures a strong, transparent and explicit organizational culture which gives employees a line of sight between their job and the vision and aims of the organization;

- engaging managers who offer clarity, appreciation of employees' effort and contribution, who treat their people as individuals and who ensure that work is organized efficiently and effectively so that employees feel they are valued, and equipped and supported to do their job;

- employees feeling they are able to voice their ideas and be listened to, both about how they do their job and in decision making in their own department, with joint sharing of problems and challenges and a commitment to arrive at joint solutions;

- a belief among employees that the organization lives its values, and that espoused behavioural norms are adhered to, resulting in trust and a sense of integrity.

Towers Perrin's 2008 Global Workforce Study of employee views found that the top driver of engagement was senior management demonstrating a sincere interest in employee well-being.

Balain and Sparrow (2009) concluded that 'To understand what really causes engagement, and what it causes in turn, we need to embed the idea in a well-founded theory. The one that is considered most appropriate is social exchange theory, which sees feelings of loyalty, commitment, discretionary effort as all being forms of social reciprocation by employees to a good employer.'

MacLeod and Clarke (2009) pointed out that engagement is a two-way process: 'organizations must work to engage the employee, who in turn has a choice about the level of engagement to offer the employer. Each reinforces the other.' They also noted that 'Engagement is about establishing mutual respect in the workplace for what people can do and be.' As a representative of the home insulation company KHI put it to them, 'Employee engagement is when the business values the employee and the employee values the business.'

Research cited by IDS (2007) has identified two key elements that have to be present if genuine engagement in its broadest sense is to exist. The first is the rational aspect, which relates to an employee's understanding of their role, where it fits in the wider organization, and how it aligns with business objectives. The second is the emotional aspect, which has to do with how the person feels about the organization, whether their work gives them a sense of personal accomplishment and how they relate to their manager.

To summarize, job engagement will be affected by work and job design, the quality of leadership exercised by line managers and the reward system. Organizational engagement will be affected by the quality of life provided by the working environment and by ensuring that the organization is an employer of choice.

Enhancing engagement

Engaging their employees is what every employer wants to do. But how can they do it? They will need to address issues concerning both aspects of engagement: job and organizational engagement. These are interrelated, and any actions taken to enhance either aspect will be mutually supporting, although it is useful to consider what can be done specifically in each area bearing in mind the particular circumstances and needs of the organization. There are no universal prescriptions, and any actions taken should be based on evidence derived from measurements of levels of engagement, trends in those levels and benchmarking. The data need to be analysed and assessed to provide information on what might be done.

Measuring engagement

Interest in engagement has been stimulated by the scope for measuring levels and trends through engagement surveys. These provide the basis for the development and implementation of engagement strategies through the 'triple-A' approach: Analysis, Assessment and Action. An example of a survey is given in Figure 9.1. The first 10 questions focus on job engagement and the next 10 are more concerned with organizational engagement.

Enhancing job engagement

Justin King (2009), CEO of Sainsbury's, has stressed that 'In our business with almost 150,000 people, engagement is a key concern. In businesses of our scale, you don't even get started without engagement.' For anyone working in Sainsbury's engagement was only possible if three conditions were met:

- they were clear about what they were expected to do;
- they had the skills to do it;
- they understood why they had to do it.

These three conditions can be satisfied through good job design, learning and development programmes, performance management, and improving the quality of leadership provided by line managers. In additions rewards in the broadest sense, that is, non-financial as well as financial, can play an important part.

Job design

As Herzberg (1968) remarked, 'If you want someone to do a good job give them a good job to do.' Intrinsic motivation and therefore increased engagement can be generated by the work itself if it provides interest and opportunities for achievement and self-fulfilment. The approaches to motivation through job design suggested by Robertson and Smith (1985) are to influence:

- *skill variety* by providing opportunities for people to do several tasks and combining tasks;
- *task identity* by combining tasks and forming natural work units;
- *task significance* by informing people of the importance of their work;

Engagement survey

Please circle the number which most closely matches your opinion

		Strongly agree	Agree	Disagree	Strongly disagree
1	I am very satisfied with the work I do	1	2	3	4
2	My job is interesting	1	2	3	4
3	I know exactly what I am expected to do	1	2	3	4
4	I am prepared to put myself out to do my work	1	2	3	4
5	I have plenty of freedom to decide how to do my work	1	2	3	4
6	I get lots of opportunities to use and develop my skills in this job	1	2	3	4
7	The facilities/equipment/tools provided are excellent	1	2	3	4
8	I get good support from my boss	1	2	3	4
9	My boss gives me helpful feedback on how well I am doing	1	2	3	4
10	I am rewarded well for my contribution	1	2	3	4
11	I think this organization is a great place in which to work	1	2	3	4
12	I would recommend this organization to people as a good employer	1	2	3	4
13	I believe I have a good future in this organization	1	2	3	4
14	I intend to go on working for this organization	1	2	3	4
15	I am happy about the values of this organization, the ways in which it conducts its business	1	2	3	4
16	I believe that the products/services provided by this organization are excellent	1	2	3	4
17	The management of this organization is really concerned about the well-being of employees	1	2	3	4
18	I have no problems in achieving a balance between my work and my private life	1	2	3	4
19	I like working for my boss	1	2	3	4
20	I get on well with my work colleagues	1	2	3	4

Figure 9.1   Example of an engagement survey

- *autonomy* by giving people responsibility for determining their own working systems;
- *feedback* on how well they are doing.

These approaches may be used when setting up new work systems and jobs, and the intrinsic motivation strategy should include provision for guidance and advice along these lines to those responsible for such developments. But the greatest impact on the design of work systems or jobs is made by line managers on a day-to-day basis. An engagement strategy should therefore include arrangements for educating them as part of a leadership development programme in the importance of good work and job design, and what they can do to improve intrinsic motivation.

The work environment

A strategy for increasing job engagement through the work environment will be generally concerned with developing a culture which encourages positive attitudes to work, promoting interest and excitement in the jobs people do, and reducing stress. Lands' End believes that staff who are enjoying themselves, who are being supported and developed, and who feel fulfilled and respected at work will provide the best service to customers.

Performance management

Performance management processes (described in Chapter 14) can be used to define expectations and to provide feedback.

Learning and development programmes

Learning and development programmes can ensure that people have the opportunity and are given the encouragement to learn and grow in their roles. This includes the use of policies which focus on role flexibility – giving people the chance to develop their roles by making better and extended use of their talents. This means going beyond talent management for the favoured few and developing the abilities of the core people on whom the organization depends The philosophy should be that everyone has the ability to succeed, and the aim should be to 'achieve extraordinary results with ordinary people'. It includes using performance management primarily as a developmental process with an emphasis on personal development planning.

The strategy should also cover career development opportunities, and how individuals can be given the guidance, support and encouragement they need if they are to fulfil their potential and achieve a successful career with the organization, in tune with their talents and aspirations. The actions required to provide men and women of promise with a sequence of learning activities and experiences that will equip them for whatever level of responsibility they have the ability to reach should be included in the strategy.

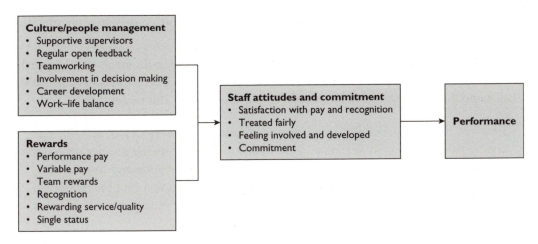

Figure 9.2   How reward policies influence performance through engagement

Line managers

Line managers play a vital and immediate part in increasing levels of job engagement. They do this by exercising leadership and ensuring that their team members are clear about what they have to do, acquire the skills required and appreciate the significance of their contribution. They have considerable influence over job and work design, and are there to provide support, encouragement and coaching with the help of the performance management system. They need guidance on what they are expected to do, and help in developing the skills they need.

Developing engagement through reward

Reilly and Brown (2008) contend that appropriate reward practices and processes, both financial and non-financial and managed in combination (in a total rewards approach) can help to build and improve employee engagement, and that badly designed or executed rewards can hinder it. Their model, based on research of how reward policies influence performance through engagement, is shown in Figure 9.2.

Enhancing organizational engagement

It was suggested by David Guest (2009) that engagement can be achieved 'through effective leadership of a strong, positive culture that ensures the enactment of organizational values; through strong management that supports employees' work and well-being; through careful design of systems and jobs to enable employees to contribute through full use of their knowledge and skills; through effective employee voice; and through provision of appropriate resources, tools and information to perform effectively'.

A basis for enhancing organizational engagements was established by the longitudinal research in 12 companies conducted by Professor John Purcell and his colleagues (Purcell *et al*, 2003). They found that the most successful companies had 'the big idea'. This meant that:

> *They had a clear vision and a set of integrated values. They were concerned with sustaining performance and flexibility. Clear evidence existed between positive attitudes towards HR policies and practices, levels of satisfaction, motivation and commitment, and operational performance. Policy and practice implementation (not the number of HR practices adopted) is the vital ingredient in linking people management to business performance and this is primarily the task of line managers.*

At Lands' End the thinking behind how the company inspires its staff is straightforward – employees' willingness to do that little bit extra arises from their sense of pride in what the organization stands for (quality, service and value). It makes the difference between a good experience for customers and a poor one.

High-involvement management

Organizational engagement can be developed through high-involvement management. This term was first used by Lawler (1986) to describe management systems based on commitment and involvement, as opposed to the old bureaucratic model based on control. The underlying hypothesis is that each employee will increase their involvement with the company if they are given the opportunity to control and understand their work. Lawler claimed that high-involvement practices worked well because they acted as a synergy and had a multiplicative effect.

High-involvement management involves treating employees as partners in the enterprise, whose interests are respected and who have a voice on matters that concern them. It is concerned with communication and participation. The aim is to create a climate in which a continuing dialogue between managers and the members of their teams takes place in order to define expectations and share information on the organization's mission, values and objectives. This establishes mutual understanding of what is to be achieved, and a framework for managing and developing people to ensure that it will be achieved.

Employee engagement: key learning points

The meaning of employee engagement

Engagement takes place when people are committed to their work and motivated to achieve high levels of performance.

Why engagement is important

Engagement is important to employers because a considerable amount of research indicates that high levels of engagement which result in behaviours such as maximizing discretionary effort, taking initiative, wanting to develop, and aligning actions with organizational needs deliver a range of organizational benefits, for example higher productivity/performance.

The factors that affect engagement

Engagement will be affected by the quality of work and job design, the quality of life provided by the working environment, and the quality of leadership and the reward system.

Methods of enhancing engagement

Financial and nonfinancial rewards can enhance engagement, but providing intrinsic motivation through the work itself, improving the work environment and ensuring that line managers play their part are equally if not more important.

Questions

1. Distinguish between the concepts of engagement, motivation and organizational citizenship.

2. What is discretionary behaviour, why is it a good thing and how can it be encouraged?

3. What is the role of line managers in enhancing engagement?

References

Balain, S and Sparrow, P (2009) *Engaged to Perform: A new perspective on employee engagement*, Lancaster University Management School, Lancaster

Bevan, S, Barber, L and Robinson, D (1997) *Keeping the Best: A practical guide to retaining key employees*, Institute for Employment Studies, Brighton

Conference Board (2006) *Employee Engagement: A review of current research and its implications*, Conference Board, New York

Corporate Leadership Council (2004) *Driving Performance and Retention through Employee Engagement*, Corporate Executive Board, Washington, DC

Emmott, M (2006) Hear me now, *People Management*, 23 November, pp 38–40

Gallup (2006a) *Feeling Good Matters in the Workplace*, Gallup Inc, Washington, DC

Gallup (2006b) *Engagement Predicts Earnings Per Share*, Gallup Inc, Washington, DC

Gallup (2009) *Workplace Audit*, Gallup Inc, Washington, DC

Guest, D (2009) *Review of Employee Engagement*, notes for a discussion (unpublished), prepared specifically for the MacLeod and Clarke 2009 review of employee engagement

Herzberg, F (1968) One more time: how do you motivate employees? *Harvard Business Review*, January–February, pp 109–20

IDS (2007) Building an engaged workforce, *HR Studies Update*, IDS, London

Katz, D and Kahn, R (1966) *The Social Psychology of Organizations*, Wiley, New York

King, J (2009) Address to DBIS employee engagement conference, 16 July, London

Lawler, E E (1986) *High Involvement Management*, Jossey-Bass, San Francisco, CA

MacLeod, D and Clarke, N (2009) *Engaging for Success: Enhancing performance through employee engagement*, Department for Business Innovation and Skills, London

Maslach, C, Schaufeli, W B and Leiter, M P (2001) Job burnout, *Annual Review of Psychology*, **52**, pp 397–422

Mowday, R, Porter, L and Steers, R (1982) *Employee-Organization Linkages: The psychology of commitment, absenteeism and turnover*, Academic Press, London

Murlis, H and Watson, S (2001) Creating employee engagement – transforming the employment deal, *Benefits and Compensation International*, **30** (8), pp 6–17

Porter, L W, Steers, R, Mowday, R and Boulian, P (1974) Organizational commitment: job satisfaction and turnover amongst psychiatric technicians, *Journal of Applied Psychology*, **59**, pp 603–09

Purcell, J, Kinnie, K, Hutchinson, S, Rayton, B and Swart, J (2003) *People and Performance: How people management impacts on organizational performance*, CIPD, London

Reilly, P and Brown, D (2008) Employee engagement: future focus or fashionable fad for reward management? *WorldatWork Journal*, **17** (4), pp 37–49

Robertson, I T and Smith, M (1985) *Motivation and Job Design*, IPM, London

Robinson, D (2008) Employee engagement: an IES perspective, presentation to the IES HR Network, unpublished

Robinson, D, Perryman, S and Hayday, S (2004) *The Drivers of Employee Engagement*, Institute for Employment Studies, Brighton

Saks, A M (2006) Antecedents and consequences of employee engagement, *Journal of Managerial Psychology*, **21** (6), pp 600–19

Towers Perrin (2008) *Global Workforce Study*, Towers Perrin, London

Truss, C, Soane, E, Edwards, C, Wisdom, K, Croll, A and Burnett, J (2006) *Working Life: Employee attitudes and engagement*, CIPD, London.

Vance, R J (2006) *Effective Practice Guidelines: Employee engagement and commitment*, SHRM Foundation, Alexandria, VA

Part III
HRM Practice

Competency-based HRM

Introduction

Competency-based HRM uses the notion of competency and the results of competency analysis to inform and improve the processes of recruitment and selection, employee development, performance management and employee reward. It therefore has an important part to play in all the major HR activities.

The concept of competency is essentially about performance. Mansfield (1999) defines competency as 'an underlying characteristic of a person that results in effective or superior performance'. Rankin (2002) describes competencies as 'definitions of skills and behaviours that organizations expect their staff to practice in their work', and explains their meaning as:

> Competencies represent the language of performance. They can articulate both the expected outcomes from an individual's efforts and the manner in which these activities are carried out. Because everyone in the organization can learn to speak this language, competencies provide a common, universally understood means of describing expected performance in many different contexts.

Types of competencies

Behavioural competencies

Behavioural competencies define behavioural expectations, in other words the type of behaviour required to deliver results under such headings as team working, communication, leadership and decision making. They are sometimes known as 'soft skills'. Behavioural competencies are usually set out in a competency framework.

The behavioural competency approach was first advocated by McClelland (1973). He recommended the use of criterion-referenced assessment. Criterion referencing or validation is the process of analysing the key aspects of behaviour which differentiate between effective and less effective performance.

The leading figure in popularizing the concept of competency was Boyatzis (1982). He conducted research which established that there is no single factor but a range of factors that differentiate successful from less successful performance. These factors included personal qualities, motives, experience and behavioural characteristics. Boyatzis (1982) defined competency as:

> A capacity that exists in a person that leads to behaviour that meets the job demands within the parameters of the organizational environment and that, in turn, brings about desired results.

The 'clusters' of competencies he identified were goal and action management, directing sub-ordinates, human resource management and leadership. He made a distinction between threshold competencies, which are the basic competencies required to do a job, and perform-ance competences, which differentiate between high and low performance.

Technical competencies

Technical competencies define what people have to know and be able to do (knowledge and skills) to carry out their roles effectively. They are related to either generic roles (groups of similar roles) or individual roles (as 'role-specific competencies').

The term 'technical competency' has been adopted to avoid the confusion that existed between the terms 'competency' and 'competence'. Competency was originally defined as being about behaviours, while Woodruffe (1991) defined competence as 'A work-related concept which refers to areas of work at which the person is competent. Competent people at work are those who meet their performance expectations.' Competences are sometimes known as 'hard skills'. The terms 'technical competencies' and 'competences' are closely related, although the latter has a particular and more limited meaning when applied to NVQs/SNVQs.

Competency frameworks

A competency framework contains definitions of the behavioural competencies used in the whole or part of an organization. It provides the basis for the use of competencies in such areas as recruitment, performance management, learning and development, and reward. A survey by Competency and Emotional Intelligence (2006/7) established that the 49 frameworks reviewed had a total of 553 competency headings. Presumably many of these overlapped. The typical number of competencies was seven, rising to eight where the frameworks applied solely to managers.

Competency headings

The most common competencies in frameworks are people skills, although outcome-based skills, such as focusing on results and solving problems, are also popular. The seven most used competency headings in the frameworks of the organizations responding to the Competency and Emotional Intelligence survey are shown in Table 10.1.

Applications of competency-based HRM

The Competency and Emotional Intelligence 2006/07 survey found that 95 per cent of respondents used behavioural competencies and 66 per cent used technical competencies. It was noted that

Table 10.1   Incidence of different competency headings

Competency heading	Summary definition	% used
Team orientation	The ability to work cooperatively and flexibly with other members of the team, with a full understanding of the role to be played as a team member.	86
Communication	The ability to communicate clearly and persuasively, orally or in writing.	73
People management	The ability to manage and develop people and gain their trust and cooperation to achieve results.	67
Customer focus	The exercise of unceasing care in looking after the interests of external and internal customers to ensure that their wants, needs and expectations are met or exceeded.	65
Results orientation	The desire to get things done well and the ability to set and meet challenging goals, create own measures of excellence and constantly seek ways of improving performance.	59
Problem solving	The capacity to analyse situations, diagnose problems, identify the key issues, establish and evaluate alternative courses of action, and produce a logical, practical and acceptable solution.	57
Planning and organizing	The ability to decide on courses of action, ensuring that the resources required to implement the action will be available, and scheduling the programme of work required to achieve a defined end result.	51

because the latter deal with specific activities and tasks they inevitably result in different sets of competencies for groups of related roles, functions or activities. The top four areas where competencies were applied are:

- selection – 85 per cent;
- learning and development – 82 per cent;
- performance management – 76 per cent;
- recruitment – 55 per cent.

Only 30 per cent of organizations linked competencies to reward. The ways in which these competencies are used are described below.

Learning and development

Role profiles which are either generic (covering a range of similar jobs) or individual (role-specific) can include statements of the technical competencies required. These can be used as the basis for assessing the levels of competency achieved by individuals, and so identifying their learning and development needs.

Career family grade structures can define the competencies required at each level in a career family. These definitions provide a career map showing the competencies people need to develop in order to progress their career.

Competencies are also used in development centres, which help participants build up their understanding of the competencies they require now and in the future so that they can plan their own self-directed learning programmes.

Performance management

Competencies in performance management are used to ensure that performance reviews do not simply focus on outcomes but also consider the behavioural aspects of how the work is carried out which determine those outcomes. Performance reviews conducted on this basis are used to inform personal improvement and development plans and other learning and development initiatives.

As noted by Rankin (2004), 'Increasingly, employers are extending their performance management systems to assess not only objectives but also qualitative aspects of the job.' The alternative approaches are, first, for the assessment to be made by reference to the whole set of core competencies in the framework, or second, the manager and the individual carry out a joint assessment of the latter's performance and agree on the competencies to be assessed, selecting those most relevant to the role. In some cases the assessment is linked to defined levels of competency.

Use of behavioural indicators

Guidance on assessing levels of competency can be provided by the use of behavioural indicators which define how the effective use of a behavioural competency can be demonstrated in a person's day-to-day work.

Recruitment and selection

The language of competencies is used in many organizations as a basis for a person specification, which is set out under competency headings as developed through role analysis. The competencies defined for a role are used as the framework for recruitment and selection.

A competencies approach can help to identify which selection techniques such as psychological testing are most likely to produce useful evidence. It provides the information required to conduct a structured interview, in which questions can focus on particular competency areas to establish the extent to which candidates meet the specification as set out in competency terms.

In assessment centres competency frameworks are used to define the competency dimensions that distinguish high performance. This indicates what exercises or simulations are required and the assessment processes that should be used.

Reward management

In the 1990s, when the competency movement came to the fore, the notion of linking pay to competencies – competency-related pay – emerged. But it has never taken off; only 8 per cent of the respondents to the e-reward 2004 survey of contingent pay used it. However, more recently, the concept of contribution-related pay has emerged, which provides for people to be rewarded according to both the results they achieve and their level of competence. The e-reward 2004 survey established that 33 per cent of respondents had introduced it. Another application of competencies in reward management is career family grade and pay structures.

Behavioural competency modelling

Behavioural competency modelling is the process used for identifying, analysing and describing behavioural competencies which define the behaviours that organizations expect their employees to practise in their work in order to reach an acceptable level of performance. The main methods of competency analysis are:

- Expert opinion: this is the basic, crudest and least satisfactory method. It involves an 'expert' member of the HR department drawing up a list from their own understanding of 'what counts' coupled with an analysis of other published lists.

- Structured interview: this method begins with a list of competencies drawn up by 'experts' and proceeds by subjecting a number of role holders to a structured interview. The basic question is 'What are the positive or negative indicators of behaviour which are conducive or non-conducive to achieving high levels of performance?' The answers are analysed under headings such as decisiveness, commercial judgement, creative thinking, leadership, interpersonal relationships and ability to communicate.

- Workshops: these bring a group of people together who have 'expert' knowledge or experience of the role – managers and role holders as appropriate – with a facilitator. The members of the workshop begin by reaching agreement on the overall purpose of the role and its key result areas. They then develop examples of effective and less effective behaviour for each area, from which are distilled competency headings and their definitions.

Keys to success in using competencies

- The competencies should reflect the goals, values and culture of the organization.
- Competencies should be identified and defined in ways which will ensure that they aid recruitment, performance management, and learning and development activities.
- Competencies must be selected and defined in ways which ensure that they can be assessed by managers.
- Frameworks should not be over-complex.
- There should not be too many headings in a framework – seven or eight will often suffice.
- The language used should be clear and jargon-free.
- Frameworks should be updated regularly.

Competency-based HRM: key learning points

The different types of competencies

The three types of competencies are behavioural competencies, technical competencies, and NVQs and SNVQs.

The contents of competency frameworks (the most popular headings)

- Team orientation.
- Communication.
- People management.
- Customer focus.
- Results orientation.
- Problem-solving.
- Planning and organizing.
- Technical skills.
- Leadership.

Coverage of competencies (Rankin, 2002)

- 22 per cent covered the whole workforce;

- 48 per cent confined competencies to specific work groups, functions or departments;

- 20 per cent have a core competency framework that covers all staff in respect of behavioural competencies, alongside sets of technical competencies in functions or departments.

Uses of competencies (Competency and Emotional Intelligence, 2006/7)

- Learning and development – 82 per cent.

- Performance management – 76 per cent.

- Selection – 85 per cent.

- Recruitment – 55 per cent.

- Reward – 30 per cent.

Behavioural competency modelling

Behavioural competency modelling is the process used for identifying, analysing and describing behavioural competencies which define the behaviours that organizations expect their staff to practise in their work in order to reach an acceptable level of performance. The emphasis is on the systematic collection and analysis of data. The three main approaches to behavioural competency analysis are expert opinion, structured interview and workshops.

Questions

1. Your managing director says to you that she is getting confused by the terms 'competency' and 'emotional intelligence'. She asks you to clarify the differences between them, if any, and what their significance is to the organization. Draft your response.

2. You have been asked to deliver a talk at a local conference on the use of competency frameworks and their advantages and disadvantages. Prepare your lecture outline.

3. It is felt by your boss that the existing competence framework in your organization is out of date. He has asked you to propose a programme for updating it which will not take too much time or trouble. Draft a programme.

References

Boyatzis, R (1982) *The Competent Manager*, Wiley, New York

Competency and Emotional Intelligence (2004), Benchmarking survey, *Competency and Emotional Intelligence*, **12** (1), pp 4–6

Competency and Emotional Intelligence (2006/7) *Raising Performance Through Competencies: The annual benchmarking survey*, Competency and Emotional Intelligence, London

e-reward (2004) *Survey of Contingent Pay*, e-reward.co.uk, Stockport

Mansfield, B (1999) What is 'competence' all about?, *Competency*, **6** (3), pp 24–28

McClelland, D C (1973) Testing for competence rather than intelligence, *American Psychologist*, **28** (1), pp 1–14

Rankin, N (2002) Raising performance through people: the ninth competency survey, *Competency and Emotional Intelligence*, January, pp 2–21

Rankin, N (2004), Benchmarking survey, *Competency and Emotional Intelligence*, **12** (1), pp 4–6

Woodruffe, C (1991) Competent by any other name, *Personnel Management*, September, pp 30–33

Job and Role Analysis and Design

Key concepts and terms

- Generic role
- Job
- Job analysis
- Job breakdown
- Job characteristics model
- Job description
- Job design

- Job enlargement
- Job enrichment
- Job rotation
- Role
- Role analysis
- Role profile

Learning outcomes

On completing this chapter you should be able to define these key concepts. You should also know about:

- The distinction between jobs and roles
- Job and role analysis methodology
- Producing job descriptions and role profiles

- Approaches to job design
- Role development

Introduction

The analysis and design of jobs and roles is one of the most important techniques in HRM. Job or role analysis provides the information required to produce job descriptions, role profiles and person and learning specifications. It is of fundamental importance in organization and job design, recruitment and selection, performance management, learning and development, management development, career management, job evaluation and the design of grade and pay structures. These constitute most of the key HRM activities. Job or role design is the means by which jobs can be made intrinsically motivating.

The terms 'job' and 'role' are often used interchangeably, but they are different, as defined below.

Job

A job is an organizational unit which consists of a group of defined tasks or activities to be carried out or duties to be performed.

Role

A role is the part played by individuals and the patterns of behaviour expected of them in fulfilling their work requirements. A role has been defined by Ivancevich *et al* (2008) as 'an organized set of behaviours'. Roles are about people as distinct from jobs, which are about tasks and duties. It is recognized more generally that organizations consist of people using their knowledge and skills to achieve results and working cooperatively together, rather than impersonal jobs contained in the boxes of an organization chart.

A generic role is a role in which essentially similar activities are carried out by a number of people, for example a team leader or a call centre agent. In effect, it covers an occupation rather than a single role.

Although reference is frequently made nowadays to roles, use is still made of the terms job analysis and job design, as discussed in this chapter.

Job and role analysis

Job analysis

Job analysis produces the following information about a job:

- Overall purpose: why the job exists and, in essence, what the job holder is expected to contribute.

- Organization: to whom the job holder reports and who reports to the job holder.

- Content: the nature and scope of the job in terms of the tasks and operations to be performed and duties to be carried out.

If the outcome of the job analysis is to be used for job evaluation purposes, the job will also be analysed in terms of the factors or criteria used in the job evaluation scheme.

The essence of job analysis is the application of systematic methods to the collection of information about job content. It is about data collection, and the basic steps are:

- Obtain documents such as existing organization, procedure or training manuals which give information about the job.

- Obtain from managers fundamental information concerning the job.

- Obtain from job holders similar information about their jobs.

Job analysis is best carried out through interviews but these can usefully be supplemented by questionnaires.

Role analysis

Role analysis uses the same techniques as job analysis but the focus is on identifying inputs (knowledge and skill and competency requirements) and required outcomes (key result areas or accountabilities) rather than simply listing the tasks to be carried out.

Job description

Job analysis provides the information required to produce a job description, which defines what job holders are required to do in terms of activities, duties or tasks. Job descriptions are prescriptive and inflexible, giving people the opportunity to say 'It's not in my job description', meaning that they only need to do the tasks listed there. They are more concerned with tasks than outcomes, and with the duties to be performed rather than the competencies required to perform them (technical competencies covering knowledge and skills, and behavioural competencies).

Role profile

A role profile defines outcomes, accountabilities and competencies for an individual role. It concentrates on outcomes rather than duties, and therefore provides better guidance than a job description on expectations, and does not constrain people to carrying out a prescribed set of tasks. Outcomes may be expressed as key result areas – elements of the role for which clear outputs and standards can be defined, each of which makes a significant contribution to achieving its overall purpose. Alternatively, they may be termed accountabilities – areas of the role for which role holders are responsible in the form of being held to account for what they do and what they achieve.

A role profile does not prescribe in detail what has to be done to achieve the required outcomes. It therefore allows for greater flexibility than a job description, and is more easily updated to reflect changing demands.

Role profiles are person-oriented. A role can be described in behavioural terms – given certain expectations, this is how the person needs to behave to meet them. Because it identifies knowledge, skill and competency requirements, it also provides a better basis for recruitment and selection, performance management, and learning and development purposes.

Generic roles are defined in a generic role profile.

Job design

Job design specifies the contents, methods and relationships of jobs in order to satisfy work requirements for productivity, efficiency and quality, meet the personal needs of the job holder and thus increase levels of employee engagement. The process of job design starts with an analysis of the way in which work needs to be organized and what work therefore needs to be done – the tasks that have to be carried out if the purpose of the organization or an organizational unit is to be achieved.

The job characteristics model

A useful perspective on the factors affecting job design and motivation is provided by Hackman and Oldham's (1974) job characteristics model. They suggest that the 'critical psychological states' of 'experienced meaningfulness of work, experienced responsibility for outcomes of work and knowledge of the actual outcomes of work' strongly influence motivation, job satisfaction and performance. They identified the following characteristics of jobs that need to be taken into account in job design:

- variety;
- autonomy;
- required interaction;
- optional interaction;
- knowledge and skill required;
- responsibility.

Approaches to job design

Job design starts with an analysis of task requirements. These requirements will be a function of the purpose of the organization, its technology and its structure. The analysis has also to take into account the decision-making process – where and how decisions are made and the extent to which responsibility is devolved to individuals and work teams. These approaches are used as the basis for the methods of job design described below.

Approaches to job design

- Influence skill variety by providing opportunities for people to do several tasks and by combining tasks.

- Influence task identity by combining tasks and forming natural work units.

- Influence task significance by forming natural work units and informing people of the importance of their work.

- Influence autonomy by giving people responsibility for determining their own working systems.

- Influence feedback by establishing good relationships and opening feedback channels.

Source: Robertson and Smith (1985)

Job rotation

This is the movement of employees from one task to another to reduce monotony by increasing variety.

Job enlargement

This means combining previously fragmented tasks into one job, again to increase the variety and meaning of repetitive work.

Job enrichment

This goes beyond job enlargement to add greater autonomy and responsibility to a job, and is based on the job characteristics approach. Job enrichment aims to maximize the interest and challenge of work by providing the employee with a job that has these characteristics:

- It is a complete piece of work in the sense that the worker can identify a series of tasks or activities that end in a recognizable and definable product.

- It affords the employee as much variety, decision-making responsibility and control as possible in carrying out the work.

- It provides direct feedback through the work itself on how well the employee is doing his or her job.

Role development

Role development is the continuous process through which roles are defined or modified as work proceeds and evolves. Job design as described above takes place when a new job is created or an existing job is substantially changed, often following a reorganization. But the part people play in carrying out their roles can evolve over time as people grow into them and grow with them, and as incremental changes take place in the scope of the work and the degree to which individuals have freedom to act (their autonomy).

Roles are developed as people develop in them – responding to opportunities and changing demands, acquiring new skills and developing competencies. Role development is a continuous process which takes place in the context of day-to-day work, and is therefore a matter between managers and the members of their teams. It involves agreeing definitions of accountabilities, objectives and competency requirements as they evolve. When these change – as they probably will in all except the most routine jobs – it is desirable to achieve mutual understanding of new expectations.

Job and role analysis: key learning points

Job
A job is an organizational unit which consists of a group of defined tasks or activities to be carried out or duties to be performed.

Role
A role is the part played by individuals and the patterns of behaviour expected of them in fulfilling their work requirements.

Job analysis methodology and techniques
The essence of job analysis is the application of systematic methods to the collection of information about job content. It is essentially about data collection, and the basic steps are:

- obtain documents such as existing organization, procedure or training manuals which give information about the job;

- obtain from managers fundamental information concerning the job;

- obtain from job holders similar information about their jobs.

Job descriptions

Job descriptions should be based on the job analysis and should be as brief and factual as possible. The headings should be: job title, reporting to, reporting to job holder, main purpose of job, main activities, tasks or duties.

Role profile

A role profile defines outcomes, accountabilities and competencies for an individual role.

Role analysis methodology

Role analysis uses the same techniques as job analysis but the focus is on identifying inputs (knowledge and skill and competency requirements) and required outcomes (key result areas) rather than simply listing the tasks to be carried out.

Job design

- Job design specifies the contents, methods and relationships of jobs in order to satisfy work requirements for productivity, efficiency and quality, meet the personal needs of the job holder and thus increase levels of employee engagement.

- The process of job design is based on an analysis of the way in which work needs to be organized and what work therefore needs to be done – the tasks that have to be carried out if the purpose of the organization or an organizational unit is to be achieved.

Questions

1. What is the difference between a job and a role?

2. What is the essence of job analysis?

3. What is the process of job design?

4. What is the job characteristics model?

5. What is job enrichment and why is it important?

References

Hackman, J R and Oldham, G R (1974) Motivation through the design of work: test of a theory, *Organizational Behaviour and Human Performance*, **16** (2), pp 250–79

Ivancevich, J M, Konopaske, R and Matteson, M T (2008) *Organizational Behaviour and Management*, 8th edn, McGraw-Hill/Irwin, New York

Robertson, I T and Smith, M (1985) *Motivation and Job Design*, IPM, London

People Resourcing

Learning outcomes

On completing this chapter you should be able to define these key concepts. You should also know about:

- People resourcing strategy
- Human resource planning
- Recruitment and selection processes
- Retention planning

- Talent management
- Flexibility planning
- Absence management

Introduction

People resourcing is about the acquisition, retention, development and effective utilization of the people the organization needs. It is based on a resourcing strategy which is linked to the business strategy, and is the basis for human resource or workforce planning activities. Human resource plans are implemented by means of the key resourcing activities of recruitment and selection, retention planning and talent management, and by learning and development programmes as described in Chapter 13. The effectiveness with which human resources are used involves providing for flexibility and controlling absenteeism.

People resourcing strategy

People resourcing strategy defines the longer-term plans an organization needs for the acquisition, retention, development and use of its human resources. Its rationale is the concept that the strategic capability of a firm depends on its resource capability in the shape of people (the resource-based view). As explained by Grant (1991):

> The firm's most important resources and capabilities are those which are durable, difficult to identify and understand, imperfectly transferable, not easily replicated, and in which the firm possesses clear ownership and control. These are the firm's 'crown jewels' and need to be protected; and they play a pivotal role in the competitive strategy which the firm pursues. The essence of strategy formulation, then, is to design a strategy that makes the most effective use of these core resources and capabilities.

Aim

The aim of people resourcing strategy is to ensure that a firm achieves competitive advantage by attracting and retaining more capable people than its rivals and employing them more effectively. These people will have a wider and deeper range of skills and will behave in ways which will maximize their contribution. The organization attracts and retains such people as an 'employer of choice' by offering a compelling 'employee value proposition' and 'employer brand', and by providing better opportunities and rewards than others. Furthermore, the organization deploys its people in ways that maximize the added value they create.

Resourcing strategy provides the framework for the resourcing activities of human resource planning, recruitment and selection, talent management, retention planning, flexibility planning and absence management, as examined in this chapter.

On being an employer of choice

The aim is to become 'an employer of choice', a firm people want to work for and stay with. The conclusions of Purcell *et al* (2003) on the basis of their research were:

> *What seems to be happening is that successful firms are able to meet peoples' needs both for a good job and to work 'in a great place'. They create good work and a conducive working environment. In this way they become an 'employer of choice'. People will want to work there because their individual needs are met – for a good job with prospects linked to training, appraisal and working with a good boss who listens and gives some autonomy but helps with coaching and guidance.*

Creating an employee value proposition

To become an employer of choice the resourcing strategy should be based on an employee value proposition. This consists of what the organization has to offer for prospective or existing employees that they are likely to value, and that would help to persuade them to join or remain with the business. It will include pay and benefits, which are important but can be over-emphasized compared with other non-financial elements. The latter elements may be crucial in attracting and retaining people, and include the attractiveness of the organization, its reputation as a good employer, the degree to which it acts responsibly, treats people with consideration and respect, and provides for diversity and inclusion, work–life balance and personal and professional growth.

Employer brand

The employee value proposition can be expressed as an employer brand, defined by Walker (2007) as 'a set of attributes and qualities – often intangible – that make an organization distinctive, promise a particular kind of employment experience and appeal to people who will thrive and perform their best in its culture'. Employer branding is the creation of a brand image of the organization for prospective employees.

Creating an employer brand

- Analyse what ideal candidates need and want and take this into account in deciding what should be offered and how it should be offered.

- Establish how far the core values of the organization support the creation of an attractive brand and ensure that these are incorporated in the presentation of the brand as long as they are 'values in use' (lived by members of the organization) rather than simply espoused.

- Define the features of the brand on the basis of an examination and review of each of the areas which affect the perceptions of people about the organization as 'a great place to work' – the way people are treated, the provision of a fair deal, opportunities for growth, work–life balance, leadership, the quality of management, competitive but equitable rewards, involvement with colleagues, and the reputation of the organization.

- Benchmark the approaches of other organizations (the *Sunday Times* list of the 100 best companies to work for is useful) to obtain ideas about what can be done to enhance the brand.

- Be honest and realistic.

Human resource planning

Organizations need to know how many people and what sort of people they should have to meet present and future business requirements. This is the function of human resource planning, or workforce planning as it is sometimes called, especially in the public sector. However, it is not always the logical and systematic process conceived when the notion of 'manpower planning' became popular in the 1960s and 1970s. Human resource planning may be well established in the HRM vocabulary but it does not seem to be embedded as a key HR activity.

Human resource planning defined

As defined by Bulla and Scott (1994), human resource planning is 'the process for ensuring that the human resource requirements of an organization are identified and plans are made for satisfying those requirements'. Reilly (2003) defined workforce planning as 'A process in which an organization attempts to estimate the demand for labour and evaluate the size, nature and sources of supply which will be required to meet the demand.'

Hard and soft human resource planning

A distinction can be made between 'hard' and 'soft' human resource planning. The former is based on quantitative analysis in order to ensure that the right number of the right sort of people are available when needed. The latter, as described by Marchington and Wilkinson (1996), 'is more explicitly focused on creating and shaping the culture of the organization so that there is a clear integration between corporate goals and employee values, beliefs and behaviours'. But as they point out, the soft version becomes virtually synonymous with the whole area of human resource management.

Link to business planning

Human resource planning is an integral part of business planning. The strategic planning process defines projected changes in the types of activities carried out by the organization and the scale of those activities. It identifies the core competences the organization needs to achieve its goals and therefore its skill and behavioural requirements.

Human resource planning interprets these plans in terms of people requirements, focusing on any problems that might have to be resolved in order to ensure that the people required will be available and will be capable of making the necessary contribution. But it may also influence the business strategy by drawing attention to ways in which people could be developed and deployed more effectively to further the achievement of business goals. As Quinn Mills (1983) wrote in his seminal *Harvard Business Review* article, 'Planning with people in mind', human resource planning is 'a decision-making process that combines three important activities: (1) identifying and acquiring the right number of people with the proper skills, (2) motivating them to achieve high performance, and (3) creating interactive links between business objectives and people-planning activities.'

Human resource planning is important because it encourages employers to integrate their business and HR plans. It allows for better control over staffing costs and numbers employed, and it enables employers to make more informed judgements about the skills mix in their organizations. Human resource planning also provides a profile of current staff in terms of age, gender, disability and other characteristics, so as to move towards being an equal opportunity organization. But organizations frequently give little time to it because of lack of resources and skills, the time and effort required, and the absence of relevant data to do so.

The process of human resource planning

Human resource planning activities

- Scenario planning: making broad assessments of future environmental developments and their likely impact on people requirements.

- Demand forecasting: estimating future needs for people and competences by reference to corporate and functional plans and forecasts of future activity levels.

- Supply forecasting: estimating the supply of people by reference to analyses of current resources and future availability, after allowing for wastage. The forecast will also take account of labour market trends relating to the availability of skills and to demographics.

- Forecasting requirements: analysing the demand and supply forecasts to identify future deficits or surpluses with the help of models, where appropriate.

- Action planning: preparing plans to deal with forecast deficits through internal promotion, training or external recruitment. If necessary, plan for unavoidable downsizing so as to avoid any compulsory redundancies, if that is possible. Develop retention and flexibility strategies.

Although the areas outlined in the box are described as separate areas, they are closely inter-related and often overlap. For example, demand forecasts are estimates of future requirements, and these may be prepared on the basis of assumptions about the productivity of employees. But the supply forecast will also have to consider productivity trends and how they might affect the supply of people.

A flow chart of the process of human resource planning is shown in Figure 12.1.

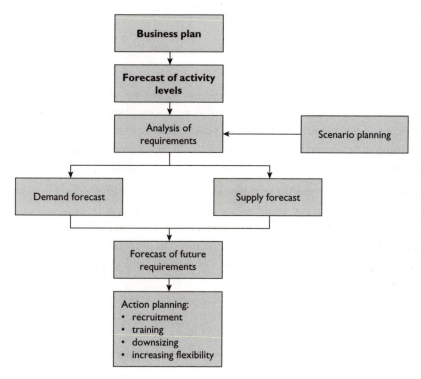

Figure 12.1   Human resource planning flow chart

Recruitment and selection

Recruitment is the process of finding and engaging the people the organization needs. Selection is an aspect of recruitment concerned with deciding which applicants or candidates should be appointed to jobs. Recruitment can be costly. The 2009 CIPD *Survey of Recruitment, Retention and Turnover* (2009a) found that the average cost per employee of filling a vacancy was £4,000.

The recruitment and selection process

The four stages of recruitment and selection are:

1. Defining requirements – preparing role profiles and person specifications; deciding terms and conditions of employment.

2. Planning recruitment campaigns.

3. Attracting candidates – reviewing and evaluating alternative sources of applicants, inside and outside the company: advertising, e-recruiting, agencies and consultants.

4. Selecting candidates – sifting applications, interviewing, testing, assessing candidates, assessment centres, offering employment, obtaining references; preparing contracts of employment.

Defining requirements

The number and categories of people required may be set out in formal human resource or workforce plans, from which are derived detailed recruitment plans. More typically requirements are expressed in the form of ad hoc demands for people because of the creation of new posts, expansion into new activities or areas, or the need for a replacement. These short-term demands may put HR under pressure to deliver candidates quickly.

Requirements are set out in the form of job descriptions or role profiles and person specifications. The latter will set out the qualities required in the shape of behavioural and technical competencies and the types of qualifications and experience that are likely to generate these competencies. These provide the information required to draft advertisements, post vacancies on the internet, brief agencies or recruitment consultants, and assess candidates by means of interviews and selection tests.

Sources of candidates

The sources of candidates and their advantages and disadvantages are set out in Table 12.1.

Table 12.1   Sources of candidates

Source	Advantages	Disadvantages
Internal candidates	• Readily available. • Demonstrate that career opportunities exist within the organization.	• Suitable people may not be available. • Does not provide an influx of 'fresh blood' into the organization.
Returns and referrals – persuade former employees to return to the organization or obtain suggestions from existing employees	• Obtain people with relevant experience. • Tap a new source of candidates.	• Hit and miss.
Advertising	• Target recruitment. • Reach a wide audience. • Controlled by organization.	• Expertise required in drafting and designing national display advertisements and media planning. • Can be expensive, especially if agencies are used. • May involve a lot of time-consuming administration. • Does not necessarily reach the right people.
Online recruitment	• Can reach an even wider range of possible applicants than advertising. • Quicker and cheaper than traditional methods of advertising. • More details of jobs and firms can be supplied on the site, CVs can be matched and applications can be submitted electronically.	• May produce too many irrelevant or poor applications. • Still not the first choice of many job seekers. • Will not reach those who do not have access to the internet.

Table 12.1   *continued*

Source	Advantages	Disadvantages
Recruitment agencies	● Reach specified candidates. ● Access agency database. ● Save time and trouble.	● May be expensive. ● May be hard to find agencies who are good at recruiting specially qualified staff.
Job centres	● No cost. ● Easily accessible.	● Limited availability of candidates for higher-level jobs.
Executive search consultants	● Source well-qualified candidates who would not necessarily respond to other media. ● Provide advice on terms and conditions and expertise in selection.	● Expensive. ● Do not always deliver.
Recruitment process outsourcing (RPO) – using providers who to take responsibility for the end-to-end delivery of the recruitment process covering all vacancies or a selection of them.	● Can save time. ● Brings outside expertise to bear on recruitment problems. ● Frees HR up for more value-adding activities.	● The perception by some HR people and line managers that the provider is too remote to deal with the real issues and that there is a danger of losing control.
Educational establishments	● A convenient source of people with good academic or practical qualifications who can be developed within the organization.	● Will only fill trainee or junior posts.

There is usually a choice between different sources or combinations of them. The criteria to use when making the choice are:

● the likelihood that it will produce good candidates;

● the speed with which the choice enables recruitment to be completed;

● the costs involved, bearing in mind that there may be direct advertising costs or consultants' fees.

The percentages of respondents to the 2009 CIPD *Survey of Recruitment, Retention and Turnover* using different types of recruitment methods were:

Own corporate website	78 per cent
Recruitment agencies	76 per cent
Local paper advertisements	70 per cent
Specialist papers/journals	55 per cent
Employee referral schemes	46 per cent
Job centres	43 per cent
Search consultants	37 per cent
National paper advertisements	31 per cent

Selection methods

The aim of selection is to assess the suitability of candidates by predicting the extent to which they will be able to carry out a role successfully. It involves deciding on the degree to which the characteristics of applicants in terms of their competencies, experience, qualifications, education and training match the person specification. It also involves using this assessment to make a choice between candidates. The main methods of selection are individual interviews and assessment centres. These can be supported by the use of selection tests.

Individual interviews

The individual interview is the most familiar method of selection. It involves face-to-face discussion, and provides the best opportunity for the establishment of close contact – rapport – between the interviewer and the candidate. A structured interview is best. This is one that is built around a set of predetermined questions related to a person specification, which sets out the knowledge and skills required, and indicates the type of experience that will be most appropriate. Competency-based interviews are structured around the competencies required for the post as defined in the person specification. Selection interviewing techniques are described in Chapter 20. If only one interviewer is used, there is more scope for a biased or superficial decision, and this is one reason for using a second interviewer or an interviewing panel.

Assessment centres

Assessment centres assemble a group of candidates and use a range of assessment techniques: interviews, group exercises and tests over a concentrated period (one or two days), with the aim of providing a more comprehensive and balanced view of the suitability of individual members of the group.

Selection tests

Selection tests are used to provide evidence of levels of abilities, intelligence, personality characteristics, aptitudes and attainments. They typically supplement the information obtained from an interview. A distinction is made between psychological or psychometric tests, which measure or assess intelligence, ability or personality, and aptitude tests, which are occupational or job-related tests that assess the extent to which people can do the work.

Intelligence tests

Intelligence tests measure a range of mental abilities which enable a person to succeed at a variety of intellectual tasks using the faculties of abstract thinking and reasoning. They are concerned with general intelligence, and are sometimes called general mental ability (GMA) tests.

Ability tests

Ability tests establish what people are capable of knowing or doing. They measure the capacity for:

- verbal reasoning – the ability to comprehend, interpret and draw conclusions from oral or written language;

- numerical reasoning – the ability to comprehend, interpret and draw conclusions from numerical information;

- spatial reasoning – the ability to understand and interpret spatial relations between objects;

- mechanical reasoning – understanding of everyday physical laws such as force and leverage.

Personality tests

Personality tests attempt to assess the personality of candidates in order to make predictions about their likely behaviour in a role. Personality is an all-embracing and imprecise term which refers to the behaviour of individuals and the way it is organized and coordinated when they interact with the environment. There are many different theories of personality, and consequently many different types of personality tests. These include self-report personality questionnaires and other questionnaires that measure interests, values or work behaviour.

Personality tests can provide interesting supplementary information about candidates, which is free from the biased reactions that frequently occur in face-to-face interviews. But they have to be used with great care.

Aptitude tests

Aptitude tests are job-specific tests that are designed to predict the potential an individual has to perform tasks within a job. They typically take the form of work sample tests which replicate an important aspect of the actual work the candidate will have to do, such as using a keyboard or carrying out a skilled task like repair work. Work sample tests can be used only with applicants who are already familiar with the task through experience or training.

Characteristics of a good test

A good test is one that provides valid data which enable reliable predictions of behaviour or performance to be made, and therefore assists in the process of making objective and reasoned decisions when selecting people for jobs. It will be based on research that has produced standardized criteria derived by using the same measure to test a number of representative people to produce a set of 'norms' for comparison purposes. The test should be capable of being scored objectively by reference to the normal or average performance of the group.

Choice of selection methods

There is a choice between selection methods. The most important criterion is the predictive validity of the method or combination of methods as measured by its predictive validity coefficient – perfect validity is 1.0, no validity is 0.0.

A meta-analysis on the validity of different selection methods was conducted by Schmidt and Hunter (1998). This covered 85 years of research findings, and produced the following predictive validity coefficients which support the use of a combination of intelligence tests and structured interviews:

Intelligence tests and structured interviews	0.63
Intelligence tests and unstructured interviews	0.55
Assessment centres and structured interviews	0.53
Intelligence tests only	0.51
Structured interviews only	0.51
Unstructured interviews only	0.38
Assessment centres only	0.37
Graphology only	0.02

Robertson and Smith (2001) added personality assessments to this list, with a validity coefficient of 0.37.

Schmidt and Hunter (1998) stated that the reason intelligence (general mental ability or GMA) is such a good predictor of job performance is because 'more intelligent people acquire job knowledge more rapidly and acquire more of and it is this knowledge of how to perform the job that causes their job performance to be higher'. Their research clearly indicates that the combination of structured interviews and intelligence tests is the most effective in terms of predictive validity.

Retention planning

It is not enough to get good people into the organization. They have to be kept there. This is the aim of retention planning, which, on the basis of information about how many people leave and why they leave, establishes what steps are required to retain those who are worth retaining.

The turnover of key employees can have a disproportionate impact on the business. The employees organizations wish to retain are often the ones most likely to leave. It was claimed by Reed in 2001 that 'Every worker is five minutes away from handing in his or her notice, and 150 working hours away from walking out of the door to a better offer. There is no such thing as a job for life and today's workers have few qualms about leaving employers for greener pastures.' Things are a bit different during economic downturns, but the risk of good people leaving still exists. Concerted action is required to retain these talented people, but there are limits to what any organization can do. It is also necessary to encourage the greatest contribution from existing talent and to value them accordingly. Retention planning has to start from an understanding of how large the problem is, and that can be achieved by analysing employee turnover.

Employee turnover

Employee turnover (sometimes known as labour turnover or wastage or attrition) is the rate at which people leave an organization. It can be disruptive and costly. The CIPD 2009 *Survey of Recruitment, Retention and Turnover* found that the average rate of labour turnover (the number of employees leaving as a percentage of the number employed) in the United Kingdom was 15.7 per cent. The average cost to the employer of every leaver was £6,150.

Measuring employee turnover

It is necessary to measure employee turnover and calculate its costs in order to forecast future losses for planning purposes and to identify the reasons that people leave the organization. Data on turnover is one of the basic metrics that can be used in human capital management and the evaluation of HRM effectiveness. There are a number of different methods of measuring turnover, which are summarized in Table 12.2.

Table 12.2   Different methods of measuring employee turnover

Method	Description	Comments
Employee (labour) turnover index	The number leaving over a period as a percentage of the average number employed over the period.	The most common method – easy to calculate and understand, and can be used readily for benchmarking (comparing rates of turnover with other organizations). But it can be misleading – the percentage may be inflated by the high turnover of a relatively small proportion of the workforce, especially in times of heavy recruitment.
Survival rate	The proportion of employees who are engaged within a certain period who remain with the organization after so many months or years of service.	A good indication of the effectiveness of recruitment procedures as well as, typically, the high proportion of people who leave after relatively short periods of service. It can therefore highlight where action is required.
Stability index	The number of employees with one year's service or more as a percentage of the number employed a year ago.	The purpose is similar to the survival index and it provides a simple, if rather limited, basis for measurement. Not much used.
Half-life index	The time taken for a group or cohort of starters to reduce to half its original size through turnover.	A variety of survival rate analysis which facilitates turnover comparisons for successive entry years or between different groups of employees. A useful approach but survival rate analysis is more popular because it is easier to grasp.

Choice of measurement

It is difficult to avoid using the conventional employee (labour) turnover index as the easiest of all methods of measurement. It is the most familiar measure in spite of its flaws, and it is therefore a good basis for comparing the performance of the business with national statistics such as those produced by the CIPD or through benchmarking. But internally it needs to be supplemented with some measure of stability. An analysis of turnover or wastage as part of a human resource planning exercise requires detailed information on the length of service of leavers to identify problem areas and to provide a foundation for supply forecasts. The best measure of stability is the survival rate.

Costing employee turnover

Estimates of the cost of employee turnover are useful as means of backing up a business case for taking action to reduce wastage. The following factors should be considered when calculating costs.

- direct cost of recruiting replacements (advertising, interviewing, testing and so on);
- direct cost of introducing replacements (induction cost);
- direct cost of training replacements in necessary skills;
- leaving costs – payroll and HR administration;
- opportunity cost of time spent by HR and line managers in recruitment, induction and training;
- loss of output from those leaving before they are replaced;
- loss of output because of delays in obtaining replacements;
- loss of output while new starters are on their learning curves acquiring the necessary knowledge and skills.

Research by Phillips (1990) found that the 'visible', or direct, costs of recruitment accounted for only 10–15 per cent of total costs. By far the highest costs were associated with the inefficiencies arising while the post was vacant (33 per cent) and the inefficiency of new workers (32 per cent). On average, 12.5 months were required for executives to be comfortable in a new position, and 13.5 months were required for a new employee to achieve maximum efficiency.

Factors affecting retention

Retention strategies should be based on an understanding of the factors that affect whether employees leave or stay. For early-career employees (30 years and under) career advancement is significant. For mid-career employees (age 31–50), the ability to manage their careers and satisfaction from their work are important. Late-career employees (over 50) will be more interested in security. It is also the case that a younger workforce will change jobs and employers more often than an older workforce, and workforces with a lot of part-timers are less stable than those with predominately full-time staff. The other factors that affect retention are:

- company image;
- the effectiveness of recruitment, selection and deployment activities;
- leadership – 'employees join companies and leave managers';
- learning opportunities;
- performance recognition and rewards.

A study by Holbeche (1998) of high flyers found that the factors that aided the retention and motivation of high performers included providing challenge and achievement opportunities (such as assignments), mentors, realistic self-assessment and feedback processes.

Basis of the retention strategy

A retention strategy takes into account the retention issues the organization is facing, as measured by employee turnover, and sets out ways in which these issues can be dealt with. This may mean accepting the reality, as mentioned by Cappelli (2000), that the market, not the company, will ultimately determine the movement of employees. Cappelli believes that it may be difficult to counter the pull of the market – 'you can't shield your people from attractive opportunities and aggressive recruiters'. He suggests that 'The old goal of HR management – to minimize overall employee turnover – needs to be replaced by a new goal: to influence who leaves and when.' This, as proposed by Bevan *et al* (1997), could be based on risk analysis to quantify the seriousness of losing key people or of key posts becoming vacant.

Risk of leaving analysis

Risk of leaving analysis can be carried out by initially identifying potential risk areas – the key people who may leave and for each of them as individuals or groups:

- Estimate the likelihood of this occurring.
- Estimate how serious the effects of a loss would be on the business.
- Estimate the ease with which a replacement could be made and the replacement costs.

Each of the estimates could be expressed on a scale, say very high, high, medium, low, very low. An overview of the ratings under each heading could then indicate where action may need to be taken to retain key people or groups of people.

Analysis of reasons for leaving

Risk analysis provides specific information on areas for concern. Reasons for leaving can include:

- more pay;
- better prospects (career move);
- more security;
- more opportunity to develop skills;
- unable to cope with job;
- better working conditions;

- poor relationship with manager/team leader;
- poor relationship with colleagues;
- bullying or harassment;
- personal – pregnancy, illness, moving away from area, etc.

Some indication of the reasons for leaving and therefore where action needs to be taken can be provided by exit interviews, but they are fallible. More reliance can be placed on the results of attitude or opinion surveys to identify any areas of dissatisfaction. The retention plan should propose actions, and would focus on each of the areas in which lack of commitment and dissatisfaction can arise.

Areas for action

Depending on the outcome of the risk analysis and the overall assessment of reasons for leaving, the possible actions that can be taken are as follows:

- Deal with uncompetitive, inequitable or unfair pay systems. But as Cappelli (2000) points out, there is a limit to the extent to which people can be bribed to stay.

- Design jobs to maximize skill variety, task significance, autonomy, control over their work and feedback, and ensure that they provide opportunities for learning and growth. Some roles can be customized to meet the needs of particular individuals.

- Increase job engagement through job design and by organizing work around projects with which people can identify more readily than with the company as a whole.

- Encourage the development of social ties within the company. In the words of Cappelli (2000), 'loyalty to companies may be disappearing but loyalty to colleagues is not'.

- Ensure that selection and promotion procedures match the capacities of individuals to the demands of the work they have to do. Rapid turnover can result simply from poor selection or promotion decisions.

- Reduce the losses of people who cannot adjust to their new job – the 'induction crisis' – by giving them proper training and support when they join the organization.

- Take steps to improve work–life balance by developing policies including flexible working which recognize the needs of employees outside work.

- Eliminate as far as possible unpleasant working conditions or the imposition of too much stress on employees.

- Select, brief and train managers and team leaders so that they appreciate the positive contribution they can make to improving retention by the ways in which they lead their teams. Bear in mind that people often leave their managers rather than their organization.

- Ensure that policies for controlling stress, bullying and harassment exist and are applied.

Talent management

Resourcing strategies are concerned with assessing the need for talented people and then recruiting and retaining them. The concept of talent management as a process of ensuring that the organization has the talented people it needs only emerged in the late 1990s. It has now been recognized as a major resourcing activity, although its elements are all familiar. Talent management has been called a fad or a fashion, but David Guest argues that 'talent management is an idea that has been around for a long time. It's been re-labelled, and that enables wise organizations to review what they are doing. It integrates some old ideas and gives them freshness, and that is good' (quoted in Warren, 2006: 29).

The meaning of talent management

Talented people possess special gifts, abilities and aptitudes which enable them to perform effectively. As defined by the CIPD (2007), 'Talent consists of those individuals who can make a difference to organizational performance, either through their immediate contribution or in the longer term by demonstrating the highest levels of potential.' Talent management is the process of identifying, developing, recruiting, retaining and deploying those talented people.

The term 'talent management' may refer simply to management succession planning and management development activities, although this notion does not really add anything to these familiar processes except a new, admittedly quite evocative, name. It is better to regard talent management as a more comprehensive and integrated bundle of activities, the aim of which is to secure the flow of talent in an organization, bearing in mind that talent is a major corporate resource.

However, there are different views about what talent management means. Some follow the lead given by McKinsey, which coined the phrase 'the war for talent' in 1997. A book on this subject by Michaels *et al* (2001) identified five imperatives that companies need to act on if they are to win the war for managerial talent. These are:

- Create a winning employee value proposition that will make your company uniquely attractive to talent.

- Move beyond recruiting hype to build a long-term recruiting strategy.

- Use job experience, coaching and mentoring to cultivate the potential in managers.

- Strengthen your talent pool by investing in A players, developing B players and acting decisively on C players.

- Central to this approach is a pervasive mindset – a deep conviction shared by leaders throughout the company that competitive advantage comes from having better talent at all levels.

The McKinsey prescription has often been misinterpreted to mean that talent management is only about obtaining, identifying and nurturing high flyers, ignoring the point they made that competitive advantage comes from having better talent at all levels.

Jeffrey Pfeffer (2001) has doubts about the war for talent concept, which he thinks is the wrong metaphor for organizational success:

> Fighting the war for talent itself can cause problems. Companies that adopt a talent war mind-set often wind up venerating outsiders and downplaying the talent already in the company. They frequently set up competitive zero-sum dynamics that make internal learning and knowledge transfer difficult, activate the self-fulfilling prophesy in the wrong direction (those labelled as less able become less able), and create an attitude of arrogance instead of an attitude of wisdom. For all these reasons, fighting the war for talent may be hazardous to an organization's health and detrimental to doing the things that will make it successful.

It is possible to have different views about talent management: on the one hand, everyone has talent and it not just about the favoured few; on the other, you need to focus on the best. Laura Ashley, director of talent at newspaper group Metro (reported by Warren, 2006), believes you must maximize the performance of your workforce as a whole if you are to maximize the performance of the organization. In contrast (also reported by Warren), Wendy Hirsh, principal associate at the Institute for Employment Studies, says it is not helpful to confuse talent management with overall employee development. Both are important, but talent management is best kept clear and focused. Another view was expressed by Thorne and Pellant (2007): 'No organization should focus all its attention on development of only part of its human capital. What is important, however, is recognizing the needs of different individuals within its community.' The general consensus seems to be that while talent management does concentrate on obtaining, identifying and developing people with high potential, this should not be at the expense of the development needs of people generally.

The process of talent management

Talent management takes the form of a 'bundle' of interrelated processes as shown in Figure 12.2.

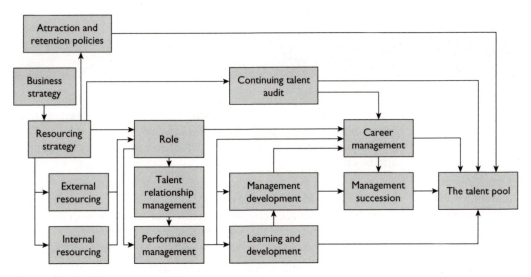

Figure 12.2   The process of talent management

Talent management starts with the business strategy and what it signifies in terms of the talented people required by the organization. Ultimately, the aim is to develop and maintain a pool of talented people. This is sometimes described as the 'talent management pipeline'. Talent management activities are summarized in Table 12.3.

Developing a talent management strategy

A talent management strategy consists of a view on how the processes described above should mesh together with an overall objective – to acquire and nurture talent, wherever it is and wherever it is needed, by using a number of interdependent policies and practices. Talent management is the notion of 'bundling' in action. The development steps required are shown below.

1. Define who the talent management programme should cover.

2. Define what is meant by talent in terms of competencies and potential.

3. Define the future talent requirements of the organization.

4. Develop the organization as an employer of choice – a 'great place to work'.

5. Use selection and recruitment procedures that ensure good-quality people are recruited who are likely to thrive in the organization and stay with it for a reasonable length of time (but not necessarily for life).

6. Develop reward policies that help to attract and retain high-quality staff.

7. Design jobs and develop roles which give people opportunities to apply and grow their skills and provide them with autonomy, interest and challenge.

Table 12.3   Talent management activities

Element	Description
The resourcing strategy	The business plan provides the basis for human resource planning, which defines human capital requirements and leads to attraction and retention policies and programmes for internal resourcing (identifying talented people within the organization and developing and promoting them).
Attraction and retention policies and programmes	Attraction policies lead to programmes for external resourcing (recruitment and selection of people from outside the organization). Retention policies are designed to ensure that people remain as committed members of the organization. The outcome of these policies is a talent flow which creates and maintains the talent pool.
Talent audit	A talent audit identifies those with potential and provides the basis for career planning and development.
Role development	Ensuring that roles provide the responsibility, challenge and autonomy required to create role engagement and motivation.
Talent relationship management	Building effective relationships with people in their roles – treating individual employees fairly, recognizing their value, giving them a voice and providing opportunities for growth. The aim is to achieve 'talent engagement', ensuring that people are committed to their work and the organization.
Performance management	Building relationships with people, identifying talent and potential, planning learning and development activities, and making the most of the talent possessed by the organization.
Learning and development	Ensuring that people acquire and enhance the skills and competencies they need. Development plans are formulated by reference to 'employee success profiles' which are described in terms of competencies and define the qualities that need to be developed.
Management succession planning	Ensure that, as far as possible, the organization has the managers it requires to meet future business needs.
Career management	Providing opportunities for people to develop their abilities and their careers in order to ensure that the organization has the flow of talent it needs and to satisfy their own aspirations.

8. Provide talented staff with opportunities for career development and growth.

9. Create a working environment in which work processes and facilities enable rewarding (in the broadest sense) jobs and roles to be designed and developed.

10. Provide scope for achieving a reasonable balance between working in the organization and life outside work.

11. Develop a positive psychological contract.

12. Develop the leadership qualities of line managers.

13. Recognize those with talent by rewarding excellence, enterprise and achievement.

14. Conduct talent audits which identify those with potential and those who might leave the organization.

15. Introduce management succession planning procedures which identify the talent available to meet future requirements and indicate what management development activities are required.

16. Apply career management procedures.

The following talent management checklist was developed by the CIPD (2006):

- How are we defining talent and talent management?

- Where do professional and specialist staff fit into our talent management process?

- What are the key features of the external environment and the labour market issues impacting on our talent management task?

- What are the main challenges faced in developing a talent pipeline?

- What are we doing to overcome them?

- How do we define and measure aspects of talent, such as potential?

- Are we benchmarking with other organizations?

- Have we clarified for everyone involved the relationship between talent management and other HR initiatives, such as succession planning?

- What tools can be used to identify the right talent and assess potential, employee engagement and so on?

- Are we prepared to train and encourage those responsible for talent management to ask serious questions about performance and potential, and to do something about those not up to the task?

- How is the success of our talent management process measured?

- Do we undertake any systematic evaluation, including calculation of the financial and other benefits of talent management to our organization?

The qualities required

The development and implementation of a talent management strategy requires high-quality management and leadership from the top, and from senior managers and the HR function. Younger *et al* (2007) suggested the approaches required involve emphasizing 'growth from within', regarding talent development as a key element of the business strategy, being clear about the competencies and qualities that matter, maintaining well-defined career paths, taking management development, coaching and mentoring very seriously, and demanding high performance.

Career management

Career management is an important aspect of talent management. It is concerned with the provision of opportunities for people to develop their abilities and their careers in order to ensure that the organization has the flow of talent it needs and to satisfy their own aspirations. It is about integrating the needs of the organization with the needs of the individual.

An important part of career management is career planning, which shapes the progression of individuals within an organization in accordance with assessments of organizational needs, defined employee success profiles, and the performance, potential and preferences of individual members of the enterprise. Career management is also concerned with career counselling to help people develop their careers to their advantage as well as that of the organization.

But career management within the organization has its limitations. It has to take into account the notion of the 'boundaryless career' which, Makela and Suutari (2009) explained, refers to the increasing tendency for individuals to achieve personal goals and to develop a level of professional excellence that gives them enough flexibility to manage their own career progression. 'Individual managers may want to be trained and developed in ways which ensure that their skills are transferable. They are ready to work for a number of organizations that need those skills. Success is measured in terms of psychologically meaningful work and career progression that comes from inter-company self-development rather than hierarchical advancement within one company.'

Flexibility planning

Resourcing strategies cover how people are employed as well as recruitment, retention planning and talent management. This might mean taking a radical look at traditional employment patterns through flexibility planning. This is the process of deciding on the scope for more flexible working arrangements such as multiskilling, job sharing, home working, teleworking, flexible hours, overtime and shift working. It might also mean developing the business as a 'flexible firm' as described below.

Developing a flexible firm

Flexibility can be enhanced by developing what has come to be known as the flexible firm, one in which there is structural and operational flexibility. The concept was originated by Doeringer and Priore (1971), but was popularized by Atkinson (1984).

Structural flexibility is present when the core of permanent employees is supplemented by a peripheral group of part-time employees, employees on short or fixed-term contracts, or subcontracted workers. The forms of operational flexibility are set out below.

- *Functional flexibility* which is sought so that employees can be redeployed quickly and smoothly between activities and tasks. Functional flexibility may require multiskilling – workers who possess and can apply a number of skills: for example, both mechanical and electrical engineering – or multitasking – workers who carry out a number of different tasks, for example in a work team.

- *Numerical flexibility* which is sought so that the number of employees can quickly and easily be increased or decreased in line with even short-term changes in the level of demand for labour.

- *Financial flexibility* which provides for pay levels to reflect the state of supply and demand in the external labour market, and also means the use of flexible pay systems which facilitate either functional or numerical flexibility.

Atkinson (1984) suggested that the growth of the flexible firm has involved the break-up of the labour force into increasingly peripheral, and therefore numerically flexible, groups of workers clustered around a numerically stable core group who will conduct the organization's key, firm-specific activities. This is usually called the 'core–periphery' view of the firm.

At the core, the focus is on functional flexibility. Shifting to the periphery, numerical flexibility becomes more important. As the market grows, the periphery expands to take up slack; as growth slows, the periphery contracts. In the core, only tasks and responsibilities change; the workers here are insulated from medium-term fluctuations in the market and can therefore enjoy a measure of job security, whereas those in the periphery are exposed to them.

Critical evaluation of the flexible firm concept

The concept of the flexible firm has created a lot of interest, but concerns about it have been raised by Marchington and Wilkinson (1996). First, it tends to fuse together description, prediction and prescription into a self-fulfilling prophesy. Second, the evidence of a significant increase in 'flexible firms' and flexibility within firms is lacking. Third, it is not a recent phenomenon – the proportion of people working part-time has grown for decades; and fourth, there are doubts about the costs and benefits of flexibility. Subcontracted workers can be expensive, and part-time workers may have higher levels of absenteeism and lack commitment.

Absence management

Absence management is the development and application of policies and procedures designed to reduce levels of absenteeism. Controlling absence is a resourcing issue in that it is concerned with making effective use of the organization's human resources.

The CIPD 2009 *Survey of Absence Management* revealed that on average employers lose 7.4 working days for each member of staff per year, and absence costs employers an average of £666 per employee per year. It also established that approximately two-thirds of working time lost to absence is accounted for by short-term absences of up to seven days, 17 per cent is caused by absences of between eight days and four weeks, and a similar proportion is caused by absences of four weeks or longer.

Something has to be done about it. This means understanding the causes of absence, and adopting comprehensive absence management (or more positively, attendance management) policies, measuring absence and implementing procedures for the management of short- and long-term absence.

Causes of absence

The causes of absence have been analyzed by Huczynski and Fitzpatrick (1989) under three headings:

- Job situation factors: scope of the job in terms of interest, stress, frequent transfers, quality of leadership, physical working conditions, work group size (the larger the group, the higher the absenteeism), and work group norms which can exert pressure for or against attendance.

- Personal factors: younger employees are more frequently absent than older ones, and some people are absence-prone (studies have noted that between 5 per cent and 10 per cent of workers account for about half of the total absence, while a few are never absent at all).

- Company policy factors: as pay increases, attendance improves, and sick pay schemes may increase absenteeism.

Absence policies

Absence policies should cover:

- methods of measuring absence;

- setting targets for the level of absence;

- deciding on the level of short-term absence that will trigger action, possibly using the Bradford factor, as explained below;

- the circumstances in which disciplinary action might be taken;
- what employees must do if they are unable to attend work;
- sick pay arrangements;
- provisions for the reduction and control of absence, such as return-to-work interviews;
- other steps that can be taken to reduce absence, such as flexible working patterns.

Recording and measuring absence

As a basis for action, absence levels need to be recorded so that they can be measured and monitored against targets for maintaining absence at a certain level or reducing absenteeism.

An HR information system (HRIS) can provide the best means of recording absenteeism. If a self-service approach is in place, managers and team leaders can have direct access to absence records showing the incidence of absenteeism (number and lengths of absence). This data can be consolidated for use by HR in compiling absence statistics and monitoring against targets.

The most common measurement is the percentage of time available that has been lost due to absence.

The Bradford factor

Another increasingly popular measure is the 'Bradford factor'. This index identifies persistent short-term absence by measuring the number and duration of spells of absence. It is calculated using the formula $S \times S \times D =$ Bradford points score, where S is the number of occasions of absence in the last 52 weeks and D is the total number of days' absence in the last 52 weeks. Thus, for employees with a total of 14 days' absence in a 52-week period, the Bradford score can vary enormously depending on the number of occasions involved.

Controlling short-term absence

Short-term absence can be controlled by the following actions:

- return-to work interviews conducted by line managers which can identify problems at an early stage and provide an opportunity for a discussion on ways of reducing absence;
- use of trigger mechanisms such as the Bradford factor to review attendance;
- invoking disciplinary procedures for unacceptable absence levels;
- training line managers in methods of controlling absence, including return-to-work interviews;
- extending the scope for flexible working.

Managing long-term absence

The CIPD (2009b) survey showed that absence of four weeks or more accounts for 17 per cent of total absenteeism. The best way to manage long-term absence is to keep in contact with employees by letter, telephone or visits to discuss the situation, and where possible, plan the return to work. This plan may include modified working hours or a modified role for a period.

People resourcing: key learning points

People resourcing strategy

People resourcing strategy defines the longer-term plans an organization needs for the acquisition, retention, development and use of its human resources. Its rationale is the concept that the strategic capability of a firm depends on its resource capability in the shape of people (the resource-based view).

Human resource planning

Organizations need to know how many people and what sort of people they should have to meet present and future business requirements. This is the function of human resource planning, or workforce planning as it is sometimes called. Human resource planning is an integral part of business planning.

Recruitment and selection processes

Recruitment is the process of finding and engaging the people the organization needs. Selection is that part of the recruitment process concerned with deciding which applicants or candidates should be appointed to jobs.

The four stages of recruitment are:

1. Define requirements.

2. Plan recruitment campaigns.

3. Attract candidates.

4. Select employees.

Retention planning

Retention planning uses information about how many people leave and why they leave to establish what steps are required to retain those who are worth retaining.

Talent management

Talent management is the process of identifying, developing, recruiting, retaining and deploying talented people. It starts with the business strategy and what it signifies in terms of the talented people required by the organization. Ultimately, the aim is to develop and maintain a pool of talented people.

Flexibility planning

Flexibility planning is the process of deciding on the scope for more flexible working arrangements such as multiskilling, job sharing, home working, teleworking, flexible hours, overtime and shift working. It may also mean developing the business as a 'flexible firm'.

Absence management

Absence management is the development and application of policies and procedures designed to reduce levels of absenteeism. Controlling absence is a resourcing issue in that it is concerned with making effective use of the organization's human resources.

Questions

1. What is the objective of a people resourcing strategy?

2. What is an employee value proposition?

3. What is the difference between hard and soft human resource planning?

4. What are the criteria when deciding on sources of applicants?

5. What are the characteristics of a good selection test?

6. Why measure employee turnover?

7. What are the main ways of measuring employee turnover?

8. What is the meaning of talent management?

9. What are the main talent management activities?

10. What is the meaning and significance of the distinction between a core and a periphery organization?

References

Atkinson, J (1984) Manpower strategies for flexible organizations, *Personnel Management*, August, pp 28–31

Bevan S, Barber, I and Robinson, D (1997) *Keeping the Best: A practical guide to retaining key employees*, Institute for Employment Studies, Brighton

Bulla, D N and Scott, P M (1994) Manpower requirements forecasting: a case example, in *Human Resource Forecasting and Modelling*, ed D Ward, T P Bechet and R Tripp, Human Resource Planning Society, New York

Cappelli, P (2000) A market-driven approach to retaining talent, *Harvard Business Review*, January–February, pp 103–11

Chartered Institute of Personnel and Development (CIPD) (2006) *Talent Management: Understanding the dimensions*, CIPD, London

CIPD (2007) Talent management fact sheet, CIPD, London

CIPD (2009a) *Survey of Recruitment, Retention and Turnover*, CIPD, London

CIPD (2009b) *Survey of Absence Management*, CIPD, London

Doeringer, P and Priore, M (1971) *Internal Labour Markets and Labour Market Analysis*, Heath, Lexington, DC

Grant, R M (1991) The resource-based theory of competitive advantage: implications for strategy formation, *California Management Review*, **33** (3), pp 14–35

Holbeche, L (1998) *Motivating People in Lean Organizations*, Butterworth-Heinemann, Oxford

Huczynski, A and Fitzpatrick, M J (1989) *Managing Employee Absence for a Competitive Edge*, Pitman, London

Makela, K and Suutari, V (2009) Global careers: a social capital paradox, *International Journal of Human Resource Management*, **20** (5), pp 992–1008

Marchington, M and Wilkinson, A (1996) *Core Personnel and Development*, Institute of Personnel and Development, London

Michaels, E G, Handfield-Jones, H and Axelrod, B (2001) *The War for Talent*, Harvard Business School Press, Boston, MA

Pfeffer, J (2001) Fighting the war for talent is hazardous to your organization's health, *Organizational Dynamics*, **29** (4), pp 248–59

Phillips, J D (1990) The price tag of turnover, *Personnel Journal*, December, pp 58–61

Purcell, J, Kinnie, K, Hutchinson, S, Rayton, B and Swart, J (2003) *People and Performance: How people management impacts on organisational performance*, CIPD, London

Quinn Mills, D (1983) Planning with people in mind, *Harvard Business Review*, November–December, pp 97–105

Reed, A (2001) *Innovation in Human Resource Management*, CIPD, London

Reilly, P (2003) *Guide to Workforce Planning in Local Authorities*, Employers' Organization for Local Government, London

Robertson, I T and Smith, M (2001) Personnel selection, *Journal of Occupational and Organizational Psychology*, **74** (4), pp 441–72

Schmidt, F L and Hunter, J E (1998) The validity and utility of selection methods in personnel psychology: practical and theoretical implications of 85 years of research findings, *Psychological Bulletin*, **124** (2), pp 262–74

Thorne, K and Pellant, A (2007) *The Essential Guide to Managing Talent*, Kogan Page, London

Walker, P (2007) Develop an effective employer brand, *People Management*, 18 October, pp 44–45

Warren, C (2006) Curtain call, *People Management*, 23 March, pp 24–29

Younger, J, Smallwood, N and Ulrich, D (2007) Developing your organization's brand as a talent developer, *Human Resource Planning*, **30** (2), pp 21–29

Learning and Development

Key concepts and terms

- Bite-sized training
- Blended learning
- Criterion behaviour
- Development
- Double-loop learning
- Experiential learning
- Just-in-time training
- Learning

- Learning culture
- Learning organization
- Personal development planning
- Reflective learning
- Self-directed learning
- Single-loop earning
- Terminal behaviour
- Training

Learning outcomes

On completing this chapter you should be able to define these key concepts. You should also know about:

- The nature of learning and development
- Learning and development strategy
- The nature and creation of a learning culture
- The learning organization
- The nature of organizational learning

- How people learn
- The planning and operation of learning programmes for individuals
- Management development
- How to evaluate learning and development programmes

Introduction

The resource-based view emphasizes the importance of having a highly qualified workforce which is different from and better than those of competitors. Learning and development programmes and activities, sometimes termed human resource development (HRD), make an important contribution to achieving this. As described in this chapter, these need to be established within the framework of a learning and development strategy and against the background of learning theory. It is necessary to create a learning culture which encourages individual and organizational learning and the associated although over-hyped notion of the learning organization. It is also necessary to understand how to plan, run and evaluate learning and development programmes, including those concerned with management development.

Learning and development defined

Learning and development is the process of acquiring and developing knowledge, skills capabilities, behaviours and attitudes through experience, events and programmes provided by the organization, guidance and coaching provided by line managers and others, and self-directed or self-managed learning activities. It is concerned with ensuring that the organization has the knowledgeable, skilled and engaged workforce it needs.

Learning

Learning is the means by which a person acquires and develops new knowledge, skills, capabilities, behaviours and attitudes. As Honey and Mumford (1996) explained it, 'Learning has happened when people can demonstrate that they know something that they did not know before (insights, realizations as well as facts) and when they can do something they could not do before (skills).'

Learning is a continuous process which not only enhances existing capabilities but also leads to the development of the knowledge and skills that prepare people for enlarged or higher-level responsibilities in the future.

Development

Development is concerned with ensuring that a person's ability and potential grows through the provision of learning experiences or through self-directed (self-managed) learning. It is an unfolding process which enables people to progress from a present state of understanding and capability to a future state in which higher-level skills, knowledge and competencies are required.

Training

Training involves the application of formal processes to impart knowledge and help people to acquire the skills necessary for them to perform their jobs satisfactorily.

Comparison of learning and training

Learning should be distinguished from training. 'Learning is the process by which a person constructs new knowledge, skills and capabilities, whereas training is one of several responses an organization can undertake to promote learning' (Reynolds *et al*, 2002).

The encouragement of learning makes use of a process model which is concerned with facilitating the learning activities of individuals and providing learning resources for them to use. Conversely, the provision of training involves the use of a content model, which means deciding in advance the knowledge and skills that need to be enhanced by training, planning the programme, deciding on training methods, and presenting the content in a logical sequence through various forms of instruction.

A distinction was made by Sloman (2003) between learning, which 'lies within the domain of the individual', and training, which 'lies within the domain of the organization'. Today the approach is to focus on individual learning, and ensure that it takes place when required – 'just-for-you' and 'just-in-time' learning.

Elements of learning and development

The elements of learning and development are shown in Figure 13.1.

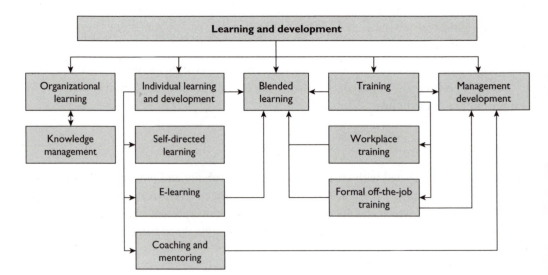

Figure 13.1 Elements of learning and development

Learning and development strategy

A learning and development strategy outlines the approach an organization adopts to ensure that now and in the future, learning and development activities support the achievement of its goals by enhancing the skills and capacities of individuals and teams. It is often called strategic human resource development.

A learning and development strategy should be business-led in the sense that it is designed to support the achievement of business goals by promoting human capital advantage. But it should also be people-led, which means taking into account the needs and aspirations of people to grow and develop. Achieving the latter aim, of course, supports the attainment of the former. The strategy will aim to develop a learning culture.

Learning culture

A learning culture is one that promotes learning because it is recognized by top management, line managers and employees generally as an essential organizational process to which they are committed and in which they engage continuously.

Reynolds (2004) describes a learning culture as a 'growth medium' which will 'encourage employees to commit to a range of positive discretionary behaviours, including learning', and which has the following characteristics: empowerment not supervision, self-managed learning not instruction, long-term capacity building, not short-term fixes. He suggested that to create a learning culture it is necessary to develop organizational practices that raise commitment amongst employees and 'give employees a sense of purpose in the workplace, grant employees opportunities to act upon their commitment, and offer practical support to learning'. The concept of a learning culture is associated with that of the learning organization.

Developing a learning culture

- Develop and share the vision – belief in a desired and emerging future.

- Empower employees – provide 'supported autonomy', freedom for employees to manage their work within certain boundaries (policies and expected behaviours) but with support available as required.

- Adopt a facilitative style of management in which responsibility for decision making is ceded as far as possible to employees.

- Provide employees with a supportive learning environment where learning capabilities can be discovered and applied, for example peer networks, supportive policies and systems, and protected time for learning.

- Use coaching techniques to draw out the talents of others by encouraging employees to identify options and seek their own solutions to problems.

- Guide employees through their work challenges and provide them with time, resources and, crucially, feedback.

- Recognize the importance of managers acting as role models: 'The new way of thinking and behaving may be so different that you must see what it looks like before you can imagine yourself doing it. You must see the new behaviour and attitudes in others with whom you can identify' (Schein, 1990).

- Encourage networks – communities of practice.

- Align systems to vision – get rid of bureaucratic systems that produce problems rather than facilitate work.

Source: Reynolds (2004)

The learning organization

The learning organization is defined as one in which provision is made for the continuous learning of its members. This concept has caught the imagination of many people since it was first popularized by Senge (1990), who described the learning organization as one:

> *where people continually expand their capacity to create the results they truly desire, where new and expansive patterns of thinking are nurtured, where collective aspiration is set free, and where people are continually learning how to learn together.*

Pedler *et al* (1991) state that a learning organization is one 'which facilitates the learning of all its members and continually transforms itself'. Wick and Leon (1995) refer to a learning organization as one that 'continually improves by rapidly creating and refining the capabilities required for future success'.

Critical evaluation of the learning organization concept

As Harrison (2000) comments, the notion of the learning organization remains persuasive because of its 'rationality, human attractiveness and presumed potential to aid organizational effectiveness and advancement'. However, Scarborough *et al* (1999) argue that 'the dominant perspective [of the learning organization concept] is that of organization systems and design'. Little attention seems to be paid to what individuals want to learn or how they learn. The idea that individuals should be enabled to invest in their own development seems to have escaped learning organization theorists, who are more inclined to focus on the imposition of learning by the organization, rather than creating a climate conducive to learning. This is a learning culture, a concept that has more to offer than that of the learning organization.

Viewing organizations as learning systems is a limited notion. Argyris and Schon (1996) contend that organizations are products of visions, ideas, norms and beliefs, so that their shape is much more fragile than the organization's material structure. People act as learning agents for the organization in ways that cannot easily be systematized. They are not only individual learners but also have the capacity to learn collaboratively. Organization learning theory, as described later, analyses how this happens, and leads to the belief that it is the culture and environment that are important, not the systems approach implied by the concept of the learning organization.

The notion of a learning organization is somewhat nebulous. It incorporates miscellaneous ideas about human resource development, systematic training, action learning, organizational development and knowledge management, with an infusion of the precepts of total quality management. But they do not add up to a convincing whole. Easterby-Smith (1997) contends that attempts to create a single best-practice framework for understanding the learning organization are fundamentally flawed. There are other problems with the concept: it is idealistic, knowledge management models are beginning to supersede it, few organizations can meet the criteria, and there is little evidence of successful learning organizations.

Organizational learning

Organizational learning theory is more relevant. It is concerned with how learning takes place in organizations. It focuses on collective learning, but takes into account the proposition made by Argyris (1992) that organizations do not perform the actions that produce the learning; it is individual members of the organization who behave in ways that lead to it, although organizations can create conditions which facilitate such learning. The concept of organizational learning recognizes that the way in which this takes place is affected by the context of the organization and its culture.

The process of organizational learning

Organizational learning can be characterized as an intricate three-stage process consisting of knowledge acquisition, dissemination and shared implementation (Dale, 1994). Knowledge may be acquired from direct experience, the experience of others or organizational memory.

Argyris (1992) suggests that organizational learning occurs under two conditions: first, when an organization achieves what is intended, and second, when a mismatch between intentions and outcomes is identified and corrected. He distinguishes between single-loop and double-loop learning. These two types of learning can be described as adaptive or generative learning.

Single-loop or adaptive learning is incremental learning which does no more than correct deviations from the norm by making small changes and improvements without challenging assumptions, beliefs or decisions. Argyris (1992) suggests that organizations where single-loop learning is the norm define the 'governing variables' – that is, what they expect to achieve in terms of targets and standards – and then monitor and review achievements and take corrective action as necessary, thus completing the loop.

Double-loop or generative learning involves challenging assumptions, beliefs, norms and decisions rather than accepting them. On this basis, learning takes place through the examination of the root causes of problems, so that a new learning loop is established which goes far deeper than the traditional learning loop provided by single-loop learning. It occurs when the monitoring process initiates action to redefine the 'governing variables' to meet the new situation, which may be imposed by the external environment. The organization has learnt something new about what has to be achieved in the light of changed circumstances and can then decide how this should be done. This learning is converted into action. The process is illustrated in Figure 13.2.

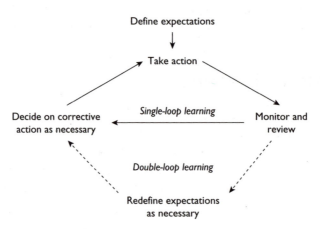

Figure 13.2   Single- and double-loop learning

As Easterby-Smith and Araujo (1999) commented, single-loop learning could be linked to incremental change, 'where an organization tries out new methods and tactics and attempts to get rapid feedback on their consequences in order to be able to make continuous adjustments and adaptations'. In contrast, double-loop learning is associated 'with radical change, which might involve a major change in strategic direction, possibly linked to replacement of senior personnel, and wholesale revision of systems'. It is generally assumed that double-loop learning is superior, but there are situations when single-loop learning may be more appropriate.

Organizational learning and the learning organization

The notion of the learning organization is sometimes confused with the concept of organizational learning. However, as Harrison (2000) points out: 'Too often... it is assumed that the terms 'the learning organization' and 'organizational learning' are synonymous. They are not.'

Easterby-Smith and Araujo (1999) explain that the literature on organizational learning focuses on the 'observation and analysis of the processes of individual and collective learning in organizations', whereas the learning organization literature is concerned with 'using specific diagnostic and evaluative tools which can help to identify, promote and evaluate the quality of the learning processes inside organizations'. In other words the learning organization concept is about what organizations should do to facilitate the learning of their members, and organizational learning is about how people learn in organizations, as discussed below.

How people learn

An understanding of how people learn is necessary if learning is to take place effectively. Learning has been defined by Kim (1993) as the process of 'increasing one's capacity to take action'. It can be described as the modification of behaviour through experience.

Types of learning

- Instrumental learning – learning how to do the job better once the basic standard of performance has been attained. Helped by learning on the job.

- Cognitive learning – outcomes based on the enhancement of knowledge and understanding.

- Affective learning – outcomes based on the development of attitudes or feelings rather than knowledge.

- Self-reflective learning – developing new patterns of understanding, thinking and behaving and therefore creating new knowledge.

Source: Harrison (2005).

The learning process

Individuals learn for themselves and learn from other people. They learn as members of teams and by interaction with their managers, co-workers and people outside the organization. They learn by doing and by instruction. The ways in which individuals learn will differ, and the extent to which they learn will depend largely on how well they are motivated or self-motivated. Discretionary learning can take place when individuals of their own volition actively seek to acquire the knowledge and skills they need to carry out their work effectively. It should be encouraged and supported.

Learning theory

Learning theory explains how people learn and provides the foundation for planning and implementing learning and development programmes. The main theories and their practical implications are summarized in Table 13.1.

Table 13.1   The implications of learning theory and concepts

Theory/concept	Content	Practical implications
The process of learning	<ul><li>Learning is complex and is achieved in many different ways.</li><li>The context is important.</li></ul>	<ul><li>Different learning needs require different learning methods, often in combination.</li><li>Learning effectiveness depends on the extent to which the organization believes in learning and supports it.</li></ul>
Reinforcement theory	Behaviours can be strengthened by reinforcing them with positive feedback (conditioning).	Reinforcement theory underpins training programmes concerned with developing skills through instruction. In these, the learner is conditioned to make a response and receives immediate feedback. Progress is made in incremental steps each directed to a positive outcome.
Cognitive learning theory	Learners acquire understanding which they internalize by being exposed to learning materials and by solving problems.	The knowledge and understanding of learners can be enriched and internalized by presenting them with learning materials (perhaps via e-learning). Case studies, projects and problem-solving activities can also be used for this purpose. Self-directed learning, personal development planning activities and discovery learning processes with help from facilitators, coaches or mentors are underpinned by cognitive learning theory.

Table 13.1 *continued*

Theory/concept	Content	Practical implications
Experiential learning theory	People learn by constructing meaning and developing their skills through experience.	Learning through experience can be enhanced by encouraging learners to reflect on and make better use of what they learn through their own work and from other people. Self-directed learning and personal development planning activities with help from facilitators, coaches or mentors are also underpinned by experiential learning theory, as is action learning.
Social learning theory	Learning is most effective in a social setting. Individual understanding is shaped by active participation in real situations.	Learning can be encouraged in communities of practice and in project teams and networks.
Learning styles	Every person has their own learning style.	Learning programmes need to be adjusted to cope with different learning styles. Trainers have also to flex their methods. People will learn more effectively if they are helped to 'learn how to learn' by making the best use of their own style but also by experimenting with other styles.
The learning curve	The time required to reach an acceptable standard of skill or competence varies between people. Learning may proceed in steps with plateaus rather than being a continuous process.	Recognize that progress may vary and may not be continuous. Enable learners to consolidate their learning, and introduce reinforcement periods in training programmes to recognize the existence of learning steps and plateaus.
The motivation to learn	People need to be motivated to learn effectively.	Learners should be helped to develop learning goals and to understand the benefits to them of achieving them. Performance management processes leading to personal development plans can provide a means of doing this.

The approaches to learning and development described below need to be based on an understanding of the applications of learning theory.

Approaches to learning and development

Learning and development can be formal or informal, and it can use computer, networked and web-based technology (e-learning). Its effectiveness is increased by joining up different methods of learning and development (blended learning) and by encouraging self-directed learning.

Formal learning

Formal learning is planned and systematic. It makes use of structured training programmes consisting of instruction and practice which may be conducted on the job or off the job. Experience may be planned to provide opportunities for continuous learning and development. Formal learning and developmental activities may be used, such as action learning, coaching, mentoring and outdoor learning. The organization may have its own training centre. Some large companies have corporate universities.

Informal learning

Informal learning is experiential learning. It takes place while people are learning on the job as they go along (workplace learning). Most learning does not take place in formal training programmes.

A study by Eraut *et al* (1998) established that in organizations adopting a learner-centred perspective, formal education and training provided only a small part of what was learnt at work. Most of the learning described to the researchers was non-formal, neither clearly specified nor planned. It arose naturally from the challenges of work. Effective learning was, however, dependent on the employees' confidence, motivation and capability. Some formal training to develop skills (especially induction training) was usually provided, but learning from experience and other people at work predominated. Reynolds (2004) noted that 'The simple act of observing more experienced colleagues can accelerate learning; conversing, swapping stories, co-operating on tasks and offering mutual support deepen and solidify the process... This kind of learning – often very informal in nature – is thought to be vastly more effective in building proficiency than more formalised training methods.'

Advantages and disadvantages of informal learning

Advantages

- Learning efforts are relevant and focused in the immediate environment.
- Understanding can be achieved in incremental steps rather than in indigestible chunks.
- Learners define how they will gain the knowledge they need – formal learning is more packaged.
- Learners can readily put their learning into practice.

Disadvantages

- It may be left to chance – some people will benefit, some will not.
- It can be unplanned and unsystematic, which means that it will not necessarily satisfy individual or organizational learning needs.
- Learners might simply pick up bad habits.

E-learning

E-learning was defined by Pollard and Hillage (2001) as 'the delivery and administration of learning opportunities and support via computer, networked and web based technology to help individual performance and development'. E-learning enhances learning by extending and supplementing face-to-face learning rather than replacing it. It enables learning to take place when it is most needed (just in time as distinct from just in case) and when it is most convenient. Learning can be provided in short segments or bites which focus on specific learning objectives. It is 'learner-centric' in that it can be customized to suit an individual's learning needs – learners can choose different learning objects within an overall package. The main potential drawbacks are the degree of access to computers, the need for a reasonable degree of literacy, the need for learners to be self-motivated, and the time and effort required to develop and update e-learning programmes.

Self-directed learning

Self-directed or self-managed learning involves encouraging individuals to take responsibility for their own learning needs, either to improve performance in their present job or to develop their potential and satisfy their career aspirations. It can also be described as self-reflective learning (Mezirow, 1985), which is the kind of learning that involves encouraging individuals to develop new patterns of understanding, thinking and behaving.

Self-directed learning can be based on a process of recording achievements and action planning, which involves individuals reviewing what they have learnt, what they have achieved, what their goals are, how they are going to achieve those goals and what new learning they need to acquire. The learning programme can be 'self-paced' in the sense that learners can decide for themselves up to a point the rate at which they work, and are encouraged to measure their own progress and adjust the programme accordingly.

Self-directed learning is based on the principle that people learn and retain more if they find things out for themselves. But they still need to be given guidance on what to look for and help in finding it. Learners have to be encouraged to define, with whatever help they may require, what they need to know to perform their job effectively. They need to be provided with guidance on where they can get the material or information that will help them to learn, and how to make good use of it. Personal development plans, as described later in this chapter, can provide a framework for this process. Learners also need support from their manager and the organization with the provision of coaching, mentoring and learning facilities, including e-learning.

Development

Development takes the form of learning activities that prepare people to exercise wider or increased responsibilities. In development programmes there is an emphasis on self-directed learning, as described above, personal development planning (together with learning contracts) and planned learning from experience.

Personal development planning

Personal development planning is carried out by individuals with guidance, encouragement and help from their managers as required. A personal development plan sets out the actions people propose to take to learn and to develop themselves. They take responsibility for formulating and implementing the plan, but receive support from the organization and their managers in doing so. The purpose is to provide what Tamkin *et al* (1995) call a 'self-organized learning framework'.

Stages of personal development planning

1. Analyse the current situation and development needs. This can be done as part of a performance management process.

2. Set goals. These could include improving performance in the current job, improving or acquiring skills, extending relevant knowledge, developing specified areas of competence, moving across or upwards in the organization, or preparing for changes in the current role.

3. Prepare an action plan. The action plan sets out what needs to be done and how it will be done under headings such as outcomes expected (learning objectives), the development activities, the responsibility for development (what individuals are expected to do and the support they will get from their manager, the HR department or other people), and timing. A variety of activities tuned to individual needs should be included in the plan, for example observing what others do, project work, planned use of e-learning programmes and internal learning resource centres, working with a mentor, coaching by the line manager or team leader, experience in new tasks, guided reading, special assignments and action learning. Formal training to develop knowledge and skills may be part of the plan but it is not the most important part.

4. Implement the plan.

A development plan can be expressed in the form of a learning contract, as described below.

Learning contracts

A learning contract is a formal agreement between the manager and the individual on what learning needs to take place, the objectives of such learning, and what parts the individual, the manager, the learning and development function or a mentor will play in ensuring that learning happens. The partners to the contract agree on how the objectives will be achieved and their roles. It will spell out learning programmes and indicate what coaching, mentoring and formal training activities should be carried out. It is, in effect, a blueprint for learning.

Planned experience

Planned experience is the process of deciding on a sequence of experience that will enable people to obtain the knowledge and skills required in their jobs and prepare them to take on increased responsibilities. This enables experiential learning to take place in order to meet a learning specification. A programme is drawn up which sets down what people are expected to learn in each department or job in which they are given experience. This should spell out what they are expected to discover for themselves. A suitable person (a mentor) should be available to see that people in a development programme are given the right experience and opportunity to learn, and arrangements should be made to check progress. A good way of stimulating people to find out for themselves is to provide them with a list of questions to answer. It is essential, however, to follow up each segment of experience to check what has been learnt and, if necessary, modify the programme.

Training

Training is the use of systematic and planned instruction activities to promote learning. The approach can be summarized in the phrase 'learner-based training'. It is one of several responses an organization can undertake to promote learning.

As Reynolds (2004) points out, training has a complementary role to play in accelerating learning: 'It should be reserved for situations that justify a more directed, expert-led approach rather than viewing it as a comprehensive and all pervasive people development solution.' He also commented that the conventional training model has a tendency to 'emphasize subject-specific knowledge, rather than trying to build core learning abilities'.

The justification for training

Formal training is indeed only one of the ways of ensuring that learning takes place, but it can be justified in the following circumstances.

- The work requires skills that are best developed by formal instruction.

- Different skills are required by a number of people which have to be developed quickly to meet new demands and cannot be acquired by relying on experience.

- The tasks to be carried out are so specialized or complex that people are unlikely to master them on their own initiative at a reasonable speed.

- Critical information must be imparted to employees to ensure they meet their responsibilities.

- A learning need common to a number of people has to be met and can readily be dealt with in a training programme: for example induction, essential IT skills, communication skills.

Systematic training

Training should be systematic in that it is specifically designed, planned and implemented to meet defined needs. It is provided by people who know how to train, and the impact of training

Figure 13.3 Systematic training model

is carefully evaluated. The concept was originally developed for the industrial training boards in the 1960s, and consists of a simple four-stage model as illustrated in Figure 13.3.

Just-in-time training

Just-in-time training is training that is closely linked to the pressing and relevant needs of people by its association with immediate or imminent work activities. It is delivered as close as possible to the time when the activity is taking place. The training is based on an identification of the latest requirements, priorities and plans of the participants, who are briefed on the live situations in which their learning has to be applied. The training programme takes account of any issues concerning the transfer of learning to the job, and aims to ensure that what is taught is seen to be applicable in the current work situation.

Bite-sized training

Bite-sized training involves the provision of opportunities to acquire a specific skill or a particular piece of knowledge in a short training session which is focused on one activity, such as using a particular piece of software, giving feedback or handling an enquiry about a product or service of the company. It is often carried out through e-learning. It can be a useful means of developing a skill or understanding which is readily put to use in the workplace through a concentrated session or learning activity without diversions.

Types of training

Training programmes or events can be concerned with any of the following:

- manual skills, including modern apprenticeships;
- IT skills;

- team leader or supervisory training;

- management training;

- interpersonal skills such as leadership, team building, group dynamics, neurolinguistic programming;

- personal skills such as assertiveness, coaching, communicating, time management;

- training in organizational procedures or practices such as induction, health and safety, performance management, equal opportunity or managing diversity policy and practice.

Blended learning

Blended learning is the use of a combination of learning methods to increase the overall effectiveness of the learning process by providing for different parts of the learning mix to complement and support one another. A blended learning programme might be planned for an individual using a mix of self-directed learning activities defined in a personal development plan, e-learning facilities, group action learning activities, coaching or mentoring, and instruction provided in an in-company course or externally. Generic training for groups of people might include e-learning, planned instruction programmes, planned experience, and selected external courses. Within a training course a complementary mix of different training activities might take place: for example a skills development course for managers or team leaders might include some instruction on basic principles, but much more time would be spent on case studies, simulations, role playing and other exercises.

Planning and delivering learning programmes and events

The actions required are:

1. *Establish learning needs* (methods of doing this are described in the next section of this chapter).

2. *Define learning objectives.* It is essential to be clear about what the programme or event is required to achieve – its learning objectives and outcomes. These are defined by reference to established learning needs, and provide the basis for planning content and evaluating results. Objectives can be defined as criterion behaviour (the performance standards or changes in behaviour on the job to be achieved if a learning process is to be regarded as successful) and terminal behaviour (what actually happened following the learning event). Any gap between criterion and terminal behaviour will indicate deficiencies in the programme. A behavioural objective could be set out as follows.

Example of a behavioural learning objective

At the end of the programme managers will be able to take greater responsibility for the development of their staff. Indicative activities will include:

- the conduct of satisfactory performance and development reviews;
- the agreement of personal development plans;
- enabling team members to carry out self-directed learning activities;
- the ability to use coaching skills to improve performance.

3. *Decide on content.* The content of the programme or event will clearly be governed by whatever those attending need to know or be able to do, as set out in the learning objectives. It is important not to try to achieve too much in any one event. There is a limit to how much people can absorb at any one time, and an even greater limit to how much they can put into effect. The content of the training should be related to the work contexts of the participants. Ideally, their work should be made a central feature of the subject matter. Every opportunity should be taken taking to embed learning at work.

4. *Decide on methods of delivery.* The methods used to deliver learning should be appropriate to the purpose of the course and to the characteristics of participants – their jobs, learning needs, previous experience, level of knowledge and skills, and how receptive they are to being taught (motivated to learn). A blended learning approach should be adopted. Account must be taken of how people learn. Every opportunity should be taken to embed learning at work. It is particularly important in management, supervisory and interpersonal skills training to provide ample time for participation and active learning through discussion, case studies and simulations. Lectures should form a minor part of the course. The design of the programme or event should take account of the principles of learning.

Guidance on the design and delivery of learning events

- Design an appropriate structure and culture – how the event will be shaped and the desirable climate of relationships.
- Stimulate the learners – ensure that learners believe that their needs are being catered for. Get them involved. Focus on key learning points.
- Help understanding – check understanding regularly and vary the learning pace to ensure that it is absorbed.

- Incorporate appropriate learning activities – these should include situations or the use of knowledge and skills which learners perceive to be relevant to their jobs.

- Build on existing learning – find out what people know and do and build on that so that they can incorporate new learning or recognize that they are irrelevant and allow them gradually to fall away.

- Guide the learners – give them regular feedback and guidance on the learning process.

- Ensure that learning is retained – enable learners to practice and consolidate their skills, bearing in mind the phenomenon of the learning curve. Provide feedback and praise as appropriate.

- Ensure transfer of learning – successful transfer of learning from the event to the workplace depends on the extent to which the event has been relevant to the learners' needs, the learners have been able to acquire the knowledge and skills covered in the programme, they have been stimulated throughout the programme and are encouraged and enabled to put their learning into practice.

Source: Harrison (2005), based on the ideas of Gagne (1977).

5. *Decide on the location and facilities required, the budget and who delivers the programme.* The programme could take place on or off the job, in-house or at an external centre. The facilities will be determined by the planned learning methods, and their availability will influence the location. At this stage it is also necessary to cost the programme and prepare a financial budget. The programme could be delivered by the organization's own learning and development staff, or outsourced in whole or in part to outside training providers. Line managers may usefully take part as long as they are reasonably proficient as instructors, trainers or coaches.

6. *Prepare information on the programme or event* – this will set out its objectives, content and methods as a guide to nominating managers and potential participants.

7. *Deliver the learning* – this should not present too many problems if the planning and preparation for the programme or event has been carried out systematically. However, a flexible approach is desirable because all learning events vary according to the characteristics of the learners, whose learning needs and reactions will vary. Fine-tuning will be necessary throughout the programme.

8. *Evaluate the learning* – the criteria for an effective learning programme or event are set out in the box. Systematic methods of evaluation are described later in this chapter.

Criteria for learning programme effectiveness

- The event or programme is based on a thorough evaluation of learning needs.

- Clear objectives have been set for the outcomes of the event or programme.

- Standards are set for the delivery of the event or programme.

- Success criteria and methods of measuring success have been established.

- A blend of learning and development methods are used – informal and formal – which are appropriate for the established needs of those taking part.

- The responsibilities for planning and delivering the programme or event have been clarified.

- Those responsible for the learning activity are well qualified in whatever role they are expected to play.

- Adequate resources have been allocated to the programme or event.

- The programme or event has the support of top management.

- The programme is implemented effectively as planned, within its budget and in accordance with the defined standards.

- The application of the programme or event is regularly monitored to ensure that it meets the defined objectives and standards.

- The achievements of the programme or event are evaluated against the success criteria and swift corrective action is taken to deal with any problems.

Identifying learning needs

All learning activities need to be based on an understanding of what needs to be done and why it needs to be done. The purpose of the activities must be defined, and this is only possible if the learning needs of the organization and the groups and individuals within it have been identified and analysed.

The basis of learning needs analysis

Learning needs analysis is often described as the process of identifying the learning gap – the gap between what is and what should be, as illustrated in Figure 13.4. But this 'deficiency model' of training – only putting things right that have gone wrong – is limited. Learning is much more positive than that. It should be concerned with identifying and satisfying

Figure 13.4   The learning gap

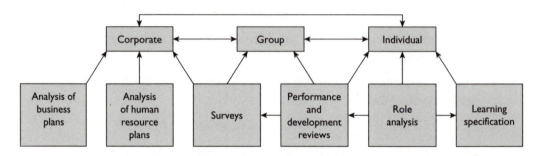

Figure 13.5   Learning needs analysis – areas and methods

development needs – fitting people to take on extra responsibilities, increasing all-round competence, equipping people to deal with new work demands, multi-skilling, and preparing people to take on higher levels of responsibility in the future.

Areas for learning needs analysis

Learning needs should be analysed, first, for the organization as a whole – corporate needs; second, for departments, teams, functions or occupations within the organization – group needs; and third, for individual employees – individual needs. These three areas are inter-connected, as shown in Figure 13.5. The analysis of corporate needs will lead to the identification of learning needs in different departments or occupations, while these in turn will indicate what individual employees need to learn. The process operates in reverse. As the needs of individual employees are analysed separately, common needs emerge which can be dealt with on a group basis. The sum of group and individual needs will help to define corporate needs, although there may be some superordinate learning requirements which can be related only to the company as a whole to meet its business development needs. So the whole learning plan may be greater than the sum of its parts. These areas of analysis are discussed below.

Analysis of business and human resource plans

Business and HR plans should indicate in general terms the types of skills and competencies that may be required in the future and the numbers of people with those skills and competencies who will be needed. These broad indicators have to be translated into more specific plans which cover, for example, the outputs from training programmes of people with particular skills or a combination of skills (multi-skilling).

Surveys

Special surveys may be carried out which analyse the information from a number of sources, such as performance reviews, to identify corporate and group learning and training needs. This information can usefully be supplemented by interviewing people to establish their views about what they need to learn. People often find it difficult to articulate learning needs, and it is best to lead with a discussion of the work they do and identify any areas where they believe that their performance and potential could be improved by a learning or training programme.

An analysis should also be made of any areas where future changes in work processes, methods or job responsibilities are planned, and of any common gaps in skills or knowledge, or weaknesses in performance, which indicate a learning need. Further information should be derived from the evaluation of training as described at the end of this chapter.

Performance and development reviews

Performance management processes (described in Chapter 14) should be a prime source of information about individual learning and development needs. The performance management approach to learning concentrates on the preparation of performance improvement programmes, personal development plans and learning contracts which lead to jointly determined action plans. The emphasis is on identifying learning needs for continuous development, which can be met by self-directed learning, or to produce specific improvements in performance.

Role analysis

Role analysis is the basis for preparing role profiles which provide a framework for analysing and identifying learning needs. Role profiles set out the key result areas of the role, and importantly also define the competencies required to perform the role. A good performance management process will ensure that role profiles are updated regularly and the performance review is built round an analysis of the results achieved by reference to the key result areas and agreed objectives.

The competency framework for the role is used to assess the level of competency displayed in achieving, or not achieving, those results. An assessment can then be made of any learning required to develop levels of competency. Ideally, this should be a self-assessment by individuals, who should be given every encouragement to identify learning needs for themselves. These can be discussed with the individual's manager and agreement reached on how the learning needs should be met, by the individuals through self-directed learning and/or with the help and support of their managers.

Learning specification

Role analysis can be the basis of a learning specification which sets out what needs to be learnt and how the learning should be carried out.

Evaluation of learning

It is important to evaluate learning, in order to assess its effectiveness in producing the outcomes specified when the activity was planned, and to indicate where improvements or changes are required to make the learning programme even more effective.

The best-known framework for evaluation was developed by Kirkpatrick (1983). His four levels, which become progressively more demanding and revealing, are as follows.

Level 1: Reaction

At this level, evaluation measures how those who participated in the training have reacted to it. In a sense, it is a measure of immediate customer satisfaction. Kirkpatrick suggests the following guidelines for evaluating reactions:

1. Determine what you want to find out.

2. Design a form that will quantify reactions.

3. Encourage written comments and suggestions.

4. Get 100 per cent immediate response.

5. Get honest responses.

6. Develop acceptable standards.

Level 2: Evaluate learning

This level obtains information on the extent to which learning objectives have been attained. It will aim to find how much knowledge was acquired, what skills were developed or improved, and the extent to which attitudes have changed in the desired direction. So far as possible, the evaluation of learning should involve the use of tests before and after the programme – paper and pencil, oral or performance tests.

Level 3: Evaluate behaviour

This level evaluates the extent to which behaviour has changed as required when people attending the programme have returned to their jobs. The question to be answered is the extent to which knowledge, skills and attitudes have been transferred from the classroom to the workplace. Ideally, the evaluation should take place both before and after the training. Time should be allowed for the change in behaviour to take place. The evaluation needs to assess the extent to which specific learning objectives relating to changes in behaviour and the application of knowledge and skills have been achieved.

Level 4: Evaluate results

This is the ultimate level of evaluation, and provides the basis for assessing the benefits of the training against its costs. The objective is to determine the added value of learning and development programmes – how they contribute to raising organizational performance above its previous level. The evaluation has to be based on before and after measures. It has to determine the extent to which there has been a satisfactory return on the investment in the learning programme, and how far its fundamental objectives have been achieved in areas such as increasing sales, raising productivity, reducing accidents or increasing customer satisfaction. Evaluating results is obviously easier when they can be quantified. However, it is not always easy to prove the contribution to improved results made by training as distinct from other factors, and as Kirkpatrick says, 'Be satisfied with evidence, because proof is usually impossible to get.'

Management and leadership development

Management development is concerned with improving the performance of managers in their present roles, preparing them to take on greater responsibilities in the future, and, importantly, developing their leadership skills. It has been described by Mumford and Gold (2004) as 'an attempt to improve managerial effectiveness through a learning process'. Management development activities are associated with talent management, described in Chapter 12.

A systematic approach to management and leadership development is necessary because the increasingly onerous demands made on line managers mean that they require a wider range of developed skills than ever before.

Formal approaches to management and leadership development

Management and leadership development should be based on the identification of development needs through performance management or a development centre making use of the following formal approaches:

- Coaching and mentoring.

- The use of performance management processes to provide feedback and satisfy development needs.

- Planned experience, which includes job rotation, job enlargement, taking part in project teams or task groups, 'action learning', and secondment outside the organization.

- Formal training by means of internal or external courses.

- Structured self-development following a self-directed learning programme set out in a personal development plan and agreed as a learning contract with the manager or a management development adviser.

- Competency frameworks can be used as a means of identifying and expressing development needs and pointing the way to self-managed learning programmes or the provision of learning opportunities by the organization.

Informal approaches to management and learning development

Informal approaches to management development make use of the learning experiences that managers meet during the course of their everyday work. Managers are learning every time they are confronted with an unusual problem, an unfamiliar task or a move to a different job. They then have to evolve new ways of dealing with the situation. They will learn if they analyse what they did to determine how and why it contributed to its success or failure. This retrospective or reflective learning will be effective if managers can apply it successfully in the future.

Experiential and reflective learning is potentially the most powerful form of learning. It comes naturally to some managers. They seem to absorb, unconsciously and by some process of osmosis, the lessons from their experience, although in fact they have probably developed a capacity for almost instantaneous analysis, which they store in their mental databank to retrieve when necessary. Ordinary mortals, however, either find it difficult to do this sort of analysis or do not recognize the need. This is where informal or at least semi-formal approaches can be used to encourage and help managers to learn more effectively.

Informal approaches to management development

- Getting managers to understand their own learning styles so that they can make the best use of their experience and increase the effectiveness of their learning activities – the manager's self-development guide by Pedler *et al* (1994) provides an excellent basis for this important activity.

- Emphasizing self-assessment and the identification of development needs by getting managers to assess their own performance against agreed objectives and analyse the factors that contributed to effective or less-effective performance – this can be provided through performance management.

- Getting managers to produce their own personal development plans – self-directed learning programmes.

- Encouraging managers to discuss their own problems and opportunities with their manager, colleagues or mentors in order to establish for themselves what they need to learn or be able to do.

Development centres

Development centres consist of a concentrated (usually one- or two-day) programme of exercises, tests and interviews designed to identify managers' development needs and to provide counselling on their careers. They offer participants the opportunity to examine and understand the competencies they require now and in the future. Because 'behaviour predicts behaviour', centres offer opportunities for competencies to be observed in practice. Simulations of various kinds are therefore important features – these are a combination of case studies and role playing designed to obtain the maximum amount of realism.

Participants are put into the position of practising behaviour in conditions very similar to those they will meet in the course of their everyday work. Important parts of the centre's activities are feedback reviews, counselling and coaching sessions conducted by the directing staff.

Criteria for management and leadership development

The effectiveness and value of any approach to management development include the extent to which it:

- links to organizational goals and context – and so has relevance for the organization as well as for individuals;

- builds on and develops the qualities, skills and attitudes of participants;

- is supported by appropriate HR policies to do with recruitment and selection, reward, talent management and succession planning;
- has the full commitment of those responsible for the operation of the process;
- is motivating to those encouraged to participate in it.

Learning and development: key learning points

Learning and development

Learning and development is the process of acquiring and developing knowledge, skills, capabilities, behaviours and attitudes through learning or developmental experiences.

Learning and development strategy

The approach an organization adopts to ensure that now and in the future, learning and development activities support the achievement of its goals by developing the skills and capacities of individuals and teams.

Learning organization

One in which the continuous learning of its members is provided for and encouraged.

Organizational learning

Organizational learning theory is concerned with how learning takes place in organizations.

How people learn

Individuals learn for themselves and learn from other people. They learn as members of teams and by interaction with their managers, co-workers and people outside the organization. They learn by doing and by instruction.

Informal and formal learning

Formal learning is planned and systematic. It makes use of structured training programmes consisting of instruction and practice which may be conducted on the job or off the job. Informal learning is experiential learning. It takes place while people are learning on the job as they go along.

E-learning

E-learning provides for learning via computer technology. It provides a means of satisfying individual learning needs through self-managed learning.

Self-directed learning

Self-directed learning involves encouraging individuals to take responsibility for their own learning needs.

Development

Development takes the form of learning activities such as personal development planning which prepare people to exercise wider or increased responsibilities.

Training

Training is the use of systematic and planned instruction activities to promote learning.

Blended learning

Blended learning is the use of a combination of learning methods to increase the overall effectiveness of the learning process.

Planning learning programmes and events

It is essential to be clear about what the programme or event is required to achieve – its learning objectives and outcomes. These are defined to satisfy established learning needs and to provide the basis for planning content and evaluating results. The methods used to deliver learning should be appropriate to the purpose of the course and to the characteristics of participants.

Identifying learning needs

All learning activities need to be based on an understanding of what needs to be done and why it needs to be done. The purpose of the activities must be defined, and this is only possible if the learning needs of the organization and the groups and individuals within it have been identified and analysed.

Evaluating learning

It is important to evaluate learning in order to assess its effectiveness in producing the outcomes specified when the activity was planned, and to indicate where improvements or changes are required to make the learning programme even more effective.

Management development

Management development is concerned with improving the performance of managers in their present roles and preparing them to take on greater responsibilities in the future.

Questions

1. What are the elements of a learning and development strategy?

2. What is a learning culture and how can it be developed?

3. Critically evaluate the concept of a learning organization.

4. What is the basis of learning needs analysis?

5. What are the potential benefits of learning and development activities?

6. What are the criteria for an effective learning and development programme?

7. Why is learning evaluation important?

8. What are the levels of learning evaluation suggested by Kirkpatrick?

References

Argyris, C (1992) *On Organizational Learning*, Blackwell, Cambridge

Argyris, C and Schon, D A (1996) *Organizational Learning: A theory of action perspective*, Addison Wesley, Reading, MA

Dale, M (1994) Learning organizations, in *Managing Learning*, ed C Mabey and P Iles, Routledge, London

Easterby-Smith, M (1997) Disciplines of organizational learning: contributions and critiques, *Human Relations*, **50** (9), pp 1085–113

Easterby-Smith, M and Araujo, L (1999) Organizational learning: current debates and opportunities, in *Organizational Learning and the Learning Organization*, ed M Easterby-Smith, J Burgoyne and L Araujo, Sage, London

Eraut, M J, Alderton, G, Cole, G and Senker, P (1998) *Development of Knowledge and Skills in Employment*, Economic and Social Research Council, London

Gagne, R M (1977) *The Conditions of Learning*, 3rd edn, Rinehart & Winston, New York

Harrison, R (2000) *Employee Development*, 2nd edn, IPM, London

Harrison, R (2005) *Learning and Development*, 4th edn, CIPD, London

Honey, P and Mumford, A (1996) *The Manual of Learning Styles*, 3rd edn, Honey Publications, Maidenhead

Kim, D H (1993) The link between individual and organizational learning, *Sloane Management Review*, **35** (1), pp 37–50

Kirkpatrick, D L (1983) Four steps to measuring training effectiveness, *Personnel Administrator*, **28** (11), pp 19–25

Mezirow, J A (1985) A critical theory of self-directed learning, in *Self-directed Learning: From theory to practice*, ed S Brookfield, Jossey-Bass, San Francisco, CA

Mumford, A and Gold, J (2004) *Management Development: Strategies for action*, CIPD, 2004

Pedler, M, Burgoyne, J and Boydell, T (1991) *The Learning Company: A strategy for sustainable development*, McGraw-Hill, Maidenhead

Pedler, M, Burgoyne, J and Boydell, T (1994) *A Manager's Guide to Self Development*, McGraw-Hill, Maidenhead

Pollard, E and Hillage, J (2001) *Explaining e-Learning*, Report No 376, Institute for Employment Studies, Brighton

Reynolds, J (2004) *Helping People Learn*, CIPD, London

Reynolds, J, Caley, L and Mason, R (2002) *How Do People Learn?* CIPD, London

Scarborough, H, Swan, J and Preston, J (1999) *Knowledge Management: A Literature Review*, Institute of Personnel and Development, London

Schein, E H (1990) Organizational culture, *American Psychologist*, **45**, pp 109–119

Senge, P (1990) *The Fifth Discipline: The art and practice of the learning organization*, Doubleday, London.

Sloman, M (2003) E-learning: stepping up the learning curve, *Impact*, CIPD, January, pp 16–17

Tamkin, P, Barber, L and Hirsh, W (1995) *Personal Development Plans: Case studies of practice*, Institute for Employment Studies, Brighton

Tamkin, P, Yarnall, J and Kerrin, M (2002) *Kirkpatrick and Beyond: A review of training evaluation*, Report 392, Institute for Employment Studies, Brighton

Wick, C W and Leon, L S (1995) Creating a learning organization: from ideas to action, *Human Resource Management*, Summer, pp 299–311

Managing Performance

Introduction

Managing performance involves taking systematic action to improve organizational, team and individual performance. It enables performance expectations to be defined, and creates the basis for developing organizational and individual capability. For individuals, performance management processes are associated with both financial and non-financial rewards.

Organizations exist to meet the needs of their stakeholders. They do this in five ways:

- by delivering high-quality goods and services;

- by acting ethically (exercising social responsibility) with regard to their employees and the public at large;

- by rewarding their employees equitably according to their contribution;

- in the private sector, by rewarding shareholders by increasing the value of their holdings, as long as this is consistent with the requirement to meet the needs of other stakeholders;

- by ensuring that the organization has the capability required to guarantee continuing success.

Managing performance is about developing organizational capability – the capacity of an organization to perform effectively in order to achieve desired results. This means achieving sustained competitive advantage and increased shareholder value in the private sector, or high-quality and cost-effective services in the public and not-for profit sectors.

The questions that will be answered in this chapter are: What is meant by performance? What are the factors that influence performance? How can high performance be achieved? What can be done to manage organizational, team and individual performance?

The meaning of performance

The Oxford English Dictionary defines performance as 'The accomplishment, execution, carrying out, working out of anything ordered or undertaken.' This refers to outputs/outcomes (accomplishment), but also states that performance is about doing the work as well as being about the results achieved.

Performance is indeed often regarded as simply the outcomes achieved: a record of a person's accomplishments. Kane (1996) argued that performance 'is something that the person leaves behind and that exists apart from the purpose'. Bernardin *et al* (1995) believe that 'Performance should be defined as the outcomes of work because they provide the strongest linkage to the strategic goals of the organization, customer satisfaction, and economic contributions.'

Borman and Motowidlo (1993) put forward the notion of contextual performance, which covers non-job specific behaviours such as cooperation, dedication, enthusiasm and persistence, and is differentiated from task performance, covering job-specific behaviours. As Fletcher (2001) mentioned, contextual performance deals with attributes that go beyond task competence, and which foster behaviours that enhance the climate and effectiveness of the organization.

Performance could therefore be regarded as behaviour – the way in which organizations, teams and individuals get work done. Campbell (1990) stated that 'Performance is behaviour and should be distinguished from the outcomes because they can be contaminated by systems factors.'

A more comprehensive view of performance is achieved if it is defined as embracing both behaviour and outcomes. This was well put by Brumbach (1988):

> *Performance means both behaviours and results. Behaviours emanate from the performer and transform performance from abstraction to action. Not just the instruments for results, behaviours are also outcomes in their own right – the product of mental and physical effort applied to tasks – and can be judged apart from results.*

Performance is a complicated notion. As Bates and Holton (1995) emphasized, 'Performance is a multi-dimensional construct.' It was pointed out by Campbell *et al* (1993) that the components of performance are:

- job-specific task proficiency;
- non-job-specific proficiency (such as organizational citizenship behaviour);
- written and oral communication proficiency;
- demonstration of effort;
- maintenance of personal discipline;
- facilitation of peer and team performance;
- supervision/leadership;
- management/administration.

This concept of performance leads to the conclusion that when managing the performance of teams and individuals, a number of factors have to be considered including both inputs (behaviour) and outputs (results).

Influences on performance

Vroom (1964) suggested that performance is a function of ability and motivation as depicted in the formula Performance = f (Ability × Motivation). The effects of ability and motivation on performance are not additive but multiplicative. People need both ability and motivation to perform well, and if either ability or motivation is zero, there will be no effective performance.

Another formula for performance was originated by Blumberg and Pringle (1982). Their equation was Performance = Individual Attributes × Work Effort × Organizational Support. By including organizational support in the formula they brought in the organizational context as a factor affecting performance.

Research carried out by Bailey *et al* (2001) in 45 establishments focused on another factor affecting performance – the opportunity to participate. They noted that 'organizing the work process so that non-managerial employees have the opportunity to contribute discretionary effort is the central feature of a high performance work system'. (This was one of the earlier uses of the term 'discretionary effort'.)

The 'AMO' formula put forward by Boxall and Purcell (2003) is a combination of the Vroom and Bailey *et al* ideas. This model posits that performance is a function of Ability + Motivation + Opportunity to Participate (note that the relationship is additive, not multiplicative).

The work system

All these above formulae are concerned with individual performance, but this is influenced by systems as well as person factors. These include the support people get from the organization, the leadership and support they get from their managers, and other contextual factors outside the control of individuals. Jones (1995) made the radical proposal that the aim should be to 'manage context not performance', and goes on to explain that:

> In this equation, the role of management focuses on clear, coherent support for employees by providing information about organization goals, resources, technology, structure, and policy, thus creating a context that has multiplicative impact on the employees, their individual attributes (competency to perform), and their work effort (willingness to perform). In short, managing context is entirely about helping people understand; it is about turning on the lights.

It was emphasized by Deming (1986) that differences in performance are largely caused by systems variations. Coens and Jenkins (2002) were even more adamant. They wrote:

> An organizational system is composed of the people who do the work but far more than that. It also includes the organization's methods, structure, support, materials, equipment, customers, work culture, internal and external environments (such as markets, the community, governments), and the interaction of these components. Each part of the system has its own purpose but at the same time is dependent on the other parts... Because of the interdependency of the parts, improvement strategies aimed at the parts, such as appraisal, do little or nothing to improve the system.

Line managers

Line managers play a crucial role in providing non-financial rewards (positive feedback, recognition, opportunity to develop and scope to exercise responsibility). They also, of course, have considerable influence on financial reward decisions – pay reviews and fixing rates of pay. Importantly, it is they who are largely responsible for operating the performance management system, job design and on-the-job coaching and development, all of which impact directly on the performance of their teams and the individuals in them.

Taking action

These activities are concerned with developing a high-performance culture, as discussed in the next section. Such a culture depends on adopting the right approach to improving organizational, team and individual performance, and getting the work system and leadership right.

High-performance cultures

A high-performance culture is one in which people are aware of the need to perform well, and behave accordingly in order to meet or exceed expectations. Such a culture embraces a number of interrelated processes which together make an impact on the performance of the organization through its people, in such areas as productivity, quality, levels of customer service, growth, profits, and ultimately, in profit-making firms, the delivery of increased shareholder value. In our more heavily service- and knowledge-based economy, employees have become the most important determinant of organizational success.

Characteristics of a high-performance culture

The following characteristics of a high-performance culture were defined by Lloyds TSB (source: e-reward, 2003):

- People know what is expected of them – they are clear about their goals and accountabilities.
- They have the skills and competencies to achieve their goals.
- High performance is recognized and rewarded accordingly.
- People feel that their job is worth doing, and that there is a strong fit between the job and their capabilities.
- Managers act as supportive leaders and coaches, providing regular feedback, performance reviews and development.

- A pool of talent ensures a continuous supply of high performers in key roles.

- There is a climate of trust and teamwork, aimed at delivering a distinctive service to the customer.

Developing a high-performance culture

There are three approaches that can be adopted to developing a high-performance culture:

- the implementation of high-performance working through a high-performance work system;

- the use of rewards;

- the use of systematic methods of managing performance.

These are discussed in the remaining sections of this chapter.

High-performance work systems

A high-performance work system (HPWS) is described by Becker and Huselid (1998) as 'An internally consistent and coherent HRM system that is focused on solving operational problems and implementing the firm's competitive strategy'. They suggest that such a system 'is the key to the acquisition, motivation and development of the underlying intellectual assets that can be a source of sustained competitive advantage'. This is because it has the following characteristics:

- It links the firm's selection and promotion decisions to validated competency models.

- It is the basis for developing strategies that provide timely and effective support for the skills demanded to implant the firm's strategies.

- It enacts compensation and performance management policies that attract, retain and motivate high-performance employees.

HPWSs provide the means for creating a performance culture. They embody ways of thinking about performance in organizations and how it can be improved. They are concerned with developing and implementing bundles of complementary practices which as an integrated whole will make a much more powerful impact on performance than if they were dealt with as separate entities.

Becker *et al* (2001) stated that the aim of such systems is to develop a 'high-performance perspective in which HR and other executives view HR as a system embedded within the larger system of the firm's strategy implementation'. As Nadler (1989) commented, they are deliberately introduced in order to improve organizational, financial and operational performance. Nadler and Gerstein (1992) characterized an HPWS as a way of thinking about organizations. It can play an important role in strategic HRM by helping to achieve a 'fit' between information, technology, people and work.

In their seminal work *Manufacturing Advantage: Why high performance work systems pay off*, Appelbaum *et al* (2000) stated that HPWS facilitate employee involvement, skill enhancement and motivation. An HPWS is 'generally associated with workshop practices that raise the levels of trust within workplaces and increase workers' intrinsic reward from work, and thereby enhance organizational commitment'. They define high performance as a way of organizing work so that front-line workers participate in decisions that have a real impact on their jobs and the wider organization.

It is sometimes believed that HPWSs are just about HR policies and initiatives. But as Godard (2004) suggested, they are based on both alternative work practices and high-commitment employment practices. He called this the high-performance paradigm, and described it as follows.

> *Alternative work practices that have been identified include: (1) alternative job design practices, including work teams (autonomous or non-autonomous), job enrichment, job rotation and related reforms; and (2) formal participatory practices, including quality circles or problem-solving groups, town hall meetings, team briefings and joint steering committees. Of these practices, work teams and quality circles can be considered as most central to the high performance paradigm. High-commitment employment practices that have been identified include: (1) sophisticated selection and training, emphasizing values and human relations skills as well as knowledge skills; (2) behaviour-based appraisal and advancement criteria; (3) single status policies; (4) contingent pay systems, especially pay-for-knowledge, group bonuses, and profit sharing; (5) job security; (6) above-market pay and benefits; (7) grievance systems; and others.*

Components of an HPWS

There is no generally accepted definition of an HPWS, and there is no standard list of the features or elements of such a system. However, an attempt to define the basic components of an HPWS was made by Shih *et al* (2005):

- Job infrastructure – workplace arrangements that equip workers with the proper abilities to do their jobs, provide them with the means to do their jobs, and give them the motivation to do their jobs. These practices must be combined to produce their proper effects.

- Training programmes to enhance employee skills – investment in increasing employee skills, knowledge and ability.

- Information sharing and worker involvement mechanisms – to understand the available alternatives and make correct decisions.

- Compensation and promotion opportunities that provide motivation – to encourage skilled employees to engage in effective discretionary decision making in a variety of environmental contingencies.

Developing an HPWS

An HPWS has to be based on a high-performance strategy which sets out intentions and plans on how a high-performance culture can be created and maintained. The strategy must be aligned to the context of the organization and to its business strategy. Every organization will therefore develop a different strategy. The approach to developing an HPWS is based on an understanding of what the goals and performance drivers of the business are, what work arrangements are appropriate to the attainment of those goals, and how people can contribute to their achievement. This leads to an assessment of what type of performance culture is required and what approach to reward is appropriate for the different segments of the workforce.

The development programme requires strong leadership from the top. Stakeholders – line managers, team leaders, employees and their representatives – should be involved as much as possible through surveys, focus groups and workshops.

An HPWS is the basis for developing a performance culture, and provides the framework for managing performance. This is sometimes assumed to be simply concerned with managing individual performance through performance management systems. But it is also very much about managing organizational and team performance, as described below.

Managing organizational performance

The management of organizational performance takes place in a number of dimensions. It is a strategic approach which has to take account of the needs of multiple stakeholders. It is the prime responsibility of top management who plan, organize, monitor and control activities and provide leadership to achieve strategic objectives and satisfy the needs and requirements of stakeholders.

As Gheorghe and Hack (2007) observed, 'Actively managing performance is simply running a business – running the entire business as one entity. It's a continuous cycle of planning, executing, measuring results and planning the next actions. In the context of a larger strategic initiative, that means continuous improvement.'

Organizational capability

The aim of managing organizational performance is to increase organizational capability – the capacity of an organization to function effectively. It is about the ability of an organization to guarantee high levels of performance, achieve its purpose (sustained competitive advantage in a commercial business), deliver results and, importantly, meet the needs of its stakeholders. It is concerned with the organization as a system, and is in line with the belief expressed by Coens and Jenkins (2002) that to 'focus on the overall "system" of the organization yields better results than trying to get individual employees to improve their performance'.

The aim is to increase organizational effectiveness by obtaining better performance from people, getting them to work well together, improving organizational processes such as the formulation and implementation of strategy and the achievement of high quality and levels of customer service, and facilitating the management of change.

This has to take place in a context in which organizations are increasingly embracing a new management culture based on inclusion, involvement and participation, rather than on the traditional command, control and compliance paradigm which Flaherty (1999) claims 'cannot bring about the conditions and competence necessary to successfully meet the challenges of endless innovation; relentless downsizing, re-engineering, and multicultural working holistically'. This new management paradigm requires the development of a high-performance work environment through management practices that value and support achievement, growth and learning. It also calls for facilitative behaviours that focus on employee empowerment, learning and development. In other words, it needs performance management.

The dimensions of managing organizational performance

Sink and Tuttle (1990) stated that managing organizational performance includes five dimensions:

- creating visions for the future;
- planning – determining the present organizational state, and developing strategies to improve that state;
- designing, developing and implementing improvement interventions;
- designing, redesigning, developing, and implementing measurement and evaluation systems;
- putting cultural support systems in place to reward and reinforce progress.

A strategic approach to managing organizational performance means taking a broad and long-term view of where the business is going, and managing performance in ways that ensure that this strategic thrust is maintained. The objective is to provide a sense of direction in an often turbulent environment, so that the business needs of the organization and the individual and collective needs of its employees can be met by the development and implementation of integrated systems for managing and developing performance.

Implementing organizational performance management

Organizational performance management systems are strategic in the sense that they are aligned to the business strategy of the organization and support the achievement of its strategic goals. They focus on developing work systems and the working environment as well as developing individuals. To develop the systems and make them function effectively it is necessary to ensure that the strategy is understood, including, as Kaplan and Norton (2000) put it, 'The crucial but perplexing processes by which intangible assets will be converted into tangible outcomes.' The notion of mapping strategy was originated by them as a development of their concept of the balanced scorecard.

Strategy maps show the cause-and-effect links by which specific improvements create desired outcomes. They are means of describing the elements of the organization's systems and their interrelationships. They therefore provide a route map for systems improvement leading to performance improvement. In addition, they give employees a clear line of sight into how their jobs are linked to the overall objectives of the organization, and provide a visual representation of a company's critical objectives and the relationships between them that drive organizational performance. Bourne *et al* (2003) call them 'success maps', which they describe as diagrams that show the logic of how the objectives of the organization interact to deliver overall performance. An example of a strategy map is given in Figure 14.1.

This map shows an overall objective to improve profitability as measured by return on capital employed. In the next line the map indicates that the main contributors to increased profitability are increases to the gross margin (the difference between the value of sales and the cost of sales), improvements to operational capability and better cost management. At the next level down the objective is to increase sales turnover in order to increase the gross margin. How this is to be achieved is set out in the next group of objectives and their interconnections, comprising increases in customer satisfaction and sales force effectiveness, innovations in product/market development and marketing, and improvements in customer service and quality levels. The key objective of improving operational capability is underpinned by developments in high-performance working and the contribution of the organization's human capital. The latter is supported by HRM objectives in the fields of performance management, reward management, talent management, levels of employee engagement, and learning and development.

The overall objective of increasing profitability in this example addresses the concerns of only one section of the stakeholders of an organization, the investors. This need would probably be given precedence by many quoted companies. But there are other objectives which they could and should have, which relate to their other stakeholders, for example those concerned with corporate social responsibility. These could be catered for in separate strategy maps. Better still, they could be linked to their commercial objectives. Public and voluntary sector organizations will certainly have objectives which relate to all their stakeholders as well as their overall purpose. A stakeholder approach to strategic performance management is required.

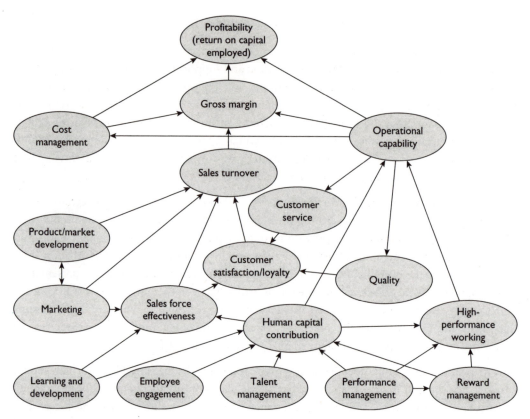

Figure 14.1   A strategy map

The performance prism

A multiple stakeholder framework for organizational performance management – the performance prism – has been formulated by Neely *et al* (2002). This framework is based on the proposition that organizations exist to satisfy their stakeholders, and their wants and needs should be considered first. Neely *et al* contend that companies in particular must assume a broader role than simply delivering value to their shareholders. To be successful over time, even for and on behalf of shareholders, businesses must address multiple stakeholders. If companies do not give each of their stakeholders the right level of focus, both their corporate reputation and their market capitalization – and therefore shareholder value – are likely to suffer in one way or another. They suggest that the performance prism can facilitate or structure the analysis of multiple stakeholders in preparation for applying performance measurement criteria.

Neely *et al* explain the term 'performance prism' as follows:

A prism refracts light. It illustrates the hidden complexity of something as apparently simple as white light. So it is with the performance prism. It illustrates the true complexity of performance measurement and management. It is a thinking aid which seeks to integrate five related perspectives and provide a structure that allows executives to think through the answers to five fundamental questions:

- *Stakeholder Satisfaction: Who are our stakeholders and what do they want and need?*

- *Stakeholder Contribution: What do we want and need from our stakeholders?*

- *Strategies: What strategies do we need to put in place to satisfy these wants and needs?*

- *Processes: What processes do we need to put in place to satisfy these wants and needs?*

- *Capabilities: What capabilities – people, practices, technology and infrastructure – do we need to put in place to allow us to operate our processes more effectively and efficiently?*

Managing team performance

As Purcell *et al* (1998) pointed out, teams supply the 'elusive bridge between the aims of the individual employee and the objectives of the organization… teams can provide the medium for linking employee performance targets to the factors critical to the success of the business'. Managing team performance involves the key activities of setting work and process objectives and conducting team reviews and individual reviews, which are described below.

Setting work objectives

Work objectives for teams are based on an analysis of the purpose of the team and its accountabilities for achieving results. Targets and standards of performance should be discussed and agreed by the team as a whole. These may specify what individual members are expected to contribute. Project teams will agree project plans which define what has to be done, who does it, the standards expected and the timescale.

Setting process objectives

Process objectives are defined by the team getting together and agreeing how they should conduct themselves as a team under headings related to team competencies including:

- interpersonal relationships;

- the quality of participation, collaborative effort and decision making;

- the team's relationships with internal and external customers;

- the capacity of the team to plan and control its activities;

- the ability of the team and its members to adapt to new demands and situations;

- the flexibility with which the team operates;

- the effectiveness with which individual skills are used;

- the quality of communications within the team and between the team and other teams or individuals.

Team performance reviews

Team performance review meetings analyse and assess feedback and control information on their joint achievements against objectives and project plans. The agenda for such meetings could be as follows.

General feedback review

- Progress of the team as a whole.

- Problems encountered by the team which have caused difficulties or hampered progress.

- Helps and hindrances to the operation of the team.

Work reviews

- How well the team has functioned.

- Review of the individual contribution made by each team member – in other words, peer review (see below).

- Discussion of any new problems encountered by individual team members.

Group problem solving:

- Analysis of reasons for any shortfalls or other problems.

- Agreement of what needs to be done to solve them and prevent their recurrence.

Update objectives

- Review of new requirements, opportunities or threats.

- Amendment and updating of objectives and project plans.

Managing individual performance

Individual performance is developed through performance management systems. They provide the framework for improving performance through the agreement of performance expectations and the formulation of performance development plans. As vehicles for feedback and recognition they have a major role in a performance and reward system. They inform contingent pay decisions.

This section starts with definitions of performance management strategy and the purpose and principles of performance management. Summaries of the processes involved follow.

Performance management strategy

Performance management strategy is based on the resource-based view that it is the strategic development of the organization's rare, hard to imitate and hard to substitute human resources that produces its unique character and creates competitive advantage. The strategic goal will be to 'create firms which are more intelligent and flexible than their competitors' (Boxall, 1996) by developing more talented staff and by extending their skills base, and this is exactly what performance management aims to do.

The purpose of performance management

The purpose of performance management is to get better results from the organization, teams and individuals by understanding and managing performance within an agreed framework of planned goals, standards and competency requirements. It is a process for establishing shared understanding about what is to be achieved, and an approach to managing and developing people in a way which increases the probability that it will be achieved in the short and longer term. It is owned and driven by line management. Performance management enhances the engagement of people by providing the foundation upon which many non-financial motivation approaches can be built.

Principles of performance management

The extensive research conducted by the CIPD (Armstrong and Baron, 1998, 2004) identified the following 10 principles of performance management as stated by practitioners:

- 'A management tool which helps managers to manage.'
- 'Driven by corporate purpose and values.'
- 'To obtain solutions that work.'
- 'Only interested in things you can do something about and get a visible improvement.'
- 'Focus on changing behaviour rather than paperwork.'

- 'It's about how we manage people – it's not a system.'

- 'Performance management is what managers do: a natural process of management.'

- 'Based on accepted principle but operates flexibly.'

- 'Focus on development not pay.'

- 'Success depends on what the organization is and needs to be in its performance culture.'

The performance management cycle

Performance management is a natural process of management. It is not an HRM technique or tool. As a natural process of management the performance management cycle as shown in Figure 14.2 corresponds with William Denning's (1965) Plan–Do–Check–Act model. The performance management processes taking place in this cycle are:

- *Plan*: agree objectives and competency requirements as expressed in role profiles; identify the required behaviours; produce plans expressed in performance agreements for meeting objectives and improving performance; prepare personal development plans to enhance knowledge, skills and competence and reinforce the desired behaviours.

- *Act*: carry out the work required to achieve objectives by reference to the plans and in response to new demands.

- *Monitor*: check on progress in achieving objectives and responding to new demands; treat performance management as a continuous process – 'managing performance all the year round' – rather than an annual appraisal event.

- *Review*: a 'stocktaking' discussion of progress and achievements held in a review meeting and identifying where action is required to develop performance as a basis for completing the cycle by continuing into the planning stage.

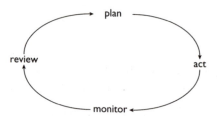

Figure 14.2   The performance management cycle

Key features of performance management

- At every stage the aim is to obtain agreement between managers and individuals on how well the latter are doing and what can be done jointly to develop strengths and deal with any weaknesses.

- Discussions between managers and individuals take the form of a dialogue. Managers should not attempt to dominate the process and it should not be perceived as an alternative method of control.

- Performance management is largely about managing expectations – both managers and individuals understand and agree what they expect of one another, developing a more positive psychological contract.

- Positive feedback is used to motivate people by recognizing their achievements and potential.

- The process is forward looking – it does not dwell on the past, and the dialogue is about what can be done in the future to develop performance and give individuals the opportunity to grow (this is an important means of motivation).

- Performance management is a continuous process, it is not an annual event; managers and individuals are there to manage performance throughout the year.

Performance management as a rewarding process

Performance management, if carried out properly, can reward people by recognition through feedback, the provision of opportunities to achieve, the scope to develop skills, and guidance on career paths. All these are non-financial rewards which can encourage job and organizational engagement, and make a longer-lasting and more powerful impact than financial rewards such as performance-related pay.

Performance management is, of course, also associated with pay by generating the information required to decide on pay increases or bonuses related to performance, competence or contribution. In some organizations this is its main purpose, but performance management is, or should be, much more about developing people and rewarding them in the broadest sense.

Managing performance: key learning points

The meaning of performance

Performance means both behaviours and results.

Influences on individual performance

Boxall and Purcell (2003) put forward the 'AMO' formula which states that performance is a function of Ability + Motivation + Opportunity to Participate.

Impact of reward on performance

In the right circumstances incentives can improve individual performance (a total of 190 studies covered individually or in meta-analyses). The assumption is that improvements in organizational performance will follow improvements in individual performance. Some research has confirmed this.

The work system

Individual performance is influenced by work systems as well as person factors. These include the support people get from the organization and their managers and other contextual factors outside the control of individuals.

High-performance cultures

A high-performance culture is one in which people are aware of the need to perform well and behave accordingly in order to meet or exceed expectations.

High-performance work systems

A high-performance work system (HPWS) is a bundle of practices that facilitate employee involvement, skill enhancement and motivation.

Managing organizational performance

The aim of managing organizational performance is to increase organizational capability, the capacity of an organization to function effectively.

Managing team performance

Managing team performance involves the key activities of setting work and process objectives and conducting team reviews.

Individual performance management

The purpose of performance management is to get better results from the organization, teams and individuals by understanding and managing performance within an agreed framework of planned goals, standards and competence requirements.

Performance management is a natural process of management. It is not an HRM technique or tool.

The performance management cycle is: plan, act, monitor and review.

Questions

1. Why is it important to be clear about the meaning of performance?

2. David Guest wrote in 1997 that 'Performance management has a poor record of success, and the temptation is to engage in a spiral of control in an attempt to extract more effort and ever higher performance from employees through policies and practices that may succeed only in further de-motivating and which are, thereby, ultimately self-defeating.' To what extent is this true today? Justify your answer by reference to experience in your organization and recent research.

3. From the managing director to the HR director: 'We went to all that time and trouble (and cost) last year to introduce your all-singing and all-dancing performance management system but what I am hearing is that with a few notable exceptions our line managers are either not capable of doing it properly or are not inclined to do it or both. What are you going to do about it?' Reply.

References

Appelbaum, E, Bailey, T, Berg, P and Kalleberg, A L (2000) *Manufacturing Advantage: Why high performance work systems pay off*, ILR Press, Ithaca, New York

Armstrong, M and Baron, A (1998) *Performance Management: The new realities*, CIPD, London

Armstrong, M and Baron, A (2004) *Managing Performance: Performance management in action*, CIPD, London

Bailey, T, Berg, P and Sandy, C (2001) The effect of high performance work practices on employee earnings in the steel, apparel and medical electronics and imaging industries, *Industrial and Labor Relations Review*, **54** (2A), pp 525–43

Bates, R A and Holton, E F (1995) Computerized performance monitoring: a review of human resource issues, *Human Resource Management Review*, Winter, pp 267–88

Becker, B E and Huselid, M A (1998) High performance work systems and firm performance: a synthesis of research and managerial implications, *Research on Personnel and Human Resource Management*, **16**, pp 53–101

Becker, B E, Huselid, M A and Ulrich, D (2001) *The HR Score Card: Linking people, strategy, and performance*, Harvard Business School Press, Boston, MA

Bernardin, H J, Hagan, C and Kane, J (1995) The effects of a 360 degree appraisal system on managerial performance, Proceedings at the 10th annual conference of the Society for Industrial and Organizational Psychology, Orlando, FL

Blumberg, M and Pringle, C (1982) The missing opportunity in organizational research: some implications for a theory of work performance, *Academy of Management Review*, 7 (4), pp 560–69

Borman, W C and Motowidlo, S J (1993) Expanding the criterion domain to include elements of contextual performance, in N Schmitt and W C Borman (eds), *Personnel Selection in Organizations*, Jossey-Bass, San Francisco, CA

Bourne, M, Franco, M and Wilkes, J (2003) Corporate performance management, *Measuring Business Excellence*, **7** (3), pp 15–21

Boxall, P F (1996) The strategic HRM debate and the resource-based view of the firm, *Human Resource Management Journal*, **6** (3), pp 59–75

Boxall, P F and Purcell, J (2003) *Strategy and Human Resource Management*, Palgrave Macmillan, Basingstoke

Brown, M P, Sturman, M C and Simmering, M J (2003) Compensation policy and organizational performance: the efficiency, operational and financial implications of pay levels and pay structure, *Academy of Management Journal*, **46** (6), pp 752–82

Brumbach, G B (1988) Some ideas, issues and predictions about performance management, *Public Personnel Management*, Winter, pp 387–402

Campbell, J P (1990) Modeling the performance prediction problem in industrial and organizational psychology, in M P Dunnette and L M Hugh (eds), *Handbook of Industrial and Organizational Psychology*, Blackwell, Cambridge, MA

Campbell, J P, McCloy, R A, Oppler, S H and Sager, C E (1993) A theory of performance, in N Schmitt and W Borman (eds), *Personnel Selection in Organizations*, Jossey-Bass, San Francisco, CA

Coens, T and Jenkins, M (2002) *Abolishing Performance Appraisals: Why they backfire and what to do instead*, Berrett-Koehler, San Francisco, CA

Curral, S C, Towler, A J, Judge, T A and Kohn, L (2005) Pay satisfaction and organizational outcomes, *Personnel Psychology*, **58** (3), pp 613–40

Deming, W E (1986) *Out of the Crisis*, Massachusetts Institute of Technology Centre for Advanced Engineering Studies, Cambridge, MA

e-reward (2003) Research Report no 17, Pay in a high performance organization: a case study of Lloyds TSB, e-reward, Stockport

e-reward (2009) Contingent Pay Survey, e-reward, Stockport

Flaherty, J (1999) *Coaching: Evoking excellence in others*, Butterworth-Heinemann, Burlington, MA

Fletcher, C (2001) Performance appraisal and management: the developing research agenda, *Journal of Occupational and Organizational Psychology*, **74** (4), pp 473–87

Gheorghe, C and Hack, J (2007) Unified performance management: how one company can tame its many processes, *Business Performance Management*, November, pp 17–19

Godard, J (2004) A critical assessment of the high-performance paradigm, *British Journal of Industrial Relations*, **42** (2), pp 349–78

Goleman, D (2000) Leadership that gets results, *Harvard Business Review*, March–April, pp 78–90

Guest, D E (1997) Human resource management and performance; a review of the research agenda, *International Journal of Human Resource Management*, **8** (3), 263–76

Jones, T W (1995) Performance management in a changing context, *Human Resource Management*, **34** (3), pp 425–42

Kane, J S (1996) The conceptualization and representation of total performance effectiveness, *Human Resource Management Review*, Summer, pp 123–45

Kaplan, R S and Norton, D P (2000) Having trouble with your strategy? Then map it, *Harvard Business Review*, September–October, pp 167–76

Lawler, E E (1986) *High Involvement Management*, Jossey-Bass, San Francisco, CA

Lawler, E E, Mohrman, S and Ledford, G (1998) *Strategies for High Performance Organizations: Employee involvement, TQM, and re-engineering programs in Fortune 1000*, Jossey-Bass, San Francisco, CA

McAdams, J and Hawks, E J (1994) *Organizational Performance and Rewards*, American Compensation Association, Scottsdale, AZ

Nadler, D A (1989) Organizational architecture for the corporation of the future, *Benchmark*, Fall, pp 12–13

Nadler, D A and Gerstein, M S (1992) Designing high-performance work systems: organizing people, technology, work and information, *Organizational Architecture*, Summer, pp 195–208

Neely, A, Adams, C and Kennerley, M (2002) *The Performance Prism: The scorecard for measuring and managing business success*, Pearson Education, Harlow

Northouse, P G (2006) *Leadership: Theory and practice*, 4th edn, Sage, Thousand Oaks, CA

Purcell, J, Hutchinson, S and Kinnie, N (1998) *The Lean Organization*, IPD, London

Shih, H-A, Chiang, Y-H and Hsu, C-C (2005) Can high performance work systems really lead to better performance? Academy of Management Conference Paper, pp 1–6

Sink, D S and Tuttle, T C (1990) The performance management question in the organization of the future, *Industrial Management*, **32** (1), pp 4–12

Vroom, V (1964) *Work and Motivation*, Wiley, New York

15

Reward Management

Key concepts and terms

- Analytical job evaluation
- Analytical matching
- Base rate
- Contingent pay
- External relativities
- Going rate
- Grade and pay structure

- Internal relativities
- Intrinsic motivation
- Job-based pay
- Job evaluation
- Market rates
- Person-based pay
- Reward system

Learning outcomes

On completing this chapter you should be able to define these key concepts. You should also know about:

- The nature and aims of reward management, the framework within which it operates and the characteristics of reward systems
- The constituents of individual reward packages
- The concepts of strategic reward and total rewards
- The nature of financial and non-financial rewards

- How jobs are valued through job evaluation and market pricing
- The characteristics of grade and pay structures and methods of pay progression within them
- The nature of recognition schemes and employee benefits

Introduction

The reward management strategies and practices of an organization contribute to the improvement of organizational performance by developing and operating reward systems which help to attract, retain and engage the people upon which the business relies. This chapter begins with a definition of reward management and its aims, and an analysis of the reward framework and systems. The key components of the reward system are then described, starting with the basic requirement to value jobs by means of job evaluation and market pricing, and continuing with the use of the information on job values to design and manage grade and pay structures. As explained in the following section, such structures usually provide for pay progression through either contingent pay (pay for performance, contribution, competency or skill) or pay related to service. In addition, as covered in the final two sections, organizations may have formal recognition schemes and will provide a range of employee benefits including pensions.

Reward management defined

Reward management is concerned with the strategies, policies and processes required to ensure that the value of people and the contribution they make to achieving organizational, departmental and team goals is recognized and rewarded. It is about the design, implementation and maintenance of reward systems (interrelated reward processes, practices and procedures) which aim to satisfy the needs of both the organization and its stakeholders, and to operate fairly, equitably and consistently. These systems include arrangements for assessing the value of jobs through job evaluation and market pricing, the design and management of grade and pay structures, performance management processes, schemes for rewarding and recognizing people according to their individual performance or contribution and/or team or organizational performance, and the provision of employee benefits.

It should be emphasized that reward management is not just about pay and employee benefits. It is equally concerned with non-financial rewards such as recognition, learning and development opportunities and increased job responsibility.

Aims of reward management

In the words of Ghoshal and Bartlett (1995), the overall aim of reward management should be to 'add value to people'. It is not just about attaching value to them. More specifically, the aims are to:

- support the achievement of business goals through high performance;
- develop and support the organization's culture;
- define what is important in terms of behaviours and outcomes;

- reward people according to the value they create;
- reward people according to what the organization values;
- align reward practices with employee needs;
- help to attract and retain the high-quality people the organization needs;
- win the engagement of people.

The reward management framework

Reward management is a complex process with many interconnecting elements and under-pinning concepts. The reward management framework expressed as a concept map is shown in Figure 15.1.

The reward package

The foundation of an individual's reward package is the base or basic rate. This is the amount of pay (the fixed salary or wage) constituting the rate for the job. It may be varied according to the grade of the job or, for manual and some service workers, the level of skill required.

Base pay is influenced by internal and external relativities (going rates). The internal relativities may be measured by some form of job evaluation. External relativities are assessed by tracking market rates. Alternatively, levels of pay may be agreed through collective bargaining with trade unions or by reaching individual agreements.

Base pay may be expressed as an annual, weekly or hourly rate. The last of these is sometimes called a time rate system of payment. The base rate may be adjusted to reflect increases in the cost of living or market rates, by the organization unilaterally or by agreement with a trade union. Pay that is related entirely to the value of the job rather than the person is called job-based pay. Where the base rate can be enhanced by payments related to a person's level of competency or skill it is known as person-based pay. This term can be extended to include contingent pay, which rewards people for their performance or contribution.

Reward systems

Reward systems consist of the interrelated processes and practices which combine to ensure that reward management is carried out effectively to the benefit of the organization and the people who work there. How a reward system operates is shown in Figure 15.2.

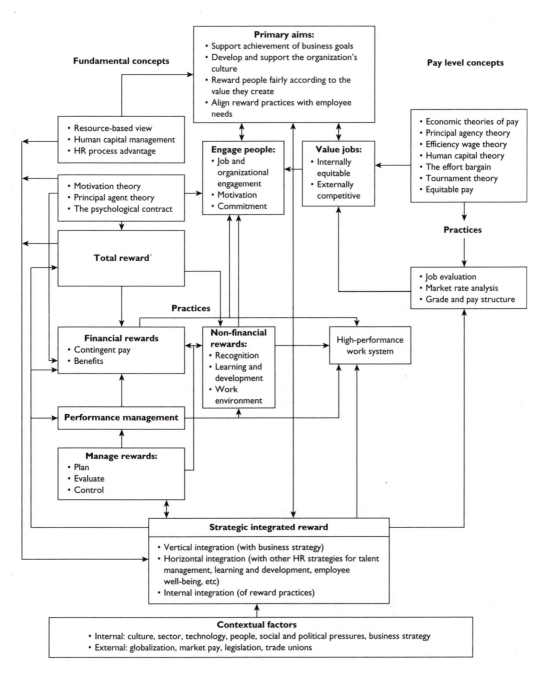

Figure 15.1   The reward management framework

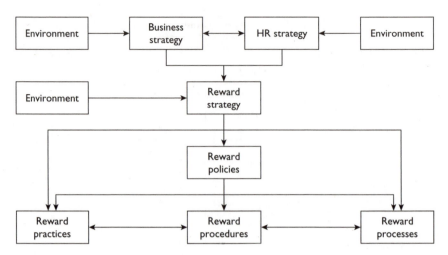

Figure 15.2 How a reward system operates

Reward systems are based on the reward strategy, which flows from the business strategy, for example to gain competitive advantage, and the HR strategy, which is influenced by the business strategy but also influences it. The HR strategy may, for example, focus on resourcing but it should also be concerned with satisfying the needs of employees as well as those of the business. All aspects of strategy are affected by the environment. Reward strategies direct the development and operation of reward practices and processes, and also form the basis of reward policies, which in turn affect reward practices, processes and procedures.

Components of a reward system

The components of a reward system and the interrelationships between them are shown in Figure 15.3. The remaining sections of this chapter describe the following key components of a reward system:

- strategic reward;
- total rewards;
- financial and non-financial rewards;
- valuing jobs through job evaluation and market pricing;
- grade and pay structures;
- pay progression through contingent and service-related pay schemes;
- recognition schemes;
- employee benefits and pensions.

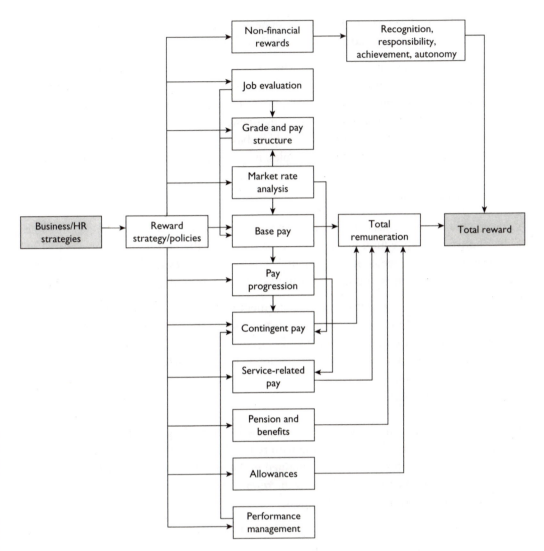

Figure 15.3   Reward system components and interrelationships

Strategic reward

Strategic reward management is the process of planning the future development of reward practices through the formulation and implementation of reward strategies. Armstrong and Brown (2006) describe how it provides answers to two basic questions: first, 'Where do we want our reward practices to be in a few years' time?' and second, 'How do we intend to get there?' It therefore deals with both ends and means. As an end it describes a vision of what reward processes will look like in a few years' time. As a means, it shows how it is expected that the vision will be realized. Strategic reward can be described as an attitude of mind – the view that it is necessary to plan ahead and make the plans happen.

Strategic reward is based on beliefs about what the organization values and wants to achieve. It does this by aligning reward practices with both business goals and employee values. As Duncan Brown (2001) emphasizes, the 'alignment of your reward practices with employee values and needs is every bit as important as alignment with business goals, and critical to the realization of the latter'. Strategic reward should be based on an articulated reward philosophy which is expressed in a set of guiding principles. It will be based on a total rewards approach.

Reward philosophy

A reward philosophy consists of belief in the need to operate in accordance with the principles of distributive and procedural justice. Reward strategies in the past have sometimes focused exclusively on business needs and alignment. Yet unless employees see and experience fairness and equity in their rewards, the strategy is unlikely to be delivered in practice.

The philosophy recognizes that reward management is a key factor in establishing a positive employment relationship, one in which there is mutuality – the state that exists when management and employees are interdependent and both benefit from this interdependency. Such a relationship provides a foundation for the development of a climate of trust.

Guiding principles

A reward philosophy can be expressed through a set of guiding principles that define the approach an organization takes to dealing with reward. They are the basis for reward policies and provide guidelines for the actions contained in the reward strategy. Importantly, they can be used to communicate to employees how the reward system operates and takes into account their interests as well as those of the business.

Reward guiding principles are concerned with matters such as:

- operating the reward system justly, fairly, equitably and transparently in the interests of all stakeholders;
- developing reward policies and practices that support the achievement of business goals;
- rewarding people according to their contribution;
- recognizing the value of everyone who is making an effective contribution, not just the exceptional performers;
- creating an attractive employee value proposition;
- providing rewards which attract and retain people and enlist their engagement;
- helping to develop a high-performance culture;

- maintaining competitive rates of pay;

- maintaining equitable rates of pay;

- allowing a reasonable degree of flexibility in the operation of reward processes and in the choice of benefits by employees;

- devolving more responsibility for reward decisions to line managers.

Developing reward strategies

Reward strategists rarely start with a clean sheet. They have to take note, and keep taking note, of constant changes in organizational requirements. They must track emerging trends and modify their views accordingly, as long as they do not leap too hastily onto the latest bandwagon. They have to ensure that reward strategy can be implemented at a pace the organization can manage and people can deal with. The fundamental change in culture often inherent in such projects takes a lot of time – and trouble – to achieve.

It may be helpful to define reward strategy formally for the record and as a basis for planning and communication. But this should be regarded as no more than a piece of paper that can be modified when needs change – as they will – not a tablet of stone. Reward strategy, like business strategy, is likely to be formulated and reformulated as it is used. An HR director told Duncan Brown and Stephen Perkins (2007) that 'We deliberately didn't have a reward strategy, it would have been a nine day wonder... we let it evolve, step-by-step.' Brown and Perkins also noted that 'Truly strategic reward approaches are not about supposed best practice or quick fixes or quick wins.'

Total rewards

The concept of total rewards describes an approach to reward management which emphasizes the need to consider all aspects of the work experience of value to employees, not just a few such as pay and employee benefits. It aims to blend the financial and non-financial elements of reward into a cohesive whole. A total rewards approach recognizes that it is necessary to get financial rewards (pay and benefits) right. But it also appreciates the importance of providing people with rewarding experiences which arise from the work they do, their work environment, how they are managed and the opportunity to develop their skills and careers. It contributes to the production of an employee value proposition which provides a clear, compelling reason why talented people should work for a company.

It is a holistic view of reward which looks at the overall reward system in order to determine how its elements should be integrated so that they provide mutual support in contributing to the overall effectiveness of the system. Reliance is not placed on one or two reward mechanisms operating in isolation; instead, account is taken of every way in which people can be rewarded and obtain satisfaction through their work. The whole is greater than the sum of its parts. The aim is to maximize the combined impact of a wide range of reward initiatives on motivation, commitment and job engagement.

The elements of total rewards are modelled in Figure 15.4.

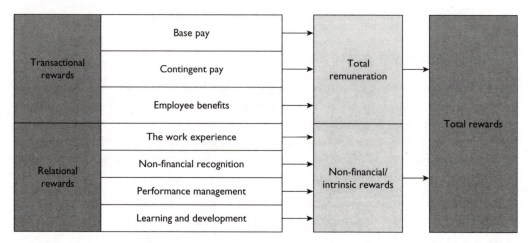

Figure 15.4　The elements of total rewards

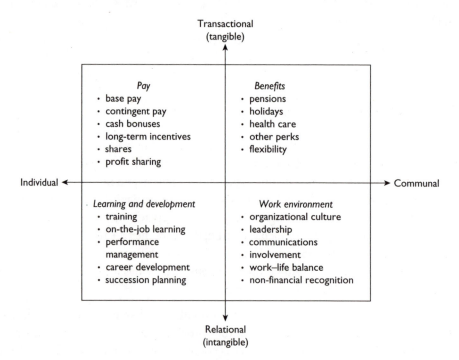

Figure 15.5　Model of total rewards: Towers Perrin

The Towers Perrin model shown in Figure 15.5 is frequently used as the basis for planning a total rewards approach. It consists of a matrix with four quadrants. The upper two quadrants – pay and benefits – represent transactional or tangible rewards. These are financial in nature, and are essential to recruit and retain staff, but can be easily copied by competitors. By contrast, the relational or intangible non-financial rewards represented in the lower two quadrants cannot be imitated so readily and can therefore create both human capital and human process advantage. They are essential to enhancing the value of the upper two quadrants. The real power, as Thompson (2002) states, comes when organizations combine relational and transactional rewards. The model also makes a useful distinction between individual and communal rewards.

The total rewards concept emphasizes the importance of both financial and non-financial rewards, and the considerations affecting them are discussed below.

Financial rewards

Financial rewards comprise all rewards that have a monetary value and add up to total remuneration – base pay, pay contingent on performance, contribution, competency or skill, pay related to service, financial recognition schemes, and benefits such as pensions, sick pay and health insurance. They are the core elements in total rewards.

The management of a reward system requires decisions on levels of pay, how jobs should be valued, the design and operation of grade and pay structures, and the choice of benefits. Such decisions can be complex and difficult, but the problems pale by comparison with the issues surrounding the use of contingent financial rewards.

Labour economists distinguish between the incentive effect of financial rewards (generating more engagement and effort) and the sorting effect (attracting better-quality employees). The fundamental issue is the extent to which financial rewards provide an incentive effect. The sorting effect is important but creates less controversy, perhaps because it is more difficult to pin down.

A vociferous chorus of disapproval has been heard on the incentive effect. One of the best-known and most influential voices was that of Alfie Kohn (1993), who stated in the *Harvard Business Review* that 'bribes in the workplace simply can't work'. He asserted that 'Rewards, like punishment, may actually undermine the intrinsic motivation that results in optimal performance. The more a manager stresses what an employee can earn for good work, the less interested that employee will be in the work itself.' Jeffrey Pfeffer (1998) concluded in his equally influential *Harvard Business Review* article 'Six dangerous myths about pay' that 'Most merit-pay systems share two attributes: they absorb vast amounts of management time and make everybody unhappy.'

There is a strong body of opinion, at least in academic circles, that financial rewards are bad – because they do not work and indeed are harmful, while non-financial rewards are good, at least when they provide intrinsic motivation – that is, motivation by the work itself. But the critics are mainly referring to financial incentives. They do not appear to recognize that incentives are not the same as rewards. They can be distinguished as follows.

Rewards offer tangible recognition to people for their achievements and contribution. Financial rewards consist of job-based pay, which provides base pay related to the value of the job, and person-based pay, which provides rewards which recognize the individual's performance, contribution, competence or skill. Rewards can also be non-financial: for example, recognition. If rewards are worth having and attainable and people know how they can attain them, they can act as motivators.

Incentives are intended to encourage people to work harder and achieve more. They are supposed to provide direct motivation: 'Do this and we will make it worth your while.' Incentives are generally financial but they can promise non-financial rewards such as promotion or a particularly interesting assignment.

If this distinction is not made it may be assumed that financial rewards only exist to provide an incentive. They might do this or, as the nay-sayers contend, they might not. But financial rewards can be justified because they are a form of tangible recognition – they are a means of informing people that they have done well, and they accord with the reasonable and generally accepted belief that people who do better should be valued more highly. However, the use of financial rewards in the shape of contingent pay has aroused strong feelings amongst those who support and those who oppose them. The arguments for and against are set out below.

Arguments for financial rewards

The most powerful argument advanced for financial rewards is that those who contribute more should be paid more. It is right and proper to recognize achievement with a financial and therefore tangible reward. This is in accordance with the principle of distributive justice which, while it states that rewards should be provided equitably, does not require them to be equal except when the value of contribution is equal. Financial rewards can also be used to highlight key performance areas and generally to emphasize the importance of high performance.

Arguments against financial rewards

The main arguments against financial rewards are that:

- The extent to which contingent pay schemes motivate is questionable – the amounts available for distribution are usually so small that they cannot act as an incentive.
- The requirements for success are exacting and difficult to achieve.
- Money by itself it will not result in sustained motivation; intrinsic motivation provided by the work itself goes deeper and lasts longer.

- People react in widely different ways to any form of motivation – it cannot be assumed that money will motivate all people equally, yet that is the premise on which contingent pay schemes are based.

- Financial rewards may possibly motivate those who receive them, but they can demotivate those that do not, and the numbers who are demotivated could be much higher than those who are motivated.

- Contingent pay schemes can create more dissatisfaction than satisfaction if they are perceived to be unfair, inadequate or badly managed.

- Employees can be suspicious of schemes because they fear that performance bars will be continuously raised; a scheme may therefore only operate successfully for a limited period.

- Schemes depend on the existence of accurate and reliable methods of measuring performance, contribution, competence, or skill, which might not exist.

- Individuals are encouraged to emphasize only those aspects of performance that are rewarded.

- Contingent pay decisions depend on the judgement of managers, which, in the absence of reliable criteria, can be partial, prejudiced, inconsistent or ill-informed.

- The concept of contingent pay is based on the assumption that performance is completely under the control of individuals when in fact it is affected by the system in which they work.

- Contingent pay, especially performance-related pay, can militate against quality and team work.

Another powerful argument against contingent pay is that it has proved difficult to manage. Organizations, including the UK Civil Service, rushed into performance-related pay in the 1980s without really understanding how to make it work. Inevitably problems of implementation arose. Studies such as those conducted by Bowey and Thorpe (1982), Kessler and Purcell (1992), Marsden and Richardson (1994) and Thompson (1992a, 1992b) have all revealed these difficulties. Failures may arise because insufficient attention has been made to fitting schemes to the context and culture of the organization, but are often rooted in implementation and operating difficulties, especially those of inadequate performance management processes, the lack of effective communication and involvement, and line managers who are not capable of or interested in carrying out the actions involved properly. Vicky Wright (1991) summed it up: 'Even the most ardent supporters of performance-related pay recognise that it is difficult to manage well.'

Criteria for effectiveness

The effectiveness of financial rewards in the shape of contingent pay depends on the following factors:

- There is accurate, consistent and fair assessment of performance or contribution.

Pay differences can be related to performance or contribution differences and can be seen to be related.

- The principles of procedural and distributive justice are upheld.

- There is a climate of trust in the organization – as Thompson (1992b) commented. 'Where there is trust, involvement and a commitment to fairness, the (PRP) schemes work.'

- Performance management systems function well.

- Line managers have the necessary skills and commitment.

- Stakeholders, including line managers, employees and employee representatives, have been involved in the design of the scheme.

- The scheme is appropriate to the context and culture of the organization.

- The scheme is not unduly complex.

- The purpose, methodology and effect of the scheme have been communicated and understood.

- There is a clear line of sight between effort and reward.

- Rewards are attainable and worth attaining.

These are demanding criteria and difficult to meet. It may be right to reward people for their contribution, and there is plenty of research evidence that financial rewards can improve performance. For example, in the United Kingdom this was established by Booth and Frank (1999), Thompson (1998), Marsden (2004) and Prentice *et al* (2007). In the United States, Gupta and Shaw (1998), Jenkins *et al* (1998), Lazear (1999) and Prendergast (1999) among others all found positive relationships between financial incentives and performance.

Critical evaluation of financial rewards

The argument that people should be rewarded in accordance with the value of their contribution is a powerful one, but it stands alone. The evidence that incentives improve performance is conflicting. In some circumstances it works, as demonstrated by a number of research projects, but in others it does not. Certainly, typical performance-related pay schemes are unlikely to provide a direct incentive simply because they do not match the demanding requirements, for example line of sight, for this to happen. Their main purpose is to recognize the level of contribution, and even this is questionable because of the difficulty of making fair and consistent assessments of performance as a basis for pay decisions. Such schemes can demotivate more people than they motivate.

But what is the alternative? Should everyone be paid the same rate in a job however well they perform? Or should pay be progressed in line with length of service – paying people for being there? For all its problems, the balance of the argument is in favour of some scheme for relating pay to contribution. But the difficulties of doing this should be recognized, and every attempt should be made to ensure that pay decisions are fair, consistent and transparent. Involving staff in the development and monitoring of contribution pay schemes can be a great help.

However, non-financial rewards, especially those intrinsic to the work being carried out, can have a longer and deeper effect, and this is the premise upon which the concept of total rewards is based.

Non-financial rewards

Non-financial rewards are those that focus on the needs people have to varying degrees for recognition, achievement, responsibility, autonomy, influence and personal growth. They incorporate the notion of relational rewards, which are the intangible rewards concerned with the work environment (quality of working life, the work itself, work–life balance), recognition, performance management, and learning and development.

Non-financial rewards can be extrinsic such as praise or recognition, or intrinsic, associated with job challenge and interest, and feelings that the work is worthwhile.

It can be said that money will motivate some of the people all of the time, and perhaps all of the people some of the time. But it cannot be relied on to motivate all of the people all of the time. To rely on it as the sole motivator is misguided. Money has to be reinforced by non-financial rewards, especially those that provide intrinsic motivation. When motivation is achieved by such means it can have a more powerful and longer-lasting effect on people, and financial and non-financial rewards can be mutually reinforcing.

Reward systems should therefore be designed and managed in such a way as to provide the best mix of all kinds of motivators according to the needs of the organization and its members.

Job evaluation

Job evaluation is a systematic and formal process for defining the relative worth or size of jobs within an organization in order to establish internal relativities. It is carried out through either an analytical or a non-analytical scheme.

Analytical job evaluation schemes

Analytical job evaluation is based on a process of breaking whole jobs down into a number of defined elements or factors such as responsibility, decisions and the knowledge and skill required. These are assumed to be present in all the jobs to be evaluated but to different degrees. In point-factor and fully analytical matching schemes, jobs are then compared factor by factor, either with a graduated scale of points attached to a set of factors, or with grade or role profiles analysed under the same factor headings.

The advantages of an analytical approach are that first, evaluators have to consider each of the characteristics of the job separately before forming a conclusion about its relative value, and second, evaluators are provided with defined yardsticks or guidelines which help to increase the objectivity and consistency of judgements. It can also provide a defence in the United Kingdom against an equal pay claim. The main analytical schemes as described below are point-factor rating and analytical matching.

Point-factor rating

Point-factor schemes are the most common forms of analytical job evaluation. They were used by 70 per cent of the respondents with job evaluation schemes to the e-reward 2007 job evaluation survey.

The basic methodology is to break jobs down into factors. These are the elements in a job such as the level of responsibility, knowledge and skill or decision making which represent the demands made by the job on job holders. For job evaluation purposes it is assumed that each of the factors will contribute to the value of the job, and is an aspect of all the jobs to be evaluated but to different degrees.

Each factor is divided into a hierarchy of levels, typically five or six. Definitions of these levels are produced to provide guidance in deciding the degree to which the factor applies in the job to be evaluated. A maximum points score is allocated to each factor. The scores available may vary between different factors in accordance with beliefs about their relative significance. This is termed 'explicit weighting'. If the number of levels varies between factors this means that they are implicitly weighted because the range of scores available will be greater in the factors with more levels.

The total score for a factor is divided between the levels to produce the numerical factor scale. The complete scheme consists of the factor and level definitions and the scoring system (the total score available for each factor and distributed to the factor levels). This comprises the 'factor plan'.

Jobs are 'scored' (that is, allocated points) under each factor heading on the basis of the level of the factor in the job. This is done by comparing the features of the job with regard to that factor with the factor level definitions to find out which definition provides the best fit. The separate factor scores are then added together to give a total score which indicates the relative value of each job and can be used to place the jobs in rank order.

Analytical job matching

Like point-factor job evaluation, analytical job matching is based on the analysis of a number of defined factors. Profiles of roles to be evaluated which have been analysed and described in terms of job evaluation factors are compared with grade, band or level profiles which have been analysed and described in terms of the same job evaluation factors. The role profiles are then 'matched' with the range of grade or level profiles to establish the best fit and thus grade the job.

Analytical matching can be used to grade jobs or place them in levels following the initial evaluation of a sufficiently large sample of benchmark jobs – representative jobs that provide a valid basis for comparisons. This can happen in big organizations when it is believed that it is not necessary to go through the whole process of point-factor evaluation for every job, especially where 'generic' roles are concerned.

Non-analytical job evaluation

Non-analytical job evaluation schemes enable whole jobs to be compared in order to place them in a grade or a rank order – they are not analysed by reference to their elements or factors. They can operate on a job-to-job basis in which a job is compared with another job to decide whether it should be valued more, less or the same (ranking and 'internal benchmarking' processes). Alternatively, they may function on a job-to-grade basis in which judgements are made by comparing a whole job with a defined hierarchy of job grades (job classification) – this involves matching a job description to a grade description. Non-analytical schemes are simple to introduce and operate but provide no defined standards of judgement. Differences between jobs are not measured and they do not provide a defence in an equal value case.

Market pricing

Market pricing is the process of obtaining information on market rates (market rate analysis) to inform decisions on pay structures and individual rates of pay. It is called 'extreme market pricing' when market rates are the sole means of deciding on internal rates of pay and relativities and conventional job evaluation is not used. An organization that adopts this method is said to be 'market driven'.

This approach has been widely adopted in the United States. It is associated with a belief that 'The market rules, OK', disillusionment with what was regarded as bureaucratic job evaluation, and the enthusiasm for broad-banded pay structures (structures with a limited number of grades or bands). It is a method which often has appeal at board level because of the focus on the need to compete in the marketplace for talent.

Market rate analysis as distinct from extreme market pricing may be associated with formal job evaluation. The latter establishes internal relativities and the grade structure, and market pricing is used to develop the pay structure – the pay ranges attached to grades. Information on market rates may lead to the introduction of market supplements for individual jobs or the creation of separate pay structures (market groups) to cater for particular market rate pressures.

The acceptability of either form of market pricing is dependent on the availability of robust market data, and when looking at external rates, the quality of the job-to-job matching process, in other words comparing like with like. It can therefore vary from analysis of data by job titles to detailed matched analysis collected through bespoke surveys focused on real market equivalence. Extreme market pricing can provide guidance on internal relativities even if these are market driven. But it can lead to pay discrimination against women where the market has traditionally been discriminatory, and it does not satisfy UK equal pay legislation.

Grade and pay structures

Grade and pay structures provide a framework within which an organization's pay policies can be implemented. They enable the organization to determine where jobs should be placed in a hierarchy, define pay levels and the scope for pay progression, and provide the basis upon which relativities can be managed, equal pay achieved, and the processes of monitoring and controlling the implementation of pay practices can take place. Grade and pay structures also enable organizations to communicate the career and pay opportunities available to employees.

Grade structures

A grade structure consists of a sequence or hierarchy of grades, bands or levels into which groups of jobs which are broadly comparable in size are placed. There may be a single structure which is defined by the number of grades or bands it contains. Alternatively the structure may be divided into a number of career or job families consisting of groups of jobs where the essential nature and purpose of the work are similar but it is carried out at different levels.

Pay structures

A grade structure becomes a pay structure when pay ranges, brackets or scales are attached to each grade, band or level. In some broad-banded structures reference points and pay zones are placed within the bands, and these define the range of pay for jobs allocated to each band.

Pay structures are defined by the number of grades they contain, and especially in narrow- or broad-graded structures, the span or width of the pay ranges attached to each grade. *Span* is the scope the grade provides for pay progression, and is usually measured as the difference between the lowest point in the range and the highest point in the range as a percentage of the lowest point. Thus a range of £20,000 to £30,000 has a span of 50 per cent.

Guiding principles for grade and pay structures

Grade and pay structures should:

- be appropriate to the culture, characteristics and needs of the organization and its employees;

- facilitate the management of relativities and the achievement of equity, fairness, consistency and transparency in managing gradings and pay;

- enable jobs to be graded appropriately and not be subject to grade drift (unjustified upgradings);

- be flexible enough to adapt to pressures arising from market rate changes and skill shortages;

- facilitate operational flexibility and continuous development;

- provide scope as required for rewarding performance, contribution and increases in skill and competence;

- clarify reward, lateral development and career opportunities;

- be constructed logically and clearly so that the basis upon which they operate can readily be communicated to employees;

- enable the organization to exercise control over the implementation of pay policies and budgets.

Types of grade and pay structures

The main types of grade and pay structures and their advantages and disadvantages are summarized in Table 15.1.

Criteria for choice

There is always a choice of structures and the criteria are given in Table 15.2.

Table 15.1   Summary description of different grade and pay structures

Type of structure	Features	Advantages	Disadvantages
Narrow-graded	• A sequence of job grades – 10 or more. • Narrow pay ranges, eg 20–40 per cent. • Progression usually linked to performance.	• Clearly indicate pay relativities. • Facilitate control. • Easy to understand.	• Create hierarchical rigidity. • Prone to grade drift. • Inappropriate in a delayered organization.
Broad-graded	• A sequence of between six and nine grades. • Fairly broad pay ranges, eg 40–50 per cent. • Progression linked to contribution and may be controlled by thresholds or zones.	As for narrow graded structures but in addition: • the broader grades can be defined more clearly; • better control can be exercised over grade drift.	• Too much scope for pay progression. • Control mechanisms can be provided but they can be difficult to manage. • May be costly.
Broad-banded	• A series of often five or six 'broad' bands. • Wide pay bands – typically between 50 and 80 per cent. • Progression linked to contribution and competence.	• More flexible. • Reward lateral development and growth in competence. • Fit new-style organizations.	• Create unrealistic expectations of scope for pay rises. • Seem to restrict scope for promotion. • Difficult to understand. • Equal pay problems.

Table 15.1   *continued*

Type of structure	Features	Advantages	Disadvantages
Career family	• Career families identified and defined. • Career paths defined for each family in terms of key activities and competence requirements. • Same grade and pay structure for each family.	• Clarify career paths within and between families. • Facilitate the achievement of equity between families and therefore equal pay. • Facilitate level definitions.	• Could be difficult to manage. • May *appear* to be divisive if 'silos' emerge.
Job family	• Separate grade and pay structures for job families containing similar jobs. • Progression linked to competence and/or contribution.	• Can appear to be divisive. • May inhibit lateral career development. • May be difficult to maintain internal equity between job families unless underpinned by job evaluation.	• Facilitate pay differentiation between market groups. • Define career paths against clear criteria.
Pay spine	• A series of incremental pay points covering all jobs. • Grades may be superimposed. • Progression linked to service.	• Easy to manage. • Pay progression not based on managerial judgement.	• No scope for differentiating rewards according to performance. • May be costly as staff drift up the spine.

Table 15.2   Grade and pay structures: criteria for choice

Type of structure	Criteria for choice – the structure may be considered more appropriate when:
Narrow-graded	<ul><li>the organization is large and bureaucratic with well-defined and extended hierarchies;</li><li>pay progression is expected to occur in small but relatively frequent steps;</li><li>the culture is one in which much significance is attached to status as indicated by gradings;</li><li>some but not too much scope for pay progression is wanted.</li></ul>
Broad-graded	<ul><li>it is believed that if there is a relatively limited number of grades it will be possible to define and therefore differentiate them more accurately as an aid to better precision when grading jobs;</li><li>an existing narrow-graded structure is the main cause of grade drift;</li><li>it is considered that pay progression through grades can be related to contribution and that it is possible to introduce effective control mechanisms.</li></ul>
Broad-banded	<ul><li>greater flexibility in pay determination and management is required;</li><li>it is believed that job evaluation should no longer drive grading decisions;</li><li>the focus is on rewarding people for lateral development;</li><li>the organization has been delayered.</li></ul>
Career family	<ul><li>there are distinct families and different career paths within and between families that can be identified and defined;</li><li>there is a strong emphasis on career development in the organization;</li><li>robust methods of defining competencies exist.</li></ul>
Job family	<ul><li>there are distinct market groups that need to be rewarded differently;</li><li>the range of responsibility and the basis upon which levels exist vary between families;</li><li>it is believed that career paths need to be defined in terms of competence requirements.</li></ul>
Pay spine	<ul><li>this is the traditional approach in a public or voluntary sector organization and it fits the culture;</li><li>it is believed to be impossible to measure different levels of contribution fairly and consistently;</li><li>ease of administration is an important consideration.</li></ul>

Pay progression

Pay progression takes place when base pay advances through pay brackets in a grade and pay structure or through promotions or upgradings. Progression through pay brackets may be determined formally by means of a contingent pay scheme or by fixed increments, as described below. Informal progression takes place when there is no contingent or incremental pay scheme and increases are arbitrary.

Contingent pay progression is typically but not inevitably governed by performance ratings which are often made at the time of the performance management review but may be made separately in a special pay review.

Contingent pay schemes

The features, advantages and disadvantages and the appropriateness of individual contingent pay schemes and service-related pay are set out in Table 15.3.

Criteria for success

The following are the five criteria for effective contingent pay:

- Individuals have a clear line of sight between what they do and what they will get for doing it.

- Rewards are worth having.

- Fair and consistent means are available for measuring or assessing performance, competence, contribution or skill.

- People are able to influence their performance by changing their behaviour and developing their competencies and skills.

- The reward follows as closely as possible the accomplishment that generated it.

These requirements are exacting and few schemes meet them in full. That is why contingent pay arrangements can often promise more than they deliver.

Service-related pay

Service-related pay is supported by many unions because they perceive it as being fair – everyone is treated equally. It is felt that linking pay to time in the job rather than performance or competence avoids the partial and ill-informed judgements about people which managers are prone to make. Some people believe that the principle of rewarding people for loyalty through continued service is a good one. It is also easy to manage; in fact, it does not need to be managed at all. But essentially service-related pay means that people are rewarded just for being there and not for the level of their contribution.

Table 15.3 Summary of contingent pay schemes

Type of scheme	Main features	Advantages	Disadvantages	When appropriate
Performance-related pay (PRP)	Increases to basic pay or bonuses are related to assessment of performance.	● May motivate (but this is uncertain). ● Links rewards to objectives. ● Meets the need to be rewarded for achievement. ● Delivers message that good performance is important and will be rewarded.	● May *not* motivate. ● Relies on judgements of performance which may be subjective. ● Prejudicial to teamwork. ● Focuses on outputs, not quality. ● Relies on good performance management processes. ● Difficult to manage well.	● For people who are likely to be motivated by money. ● In organizations with a performance-oriented culture. ● When performance can be measured objectively.
Competency-related pay	Pay increases are related to the level of competency.	● Focuses attention on need to achieve higher levels of competency. ● Encourages competency development. ● Can be integrated with other applications of competency-based HR management.	● Assessment of competency levels may be difficult. ● Ignores outputs – danger of paying for competencies that will not be used. ● Relies on well-trained and committed line managers.	● As part of an integrated approach to HRM where competencies are used across a number of activities. ● Where competency is a key factor and it may be inappropriate or hard to measure outputs. ● Where well-established competency frameworks exist.
Contribution-related pay	Increases in pay or bonuses are related both to inputs (competency) and outputs (performance).	Rewards people not only for what they do but how they do it.	As for both PRP and competence-related pay, it may be hard to measure contribution and it is difficult to manage well.	When it is believed that a well-rounded approach covering both inputs and outputs is appropriate.
Skill-based pay	Increments related to the acquisition of skills.	Encourages and rewards the acquisition of skills.	Can be expensive when people are paid for skills they do not use.	On the shop floor or in retail organizations.

Recognition schemes

Recognition schemes as part of a total reward package enable appreciation to be shown to individuals for their achievements either informally on a day-to-day basis or through formal recognition arrangements. They can take place quietly between managers and individuals in their teams, or be visible celebrations of success.

A recognition scheme can be formal and organization-wide, providing scope to recognize achievements by gifts or treats or by public applause. Typically, the awards are non-financial but some organizations provide cash awards. Importantly, recognition is also given less formally when managers simply say 'well done', 'thank you' or 'congratulations' face to face or in a brief note of appreciation.

Employee benefits

Employee benefits consist of arrangements made by employers for their employees which enhance the latter's well-being. They are provided in addition to pay, and form important parts of the total reward package. As part of total remuneration, they may be deferred or contingent like a pension scheme, insurance cover or sick pay, or they may be immediate like a company car or a loan. Employee benefits also include holidays and leave arrangements which are not strictly remuneration. Benefits are sometimes referred to dismissively as 'perks' (perquisites) or 'fringe benefits', but when they cater for personal security or personal needs they could hardly be described as 'fringe'.

Flexible benefit schemes give employees a choice within limits of the type or scale of benefits offered to them by their employers.

Employee benefits are a costly part of the remuneration package. They can amount to one-third or more of basic pay costs and therefore have to be planned and managed with care.

Reward management: key learning points

Reward management defined
Reward management is concerned with the strategies, policies and processes required to ensure that the value of people and the contribution they make to achieving organizational, departmental and team goals is recognized and rewarded.

Key aims of reward management

- Support the achievement of business goals through high performance.

- Reward people according to the value they create.

- Help to attract, retain and engage the high-quality people the organization needs.

Content of individual reward packages

The base rate for the job plus contingent pay (where applicable) and employee benefits.

Strategic reward

Strategic reward management is the process of planning the future development of reward practices through the development and implementation of reward strategies.

Total rewards

The aim of total rewards is to blend the financial and non-financial elements of reward into a cohesive whole.

Financial rewards

All rewards that have a monetary value and add up to total remuneration – base pay, contingent pay and employee benefits.

Non-financial rewards

Rewards not involving the payment of salaries, wages or cash which focus on the needs people have to varying degrees for achievement, recognition, responsibility, autonomy, influence and personal growth.

Job evaluation

A systematic and formal process for defining the relative worth or size of jobs within an organization in order to establish internal relativities.

Market pricing

The process of establishing market or going rates.

Grade and pay structures

A hierarchy of job grades to which are attached pay ranges which provide scope for pay progression based on performance, contribution, competence or service.

Pay progression

The basis upon which pay increases within a pay structure. It may be contingent on performance, contribution or skill or it may take place in the form of fixed increments related to service.

Recognition schemes

An arrangement to recognize a person's achievement publicly or by a gift or a treat.

Employee benefits

Arrangements for providing personal security, financial assistance, or company cars and for satisfying personal needs.

Questions

1. In his influential book, *Strategic Pay* (1990), Ed Lawler wrote that 'The challenge is to develop pay programmes that support and reinforce the business objectives of the organization and the kind of culture, climate and behaviour that are needed for the organization to be effective.' How can reward policies and practices support the achievement of business goals?

2. Duncan Brown wrote that 'The alignment of your reward practices with employee values and needs is every bit as important as alignment with business goals, and critical to the realization of the latter.' How can this advice be put into effect in the development and operation of a reward system?

3. Marc Thompson claimed in 1992 that 'It is possible that performance pay may be more successful in demotivating the very employees it needs to stimulate most – the average performers – and may, in practice, contribute to a downward spiral of motivation among such employees.' Evaluate the evidence on the extent to which this applies.

4. Using examples from contemporary organizational practice show how performance pay can be used effectively to support changes in employee behaviour.

5. Make the business case for a switch from multi-graded pay spines to broadbanding in a government agency which has 'delayered' its organization, intends to operate more flexibly and wants to develop a performance culture. It is in position to take advantage of the freedom offered under the 'delegated pay' policy to determine its own pay structures.

6. Duncan Brown wrote that 'The alignment of your reward practices with employee values and needs is every bit as important as alignment with business goals, and critical to the realization of the latter.' How can this advice be put into effect in the development and operation of a reward system?

References

Armstrong, M and Brown, D (2006) *Strategic Reward: Making it happen*, Kogan Page, London

Booth, A L and Frank, J (1999) Earnings, productivity and performance related pay, *Journal of Labor Economics*, **17** (3), pp. 447–463

Bowey, A and Thorpe, R (1982) *The Effects of Incentive Pay Systems*, Department of Employment, London

Brown, D (2001) *Reward Strategies: From intent to impact*, CIPD, London

Brown, D and Perkins, S (2007) Reward strategy: the reality of making it happen, *WorldatWork Journal*, **16** (2), pp 82–93

Ghoshal, S and Bartlett, C A (1995) Changing the role of top management: beyond structure to process, *Harvard Business Review*, January–February, pp 86–96

Gupta, N and Shaw, J D (1998) Financial incentives, *Compensation and Benefits Review*, March–April, pp 26, 28–32

Jenkins, D G, Mitra, A, Gupta, N and Shaw, J D (1998) Are financial incentives related to performance? A meta-analytic review of empirical research, *Journal of Applied Psychology*, **3**, pp 777–87

Kessler, I and Purcell, J (1992) Performance-related pay: objectives and application, *Human Resource Management Journal*, **2** (3), pp 16–33

Kohn, A (1993) Why incentive plans cannot work, *Harvard Business Review*, September–October, pp 54–63

Lawler, E E (1990) *Strategic Pay: Aligning organisational strategies and pay systems*, Jossey-Bass, San Francisco, CA

Lazear, E P (1999) Performance pay and productivity, *American Economic Review*, **90**, pp 1346–61

Marsden, D (2004) The role of performance-related pay in renegotiating the 'effort bargain': the case of the British public service, *Industrial and Labor Relations Review*, **57** (3), pp 350–70

Marsden, D and Richardson, R (1994) Performing for pay? The effects of 'merit pay' on motivation in a public service, *British Journal of Industrial Relations*, **32** (2), pp 243–61

Pfeffer, J (1998) Six dangerous myths about pay, *Harvard Business Review*, May–June, pp 109–19

Prendergast, C (1999) The provision of financial incentives in firms, *Journal of Economic Literature*, **37**, pp 7–63

Prentice, G, Burgess, S and Propper, C (2007) *Performance Pay in the Public Sector: A review of the issues and evidence*, Office of Manpower Economics, London

Thompson, M (1992a) *Pay and Performance: The employer experience*, IMS, Brighton

Thompson, M (1992b) *Pay and Performance: The employee experience*, IMS, Brighton

Thompson, M (1998) HR and the bottom line, *People Management*, 16 April, pp 38–41

Thompson, P (2002) *Total Reward*, CIPD, London

Wright, V (1991) Performance-related pay, in *The Performance Management Handbook*, ed E Neale, Institute of Personnel Management, London

16

Employee Relations

Key concepts and terms

- Arbitration
- Bargaining power
- Collective agreements
- Collective bargaining
- Conciliation
- Employee relations
- Employee voice
- Employment relationship

- Mediation
- New realism
- New-style agreement
- Pluralism
- Psychological contract
- Social partnership
- Stakeholder
- Unitarism

Learning outcomes

On completing this chapter you should be able to define these key concepts. You should also know about:

- The nature of the employment relationship
- Employee relations policies
- Managing employee relations
- Collective bargaining

- Collective agreements
- Disputes resolution
- Employee voice
- Communications

Introduction

Employee relations are concerned with generally managing the employment relationship and developing a positive psychological contract. In particular they deal with terms and conditions of employment, issues arising from employment, providing employees with a voice and communicating with employees. Employees are dealt with either directly or through collective agreements where trade unions are recognized.

Employee relations cover a wider spectrum of the employment relationship than industrial relations, which are essentially about what goes on between management and trade union representatives and officials. The wider definition of employee relations recognizes the move away from collectivism towards individualism in the ways in which employees relate to their employers. The concepts of joint control and rule-making belong to a historical era. To a large extent, especially in the private sector, employers are in charge. Union membership has gone down in the United Kingdom from a peak of some 12 million to around 7 million today, largely for structural reasons – the decline of large manufacturing firms and the rise in the service industries, and the growing numbers of part-time workers. Between 1980 and 2000 the coverage of collective agreements contracted from over three-quarters to under a third of the workforce. There has been a dramatic reduction in industrial action.

This chapter is organized as follows. It starts with an analysis of the fundamental concepts that explain the nature of employee relations – the employment relationship and the psychological contract. Against the background of these concepts, employee relations philosophies and the employee relations policies that evolve from them are then considered. Employee relations policies, although they may not be articulated, provide the basis for managing employee relations with or without trade unions, and for informal employee relationships (examined in the next section). If trade unions are recognized and have negotiating rights, industrial relations (considered in the next two sections) will involve collective bargaining and reaching collective agreements. Whatever policies and agreements exist, workplace conflict can still take place, and the next section of the chapter therefore deals with methods of resolving disputes. Finally, there are two sections on dealing with employees generally by giving them a voice (involvement and participation) and through communications policies and practices.

The employment relationship

Organizations consist of employers and employees who work together. This is the employment relationship, which may be expressed formally in what Rubery *et al* (2002) regarded as its cornerstone, namely the contract of employment. In law an employee is someone working for an employer who has the ultimate right to tell the worker what to do. In the United Kingdom, the Employment Rights Act (1996) defines an 'employee' as a person who works under a contract of employment, the tacit assumption being that 'the employer' is the other party to the contract. The employment relationship can be defined formally by procedure agreements and work rules.

But the employment relationship is also an informal process which happens whenever an employer has dealings with an employee and vice versa. Underpinning the employment relationship is the psychological contract, which expresses certain assumptions and expectations about what managers and employees have to offer and are willing to deliver (see Chapter 8).

The dimensions of the employment relationship

The dimensions of the employment relationship as described by Kessler and Undy (1996) are shown in Figure 16.1.

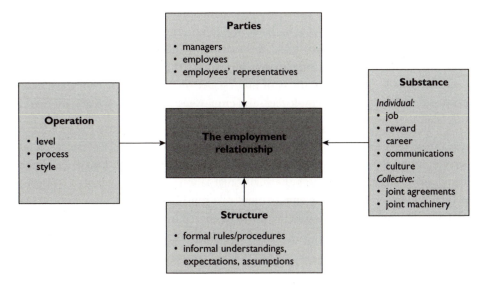

Figure 16.1   The employment relationship

The basis of the employment relationship

The starting point of the employment relationship is an undertaking by an employee to provide skill and effort to the employer, in return for which the employer provides the employee with a salary or a wage (the pay–work bargain). Initially the relationship is founded on a legal contract. This may be a written contract but the absence of such a contract does not mean that there is no contractual relationship. Employers and employees still have certain implied legal rights and obligations. The employer's obligations include the duty to pay salary or wages, provide a safe workplace, to act in good faith towards the employee and not to act in such a way as to undermine the trust and confidence of the employment relationship. The employee has corresponding obligations, which include obedience, competence, honesty and loyalty.

As Marsden (2007) points out, 'At the heart of the employment relationship lies a "zone of acceptance" within which employees agree to let management direct their labour. This may relate to the range of tasks that employees are willing to undertake at management's direction, but it may also include the priority to be accorded to different types of work, and the willingness to vary working time according to management's requirements.'

The employment relationship exists at different levels in the organization (management to employees generally, and managers to individual employees and their representatives or groups of people). The operation of the relationship will also be affected by processes such as communications and consultation, and by the management style prevailing throughout the organization or adopted by individual managers.

An important point to remember about the employment relationship is that generally it is the employer who has the power to dictate the contractual terms unless they have been fixed by collective bargaining. Except when they are in demand and can strike a bargain with their employer, individuals have little scope to vary the terms of the contract imposed upon them by employers. Inevitably there are conflicts of interest between employers, who want to control compliant and high-performing employees, and employees, who want to maintain their rights to self-determination and 'a fair day's pay for a fair day's work'.

It was claimed by Edwards (1990), in line with labour process theory, that relationships between employers representing capital and employees representing labour are usually ones of 'structured antagonism'. However, as the revisionist labour process theorists Thompson and Harley (2007) commented, 'In the employment relationship there will always be (actual and potential) conflict, but simultaneously there will be shared interests.'

The employment relationship and the psychological contract

The concept of the employment relationship is linked to that of the psychological contract. As described by Guest *et al* (1996), the psychological contract may provide some indication of the answers to the two fundamental employment relationship questions that individuals pose: 'What can I reasonably expect from the organization?' and 'What should I reasonably be expected to contribute in return?' But it is unlikely that the psychological contract and therefore the employment relationship will ever be fully understood by either party.

The aspects of the employment relationship covered by the psychological contact will include from the employee's point of view:

- how they are treated in terms of fairness, equity and consistency;
- security of employment;

- scope to demonstrate competence;

- career expectations and the opportunity to develop skills;

- involvement and influence;

- trust in the management of the organization to keep their promises.

From the employer's point of view, the psychological contract covers such aspects of the employment relationship as competence, effort, compliance, commitment and loyalty.

Underpinning employment relations philosophies

Relationships between employers and employees are founded on underpinning but seldom articulated philosophies. These are the unitary and pluralist views, the concept of social partnership and, on the part of employers, belief in a collective or individual approach.

The unitary view

The unitary view is one typically held by management, who sees its function as that of directing and controlling the workforce to achieve economic and growth objectives. To this end, management believes that it is the rule-making authority. Management tends to view the enterprise as a unitary system with one source of authority – itself – and one focus of loyalty – the organization. It extols the virtue of teamwork, where everyone strives jointly to a common objective, everyone pulls their weight to the best of their ability, and everyone accepts their place and function gladly, following the leadership of the appointed manager or supervisor. These are admirable sentiments, but they sometimes lead to what McClelland (1963) referred to as an orgy of 'avuncular pontification' on the part of the leaders of industry.

The unitary view, which is essentially autocratic and authoritarian, has sometimes been expressed in agreements as 'management's right to manage'. The philosophy of HRM with its emphasis on commitment and mutuality owes much to the unitary perspective.

The pluralist view

The pluralist view, as described by Fox (1966), is that an industrial organization is a plural society, containing many related but separate interests and objectives which must be maintained in some kind of equilibrium. In place of a corporate unity reflected in a single focus of authority and loyalty, management has to accept the existence of rival sources of leadership and attachment. It has to face the fact that, in Drucker's (1951) phrase, a business enterprise has a triple personality: it is at once an economic, a political and a social institution. In the first sense, it produces and distributes incomes. In the second, it embodies a system of government in which managers collectively exercise authority over the managed, but are also themselves involved in an intricate pattern of political relationships. Its third personality is revealed in the organization's community which evolves from below out of face-to-face relations based on shared interests, sentiments, beliefs and values among various groups of employees.

Pluralism conventionally regards the workforce as being represented by 'an opposition that does not seek to govern' (Clegg, 1976).

The concept of social partnership

Social partnership is the concept that the parties involved in employee relations should aim to work together to the greater good of all. It is based on the mutual gains theory of Kochan and Osterman (1994), which states that employers, employees and trade unions gain from cooperative forms of employment relationships.

Social partnership has been defined by Ackers and Payne (1998) as 'a stable, collaborative relationship between capital and labour, as represented by an independent trade union, providing for low social conflict and significant worker influence on business decision making through strong collective bargaining'. It provides the rationale for partnership agreements, described later in this chapter.

The concept of social partnership is rooted in stakeholder theory, originally formulated by Freeman (1984). Donaldson and Preston (1995) defined the theory as representing the corporation as a 'constellation of cooperative and competitive interests'. They explained that 'stakeholders are identified by their interest in the corporation, whether or not the corporation has any interests in them. Each group of stakeholder merits consideration because of its own sake and not merely because of its ability to further the interests of some other group, such as the shareholders.' As Hampden-Turner (1996) commented, 'Stakeholders include at least five parties: employees, shareholders, customers, community and government. Wealth is created when all work together.'

Collectivism and individualism

Employers will have views about the extent to which they want to relate to their employees collectively through trade unions or individually. This will determine the use of collective agreements on the one hand, or a focus on individual contracts on the other.

Employee relations policies

Employee relations policies express the philosophy of the organization on what sort of relationships between management and employees are wanted, and how the pay–work bargain should be managed. The overall objectives of employee relations policies should be to create and maintain a positive, productive, cooperative and trusting climate of employee relations. The areas that can be covered are:

- The employment relationship: the extent to which terms and conditions of employment should be governed by collective agreements or based on individual contracts of employment (in other words, collectivism versus individualism).

- Trade union recognition: whether trade unions should be recognized or derecognized, which union or unions the organization would prefer to deal with, and whether or not it is desirable to recognize only one union for collective bargaining and/or employee representational purposes.

- Collective bargaining: if unions are recognized with negotiating rights, the scope of areas to be covered by collective bargaining.

- Managing workplace conflict: how grievances should be settled and disputes resolved.

- Participation and involvement: the extent to which the organization is prepared to give employees a voice on matters that concern them.

- Partnership: the extent to which a partnership approach is thought to be desirable.

- Harmonization of terms and conditions of employment for staff and manual workers.

- Working arrangements: the degree to which management has the prerogative to determine working arrangements without reference to employees or, if they are recognized, trade unions.

Employee relations policies provide the basis for managing employee relations with or without trade unions, and can affect informal employee relationships.

Managing employee relations

The ways in which employee relations are managed will depend on whether or not trade unions are recognized. To a large extent day-to-day management is carried out informally.

Managing with trade unions

Trade unions can be recognized with full negotiating and representational rights, or they can only have representational rights, in other words the right to represent employees over grievances, disciplinary matters and redundancy. Trade union members may also take part in joint consultation, and act as health and safety or learning and development representatives.

Ideally, managements and trade unions learn to live together, often on a give and take basis, the presumption being that neither would benefit from a climate of hostility or by generating constant confrontation. It would be assumed in this ideal situation that mutual advantage comes from first, acting in accordance with the spirit as well as the letter of agreed joint regulatory procedures reached in collective agreements, and second, believing that with goodwill on both sides, disagreements can be settled without resource to industrial action. In practice, both parties are likely to adopt a more realistic pluralist viewpoint, recognizing the inevitability of differences of opinion, even disputes, arising because the interests and viewpoints of employers and employees can never be identical.

In the 1960s and 1970s things were different. In certain businesses, for example the motor and shipbuilding industries, hostility and confrontation were rife. And newspaper proprietors tended to let their unions walk all over them in the interests of peace and profit.

Times have changed. Trade union power has diminished in the private sector, if not in the public sector. Managements in the private sector have tended to seize the initiative. They may be content to live with trade unions but they give industrial relations lower priority. They may feel that it is easier to continue to operate with a union because it provides a useful, well-established channel for communication and for the handling of grievance, discipline and safety issues. In the absence of a union, management need to develop alternatives, which can be costly and difficult to operate effectively.

Managing without trade unions

Managements can manage perfectly well without trade unions. It may make no obvious difference to many employees, but some will not do so well. Millward *et al* (1992) established the characteristics of union-free employee relations from the third Workshop Industrial Relations Survey:

- Employee relations were generally seen by managers as better in the non-union sector than in the union sector.
- Strikes were almost unheard of.
- Labour turnover was high but absenteeism was no worse.
- Pay levels were generally set unilaterally by management.
- The dispersion of pay was higher, it was more market related and there was more performance-related pay. There was also a greater incidence of low pay.
- In general, no alternative methods of employee representation existed as a substitute for trade union representation.
- Employee relations were generally conducted with a much higher degree of informality than in the union sector. In a quarter of non-union workplaces there were no grievance procedures, and about a fifth had no formal disciplinary procedures.
- Managers generally felt unconstrained in the way in which they organized work.

- There was more flexibility in the use of labour than in the union sector, and this included the greater use of freelance and temporary workers.

- Employees in the non-union sector are two-and-a-half times more likely to be dismissed than those in unionized firms, and the incidence of compulsory redundancies is higher.

The survey concluded that many of the differences between unionized and non-unionized workplaces could be explained by the generally smaller size of the non-union firms, and the fact that many such workplaces were independent, rather than being part of a larger enterprise.

Another characteristic not mentioned by the survey is the use by non-unionized firms of personal contracts as an alternative to collective bargaining.

Informal employee relations processes

Where there are formal processes of collective bargaining and dispute resolution, as described later in this chapter, a framework for industrial relations is provided in so far as this is concerned with agreeing terms and conditions of employment and working arrangements and handling workplace conflict. But within or outside that framework, informal employee relations processes are taking place continuously.

These happen whenever a line manager or team leader is handling an issue in contact with an individual employee, a group of employees, an employee representative or a shop steward. The issue might concern methods of work, allocation of work and overtime, working conditions, health and safety, achieving output and quality targets and standards, discipline or pay (especially if a payment-by-results scheme is in operation).

Line managers and supervisors handle day-to-day grievances arising from any of these issues, and are expected to resolve them to the satisfaction of all parties without invoking a formal disputes or grievance procedure. The thrust for devolving responsibility for HR matters to line managers has increased the onus on the latter to handle employee relations well. Effective team leaders establish good working relationships with their staff, or where they exist staff representatives, which enable issues to be settled amicably before they become a problem.

Creating and maintaining a good employee relations climate – one of cooperation, trust and mutuality – in an organization may be the ultimate responsibility of top management, advised by HR specialists. But the climate will be strongly influenced by the behaviour of line managers and team leaders.

Collective bargaining

Managing with unions, as described earlier, involves collective bargaining – the establishment by negotiation and discussion of agreements on matters of mutual concern to employers and unions, covering the employment relationship and terms and conditions of employment. Collective bargaining is a joint regulating process, dealing with the regulation of management in its relationships with work people as well as the regulation of conditions of employment. It was described by Flanders (1970) as a social process which 'continually turns disagreements into agreements in an orderly fashion'.

Collective bargaining can also be seen as a political relationship in which trade unions, as Chamberlain and Kuhn (1965) noted, share industrial sovereignty or power over those who are governed, the employees. The sovereignty is held jointly by management and union in the collective bargaining process.

Above all, collective bargaining is a power relationship which takes the form of a measure of power sharing between management and trade unions (although recently the balance of power has shifted markedly in the direction of management, at least in the private sector). Bargaining power is the ability to induce the other side to make a decision or take a course of action that it would otherwise be unwilling to make. Each side is involved in assessing the bargaining preferences and bargaining power of the other side. As Fox and Flanders (1969) commented, 'Power is the crucial variable which determines the outcome of collective bargaining.' It has been suggested by Hawkins (1979) that the main test of bargaining power is 'whether the cost to one side in accepting a proposal from the other is higher than the cost of not accepting it'.

Forms of collective bargaining

Collective bargaining takes two basic forms, identified by Chamberlain and Kuhn (1965): first, conjunctive bargaining, in which both parties are seeking to reach agreement, and second, cooperative bargaining, in which it is recognized that each party is dependent on the other and can achieve its objectives more effectively if it wins the support of the other.

Walton and McKersie (1965) made the distinction between distributive bargaining, defined as the 'complex system of activities instrumental to the attainment of one party's goals when they are in basic conflict with those of the other party', and integrative bargaining, defined as the 'system of activities which are not in fundamental conflict with those of the other party and which therefore can be integrated to some degree'. These activities aim to define 'an area of common concern, a purpose'.

Collective agreements

The formal outcomes of collective bargaining are substantive agreements, procedural agreements, new style agreements, partnership agreements and employee relations procedures.

Substantive agreements

Substantive agreements set out agreed terms and conditions of employment, covering pay, allowances and overtime regulations, working hours, holidays and flexibility arrangements, and the achievement of single status or harmonization. Single status means that there are no differences in basic conditions of employment. Harmonization is the adoption of a common approach to pay and conditions for all employees, for example, placing all employees in the same grade and pay structure.

Procedural agreements

Procedural agreements set out the methods to be used and the procedures or rules to be followed in the processes of collective bargaining and the settlement of industrial disputes. Their purpose is to regulate the behaviour of the parties to the agreement, but they are not legally enforceable, and the degree to which they are followed depends on the goodwill of both parties or the balance of power between them. Like substantive agreements, procedural agreements are seldom broken, and if so, never lightly – the basic presumption of collective bargaining is that both parties will honour agreements that have been made freely between them.

The scope and content of such agreements can vary widely. Some organizations have given limited recognition to the provision of representational rights only, while others have taken an entirely different line in concluding single-union deals which, when they first emerged in the 1980s, were sometimes referred to as the 'new realism'.

Single-union deals

Single-union deals typically agree that there should be a single union representing all employees, and cover flexible working practices, the harmonization of terms and conditions between manual and non-manual employees, the commitment of the organization to involvement and the disclosure of information, the resolution of disputes by such means as arbitration, a commitment to continuity of production and a 'no-strike' provision.

New-style agreements

The so-called 'new-style agreements' emerged in the 1990s. These stipulate that negotiating and disputes procedures should be based on the mutually accepted 'rights' of the parties expressed in the recognition agreement. They typically included provision for single-union recognition, single status, labour flexibility, a company council and a no-strike clause to the effect that issues should be resolved without resource to industrial action.

Partnership agreements

Partnership agreements are based on the concept of social partnership, discussed earlier. Both parties (management and the trade union) agree to collaborate to their mutual advantage and to achieve a climate of more cooperative and therefore less adversarial industrial relations. Management may offer job security linked to productivity, and the union may agree to more flexible working.

The perceived benefits of partnership agreements are that management and unions work together, in a spirit of cooperation and mutuality which is clearly preferable to an adversarial relationship. Provision is made for change to be introduced through discussion and agreement rather than by coercion or power.

Guest and Peccei (2001) found that the balance of advantage in partnership arrangements commonly appears to favour employees. Furthermore, an analysis by Guest *et al* (2008) of evidence from the 2004 Workshop Employee Relations Survey (DTI, 2004) suggested that partnership practice remains relatively undeveloped, and that it is only weakly related to trust between management and employee representatives and to employees' trust in management. Direct forms of participation generally have a more positive association with trust than representative forms.

However, data gathered by Roche (2009) from a large representative sample of employees in Ireland showed that some mutual gains are associated with partnership. Employees gained from enhancement to the intrinsic aspects of their work, for example autonomy, but did not gain security or more pay, and did not seem to be more willing to accept change. Employers gained more commitment, an improved climate of employee relations and better supervisor/ employee relationships. Unions gained influence and more members.

Dispute resolution

The aim of collective bargaining is of course to reach agreement, preferably to the satisfaction of both parties. Grievance or negotiating procedures provide for various stages of 'failure to agree', and often include a clause providing for some form of dispute resolution in the event of the procedure being exhausted. The types of dispute resolution are conciliation, arbitration and mediation.

Conciliation

Conciliation is the process of reconciling disagreeing parties. It is carried out by a third party, in the United Kingdom often an ACAS conciliation officer, who acts in effect as a go-between, attempting to get the employer and trade union representatives to agree on terms. Conciliators can only help the parties to come to an agreement. They do not make recommendations on what that agreement should be. That is the role of an arbitrator.

The incentives to seek conciliation are the hope that the conciliator can rebuild bridges and the belief that a determined, if last-minute, search for agreement is better than confrontation, even if both parties have to compromise.

Arbitration

Arbitration is the process of settling disputes by getting a third party, the arbitrator, to review and discuss the negotiating stances of the disagreeing parties and make a recommendation on the terms of settlement which is binding on both parties, who therefore lose control over the settlement of their differences. The arbitrator is impartial, and the role is often undertaken in the United Kingdom by ACAS officials, although industrial relations academics are sometimes asked to act in this capacity. Arbitration is the means of last resort for reaching a settlement, where disputes cannot be resolved in any other way. Procedure agreements may provide for either side unilaterally to invoke arbitration, in which case the decision of the arbitrator is not binding on both parties. The process of arbitration in its fullest sense, however, only takes place at the request of both parties, who agree in advance to accept the arbitrator's findings. ACAS will not act as an arbitrator unless the consent of both parties is obtained, conciliation has been considered, any agreed procedures have been used to the full and a failure to agree has been recorded.

The notion of pendulum or final offer arbitration emerged in the 1980s and 1990s. It increases the rigidity of the arbitration process by allowing an arbitrator no choice but to recommend either the union's or the employer's final offer – there is no middle ground. The aim is to get the parties to avoid adopting extreme positions. But the evidence from the Workshop Employee Relations Survey (2004) was that the full version of pendulum arbitration, as defined above, was rare.

Mediation

Mediation is a form of arbitration which is stronger than conciliation. It takes place when a third party (often ACAS) helps the employer and the union by making recommendations which, however, they are not bound to accept. It is a cheap and informal alternative to an employment tribunal and offers a quick resolution to problems, with privacy and confidentiality.

Employee voice

Employee voice is the say employees have in matters of concern to them in their organization. Boxall and Purcell (2003) defined it: 'Employee voice is the term increasingly used to cover a whole variety of processes and structures which enable, and sometimes empower employees, directly and indirectly, to contribute to decision making in the firm.' Employee voice can be seen as 'the ability of employees to influence the actions of the employer' (Millward *et al*, 1992). The concept covers the provision of opportunities for employees to register discontent, express complaints or grievances, and modify the power of management. It sometimes brings collective and individual techniques into one framework. Direct employee voice involves contacts between management and employees without the involvement of trade unions. Union voice is expressed through representatives and can be power-based.

The forms of employee voice

Employee voice takes the following forms:

- *Participation*, which is about employees playing a greater part in the decision-making process by being given the opportunity to influence management decisions and to contribute to the improvement of organizational performance. As Williams and Adam-Smith (2006) explain, the term 'participation' refers to arrangements that give workers some influence over organizational and workplace decisions.

- *Involvement*, which is the process through which managers allow employees to discuss with them issues that affect them. Williams and Adam-Smith (2006) suggest that this term is most usefully applied to management initiatives that are designed to further the flow of communication at work as a means of enhancing the organizational commitment of employees.

Marchington *et al* (2001) categorized these elements of employee voice as representative participation and upward problem solving.

Representative participation

Representative participation can take the following forms:

- Joint consultation: a formal mechanism which provides the means for management to consult employee representatives on matters of mutual interest.

- Partnership schemes: these emphasize mutual gains and tackling issues in a spirit of cooperation rather than through traditional, adversarial relationships.

- European Works Councils: these may be set up across European sites as required by EU legislation.

- Collective representation: the role of trade unions or other forms of staff association in collective bargaining and representing the interests of individual employees and groups of employees. This includes the operation of grievance procedures.

Upward problem solving

Upward problem solving takes the following forms:

- *Upward communication* – which is any means through which employees can make representations to management about their concerns through their representatives, through established channels (consultative committees, grievance procedures, 'speak-up' programmes and so on) or informally.

- *Attitude surveys* – seeking the opinions of staff through questionnaires.

- *Suggestion schemes* – the encouragement of employees to make suggestions, often accompanied by rewards for accepted ideas.

- *Project teams* – getting groups of employees together with line managers to develop new ideas, processes, services or products, or to solve problems. (Quality circles and improvement groups come into this category, although the former have often failed to survive as a specific method of involvement.)

Communications

Employee communication processes and systems provide for 'two-way communication'. In one direction they enable organizations to inform employees about matters that will interest them. In the other, they provide for upward communication by giving employees a voice, as described above.

Communications should be distinguished from consultation. As the ACAS (2005) guide states, communication is concerned with the exchange of information and ideas within an organization, while consultation goes beyond this, and involves managers actively seeking and then taking account of the views of employees before making a decision.

The importance of employee communications

Good communications are important for three reasons. First, they are a vital part of any change management programme. If any change is proposed in terms and conditions of employment, HR processes such as contingent pay, working methods, technologies, products and services, or the organization structure (including mergers and acquisitions), employees need to know what is proposed and how it will affect them. Resistance to change often arises simply because people do not know what the change is or what it implies. Second, organizational engagement or commitment will be enhanced if employees know what the organization has achieved, or is trying to achieve, and how this benefits them. Third, effective communications generate trust, as organizations take trouble to explain what they are doing and why. However, it should be emphasized that these three benefits of good communications will only be realized in full if employees are given a voice – the opportunity to comment and respond to the information they obtain from management.

What should be communicated

Managements and individual managers need to communicate to employees about terms and conditions of employment, what they are expected to do, learning and development opportunities, the objectives, strategies, policies and performance of the organization, and any proposed changes to conditions of employment, working arrangements and requirements, or the structure and policies of the organization.

Employees need the opportunity to communicate upwards their comments and reactions to what is proposed will happen or what is actually happening in matters that affect them, for example, pay and other terms of employment, working conditions, work–life balance, equal opportunity, job security, health and safety, and learning and development programmes.

Approach to communication

To be effective, communication needs to be clear, easily understood and concise. Information should be presented systematically on a regular basis, and be as relevant, local and timely as possible. Empathy is required by management in the sense of appreciating the concerns of employees, and what they want and need to hear. Possible reactions to proposed changes should be assessed and anticipated in the communication. Attitude surveys can be used to find out what information employees want, and where they feel there are any gaps that need to be filled.

A variety of communication methods will be needed, both spoken and written, direct and indirect. Face-to-face communication to individuals or groups is direct and swift, and provides an opportunity to gauge the reactions of people who can respond on the spot and ask questions. But it should be supplemented by written material or intranet communications where the information is particularly important or complex.

Employee relations: key learning points

The nature of the employment relationship

The employment relationship describes how employees and employees work together. It may be expressed in a formal contract, but it is also an informal process which happens whenever an employer has dealings with an employee and vice versa.

The nature and significance of the psychological contract

The psychological contract is a set of unwritten expectations which exist between individual employees and their employers. Its significance arises because it can strongly affect the behaviour of both parties.

Employee relations philosophies

Relationships between employers and employees are founded on underpinning but seldom articulated philosophies. These are the unitary and pluralist views, the concept of social partnership, and on the part of employers, the extent to which a collective or individual approach should be adopted.

Employee relations policies

Employee relations policies express the philosophy of the organization on what sorts of relationships between management and employees are wanted, and how the pay–work bargain should be managed.

Managing employee relations

Managements and trade unions need to learn to live together, often on a give and take basis, the presumption being that neither would benefit from a climate of hostility or by generating constant confrontation.

Managements tend to manage perfectly well without trade unions. It may make no obvious difference to many employees but some will not do quite so well.

Informal employee relations processes take place whenever a line manager or team leader is handling an issue in contact with an individual employee, a group of employees, an employee representative or a shop steward.

Collective bargaining

Collective bargaining is a joint regulating process establishing by negotiation and discussion agreements on matters of mutual concern to employers and unions, covering the employment relationship and terms and conditions of employment.

Collective agreements

The formal outcomes of collective bargaining are substantive agreements, procedural agreements, new-style agreements, partnership agreements and employee relations procedures.

Disputes resolution

The processes of dispute resolution are conciliation, arbitration and mediation.

Employee voice

Employee voice is the say employees have in matters of concern to them in their organization. The main forms of employee voice are participation and joint consultation.

Communications

Employee communication processes and systems provide for 'two-way communication'. In one direction they enable organizations to inform employees on matters that will interest them. In the other, they provide for upward communication by giving employees a voice.

Questions

1. You have been asked by your managing director to provide a brief report on what your company can do to develop a more positive psychological contract. Prepare the report.

2. A tutor at the local further education college sends you a message, 'I should be most grateful if you would talk to my business management students on the subject of "Obtaining added value from good employee relations".' Prepare an outline of your talk.

3. Your chief executive asks 'What is the case for and against our entering into a partnership agreement with the trade union? I would be interested in any evidence you can get from research or experience elsewhere.' Reply.

References

ACAS (2005) *Guide to Communications*, ACAS, London

Ackers, P and Payne, J (1998) British trade unions and social partnership: rhetoric, reality and strategy, *International Journal of Human Resource Management*, **9** (3), pp 529–49

Boxall, P F and Purcell, J (2003) *Strategy and Human Resource Management*, Palgrave Macmillan, Basingstoke

Chamberlain, N W and Kuhn, J (1965) *Collective Bargaining*, McGraw-Hill, New York

Clegg, H (1976) *The System of Industrial Relations in Great Britain*, Blackwell, Oxford

Department of Trade and Industry (DTI) (2004) *Workplace Employment Relations Survey*, DTI, London

Donaldson, T and Preston, L E (1995) The stakeholder theory of the corporation: concepts, evidence and implications, *Academy of Management Review*, **20** (1), pp 65–91

Drucker, P (1951) *The New Society*, Heinemann, London

Edwards, P K (1990) Understanding conflict in the labor process: the logic and anatomy of struggle, in *Labor Process Theory*, Macmillan, London

Flanders, A (1970) *Management and Unions: The theory and reform of industrial relations*, Faber and Faber, London

Fox, A (1966) *Industrial Sociology and Industrial Relations*, Royal Commission Research Paper No 3, HMSO, London

Fox, A and Flanders, A (1969) Collective bargaining: from Donovan to Durkheim, in *Management and Unions*, ed A Flanders, Faber and Faber, London

Freeman, R E (1984) *Strategic Management: A stakeholder perspective*, Prentice Hall, Englewood Cliffs, NJ

Guest, D E and Peccei, R (2001) Partnership at work: mutuality and the balance of advantage, *British Journal of Industrial Relations*, **39** (2), pp 207–36

Guest, D E, Conway, N and Briner, T (1996) *The State of the Psychological Contract in Employment*, IPD, London

Guest, D E, Brown, W, Peccei, R and Huxley, K (2008) Does partnership at work increase trust? An analysis based on the 2004 Workplace Employment Relations Survey, *Industrial Relations Journal*, **39** (2), pp 124–52

Hampden-Turner, C (1996) The enterprising stakeholder, *Independent*, 5 February, p 8

Hawkins, K A (1979) *A Handbook of Industrial Relations Practice*, Kogan Page, London

Kessler, S and Undy, R (1996) *The New Employment Relationship: Examining the psychological contract*, IPM, London

Kochan, T and Osterman, P (1994) *The Mutual Gains Enterprise: Forging a winning partnership among labor, management and government*, Harvard Business School Press, Boston, MA

Marchington, M, Wilkinson, A, Ackers, P and Dundon, A (2001) *Management Choice and Employee Voice*, CIPD, London

Marsden, D (2007) Individual employee voice: renegotiation and performance management in public services, *International Journal of Human Resource Management*, **18** (7), pp 1263–78

McClelland, G (1963) Editorial, *British Journal of Industrial Relations*, June, p 278

Millward, N, Stevens, M, Smart, D and Hawes, W R (1992) *Workplace Industrial Relations in Transition*, Dartmouth, Hampshire

Roche, W K (2009) Who gains from workforce partnership? *International Journal of Human Resource Management*, **20** (1), pp 1–33

Rubery, J, Earnshaw, J, Marchington, M, Cooke, F L and Vincent, S (2002) Changing organizational forms and the employment relationship, *Journal of Management Studies*, **39** (5), pp 645–72

Thompson, P and Harley, B (2007) HRM and the worker: labour process perspectives, in *Oxford Handbook of Human Resource Management*, ed P Boxall, J Purcell and P Wright, Oxford University Press, Oxford

Walton, R E and McKersie, R B (1965) *Behavioural Theory of Labour Negotiations*, McGraw-Hill, New York

Williams, S and Adam-Smith, D (2006) *Contemporary Employment Relations: A critical introduction*, Oxford University Press, Oxford

17

Employee Well-being

Key concepts and terms

- Employee assistance programme (EAP)
- Hazard
- Health and safety audit
- Health and safety inspection
- Incidence rate
- Occupational health programme
- Occupational hygiene
- Occupational medicine
- Quality of working life
- Risk
- Risk assessment
- Work environment
- Work–life balance

Learning outcomes

On completing this chapter you should be able to define these key concepts. You should also know about:

- Approaches to achieving the well-being of employees by managing the work environment
- Approaches to achieving a healthy and safe system of work

Introduction

The well-being of employees depends on the quality of working life provided by their employers – the feelings of satisfaction and happiness arising from the work itself, and the work environment, including the provisions made for their health and safety. There are three reasons why organizations should be concerned with the well-being of their employees. First, and most importantly, they have a duty of care, and this means adopting a socially responsible approach to looking after their people. Second, employers need to concentrate on creating a good work environment not only because it is their duty to do so, but also as a means of enhancing organizational engagement. Third, it is in the interests of employers to do so because this will increase the likelihood of their employees being committed to the organization and help to establish it as a 'best place to work'.

Managing the work environment

The work environment consists of the system of work, the design of jobs, working conditions, and the ways in which people are treated at work by their managers and co-workers. Well-being is achieved when account is taken of the needs of the people concerned, in designing the work system and the jobs in it. Working conditions need to meet health and safety requirements. The way people are treated is a matter of managerial behaviour, achieving work–life balance and dealing with issues such as stress, harassment and bullying (discussed below).

Managerial behaviour

Ed Lawler (2003) suggests that what managers have to do is 'to treat people right'. This means respecting them as individuals, recognizing their different needs and wants, rewarding their achievements, helping them to develop, and treating them with consideration as human beings.

Work–life balance

Work–life balance employment practices are concerned with providing scope for employees to balance what they do at work with the responsibilities and interests they have outside work. The aim is to reconcile the often competing claims of work and home by meeting the needs of employees as well as those of their employers. As Kodz *et al* (2002) explain, the principle of work–life balance is that 'There should be a balance between an individual's work and their life outside work, and that this balance should be healthy.'

The Work Foundation (2003) defined the concept of work–life balance as 'about employees achieving a satisfactory equilibrium between work and non-work activities (ie parental responsibilities and wider caring duties, as well as other activities and interests)'. The Work Foundation recommends that practical day-to-day business and related needs should be considered when organizations set about selecting the range of work–life options that should be made available to staff, whether on a collective basis (as for example flexitime arrangements) or on an individual level (say, allowing individuals flexibility to change hours of work during term time).

Individual requests for a particular working arrangement generally need to be considered on a case-by-case basis, but it is important for a culture to exist which does not discourage employees from making such requests. In addition to fearing the reaction of line managers, the risk of career-damage is a common reason for poor take-up of work–life balance arrangements in the form of flexible hours. Line management will need to be convinced that work–life balance measures are important and pay off in terms of increased engagement.

Managing stress

There are four main reasons why organizations should take account of stress and do something about it: first, because they have the social responsibility to provide a good quality of working life; second, because excessive stress causes illness; third, because it can result in inability to cope with the demands of the job, which, of course, creates more stress; and finally because excessive stress can reduce employee effectiveness and therefore organizational performance.

The ways in which stress can be managed by an organization include:

- Job design: clarifying roles, reducing the danger of role ambiguity and conflict, and giving people more autonomy within a defined structure to manage their responsibilities.

- Targets and performance standards: setting reasonable and achievable targets which may stretch people but do not place impossible burdens on them.

- Job placement: taking care to place people in jobs that are within their capabilities.

- Career development: planning careers and promoting staff in accordance with their capabilities, taking care not to over- or under-promote.

- Performance management processes: which allow a dialogue to take place between managers and individuals about the latter's work problems and ambitions.

- Counselling: giving individuals the opportunity to talk about their problems with a member of the HR department, or through an employee assistance programme which provides counselling services to employees.

- Anti-harassment campaigns: harassment is a major cause of stress.

- Anti-bullying campaigns: bullying at work is another major cause of stress.

- Management training in what managers can do to alleviate their own stress and reduce it in others.

Health and safety management

Health and safety policies and programmes are concerned with protecting employees – and other people affected by what the company produces and does – against the hazards arising from their employment or their links with the company.

The elements of health and safety management

Occupational health programmes deal with the prevention of ill-health arising from working conditions. There are two elements:

- *Occupational medicine*, which is a specialized branch of preventive medicine concerned with the diagnosis and prevention of health hazards at work, and dealing with any ill-health or stress that has occurred in spite of preventive actions.

- *Occupational hygiene*, which is the province of the chemist and the engineer or ergonomist engaged in the measurement and control of environmental hazards.

Safety programmes deal with the prevention of accidents and with minimizing the resulting loss and damage to persons and property.

Health and safety policies

Written health and safety policies are required to demonstrate that top management is concerned about the protection of the organization's employees from hazards at work, and to indicate how this protection will be provided. They are therefore first, a declaration of intent, second, a definition of the means by which that intent will be realized, and third, a statement of the guidelines that should be followed by everyone concerned – which means all employees – in implementing the policy.

The policy statement should consist of three parts:

- the general policy statement;

- the description of the organization for health and safety;

- details of arrangements for implementing the policy.

The general policy statement

The general policy statement should be a declaration of the intention of the employer to safeguard the health and safety of employees. It should emphasize four fundamental points:

- that the safety of employees and the public is of paramount importance;

- that safety takes precedence over expediency;

- that every effort will be made to involve all managers, team leaders and employees in the development and implementation of health and safety procedures;

- that health and safety legislation will be complied with in the spirit as well as the letter of the law.

Organization

This section of the policy statement should describe the health and safety organization of the business through which high standards are set and achieved by people at all levels in the organization.

This statement should underline the ultimate responsibility of top management for the health and safety performance of the organization. It should then indicate how key management personnel are held accountable for performance in their areas. The role of safety representatives and safety committees should be defined, and the duties of specialists such as the safety adviser and the medical officer should be summarized.

Conducting risk assessments

Risk assessments are concerned with the identification of hazards and the analysis of the risks attached to them. A hazard is anything that can cause harm (such as working on roofs, lifting heavy objects, handling chemicals, working with electricity). A risk is the chance, large or small, of harm being actually done by the hazard.

The purpose of risk assessments is to initiate preventive action. They enable control measures to be devised on the basis of an understanding of the relative importance of risks. Risk assessments must be recorded if there are five or more employees.

There are two types of risk assessment. Quantitative risk assessment produces an objective probability estimate based upon risk information that is immediately applicable to the circumstances in which the risk occurs. Qualitative risk assessment is more subjective, and is based on judgement backed by generalized data. Qualitative risk assessment is preferable if the specific data are available. Qualitative risk assessment may be acceptable if there is little or no specific data as long as it is made systematically on the basis of an analysis of working conditions and hazards, and informed judgement of the likelihood of harm actually being done.

Risk assessments seek to identify typical hazards – activities where accidents happen, such as:

- receipt of raw materials, for instance lifting, carrying;

- stacking and storage, such as the risk of falling materials;

- movement of people and materials, for instance falls, collisions;

- processing of raw materials, with a risk of exposure to toxic substances;

- maintenance of buildings, such as roof work, gutter cleaning;

- maintenance of plant and machinery, such as lifting tackle, installation of equipment;

- using electricity, for example using hand tools, extension leads;

- operating machines, for example operating without sufficient clearance, or at an unsafe speed; not using safety devices;

- failure to wear protective equipment, such as hats, boots and clothing;

- distribution of products or materials, for example the movement of vehicles;

- dealing with emergencies, such as spillages, fires, explosions;

- health hazards arising from the use of equipment or methods of working, for example VDUs, repetitive strain injuries from badly designed work stations or working practices.

Most accidents are caused by a few key activities. Assessors should concentrate initially on those that could cause serious harm. Operations such as roof work, maintenance and transport movement cause far more deaths and injuries each year than many mainstream activities.

When the hazards have been identified it is necessary to assess how high the risks are. This involves answering three questions:

- What is the worst result?

- How likely is it to happen?

- How many people could be hurt if things go wrong?

A probability rating system can be used such as:

- probable – likely to occur immediately or shortly;

- reasonably probable – probably will occur in time;

- remote – may occur in time;

- extremely remote – unlikely to occur.

Health and safety audits

Risk assessments identify specific hazards and quantify the risks attached to them. Health and safety audits provide for a much more comprehensive review of all aspects of health and safety policies, procedures and practices. They cover the following.

Policies

- Do health and safety policies meet legal requirements?

- Are senior managers committed to health and safety?

- How committed are other managers, team leaders and supervisors to health and safety?

- Is there a health and safety committee? If not, why not?

- How effective is the committee in getting things done?

Procedures

How effectively do the procedures:

- support the implementation of health and safety policies?

- communicate the need for good health and safety practices?

- provide for systematic risk assessments?

- ensure that accidents are investigated thoroughly?

- record data on health and safety which is used to evaluate performance and initiate action?

- ensure that health and safety considerations are given proper weight when designing systems of work or manufacturing and operational processes (including the design of equipment and work stations, the specification for the product or service, and the use of materials)?

- provide safety training, especially induction training and training when jobs or working methods are changed?

Safety practices

- To what extent do health and safety practices in all areas of the organization conform to the general requirements of the Health and Safety at Work Act and the specific requirements of the various regulations and codes of practice?

- What risk assessments have been carried out? What were the findings? What actions were taken?

- What is the health and safety performance of the organization as shown by performance indicators?

- Is the trend positive or negative? If the latter, what is being done about it?

- How thoroughly are accidents investigated? What steps have been taken to prevent their recurrence?

- What is the evidence that managers and supervisors are really concerned about health and safety?

Health and safety inspections

Health and safety inspections are designed to examine a specific area of the organization – an operational department or a manufacturing process – in order to locate and define any faults in the system, equipment, plant or machines, or any operational errors that might be a danger to health or the source of accidents. Health and safety inspections should be carried out on a regular and systematic basis by line managers and supervisors, with the advice and help of health and safety advisors.

Accident prevention

The prevention of accidents is achieved by the following actions:

- Identify the causes of accidents and the conditions under which they are most likely to occur.

- Take account of safety factors at the design stage – build safety into the system.

- Design safety equipment and protective devices, and provide protective clothing.

- Carry out regular risk assessments audits, inspections and checks, and take action to eliminate risks.

- Investigate all accidents resulting in damage to establish the cause and to initiate corrective action.

- Maintain good records and statistics in order to identify problem areas and unsatisfactory trends.

- Conduct a continuous programme of education and training on safe working habits and methods of avoiding accidents.

- Encourage approaches to leadership and motivation that do not place excessive demands on people.

Occupational health programmes

Occupational health programmes are designed to minimize the impact of work-related illnesses arising from work. The following actions are required:

- Eliminate the hazard at source through design and process engineering.

- Isolate hazardous processes and substances so that workers do not come into contact with them.

- Change the processes or substances used to promote better protection or eliminate the risk.

- Provide protective equipment, but only if changes to the design, process or specification cannot completely remove the hazard.

- Train workers to avoid risk.

- Maintain plant and equipment to eliminate the possibility of harmful emissions, controlling the use of toxic substances and eliminating radiation hazards.

- Adopt good housekeeping practices to keep premises and machinery clean and free from toxic substances.

- Conduct regular inspections to ensure that potential health risks are identified in good time.

- Carry out pre-employment medical examinations and regular checks on those exposed to risk.

- Ensure that ergonomic considerations (that is, those concerning the design and use of equipment, machines, processes and workstations) are taken into account in design specifications, establishing work routines and training. This is particularly important as a means of minimizing the incidence of repetitive strain injury (RSI).

- Maintain preventive medicine programmes which develop health standards for each job and involve regular audits of potential health hazards and regular examinations for anyone at risk.

Particular attention needs to be exercised on the control of stress, considered earlier in this chapter. Noise and fatigue should also be matters of concern.

Employee well-being: key learning points

Reasons for concern with well-being

Employers have a duty of care, and this means adopting a socially responsible approach to looking after their people.

Employers are responsible for creating a good work environment not only because it is their duty to do so, but also as part of the total reward system.

It is in the interests of employers to do so because this will increase the likelihood of their employees being committed to the organization, and help to establish it as a 'best place to work'.

The significance of the work environment

The work environment consists of the system of work, the design of jobs, working conditions and the ways in which people are treated at work by their managers and co-workers. Well-being is achieved when account is taken in designing the work system and the jobs in it of the needs of the people concerned. Working conditions need to meet health and safety requirements. The way people are treated is a matter of managerial behaviour, achieving work–life balance and dealing with issues such as stress, harassment and bullying.

The achievement of work–life balance

Flexible working is the most practical solution to establishing an effective work–life balance. This covers flexitime, home working, part-time working, compressed working weeks, annualized hours, job sharing and term-time-only working. It also refers to special leave schemes which provide employees with the freedom to respond to a domestic crisis or to take a career break without jeopardizing their employment status.

Managing stress

Employers have the social responsibility to provide a good quality of working life.

Excessive stress causes illness. Stress can result in inability to cope with the demands of the job, which creates more stress. Excessive stress can reduce employee effectiveness and therefore organizational performance.

Managing health and safety

Conduct risk assessments to identify hazards and analyse the risks attached to them.

Conduct health and safety audits to provide for a more comprehensive review of all aspects of health and safety policies, procedures and practices.

Conduct health and safety inspections to identify and deal with specific risks and hazards.

Health and safety inspections should be carried out on a regular and systematic basis by line managers and supervisors, with the advice and help of health and safety advisors.

Questions

1. What is work–life balance, and what can be done about it?

2. How can stress be managed?

3. What is the distinction between risk assessments, health and safety audits and health and safety inspections?

References

Kodz, J, Harper, H and Dench, S (2002) *Work–Life Balance: Beyond the rhetoric*, Report 384, Institute for Employment Studies, Brighton

Lawler, E E (2003) *Treat People Right! How organisations and individuals can propel each other into a virtuous spiral of success*, Jossey-Bass, San Francisco, CA

Work Foundation (2003) *Work–Life Balance*, Work Foundation, London

Part IV

People Management Skills

18

Managing Change

Introduction

Change management is defined as the process of achieving the smooth implementation of change by planning and introducing it systematically, taking into account the likelihood of it being resisted. To manage change, it is first necessary to understand how the process works. It is important to bear in mind that while those wanting change need to be constant about ends, they have to be flexible about means. This requires them to come to an understanding of the various models of change that have been developed, and of the factors that create resistance to change, and how to minimize such resistance. In the light of an understanding of these models and the phenomenon of resistance to change, they will be better equipped to make use of the guidelines for change set out in this chapter.

The change process

Conceptually, the change process starts with an awareness of the need for change. An analysis of this situation and the factors that have created it leads to a diagnosis of their distinctive characteristics, and an indication of the direction in which action needs to be taken. Possible courses of action can then be identified and evaluated, and a choice made of the preferred action.

It is then necessary to decide how to get from here to there. Managing change during this transition state is a critical phase in the change process. It is here that the problems of introducing change emerge and have to be managed. These problems can include resistance to change, low stability, high levels of stress, misdirected energy, conflict and loss of momentum. Hence the need to do everything possible to anticipate reactions and likely impediments to the introduction of change.

The installation stage can also be painful. When planning change there is a tendency for people to think that it will be an entirely logical and linear process of going from A to B. It is not like that at all. As described by Pettigrew and Whipp (1991), the implementation of change is an 'iterative, cumulative and reformulation-in-use process'.

Change models

The best known change models are those developed by Lewin (1951), Beckhard (1969), and Beer *et al* (1990).

Lewin

The basic mechanisms for managing change set out by Lewin are:

1. *Unfreezing* – altering the present stable equilibrium which supports existing behaviours and attitudes. This process must take account of the inherent threats change presents to people and the need to motivate those affected to attain the natural state of equilibrium by accepting change.

2. *Changing* – developing new responses based on new information.

3. *Refreezing* – stabilizing the change by introducing the new responses into the personalities of those concerned.

Lewin also suggested a methodology for analysing change which he called 'field force analysis'.

1. Analyse the restraining or driving forces that will affect the transition to the future state. These restraining forces will include the reactions of those who see change as unnecessary or as constituting a threat.

2. Assess which of the driving or restraining forces are critical.

3. Take steps both to increase the critical driving forces and to decrease the critical restraining forces.

Beckhard

According to Beckhard, a change programme should incorporate the following processes:

1. Set goals and define the future state or organizational conditions desired after the change.

2. Diagnose the present condition in relation to these goals.

3. Define the transition state activities and commitments required to meet the future state.

4. Develop strategies and action plans for managing this transition in the light of an analysis of the factors likely to affect the introduction of change.

Beer et al

Michael Beer and his colleagues suggested in a seminal *Harvard Business Review* article 'Why change programs don't produce change', that most such programmes are guided by a theory of change that is fundamentally flawed. This theory states that changes in attitudes lead to changes in behaviour. 'According to this model, change is like a conversion experience. Once people get religion, changes in their behaviour will surely follow.' They believe that this theory gets the change process exactly backwards, and commented:

> In fact, individual behaviour is powerfully shaped by the organizational roles people play. The most effective way to change behaviour, therefore, is to put people into a new organizational context, which imposes new roles, responsibilities and relationships on them. This creates a situation that in a sense 'forces' new attitudes and behaviour on people.

They prescribe six steps to effective change, which concentrate on what they call 'task alignment' – reorganizing employee's roles, responsibilities and relationships to solve specific business problems in small units where goals and tasks can be clearly defined. The aim of following the overlapping steps is to build a self-reinforcing cycle of commitment, coordination and competence.

1. Mobilize commitment to change through the joint analysis of problems.

2. Develop a shared vision of how to organize and manage to achieve goals such as competitiveness.

3. Foster consensus for the new vision, competence to enact it, and cohesion to move it along.

4. Spread revitalization to all departments without pushing it from the top – don't force the issue, let each department find its own way to the new organization.

5. Institutionalize revitalization through formal policies, systems and structures.

6. Monitor and adjust strategies in response to problems in the revitalization process.

Resistance to change

People resist change because it is seen as a threat to familiar patterns of behaviour as well as to status and financial rewards. Joan Woodward (1968) made this point clearly:

> When we talk about resistance to change we tend to imply that management is always rational in changing its direction, and that employees are stupid, emotional or irrational in not responding in the way they should. But if an individual is going to be

worse off, explicitly or implicitly, when the proposed changes have been made, any resistance is entirely rational in terms of his own best interest. The interests of the organization and the individual do not always coincide.

However, some people will welcome change as an opportunity. These need to be identified, and where feasible they can be used to help in the introduction of change as change agents.

Specifically, the main reasons for resisting charge are:

- the shock of the new – people are suspicious of anything that they perceive will upset their established routines, methods of working or conditions of employment;

- economic fears – loss of money, threats to job security;

- inconvenience – the change will make life more difficult;

- uncertainty – change can be worrying because of uncertainty about its likely impact;

- symbolic fears – a small change that affects a treasured symbol, such as a separate office or a reserved parking space, might symbolize a larger one, especially when employees are uncertain about how extensive the programme of change will be;

- threat to interpersonal relationships – anything that disrupts the customary social relationships and standards of the group will be resisted;

- threat to status or skill – the change is perceived as reducing the status of individuals or as deskilling them;

- competence fears – concern about the ability to cope with new demands or to acquire new skills.

Overcoming resistance to change

Resistance to change can be difficult to overcome even when the change is not detrimental to those concerned, but the attempt must be made. The first step is to analyse the potential impact of change by considering how it will affect people in their jobs. The reasons for resisting change set out above can be used as a checklist on where they might be problems, generally, with groups or with individuals.

The analysis should indicate which aspects of the proposed change might be supported generally or by specified individuals, and which aspects might be resisted. So far as possible, the potentially hostile or negative reactions of people and the reasons for them should be identified. It is necessary to try to understand the likely feelings and fears of those affected, so that unnecessary worries can be relieved, and as far as possible ambiguities can be resolved. In making this analysis, the individual introducing the change – the change agent – should recognize that new ideas are likely to be suspect, and should make ample provision for the discussion of reactions to proposals to ensure complete understanding of them.

Involvement in the change process gives people the chance to raise and resolve their concerns, and make suggestions about the form of the change and how it should be introduced. The aim is to get 'ownership' – a feeling among people that the change is something that they are happy to live with because they have been involved in its planning and introduction – it has become *their* change.

A communication strategy to explain the proposed change should be prepared and implemented so that unnecessary fears are allayed. All the available channels should be used, but face-to-face communications direct from managers to individuals or through a team-briefing system are best.

Implementing change

The change process will take place more smoothly with the help of credible change agents, internal or external – people who facilitate change by providing advice and support on its introduction and management. It is often assumed that only people from outside the organization can take on the change agent role because they are independent and do not 'carry any baggage'. They can be useful, but people from within the firm who are respected and credible can do the job well. This is often the role of HR specialists, but the use of line managers adds extra value.

Guidelines for change management

- The achievement of sustainable change requires strong commitment and visionary leadership from the top.

- It is necessary to understand the culture of the organization and the levers for change that are most likely to be effective in that culture.

- Those concerned with managing change at all levels should have the temperament and leadership skills appropriate to the circumstances of the organization and its change strategies.

- Change is more likely to be successful if there is a 'burning platform' to justify it, in other words, a powerful and convincing reason for change.

- It is important to build a working environment that is conducive to change. This means developing the firm as a 'learning organization'.

- People support what they help to create. Commitment to change is improved if those affected by change are allowed to participate as fully as possible in planning and implementing it. The aim should be to get them to 'own' the change as something they want and will be glad to live with.

- The reward system should encourage innovation and recognize success in achieving change.

- Change will always involve failure as well as success. The failures must be expected and learnt from.

- Hard evidence and data on the need for change are the most powerful tools for its achievement, but establishing the need for change is easier than deciding how to satisfy it.

- It is easier to change behaviour by changing processes, structure and systems than to change attitudes or the organizational culture.

- There are always people in organizations who can act as champions of change. They will welcome the challenges and opportunities that change can provide. They are the ones to be chosen as change agents.

- Resistance to change is inevitable if the individuals concerned feel that they are going to be worse off – implicitly or explicitly. The inept management of change will produce that reaction.

- In an age of global competition, technological innovation, turbulence, discontinuity, even chaos, change is inevitable and necessary. The organization must do all it can to explain why change is essential and how it will affect everyone. Moreover, every effort must be made to protect the interests of those affected by change.

References

Beckhard, R (1969) *Organization Development: Strategy and models*, Addison-Wesley, Reading, MA

Beer, M, Eisenstat, R and Spector, B (1990) Why change programs don't produce change, *Harvard Business Review*, November–December, pp 158–66

Lewin, K (1951) *Field Theory in Social Science*, Harper & Row, New York

Pettigrew, A and Whipp, R (1991) *Managing Change for Competitive Success*, Blackwell, Oxford

Woodward, J (1968) Resistance to change, *Management International Review*, **8**, pp 78–93

19

Leadership Skills

Leadership is the process of setting the direction and ensuring that the members of the leader's organization or team give of their best to achieve the desired result.

What leadership involves

Leaders have three essential roles. They should:

- *Define the task* – they make it quite clear what the group is expected to do.
- *Achieve the task* – that is why the group exists. Leaders ensure that the group's purpose is fulfilled. If it is not, the result is frustration, disharmony, criticism, and eventually perhaps disintegration of the group.
- *Maintain effective relationships* – between themselves and the members of the group, and between the people within the group. These relationships are effective if they contribute to achieving the task. They can be divided into those concerned with the team and its morale and sense of common purpose, and those concerned with individuals and how they are motivated.

These roles can be described in a number of ways, as discussed below.

The John Adair three circle model

John Adair (1973), the leading British expert on leadership, explained that demands on leaders are best expressed as three areas of need which they must satisfy. These are:

- task needs – to get the job done;
- individual needs – to harmonize the needs of the individual with the needs of the task and the group;
- group maintenance needs – to build and maintain team spirit.

Figure 19.1   Leadership needs

As shown in Figure 19.1, he modelled these demands as three interlocking circles.

This model suggests that the task, individual and group needs are interdependent. Satisfying task needs will also satisfy group and individual needs. Task needs, however, cannot be met unless attention is paid to individual and group needs, and looking after individual needs will also contribute to satisfying group needs and vice versa. There is a danger in becoming so task-oriented that you ignore individual and group or team needs. It is just as dangerous to be too people-oriented, focusing on meeting individual or group needs at the expense of the task. The best leaders are those who keep these three needs satisfied and in balance according to the demands of the situation.

The path–goal model

The path–goal model states that leaders are there to define the path that should be followed by their team in order to achieve its goals. It is the leader's job to guide and help team members to select the best paths towards achieving their own goals and those of the group.

The Welch way

Jack Welch, former chief executive of General Electric, has his own prescription for leadership. He wrote (2007):

> *Being a leader changes everything. Before you are a leader success is all about you – your performance, contributions and solutions. Once you become a leader, success is all about growing others. It's about making the people who work for you smarter, bigger and bolder. Nothing you do as an individual matters, except how you nurture and*

support your team and increase their self-confidence. Your success as a leader will come not from what you do, but from the reflected glory of your team.

This is in line with the belief expressed by Charles Handy (1994) that the post-heroic leader has come to the fore: someone who 'asks how every problem can be solved in a way that develops other people's capacity to handle it'. The Welch way also draws attention to the well-known phenomenon of people who are excellent at their non-managerial job but fail when they are promoted, for example successful sales representatives who become unsuccessful sales managers.

Leaders and followers

Successful leaders depend on followers who want to feel that they are being led in the right direction. They need to know where they stand, where they are going and what is in it for them. They want to feel that it is all worthwhile.

Kelley (1991) suggested that the role of the follower should be studied as carefully as that of the leader. Leaders need effective followers. Grint (2005) pointed out that 'the trick of the leader is to develop followers who privately resolve the problems leaders have caused or cannot resolve, but publicly deny their intervention'.

Ulrich's leadership brand

Ulrich and Smallwood (2007) emphasized that businesses are responsible for establishing a leadership brand as an organizational capability by introducing and maintaining processes that help leaders to grow and develop. The leadership brand is pervasive through all levels of leadership in the organization. It endures by not being tied to one person or a strategic era. Every leader must contribute to the creation of this leadership brand, which defines their identity as leaders, translates customer expectations into employee behaviours, and outlasts them.

A leadership brand statement is necessary. It is developed using the following steps:

1. Start by defining the organization's strategy.
2. Translate the strategy into the firm's brand.
3. Identify desired outcomes for employees, customers and investors.
4. Define the desired leadership code.
5. Combine attributes and results into a leadership brand statement.
6. Create a set of expectations based on the leadership brand statement.

Leadership styles

There are many styles of leadership, and no one style is necessarily better than the other in any situation. Leaders can be classified as:

- *Charismatic/non-charismatic.* Charismatic leaders rely on their personality, their inspirational qualities and their 'aura'. They are visionary leaders who are achievement-oriented, calculated risk takers and good communicators. Non-charismatic leaders rely mainly on their know-how (authority goes to the person who knows), their quiet confidence and their cool, analytical approach to dealing with problems.

- *Autocratic/democratic.* Autocratic leaders impose their decisions, using their position to force people to do as they are told. Democratic leaders encourage people to participate and involve themselves in decision-taking.

- *Enabler/controller.* Enablers inspire people with their vision of the future and empower them to accomplish team goals. Controllers command people to obtain their compliance.

- *Transactional/transformational.* Transactional leaders trade money, jobs and security for compliance. Transformational leaders motivate people to strive for higher-level goals.

There is no such thing as an ideal leadership style. The situation in which leaders and their teams function will influence the approaches that leaders adopt. It all depends. The factors affecting the degree to which a style is appropriate are the type of organization, the nature of the task, the characteristics of the group, and importantly, the personality of the leader.

An achievement-oriented approach may be appropriate when expectations of the results the team has to produce are high and team members can be encouraged to rise to the occasion.

A task-oriented approach (autocratic, controlling, directive) may be required in emergency or crisis situations. It can work, but not always well, when the leader has power, formal backing and a relatively well-structured task. In these circumstances some but not all groups may be more ready to be directed and told what to do, although a more democratic approach can work better. In less well-structured or ambiguous situations, where results depend on the group working well together with a common sense of purpose, leaders who are concerned with maintaining good relationships (democratic, participative or supportive) are more likely to obtain good results.

Good leaders are capable of flexing their style to meet the demands of the situation. Normally democratic or participative leaders may have to shift into more of a directive mode when faced with a crisis, but they make clear what they are doing and why. Poor leaders change their style arbitrarily, so that their team members are confused and do not know what to expect next.

Effective leaders may also flex their style when dealing with individual team members according to their characteristics. Some people need more positive directions than others. Others respond best if they are involved in decision making with their boss. But there is a limit to the degree of flexibility that should be used. It is unwise to differentiate too much between the ways in which individuals are treated or to be inconsistent in your approach.

The kind of leadership you exercise will indeed be related to the nature of the task and the people being led. But it also depends on the context and, of course, on the leaders themselves. If you have a natural leadership style and it works you should be careful about changing it arbitrarily or substantially: modification yes, to a degree; transformation, no. And you can learn how to improve it as discussed towards the end of this chapter so that it fits the demands of the situation.

What makes a good leader

What makes a good leader? There is no universal answer to this question. But Lao-Tzu in the 6th century BC had a pretty good stab at it:

> *A leader is best*
> *When people barely know that he exists.*
> *Not so good when people obey and acclaim him.*
> *Worst when they despise him.*
> *Fail to honour people, they fail to honour you.*
> *But a good leader who talks little,*
> *When his work is done, his aim fulfilled,*
> *They will all say, 'We did this ourselves.'*

More recent thinking about leadership has indicated that good leaders are confident and know where they want to go and what they want to do. They have the ability to take charge, convey their vision to their team, get their team members into action and ensure that they achieve their agreed goals. They are trustworthy, effective at influencing people, and earn the respect of their team. They are aware of their own strengths and weaknesses, and are skilled at understanding the needs, attitudes and perspectives of team members. They appreciate the advantages of consulting and involving people in decision making. They can switch flexibly from one leadership style to another to meet the demands of different situations and people.

Leadership and emotional intelligence

According to Goleman (2001), emotional intelligence (defined in Chapter 8) is a critical ingredient in leadership. He claimed that effective leaders are alike in one crucial way: they have a high degree of emotional intelligence, which plays an increasingly important part at higher levels in organizations where differences in technical skills are of negligible importance. Although doubts have been expressed about Goleman's theory (see Chapter 8), it is obvious that leaders have to be good at relating to people, and emotional intelligence is a convenient label to attach to the skills involved.

Developing leadership skills

It is often said that leaders are born, not made. This is a rather discouraging statement for those who are not leaders by birthright. It may be true to the extent that some exceptional people seem to be visionaries, have built-in charisma and a natural ability to impose their personality on others. However, even they have probably to develop and hone these qualities when confronted with a situation demanding leadership. Ordinary mortals need not despair. They too can build on their natural capacities and develop their leadership abilities. A 10-point plan for doing this is given below.

1. Understand what is meant by leadership.

2. Appreciate the different leadership styles available.

3. Assess what you believe to be your fundamental leadership style.

4. Get other people, colleagues and indeed your own team members, to tell you what they think your leadership style is and how well it works.

5. In the light of this information, consider what you need to do and can do to modify your style, bearing in mind that you have to go on being the same person. In other words, your style should still be a natural one.

6. Think about the typical situations and problems with which you are confronted as a leader. Will your leadership style, modified as necessary, be appropriate for all of them? If not, can you think of any of those situations where a different style would have been better? If so, think about what you need to do to be able to flex your style as necessary without appearing to be inconsistent to your team.

7. Examine the various explanations of the qualities that make a good leader, and assess your own performance using the checklists set out below. Decide what you need to do – what you can do – about any weaknesses.

8. Think about or observe any managers whom you have worked for or with.

9. Assess each of them using the checklist.

10. Consider what you can learn from them about effective and less-effective leadership behaviours. In the light of this, assess where you could usefully modify your own leadership behaviours.

Leadership checklists

Task

- What needs to be done and why?
- What results have to be achieved and by when?
- What problems have to be overcome?
- To what extent are these problems straightforward?
- Is there a crisis situation?
- What has to be done now to deal with the crisis?
- What are these priorities?
- What pressures are likely to be exerted?

Individuals

- What are their strengths and weaknesses?
- What are likely to be the best ways of motivating them?
- What tasks are they best at doing?
- Is there scope to increase flexibility by developing new skills?
- How well do they perform in achieving targets and performance standards?
- To what extent can they manage their own performance and development?
- Are there any areas where there is a need to develop skill or competence?
- How can I provide them with the sort of support and guidance which will improve their performance?

Teams

- How well is the team organized?
- Does the team work well together?
- How can the commitment and motivation of the team be achieved?
- What is the team good and not so good at doing?
- What can I do to improve the performance of the team?

- Are team members flexible – capable of carrying out different tasks?

- To what extent can the team manage its own performance?

- Is there scope to empower the team so that it can take on greater responsibility for setting standards, monitoring performance and taking corrective action?

- Can the team be encouraged to work together to produce ideas for improving performance?

References

Adair, J (1973) *The Action-Centred Leader*, McGraw-Hill, London

Goleman, D (2001) What makes a leader? in *What Makes a Leader*, Harvard Business School Press, Boston, MA

Grint, K (2005) *Leadership: Limits and possibilities*, Palgrave Macmillan, Basingstoke

Handy, C (1994) *The Empty Raincoat*, Hutchinson, London Industrial Society

Kelley, R E (1991) In praise of followers, in *Managing People and Organizations*, ed J J Gabarro, Harvard Business School Press, Boston, MA

Ulrich, D and Smallwood, N (2007) *Leadership Brand: Developing customer-focused leaders to drive performance and build lasting value*, Harvard Business School Press, Boston, MA

Welch, J (2007) Mindset of a leader, *Leadership Excellence*, **24** (1), pp 8–9

20

Selection Interviewing Skills

One of the most important people management tasks carried out by managers is to interview candidates for a position on their team. Even when an HR (human resources) department or a recruitment agency is involved, managers usually make the final decision. The problem is that many managers think that they are good at selecting people but actually they are not. This is often revealed by an analysis of leavers, which shows that a large proportion leave in the first six months – about one in five according to a recent national survey.

Interviewing is a skilled process, and the aim of this chapter is to help you develop the skills required, by first defining the nature of a selection interview and its content, then providing guidance on preparing for and planning the interview, interviewing techniques and assessing the data.

The nature of a selection interview

A selection interview should provide you with the answers to three fundamental questions:

- Can the individual do the job? Is the person capable of doing the work to the standard required?

- Will the individual do the job? Is the person well motivated?

- How is the individual likely to fit into the team? Will I and other team members be able to work well with this person?

It should take the form of a conversation with a purpose. It is a conversation because candidates should be given the opportunity to talk freely about themselves and their careers. But the conversation has to be planned, directed and controlled to achieve your aims in the time available.

Your task as an interviewer is to draw candidates out to ensure that you get the information you want. Candidates should be encouraged to do most of the talking – one of the besetting sins of poor interviewers is that they talk too much. But you have to plan the structure of the interview to achieve its purpose, and decide in advance the questions you need to ask – questions which will give you what you need to make an accurate assessment.

Overall, an effective approach to interviewing can be summed up as the three Cs:

- Content: the information you want and the questions you ask to get it.

- Contact: your ability to make and maintain good contact with candidates; to establish the sort of rapport that will encourage them to talk freely, thus revealing their strengths and their weaknesses.

- Control: your ability to control the interview so that you get the information you want.

All this requires you to plan the interview thoroughly in terms of content, timing, structure and use of questions.

The content of an interview

The content of an interview can be analysed into three sections; its beginning, middle and end.

Beginning

At the start of the interview you should put candidates at their ease. You want them to talk freely in response to your questions. They will not do this if you plunge in too abruptly. Welcome them and thank them for coming to the interview, expressing genuine pleasure about the meeting. But do not waste too much time talking about their journey or the weather.

Some interviewers start by describing the company and the job. Wherever possible it is best to eliminate this part of the interview by sending candidates a brief job description and something about the organization.

If you are not careful you will spend far too much time at this stage, especially if the candidate later turns out to be clearly unsuitable. A brief reference to the job should suffice, and this can be extended at the end of the interview.

Middle

The middle part of the interview is where you find out what you need to know about candidates. It should take at least 80 per cent of the time, leaving, say, 5 per cent at the beginning and 15 per cent at the end.

This is when you ask questions designed to provide information on:

- the extent to which the knowledge, skills, capabilities and personal qualities of candidates meet the person specification;

- the career history and ambitions of candidates;

- sometimes, certain aspects of the individual's behaviour at work such as sickness and absenteeism.

End

At the end of the interview you should give candidates the opportunity to ask about the job and the company. How they do this can often give you clues about the degree to which applicants are interested and their ability to ask pertinent questions.

You may want to expand a little on the job. If candidates are promising, some interviewers at this stage extol the attractive features of the job. This is fine as long as these are not exaggerated. To give a realistic preview, the possible downsides should be mentioned: for example the need to travel or unsocial working hours. If candidates are clearly unsuitable you can tactfully help them to deselect themselves by referring to aspects of the work that might not appeal to them, or for which they are not really qualified. It is best not to spell out these points too strongly. It is often sufficient simply to put the question 'This is a key requirement of the job. How do you feel about it?' You can follow up this general question by more specific questions: 'Do you feel you have the right sort of experience?' 'Are you happy about (this aspect of the job)?'

At this stage you should ask a question about the availability of the candidate, if they are promising. You can ask when they would be able to start and about any holiday arrangements to which they are committed.

You should also ask their permission to obtain references from their present and previous employers. They might not want you to approach their present employer, but you should tell them that if they are made an offer of employment it would be conditional on a satisfactory reference from that employer. It is useful to ensure that you have the names of people you can approach.

Finally, you should inform candidates of what will happen next. If some time could elapse before they hear from you, they should be told that you will be writing as soon as possible, but that there will be some delay. (Do not make a promise you will be unable to keep.)

It is not normally good practice to inform candidates of your decision at the end of the interview. You should take time to reflect on their suitability, and you do not want to give them the impression that you are making a snap judgement.

Preparing for the interview

Initial preparations

Your first step in preparing for an interview is to familiarize or refamiliarize yourself with the person specification, which defines the sort of individual you want in terms of qualifications, competencies required, experience and person qualities. It is also advisable at this stage to prepare questions that you can put to all candidates to obtain the information you require. If you ask everyone some identical questions you will be able to compare the answers.

You should then read the candidates' CVs and application forms or letters. This will identify any special questions you should ask about their career, or to fill in the gaps. For example you might want to know 'What does this gap between jobs C and D signify?', although you would not put the question as baldly as that. It is better to say something like 'I see there was a gap of six months between when you left your job in C and started in D. Would you tell me what you were doing during this time?'

Timing

You should decide at this stage how long you want to spend on each interview. As a rule of thumb, 45 to 60 minutes are usually required for senior professional or technical appointments. Middle-ranking jobs need about 30 to 45 minutes. The more routine jobs can be covered in 20 to 30 minutes. But the time allowed depends on the job, and you do not want to insult a candidate by conducting a superficial interview.

Planning the interview

When planning interviews you should give some thought to how you are going to sequence your questions, especially in the middle part. There are two basic approaches, as described below.

Biographical approach

The biographical approach is probably the most popular because it is simple to use and appears to be logical. The interview can be sequenced chronologically, starting with the first job or even before that with school, and if relevant college or university. The person's succeeding jobs, if any, are then dealt with in turn, ending with the present job, on which most time is spent if the candidate has been in it for a reasonable time. If you are not careful, however, using the chronological method for someone who has had a number of jobs can mean spending too much time on their earlier jobs, leaving insufficient time for the most important recent experiences.

To overcome this problem, an alternative biographical approach is to start with the present job, which is discussed in some depth. The interviewer then works backwards, job by job, but only concentrating on particularly interesting or relevant experience in earlier jobs.

The problem with the biographical approach is that it is predictable. Experienced candidates are familiar with it and have their story ready, glossing over any weak points. It can also be unreliable. You can easily miss an important piece of information by concentrating on a succession of jobs rather than focusing on key aspects of the candidates' experience which illustrate their capabilities.

Criteria-based or targeted approach (competency-based interviews)

This approach is based on an analysis of the person specification with particular reference to the competencies required (this is sometimes referred to as a competency-based interview). You can then select the criteria for judging the suitability of the candidate, and this will put you in a position to target these key criteria during the interview. You can decide on the questions you need to ask to draw out from candidates information about their knowledge, skills, competencies, capabilities and personal qualities, which can be compared with the criteria to assess the extent to which candidates meet the specification. This is probably the best way of focusing your interview to ensure that you get all the information you require about candidates for comparison with the person specification.

Interviewing techniques – asking questions

As mentioned earlier, an interview is a conversation with a purpose. The interviewer's job is to draw the candidate out, at the same time ensuring that the information required is obtained. To this end it is desirable to ask a number of open-ended questions – questions which cannot be answered by a yes or no, and which promote a full response. A good interviewer will have an armoury of other types of questions to be asked when appropriate, as described below.

Open questions

Open questions are phrased generally, give no indication of the expected reply, and cannot be answered by a yes or no. They encourage candidates to talk, drawing them out and obtaining a full response. Single-word answers are seldom illuminating. It is a good idea to begin the interview with some open questions to obtain a general picture of candidates, helping them to settle in. Open questions or phrases inviting a response can be phrased like this:

I'd like you to tell me about the sort of work you are doing in your present job.
What do you know about…?
Could you give me some examples of…?
In what ways do you think your experience fits you to do the job for which you have
  applied?
How have you tackled…?
What have been the most challenging aspects of your job?
Please tell me about some of the interesting things you have been doing at work recently.

Open questions can give you a lot of useful information, but you may not get exactly what you want, and answers can go into too much detail. For example, the question 'What has been the main feature of your work in recent months?' might result in a one-word reply – 'Marketing.' Or it might produce a lengthy explanation which takes up too much time. Replies to open questions can get bogged down in too much detail, or miss out some key points. They can come to a sudden halt or lose their way. You need to ensure that you get all the facts, keep the flow going and maintain control. Remember that you are in charge. Hence the value of probing, closed and the other types of questions, which are discussed below.

Probing questions

Probing questions ask for further details and explanations to ensure that you are getting all the facts. You ask them when answers have been too generalized or when you suspect that there may be some more relevant information which candidates have not disclosed. If a candidate claims to have done something which clearly involved teamwork, for instance, it might be useful to find out more about the nature of their own contribution. Poor interviewers tend to let general and uninformative answers pass by without probing for further details, simply because they are sticking rigidly to a predetermined list of open questions. Skilled interviewers are able to flex their approach to ensure they get the facts, while still keeping control to ensure that the interview is completed on time.

A candidate could say to you something like 'I was involved in a major exercise that produced significant improvements in the flow of work through the factory.' This statement conveys nothing about what the candidate actually did. You have to ask probing questions such as:

> *You've informed me that you have had experience in... Could you tell me more about what you did?*
> *What sort of targets or standards have you been expected to achieve?*
> *How successful have you been in achieving those targets or standards? Please give examples.*
> *Could you give an example of any project you have undertaken?*
> *What was your precise role in this project?*
> *What exactly was the contribution you made to its success?*
> *What knowledge and skills were you able to apply to the project?*
> *Were you responsible for monitoring progress?*
> *Did you prepare the final recommendations in full or in part? If in part, which part?*
> *Could you describe in more detail the equipment you used?*

Closed questions

Closed questions aim to clarify a point of fact. The expected reply will be an explicit single word or brief sentence. In a sense, a closed question acts as a probe but produces a succinct factual statement without going into detail. When you ask a closed question you intend to find out:

- what the candidate has or has not done – 'What did you do then?'
- why something took place – 'Why did that happen?'
- when something took place – 'When did that happen?'
- how something happened – 'How did that situation arise?'
- where something happened – 'Where were you at the time?'
- who took part – 'Who else was involved?'

Hypothetical questions

Hypothetical questions are used in structured situational-based interviews when a situation is described to candidates and they are asked how they would respond. Hypothetical questions can be prepared in advance to test how candidates would approach a typical problem. Such questions may be phrased: 'What do you think you would do if…?' When such questions lie well within the candidate's expertise and experience the answers can be illuminating. But it could be unfair to ask candidates to say how they would deal with a problem without their knowing more about the context in which the problem arose. It can also be argued that what candidates say they would do and what they actually would do could be quite different. Hypothetical questions can produce hypothetical answers. The best information on which judgements about candidates can be made involves what they have actually done or achieved. You need to find out whether they have successfully dealt with the sort of issues and problems they may be faced with if they join your organization.

Behavioural event questions

Behavioural event questions as used in behavioural-based structured interviews aim to get candidates to tell you how they would behave in situations that have been identified as critical to successful job performance. The assumption upon which such questions are based is that past behaviour in dealing with or reacting to events is the best predictor of future behaviour.

These are some typical behavioural event questions:

Could you give an instance when you persuaded others to take an unusual course of action?

Could you describe an occasion when you completed a project or task in the face of great difficulties?

Could you describe any contribution you have made as a member of a team in achieving an unusually successful result?

Could you give an instance when you took the lead in a difficult situation in getting something worthwhile done?

Capability questions

Capability questions aim to establish what candidates know, the skills they possess and use, and their competencies – what they are capable of doing. They can be open, probing or closed, but they will always be focused as precisely as possible on the contents of the person specification referring to knowledge, skills and competences. Capability questions are used in behavioural-based structured interviews.

Capability questions should therefore be explicit – focused on what candidates must know and be able to do. Their purpose is to obtain evidence from candidates which shows the extent to which they meet the specification in each of its key areas. Because time is always limited it is best to concentrate on the most important aspects of the work, and it is always best to prepare the questions in advance. The types of capability questions you can ask are:

> *What do you know about…?*
> *How did you gain this knowledge?*
> *What are the key skills you are expected to use in your work?*
> *How would your present employer rate the level of skill you have reached in…?*
> *Could you please tell me exactly what sort and how much experience you have had in…?*
> *Could you tell me more about what you have actually been doing in this aspect of your work?*
> *Can you give me any examples of the sort of work you have done which would qualify you to do this job?*
> *What are the most typical problems you have to deal with?*
> *Please tell me about any instances when you have had to deal with an unexpected problem or a crisis.*

Questions about motivation

The degree to which candidates are motivated is a personal quality to which it is necessary to give special attention if it is to be properly assessed. This is usually achieved by inference rather than direct questions. 'How well are you motivated?' is a leading question that will usually produce the response 'Highly'. You can make inferences about the level of motivation of candidates by asking questions on the following subjects.

- Their career – replies to such questions as 'Why did you decide to move on from there?' can give an indication of the extent to which they have been well motivated in progressing their career.

- Achievements – not just 'What did you achieve?' but 'How did you achieve it?' and 'What difficulties did you overcome?'

- Triumphing over disadvantages – candidates who have done well in spite of an unpromising upbringing and relatively poor education may be more highly motivated than those with all the advantages that upbringing and education can bestow, but who have not made good use of these advantages.

- Spare-time interests – don't accept at its face value a reply to a question about spare-time interests which, for example, reveals that a candidate collects stamps. Find out whether the candidate is well-motivated enough to have pursued the interest with determination and achieved something in the process.

Continuity questions

Continuity questions aim to keep the flow going in an interview, and encourage candidates to enlarge on what they have told you, within limits. Here are some examples of continuity questions.

> *What happened next?*
> *What did you do then?*
> *Can we talk about your next job?*
> *Can we move on now to...?*
> *Could you tell me more about...?*

It has been said that to keep the conversation going during an interview, the best thing an interviewer can do is to make encouraging grunts at appropriate moments. There is more to interviewing than that, but single words or phrases like 'Good', 'Fine', 'That's interesting' and 'Carry on' can help things along.

Play-back questions

Play-back questions test your understanding of what candidates have said, and give an opportunity to check on misunderstandings or hidden meanings. You repeat in your own words what you think they have told you, and ask them if they agree or disagree with your version. For example, you could say 'As I understand it, you resigned from your last position because you disagreed with your boss on a number of fundamental issues. Have I got that right?' The answer might simply be yes to this closed question, in which case you might probe to find out more about what happened. Or the candidate may reply 'Not exactly', in which case you ask for the full story.

Career questions

As mentioned earlier, questions about the career history of candidates can provide some insight into motivation as well as establishing how they have progressed in acquiring useful and relevant knowledge, skills and experience. You can ask questions such as:

What did you learn from that new job?
What different skills had you to use when you were promoted?
Why did you leave that job?
What happened after you left that job?
In what ways do you think this job will advance your career?

Focused work questions

These are questions designed to tell you more about particular aspects of the candidate's work history, such as:

How many days absence from work did you have last year?
How many times were you late last year?
Have you been absent from work for any medical reason not shown on your application form?
Have you a clean driving licence? (for those whose work will involve driving)

Unhelpful questions

Multiple questions such as 'What skills do you use most frequently in your job? Are they technical skills, leadership skills, teamworking skills or communicating skills?' will only confuse candidates. You will probably get a partial or misleading reply. Ask only one question at a time.

Leading questions which indicate the reply you expect are also unhelpful. If you ask a question such as 'That's what you think, isn't it?', you will get the reply 'Yes, I do.' If you ask a question such as 'I take it that you don't really believe that...?', you will get the reply 'No, I don't.' Neither of these replies will get you anywhere.

Questions to be avoided

Avoid any questions that could be construed as being biased on the grounds of sex, race, disability or age.

Some examples of questions you must not ask

Who is going to look after the children?

Are you planning to have any more children?

Are you concerned at all about racial prejudice?

Would it worry you being the only immigrant around here?

With your disability, do you think you can cope with the job?

Do you think that at your time of life you will be able to learn the new skills associated with this job?

Ten useful questions

What are the most important aspects of your present job?

What do you think have been your most notable achievements in your career to date?

What sort of problems have you successfully solved recently in your job?

What have you learned from your present job?

What has been your experience in…?

What do you know about…?

What particularly interests you in this job and why?

Now you have heard more about the job, would you please tell me which aspects of your experience are most relevant.

What do you think you can bring to this job?

Is there anything else about your career which hasn't come out yet in this interview but you think I ought to hear?

Key interviewing skills

The key interviewing skills are establishing rapport, listening, maintaining continuity, keeping control and note taking.

Establishing rapport

Establishing rapport means establishing a good relationship with candidates – getting on their wavelength, putting them at ease, encouraging them to respond and generally being friendly. This is not just a question of being 'nice' to candidates. If you achieve rapport you are more likely to get them to talk freely about both their strengths and weaknesses.

Good rapport is created by the way in which you greet candidates, how you start the interview and how you put your questions and respond to replies. Questions should not be posed aggressively or imply that you are criticizing some aspect of the candidate's career. Some people like the idea of 'stress' interviews but they are counterproductive. Candidates clam up and gain a negative impression of you and the organization.

When responding to answers you should be appreciative, not critical. Say 'Thank you, that was very helpful. Now can we go on to…?' Do not say anything like 'Well, it seems to me that things did not go according to plan there.'

Body language can also be important. If you maintain natural eye contact, avoid slumping in your seat, nod and make encouraging comments when appropriate, you will establish better rapport and get more out of the interview.

Listening

If an interview is a conversation with a purpose, listening skills are important. You need not only to hear but also to understand what candidates are saying. When interviewing you must concentrate on what candidates are telling you. Summarizing at regular intervals forces you to listen. If you play back to candidates your understanding of what they have told you for them to confirm or amend, it will ensure that you have fully comprehended the messages they are delivering.

Maintaining continuity

As far as possible, link your questions to a candidate's last reply so that the interview progresses logically and a cumulative set of data is built up. You can put bridging questions to candidates such as 'Thank you, that was an interesting summary of what you have been doing in this aspect of your work. Now could you tell me something about your other key responsibilities?'

Keeping control

You want candidates to talk, but not too much. When preparing for the interview you should have drawn up an agenda, and you must try to stick to it. Do not cut candidates short too brutally, but you should interrupt when you feel it is necessary. Say something like 'Thank you, I've got a good picture of that. Now what about…?'

Focus on specifics as much as you can. If candidates ramble on, ask a pointed question (a 'probe' question) which asks for an example of what they are describing.

Note taking

You will not remember everything that candidates tell you. It is useful to take notes of the key points they make, discreetly but not surreptitiously. However, do not put candidates off by frowning or tut-tutting when you are making a negative note. It may be helpful to ask candidates whether they mind if you take notes. They cannot really object but will appreciate the fact that they have been asked.

Coming to a conclusion

It is essential not to be beguiled by a pleasant, articulate and confident interviewee who is all surface without substance. Beware of the 'halo' effect which occurs when people seize onto one or two early good points, and neglect later negative indicators. The opposite 'horns' effect of focusing on the negatives should also be avoided.

Individual candidates should be assessed against the criteria. These could be set under the headings of knowledge and skills, competencies, education, qualifications, training, experience and overall suitability. Ratings can be given against each heading, for example very acceptable, acceptable, marginally acceptable, unacceptable. If you have used situational or behaviourally based questions you can indicate against each question whether the reply was good, acceptable or poor. These assessments can inform your overall assessment of the candidate's knowledge, skills and competencies.

Next, compare your own assessments of each of the candidates with those of the other interviewers. You can do this heading by heading to try to come to a composite judgement.

In the end, your decision between qualified candidates may well be a matter of fine judgement. There could be one outstanding candidate, but quite often there are two or three who seem equally suitable. In these circumstances you have to come to a balanced view on which one is more likely to fit the job and the organization, and have the potential for a long-term career, if this is possible. Do not, however, settle for second best in desperation. It is better to try again.

Remember to make and keep notes of the reasons for your choice, and why candidates have been rejected. These, together with the applications, should be kept for at least six months just in case your decision is challenged as being discriminatory. An example of an interview rating form is given in Table 20.1.

Table 20.1   Example of an interview rating form

	very acceptable	acceptable	marginally acceptable	unacceptable	comments
knowledge and skills					
competencies					
education and qualifications					
training					
experience					
overall suitability					

Dos and don'ts of selection interviewing

Do:

- Plan the interview.
- Give yourself sufficient time.
- Use a structured interview approach wherever possible.
- Create the right atmosphere.
- Establish an easy and informal relationship – start with open questions.
- Encourage the candidate to talk.
- Cover the ground as planned, ensuring that you complete a prepared agenda and maintain continuity.
- Analyse the candidate's career to reveal strengths, weaknesses and patterns of interest.
- Ask clear, unambiguous questions.
- Get examples and instances of the successful application of knowledge, skills and the effective use of capabilities.
- Make judgements on the basis of the factual information you have obtained about candidates' experience and attributes in relation to the person specification.
- Keep control over the content and timing of the interview.

Don't:

- Start the interview unprepared.

- Plunge too quickly into demanding (probe) questions.

- Ask multiple or leading questions.

- Pay too much attention to isolated strengths or weaknesses.

- Allow candidates to gloss over important facts.

- Talk too much or allow candidates to ramble on.

- Allow your prejudices to get the better of your capacity to make objective judgements.

- Fall into the halo or horns effect trap.

- Ask questions or make remarks that could be construed as in any way discriminatory.

- Attempt too many interviews in a row.

21
Performance Management Skills

One of the most important, if not the most important, of the responsibilities undertaken by managers is to ensure that the members of their team achieve high levels of performance. They have to know how to agree expectations and review results against those expectations, and how to decide what needs to be done to develop knowledge and skills, and where necessary performance.

The organization may well have a performance management system which provides guidance on how this should be done, but ultimately it is up to managers. They are the people on the spot. Performance management systems only work if managers want them to work and are capable of making them work. They have to believe that their time is well spent in the process of managing performance. They need the skills required to set objectives, conduct formal performance reviews and provide feedback.

Setting objectives

Objective or goal setting (the terms are interchangeable) results in an agreement on what the role holder has to achieve. It is an important part of the performance management processes of defining and managing expectations, and forms the point of reference for performance reviews. It requires the use of skills based on an understanding of what the different types of objectives are, what makes a good objective, how managers reach agreement with individuals on what their objectives should be, and how those objectives should be achieved.

What objectives are

Objectives describe something that has to be accomplished. They define what organizations, functions, departments, and individuals are expected to achieve over a period of time. There are several different types of objectives.

Ongoing role or work objectives

All roles have built-in objectives which may be expressed as key result areas in a role profile. A key result area states what the role holder is expected to achieve in this particular aspect of the role, for example 'Identify database requirements for all projects that require data management in order to meet the needs of internal customers' or 'Deal quickly with customer queries in order to create and maintain high levels of satisfaction'.

Good role or work objectives will clearly define the activity in terms of the results and standards to be achieved. They may be supplemented by targets or standards which can be quantified or qualitative. Although described as ongoing, role objectives need to be reviewed regularly and modified as necessary.

Targets

Targets provide measures for the quantifiable results to be attained, in such terms as output, throughput, income, sales, levels of service delivery, cost reduction, reduction of reject rates. Thus a customer service target could be to respond to 90 per cent of queries within two working days.

Tasks/projects

Objectives can be set for the completion of tasks or projects by a specified date or to achieve an interim result. A target for a database administrator could be to develop a new database to meet the need of the HR department by the end of the year.

Performance standards

A performance standard definition takes the form of a statement that performance will be up to standard if a desirable, specified and observable result happens. It should preferably be quantified, in terms of, for example, level of service or speed of response. Where this is not possible, a more qualitative approach may have to be adopted, in which case the standard of performance definition would in effect state: 'This job or task will have been well done when (the following things happen).'

Behaviour

Behavioural expectations are often set out generally in competency frameworks but they may also be defined individually under the framework headings. Competency frameworks may deal with areas of behaviour associated with core values, for example teamwork, but they often convert the aspirations contained in value statements into more specific examples of desirable and undesirable behaviour which can help in planning and reviewing performance.

Values

Expectations can be defined for upholding the core values of the organization. The aim is to ensure that espoused values become values in use.

Performance improvement

Performance improvement goals define what has to be done to achieve better results. They may be expressed in a performance improvement plan which specifies what actions need to be taken by role holders and their managers.

Developmental/learning

Developmental or learning objectives specify areas for personal development and learning in the shape of enhanced knowledge and skills.

What makes a good objective

Many organizations use the 'SMART' mnemonic to summarize the desirable characteristics of an objective:

> S = *Specific/stretching* – *clear, unambiguous, straightforward, understandable and challenging.*
> M = *Measurable* – *quantity, quality, time, money.*
> A = *Achievable* – *challenging but within the reach of a competent and committed person.*
> R = *Relevant* – *relevant to the objectives of the organization so that the goal of the individual is aligned to corporate goals.*
> T = *Time-framed* – *to be completed within an agreed timescale.*

How to set objectives

Objectives are defined by reference to an agreed role profile which sets out key result areas. Role profiles are amended at the time any changes are made to these areas, and are also formally reviewed and updated at the planning and agreement stage of the performance management cycle. It is essential that individuals should participate in reviewing and agreeing their own objectives in order to ensure that they are committed to them. In the box is a checklist for objective-setting.

Checklist for objective-setting

1. Has the objective-setting process been based on an agreed and up-to-date role profile which sets out key result areas?

2. Have the objectives been agreed after an objective-setting process carried out jointly by the manager and the individual?

3. Are standards and targets clearly related to the key result areas in the role profile?

4. Do objectives support the achievement of team and corporate objectives?

5. Are the objectives specific?

6. Are they challenging?

7. Are they realistic and attainable?

8. Has a time limit for their achievement been agreed?

9. How will the achievement of objectives be measured?

10. Have any problems in attaining the objectives been identified, and has action to overcome these problems been agreed?

Formal review meetings

Formal review meetings are a vital part of the process of managing performance. They provide managers with the opportunity to give feedback, to sound out individuals on how they feel about their job, and to plan for improvements in performance or activities to meet the learning and development needs identified during the review. The feedback will summarize and draw conclusions from what has been happening since the last review, but it will be based on events and observations rather than opinion. These should have been discussed at the time – there should not be any surprises during the formal discussion.

A review should take the form of a dialogue in which the two parties exchange comments and ideas and develop agreed plans. The conversation – and that is what it should be – concentrates on analysis and review of the significant points emerging from the period under consideration. The review should be rooted in the reality of what the individual has been doing. It is concrete, not abstract. It will recognize successes and identify things that have gone wrong in order to learn lessons for the future. It should be a joint affair: both parties are involved, and self-assessment by individuals can be a valuable part of the process.

A performance review meeting provides an ideal opportunity for discussing work issues away from the hurly-burly of everyday working life. It can motivate people by providing a means of recognizing good performance. It can help to indicate areas in which performance needs to improve and how this should be done. And, importantly, it can help to identify learning and development needs and the means of satisfying them.

Preparing for the meeting

Formal review meetings should be initiated by letting the individual know some time in advance (a week or so) when it is going to take place. The individual should be told the purpose of the meeting and the points to be covered. The aim should be, as far as possible, to emphasize the positive nature of the process and to dispel any feelings of trepidation.

The individual can then be asked to prepare for the meeting by assessing their level of performance achieved and identifying any work issues.

You should work your way through the following checklist of questions:

- How well has the individual done in achieving agreed objectives during the review period?

- How well have any improvement, development or training plans agreed at the last review meeting been put into effect?

- What should be the individual's objectives for the next review period?

- Are you satisfied that you have given the individual sufficient guidance or help on what they are expected to do? If not, what extra help/guidance could you provide?

- Is the best use being made of the individual's skills and abilities?

- Is the individual ready to take on additional responsibilities?

- Would the individual benefit from further experience?

- Are there any special projects the individual could take part in which would help with their development?

- What direction do you think the individual's career could take within the organization?

- Does the individual need any further training?

Conducting the meeting

One or two uninterrupted hours should be allowed for the performance review meeting. In a sense this a stocktaking exercise answering the questions 'Where have we got to?' and 'How did we get here?' But there is much more to it than that. It is not just an historical affair, dwelling on the past and taking the form of a post-mortem. The true purpose of the review is to answer the question 'Where do we go from here?', which means looking forward to what needs to be done by people to achieve the overall purpose of their jobs, to meet new challenges, to make even better use of their skills, knowledge and abilities, and to develop their skills and competencies to further their career and increase their employability, within and outside the organization.

A constructive review meeting is most likely to take place if you:

- encourage individuals to do most of the talking: the aim should be to conduct the meeting as a dialogue rather than use it to make 'top-down' pronouncements;

- listen actively to what they say;

- allow scope for reflection and analysis;

- analyse performance, not personality – concentrate on what individuals have done, not the sort of people they are;

- keep the whole period under review, and do not concentrate on isolated or recent events;

- adopt a 'no surprises' approach – performance problems should have been identified and dealt with at the time they occurred;

- recognize achievements and reinforce strengths;

- discuss any work problems, how they have arisen and what can be done about them;

- end the meeting positively with any necessary agreed action plans (learning and development and performance improvement).

Performance review skills

The main skills needed to conduct performance reviews are asking the right questions, listening actively, providing feedback and dealing with any issues.

Asking the right questions

Only one question should be asked at a time, and if necessary unclear responses should be played back to check understanding. The two main approaches are to use open and probe questions.

Open questions are general, not specific. They provide room for people to decide how they should be answered, and encourage them to talk freely. They set the scene for the more detailed analysis of performance that will follow later, and can be introduced at any point to open up a discussion on a new topic. Open questions help to create an atmosphere of calm and friendly enquiry, and can be expressed quite informally, for example:

- How do you think things have been going?

- What do you feel about that?

- How can we build on that in the future?
- What can we learn from that?

Open questions can be put in a 'tell me' form such as:

- 'Tell me, why do you think that happened?'
- 'Tell me, how did you handle that situation?'
- 'Tell me, how is this project going?'
- 'Tell me, what do you think your key objectives are going to be next year?'

Probe questions seek specific information on what has happened and why. You can use them to:

- show interest and encouragement by making supportive statements followed by questions: 'I see, and then what?'
- seek further information by asking 'Why?' or 'Why not?' or 'What do you mean?'
- explore attitudes: 'To what extent do you believe that...?'
- reflect views: 'Have I got the right impression? Do you feel that...?'

Listening

In a review meeting it is necessary to listen carefully. Good listeners:

- concentrate on the speaker; they are alert at all times to the nuances of what is being said;
- respond quickly when appropriate but do not interrupt unnecessarily;
- ask questions to clarify meaning;
- comment as necessary on the points made to demonstrate understanding but not at length.

Providing feedback

As far as possible feedback on how well individuals are doing should be built into their jobs – they should have access to all the information they need to measure their own performance. But it is also necessary to provide feedback during the performance review meeting as part of the stocktaking exercise. Guidelines on providing feedback are provided in the next section of this chapter.

Dealing with issues

A review meeting addresses performance issues. Some will be positive, others may be negative. Dealing with negative points is often the area of greatest concern to line managers, many of whom do not like handing out criticisms. But this is not what performance reviews are about. They should not be regarded simply as an opportunity for attaching blame for something that has gone wrong in the past. If there has been a problem it should have been discussed when it happened. But this does not mean that persistent under-performance should go unnoticed during the review meeting. Specific problems may have been dealt with at the time, but it might still be necessary to discuss a pattern of under-performance. The first step, and often the most difficult one, is to get people to agree that there is room for improvement. This will best be achieved if the discussion focuses on factual evidence of performance problems. Some people will never admit to being wrong, and in those cases it may be necessary to say in effect 'Here is the evidence. I have no doubt that this is correct. I am afraid you have to accept from me on the basis of this evidence that your performance in this respect has been unsatisfactory.'

The positive elements should not be neglected. Too often they are overlooked or mentioned briefly, then put on one side. A sequence of comments like this should be avoided:

- Objective number one – fantastic.

- Objective number two – that was great.

- Objective number three – couldn't have been done better.

- Now objective number four is what we really need to talk about. What went wrong?

If this sort of approach is adopted, the discussion will focus on the failure, the negatives, and the individual will become defensive. This can be destructive, and explains why some people feel that the annual review meeting is going to be a 'beat me over the head' session or part of a blame culture.

To underemphasize the positive aspects reduces the scope for action and motivation. More can be achieved by building on success than by concentrating on failure. In the words of the song, 'Accentuate the positive, eliminate the negative.'

Guidelines on providing feedback

Feedback is an important part of a review meeting, but it can take place at any time. You should be managing performance throughout the year rather than during one annual event. Every time a task is accomplished provides an opportunity for feedback which recognizes success or suggests ways of doing even better next time. Here are some guidelines on providing feedback.

Build feedback into the job

To be effective, feedback should be built into the job or provided soon after the activity has taken place.

Provide feedback on actual events

Feedback should be provided on actual results or observed behaviour. It should be backed up by evidence. It should not be based on supposition about the reason for the behaviour. For example, it is much better to say something like 'We have received the following complaint from a customer about you. Would you like to comment?' rather than 'You tend to be aggressive.'

Describe, don't judge

The feedback should be presented as a description of what has happened. It should not be accompanied by a judgement. If you start by saying 'I have been informed that you have been rude to one of our customers. We can't tolerate that sort of behaviour', you will instantly create resistance and prejudice an opportunity to encourage improvement.

Refer to and define specific behaviours

Relate all your feedback to specific items of behaviour. Don't indulge in transmitting general feelings or impressions.

Define good work or behaviour

When commenting on someone's work or behaviour, define what you believe to be good work or effective behaviour with examples.

Ask questions

Ask questions rather than make statements – 'Why do you think this happened?' 'On reflection is there any other way in which you think you could have handled the situation?' 'How do you think you should tackle this sort of situation in the future?'

Select key issues

Select key issues and restrict yourself to them. There is a limit to how much criticism anyone can take. If you overdo it, the shutters will go up and you will get nowhere.

Focus

Focus on aspects of performance the individual can improve. It is a waste of time to concentrate on areas that the individual can do little or nothing about.

Provide positive feedback

Provide feedback on the things that the individual did well in addition to areas for improvement. People are more likely to work positively at improving their performance and developing their skills if they feel empowered by the process.

Provide constructive feedback

Focus on what can be done to improve rather than criticism.

Ensure feedback leads to action

Feedback should indicate any actions required to develop performance or skills.

22
Learning and Development Skills

Managers have a vital role in helping their people to learn and develop. Most learning takes place on the job but it will be more effective if managers provide the coaching, guidance and support people need. To do this they need to know about induction training, how to ensure continuous learning, and personal development planning processes, as covered in the next three sections of this chapter. They also need to use coaching, mentoring and giving instruction skills as described in later sections.

Induction training

You are involved in helping people to learn every time you welcome new employees, plan how they are going to acquire the know-how required (preferably as recorded in a learning specification), provide for them to receive systematic guidance and instruction on the tasks they have to carry out, and see that the plan is implemented. You may delegate the responsibility for providing this induction training to a team leader, or team leaders may carry it out themselves – the ideal method – or delegate it to a team member. Whichever approach is used you should be confident that the individual responsible for the induction has the right temperament and skills to do it.

Continuous learning

You provide learning opportunities for team members every time you delegate tasks to them. At the briefing stage you should ensure that team members are fully aware of what they have to do and have the knowledge and skills to do it. If appropriate, you ask them to tell you what they need to know and be able to do to carry out the task. If you are unsure that their staff have all the skills required but still believe that they can do it with additional guidance or help, then you will need to provide the support yourself or arrange for someone else to do so.

As you monitor progress to whatever degree is necessary (you can just let some people get on with it; less experienced people you might need to monitor more closely), you can follow up to find out whether the best approach is being used, and if not, give them any further help they need. But you must be careful. People will not learn if everything is done for them. They have to be given a chance to find things out for themselves and even make mistakes as long as things are not going badly wrong.

When outcomes are reviewed with people, preferably immediately after the event, it is a good idea to ask them what they have learnt so that it is reinforced for future use. They can also be asked whether their experience has shown that they need to learn more. This is a good opportunity for you to get individuals to develop their own learning plans (self-directed learning), but it also means that you can step in and offer your support.

Personal development planning

Personal development planning is carried out by individuals with guidance, encouragement and help from their manager as required. A personal development plan sets out the actions people propose to take to learn and to develop themselves. They take responsibility for formulating and implementing the plan, but they receive support from their managers in doing so.

The stages of personal development planning are:

1. Analyse the current situation and development needs. This can be done as part of a performance management process.

2. Set goals. These could include improving performance in the current job, improving or acquiring skills, extending relevant knowledge, developing specified areas of competence, moving across or upwards in the organization, or preparing for changes in the current role.

3. Prepare an action plan. The action plan sets out what needs to be done and how it will be done, under headings such as outcomes expected (learning objectives), the development activities, the responsibility for development (what individuals are expected to do and the support they will get from their manager, the HR department or other people), and timing. A variety of activities tuned to individual needs should be included in the plan, for example observing what others do, project work, planned use of e-learning programmes and internal learning resource centres, working with a mentor, coaching by the line manager or team leader, experience in new tasks, guided reading, and special assignments. Formal training to develop knowledge and skills may be part of the plan but it is not the most important part.

4. Implement the plan.

The plan can be expressed in the form of a learning contract, which is a formal agreement between the manager and the individual on what learning needs to take place, the objectives of such learning and what part the individual, the manager, the learning and development department (if one exists) or a mentor will play in ensuring that learning happens. The partners to the contract agree on how the objectives will be achieved and their roles. It will spell out learning programmes and indicate what coaching, mentoring and formal training activities should be carried out. It is, in effect, a blueprint for learning.

Coaching

Coaching is a one-to-one method of helping people develop their skills and competences. Coaching is often provided by specialists from inside or outside the organization who concentrate on specific areas of skills or behaviour, for example leadership, but it is also something that can happen in the workplace. You should be prepared and able to act as a coach when necessary to see that learning takes place.

The need for coaching may arise from formal or informal performance reviews, but opportunities for coaching also emerge during day-to-day activities. As part of the normal process of management, coaching consists of:

● making people aware of how well they are performing by, for example, asking them questions to establish the extent to which they have thought through what they are doing;

● controlled delegation – ensuring that individuals not only know what is expected of them but also understand what they need to know and be able to do to complete the task satisfactorily (this gives managers an opportunity to provide guidance at the outset, although guidance at a later stage may be seen as interference);

● using situations that arise as opportunities to promote learning;

● encouraging people to look at higher-level problems and how they would tackle them.

A common framework used by coaches is the GROW model:

'G' is for the *goal* of coaching, which needs to be expressed in specific measurable terms which represent a meaningful step towards future development.
'R' is for the *reality check* – the process of eliciting as full a description as possible of what the person being coached needs to learn.
'O' is for *option generation* – the identification of as many solutions and actions as possible.
'W' is for *wrapping up* – when the coach ensures that the individual being coached is committed to action.

To succeed in coaching you need to understand that your role is to help people to learn and see that they are motivated to learn. They should be aware that their present level of knowledge, skill or behaviour needs to be improved if they are to perform their work satisfactorily. Individuals should be given guidance on what they should be learning and feedback on how they are doing, and, because learning is an active not a passive process, they should be actively involved with their manager in the latter's role as a coach.

Coaching may be informal but it has to be planned. It does not involve simply checking from time to time on what people are doing and then advising them on how to do it better. Nor does it mean occasionally telling people where they have gone wrong and throwing in a lecture for good measure. As far as possible, coaching should take place within the framework of a general plan of the areas and direction in which individuals will benefit from further development. Coaching plans can and should be incorporated into the personal development plans set out in a performance agreement.

Coaching should provide motivation, structure and effective feedback. As a coach, you should believe that people can succeed and that they can contribute to their own success.

Mentoring

Mentoring is the process of using specially selected and trained individuals to provide guidance, pragmatic advice and continuing support which will help the individuals allocated to them to learn and develop. It can be regarded as a method of helping people to learn, as distinct from coaching, which is a relatively directive means of increasing people's competence.

Mentoring involves learning on the job, which must always be the best way of acquiring the particular skills and knowledge the job holder needs. It also complements formal training by providing those who benefit from it with individual guidance from experienced managers who are 'wise in the ways of the organization'.

Mentors provide people with:

- advice in drawing up self-development programmes or learning contracts:
- general help with learning programmes:
- guidance on how to acquire the necessary knowledge and skills to do a new job;
- advice on dealing with any administrative, technical or people problems individuals meet, especially in the early stages of their careers;
- information on 'the way things are done around here' – the corporate culture in terms of expected behaviour;
- coaching in specific skills;
- help in tackling projects – not by doing it for them but by pointing them in the right direction, helping people to help themselves;

● a parental figure with whom individuals can discuss their aspirations and concerns and who will lend a sympathetic ear to their problems.

Mentors need to adopt the right non-directive but supportive approach to provide help to those they are dealing with. They must be carefully briefed and trained in their role.

Managers may be asked to act as mentors, and should receive guidance on what is involved. But they may be able to call on an organizational mentor to provide help with an individual case.

Job instruction

When people learn specific tasks, especially those involving manual skills, the learning will be more effective if job instruction techniques are used. The sequence of instruction should consist of the following stages.

Preparation

Preparation for each instruction period means that the trainer must have a plan for presenting the subject matter, using appropriate teaching methods, visual aids and demonstration aids. It also means preparing trainees for the instruction that is to follow. They should want to learn. They must perceive that the learning will be relevant and useful to them personally. They should be encouraged to take pride in their job and to appreciate the satisfaction that comes from skilled performance.

Presentation

Presentation should consist of a combination of telling and showing – explanation and demonstration. Explanation should be as simple and direct as possible: the trainer explains briefly the ground to be covered and what to look for. They make the maximum use of charts, diagrams and other visual aids. The aim should be to teach first things first and then proceed from the known to the unknown, the simple to the complex, the concrete to the abstract, the general to the particular, the observation to reasoning, and the whole to the parts and back to the whole again.

Demonstration

Demonstration is an essential stage in instruction, especially when the skill to be learned is mainly a doing skill. Demonstration can take place in three stages:

1. The complete operation is shown at normal speed to show the trainee how the task should be carried out eventually.

2. The operation is demonstrated slowly and in correct sequence, element by element, to indicate clearly what is done and the order in which each task is carried out.

3. The operation is demonstrated again slowly, at least two or three times, to stress the how, when and why of successive movements.

The earner then practises by imitating the instructor and constantly repeating the operation under guidance. The aim is to reach the target level of performance for each element of the total task, but the instructor must constantly strive to develop coordinated and integrated performance; that is, the smooth combination of the separate elements of the task into a whole job pattern.

Follow-up

Follow-up continues during the training period for all the time required by the learner to reach a level of performance equal to that of the normal experienced worker in terms of quality, speed and attention to safety. During the follow-up stage, the learner will continue to need help with particularly difficult tasks or to overcome temporary setbacks which result in a deterioration in performance. The instructor may have to repeat the presentation for the elements and supervise practice more closely until the trainee regains confidence or masters the task.

23

Managing Conflict

Introduction

Conflict is inevitable in organizations because the goals, needs and values of groups and individuals do not always coincide. Conflict may be a sign of a healthy organization. Bland agreement on everything would be unnatural and enervating. There should be clashes of ideas about tasks and projects, and disagreements should not be suppressed. They should come out into the open because that is the only way to ensure that issues are explored and conflicts resolved.

There is such a thing as creative conflict – new or modified ideas, insights, approaches and solutions can be generated by a joint examination of different points of view as long as this is based on an objective and rational exchange of information and ideas. But conflict becomes counterproductive when it is based on personality clashes, or when it is treated as an unseemly mess to be cleared away, rather than a problem to be worked through.

Managing conflict is a matter of resolving the issues that create disagreement, whether it arises between groups (inter-group conflict) or between individuals.

Managing inter-group conflict

There are four ways of managing inter-group conflict: peaceful coexistence, compromise, problem-solving, and, as an aspect of organizational development, conflict interventions.

Peaceful coexistence

The aim here is to smooth out differences and emphasize common ground. People are encouraged to learn to live together; there is a great deal of information, contact and exchange of views, and individuals move freely between groups (for example, between headquarters and the field, or between marketing and operations).

This is a pleasant ideal, but it may not be practicable in many circumstances. There is much evidence that conflict is not resolved by bringing people together. Improved communications and techniques such as briefing groups may appear to be good ideas, but are useless if management has nothing to say that people want to hear. There is also a danger that the real issues, submerged for the moment in an atmosphere of superficial bonhomie, will surface again later.

Compromise

Comprise means resolving the issue by negotiation or bargaining, and the essentially pessimistic process of splitting the difference. The hallmark of this process is that there is no 'right' or 'best' answer. Agreements only accommodate differences. Real issues are unlikely to be solved.

Problem solving

Problem solving involves attempting to find a genuine solution to the problem rather than just accommodating different points of view. This is where the apparent paradox of 'creative conflict' comes in. Conflict solving aims to integrate and build on different contributions in order to create better solutions.

If solutions are to be developed by problem solving, they have to be generated by those who share the responsibility for seeing that the solution works. The sequence of actions is:

1. Those concerned work to define the problem and agree on objectives to be attained by a solution.

2. The group develops alternative solutions and debates their merits.

3. Agreement is reached on the preferred course of action and how it should be implemented.

This process can usefully be facilitated by a third party, as described at the end of this chapter.

Inter-group conflict interventions

As developed by Blake *et al* (1964), these aim to improve inter-group relations by getting groups to share their perceptions of one another and to analyse what they have learnt about themselves and the other group. The groups involved meet each other to share what they have learnt, and to agree on the issues to be resolved and the actions required.

Managing conflict between individuals

Handling conflict between individuals can be even more difficult than resolving conflicts between groups. Whether the conflict is openly hostile or subtly covert, strong personal feelings may be involved. Like inter-group conflict, interpersonal conflict is an organizational reality which is not necessarily good or bad. It can be either productive or non-productive. Problems usually arise when potential conflict is artificially suppressed, or when it increases beyond the control of the adversaries or third-party intermediaries.

Approaches to resolution

Ware and Barnes (1991) identified the following methods of resolving conflict.

Withdrawal

Either party may withdraw, leaving the other one to hold the field. This is the classic win/lose situation or zero-sum game. The winner may be triumphant but the loser will be aggrieved and either demotivated or resolved to fight another day. There will have been a lull in the conflict, but not an end to it.

Smooth out differences

Pretend the conflict does not exist, although no attempt has been made to tackle the root causes. Again, this is unsatisfactory. The issue is likely to re-emerge and the battle will recommence.

Bargaining

An attempt may be made to reach a compromise through bargaining. This means that both sides are prepared to lose as well as win some points, and the aim is to reach a solution acceptable to both sides. However, bargaining involves all sorts of tactical and often counterproductive games, and the parties are often more anxious to seek acceptable compromises than to achieve sound solutions.

Preventing interaction

Conflict is controlled by keeping people apart so that, although the differences still exist, those involved have the chance to cool down and consider more constructive approaches. But this may only be a temporary expedient, and the eventual confrontation could be even more explosive.

Structuring interaction

Ground rules are developed to deal with the issues. But this may also be a temporary expedient if the strong underlying feelings are only suppressed rather than resolved.

Personal counselling

This may give the parties a chance to release pent-up feelings and encourage them to think about new ways of resolving the conflict. But it might not deal with the essential nature of the conflict, which is the relationship between two people.

Constructive confrontation

This is a method of bringing the conflicting individuals together, ideally with a third party whose function is to help build an exploratory and cooperative climate by getting them to understand and explore the other's perceptions and feelings. The issues will be confronted but by means of a joint analysis of factors relating to the situation and the behaviour of those involved. Feelings will be expressed but they will be analysed by reference to specific events rather than inferences or speculation about motives.

Constructive confrontation is the approach most likely to deal with conflict, but it is not an easy option. Much depends on the third party using exacting skills, as described below.

The role of the third party in managing conflict

Ideally, those involved in conflict will resolve it by discussing the issues sensibly and reaching an integrated and constructive solution. But life is not always like that. As mentioned above, problem-solving solutions to resolve inter-group conflict, and constructive confrontation to manage conflict between individuals, provide more hope of success, but they may need the services of a third party. This could be a member of the HR function or an outside consultant. The skills needed are facilitating when dealing with groups and counselling when handling individuals.

Facilitating skills

Dealing with inter-group conflict may mean facilitating meetings of the groups involved separately and/or bringing them together to discuss their problems and, it is hoped, come to an agreed conclusion. Getting groups together is desirable, but the facilitating skills required are considerable. The principal ones a facilitator needs when dealing with any group are:

- Building rapport: creating a harmonious and understanding relationship in which everyone is at ease. This is done by gaining an understanding of how the group is functioning and the issues with which its members are concerned, and by 'matching' your language and behaviour with theirs.

- Setting the scene: ensuring that everyone knows why the group has assembled and getting them to develop ground rules on how it should function.

- Progressing: helping the group to agree what it is there to achieve, reviewing progress with it from time to time, and summarizing what has been achieved, making suggestions for the group to consider on future directions.

- Controlling with a light touch: acting as a calming influence if the discussion gets too heated.

- Getting everyone involved: ensuring that everyone in the group has the opportunity to have a say without allowing anyone to hog the discussion.

- Actively listening: giving people your full attention, reflecting back to people what they have said, and making it clear that you understand what they are saying and their point of view.

- Asking questions: creating better understanding of the situation and encouraging members of the group to think through the issues by asking for information on the factors involved, the behaviours of those concerned and their feelings about them.

- Being non-judgemental: not making comments, adverse or otherwise, on the situation or behaviours; eliciting the facts and allowing them to speak for themselves.

- Helping the group to function: providing help as required by suggesting possible ways for the group to tackle the issues facing it (but not telling them how to do it).

- Encouraging the group to develop its own solutions: as a facilitator your prime role is to get group members to think cooperatively for themselves and come up with the answers. You are not there to do their thinking for them.

Counselling skills

The counselling skills you need when dealing with individuals are similar in many ways to the facilitating skills needed when handling group conflict. They are:

- Listen actively.

- Observe as well as listen.

- Help people to understand and define the problem by asking pertinent, open-ended questions.

- Recognize feelings and allow them to be expressed.

- Help people define problems for themselves.

- Encourage people to explore alternative solutions.

- Get people to develop their own implementation plans but provide help and advice if asked.

Conclusion

Conflict is in itself not to be deplored: it is an inevitable concomitant of progress and change. What is regrettable is a failure to use conflict constructively. Effective problem solving, constructive confrontation and the use of facilitating and counselling skills can also open up channels of discussion and cooperative action.

Many years ago one of the pioneering writers on management, Mary Parker Follett (1924), wrote something on managing conflict which is as valid today as it was then:

> *Differences can be made to contribute to the common cause if they are resolved by integration rather than domination or compromise.*

References

Blake, R, Shepart, H and Mouton, J (1964) Breakthrough in organizational development, *Harvard Business Review*, **42**, pp 237–58

Follett, M P (1924) *Creative Experience*, Longmans Green, New York

Ware, J and Barnes, L (1991) Managing interpersonal conflict, in managing *People and Organizations*, ed J Gabbarro, Harvard Business School Publications, Boston, MA

24

Handling People Problems

If you manage people you have to manage people problems. They are bound to happen, and you will be the person on the spot who has to handle them. The basic approach you should use in tackling people problems is to:

1. *Get the facts.* Make sure that you have all the information or evidence you need to understand exactly what the problem is.

2. *Weigh and decide.* Analyse the facts to identify the causes of the problem. Consider any alternative solutions to the problem, and decide which is likely to be the most successful.

3. *Take action.* Plan what you are going to do, establish goals and success criteria, and put the plan into effect.

4. *Check results.* Monitor the implementation of the plan.

This chapter looks at some common and typical people management problems:

- absenteeism;
- disciplinary issues;
- negative behaviour;
- poor timekeeping;
- underperformance.

Absenteeism

A frequent people problem you probably have to face is absenteeism. A survey on absence management by the Chartered Institute of Personnel and Development (CIPD) in 2009 revealed that on average employers lost 7.4 working days for each member of staff per year, and absence cost employers on average £666 per employee per year. Your own organization should have figures on average absence levels. If the levels in your department are below the average for the organization, or in the absence of that information, below the national average, you should not be complacent. You should continue to monitor individuals to find out whose absence levels are above the average and why. If your department's absence figures are significantly higher than the norm, you may have to take more direct action, such as discussing with individuals whose absence rates are high the reasons for their absences, especially when it has been self-certified. You may have to deal with recurrent short-term (one- or two-day) absence or longer-term sickness absence.

Recurrent short-term absence

Dealing with people who are repeatedly absent for short periods can be difficult. This is because it can be hard to determine whether the absences are justifiable, perhaps on medical grounds.

Many organizations provide guidelines to managers on the 'trigger points' for action (the amount of absence that needs to be investigated), perhaps based on analyses of the incidence of short-term absence and the level that is regarded as acceptable. (It might be possible to use software to generate analyses and data which can be made available direct to managers through a self-service system.) If guidelines do not exist you can seek advice from an HR specialist, if one is available. In the absence of either of these sources of help and in particularly difficult cases, it may be advisable to recommend to higher management that advice is obtained from an employment law expert.

This sort of guidance is not always available, though, and you may have to make up your own mind when to do something and what to do. A day off every other month might not be too serious, although if it happens regularly on a Monday (after weekends in Prague or Barcelona, perhaps?) or a Friday (before such weekends?) you might choose to have a word with the individual, not as a formal warning but just to let them know you are aware what is going on. There might be a medical or other acceptable explanation. Return-to-work interviews can provide valuable information: they give the individual ample opportunity to explain their absence.

In persistent cases of absenteeism you can hold an absence review meeting. Although this is more comprehensive than a return-to-work interview, it should not at this stage be presented as part of a disciplinary process. The meeting should be positive and constructive. If absence results from a health problem, you can find out what the employee is doing about it, and if necessary suggest that a doctor be consulted. Absences might alternatively be caused by problems facing a parent or a carer. In such cases you should be sympathetic, but you can reasonably discuss with the individual what steps can be taken to reduce the problem. You might be able to agree on flexible working if that can be arranged. The aim is to get the employee to discuss as openly as possible any factors affecting their attendance, and to agree any constructive steps that can be taken.

If you have held an attendance review meeting and agreed on the steps necessary to reduce the number of absences, but short-term absences persist without a satisfactory explanation, then another meeting can be held which emphasizes the employee's responsibility to attend work. Depending on the circumstances (each case should be dealt with on its merits), at this meeting you can link any positive support with an indication that following the provision of support, you expect absence levels to improve over a defined timescale (an improvement period). If this does not happen, the individual can expect more formal disciplinary action.

Long-term absence

Dealing with long-term absence can be difficult. The aim should be to facilitate the employee's return to work at the earliest reasonable point, while recognizing that in extreme cases the person might not be able to come back. In that case they can fairly be dismissed for lack of capability provided:

- the employee has been consulted at all stages;

- contact has been maintained with the employee – this is something you can usefully do as long as you do not appear to be pressing them to return to work before they are ready;

- appropriate medical advice has been sought from the employee's own doctor: note that the employee's consent is needed, the employee has the right to see the report, and it might be desirable to obtain a second opinion;

- all reasonable options for alternative employment have been reviewed, as well any other means of facilitating a return to work.

The decision to dismiss should only be taken if these conditions are satisfied. This is a tricky situation, and you should seek advice before taking action, from HR if available, or from an employment law expert.

Disciplinary issues

Employees can be dismissed because they are not capable of doing their assigned work, or for misconduct. It is normal to go through a formal disciplinary procedure containing staged warnings, but instant dismissal can be justified for gross misconduct (such as serious theft), which should be defined in the company's disciplinary procedure or employee handbook. Anyone with a year's service or more can claim unfair dismissal if their employer cannot show that one of these reasons applied, if the dismissal was not reasonable in the circumstances, if a constructive dismissal has taken place, or if there has been a breach of a customary or agreed redundancy procedure and there are no valid reasons for departing from that procedure.

Even if the employer can show to an employment tribunal that there was good reason to dismiss the employee, the tribunal will still have to decide whether or not the employer acted in a reasonable way at the time of dismissal. The principles defining 'reasonable' behaviour are in line with the principles of natural justice:

- The employee should be informed of the nature of the complaint.

- The employee should be given the chance to explain.

- The employee should be given the opportunity to improve, except in particularly gross cases of incapability or misconduct.

- The employee should be warned that dismissal will be a likely outcome if specified improvements do not take place.

- The employer's decision to dismiss should be based on sufficient evidence.

- The employer should take any mitigating circumstances into account.

- The offence or misbehaviour should merit the penalty of dismissal rather than some lesser penalty.

Your organization may have a statutory disciplinary procedure. You need to know what that procedure is and the part you are expected to play in implementing it. Whether or not there is a formal procedure, if you believe that disciplinary action is necessary you need you take the following steps when planning and conducting a disciplinary interview.

1. Get all the facts in advance, including statements from all the people involved.

2. Invite the employee to the meeting in writing, explaining why it is being held and that they have the right to have someone present at the meeting to speak on their behalf.

3. Ensure that the employee has reasonable notice (ideally at least two days).

4. Plan how you will conduct the meeting.

5. Line up another member of management to attend the meeting with you to take notes (they can be important if there is an appeal) and generally provide support.

6. Start the interview by stating the complaint to the employee and referring to the evidence.

7. Give the employee plenty of time to respond and state their case.

8. Take a break as required to consider the points raised and to relieve any pressure in the meeting.

9. Consider what action is appropriate, if any. Actions should be staged, starting with a recorded warning, followed if the problem continues by a first written warning, then a final written warning and lastly, if the earlier stages have been exhausted, disciplinary action, which can be dismissal in serious cases.

10. Deliver the decision, explaining why it has been taken, and confirm it in writing.

If all the stages in the disciplinary procedure have been completed and the employee has to be dismissed, or immediate dismissal can be justified on the grounds of gross misconduct, you might have to carry out the unpleasant duty of then dismissing the employee. Again, you should have a colleague or someone from HR with you when you do this. You should:

1. If possible, meet when the office is quiet, preferably on a Friday.

2. Keep the meeting formal and organized.

3. Write down what you are going to say in advance, giving the reasons and getting your facts, dates and figures right.

4. Be polite but firm. Read out what you have written down and make it clear that it is not open for discussion.

5. Ensure that the employee clears their desk and has no opportunity to take away confidential material or use their computer.

6. See the employee off the premises. Some companies use security guards as escorts but this is rather heavy-handed, although it might be useful to have someone on call in case of difficulties.

Negative behaviour

You may well come across negative behaviour from time to time on the part of one of the members of your team. This might take the form of lack of interest in the work, unwillingness to cooperate with you or other members of the team, complaining about the work or working conditions, grumbling at being asked to carry out a perfectly reasonable task, objecting strongly to being asked to do something extra (or even refusing to do it – 'It's not in my job description') or, in extreme cases, insolence. People exhibiting negative behaviour may be quietly resentful rather than openly disruptive. They mutter away in the background at meetings and lack enthusiasm.

As a manager you can tolerate a certain amount of negative behaviour as long as the individual works reasonably well and does not upset other team members. You have simply to say to yourself 'It takes all sorts', and put up with it, although you might quietly say during a review meeting 'You're doing a good job but...' If however you do take this line, you need to be specific. You must cite actual instances. It is no good making generalized accusations which will be either openly refuted or internalized by the receiver, making them even more resentful.

If the negative behaviour means that the individual's contribution is not acceptable and they are disruptive, then you must take action. Negative people can be quiet, but they are usually angry about something; their negative behaviour is an easy way of expressing their anger. To deal with the problem it is necessary to find out what has made the person angry.

Causes of negative behaviour

There are many possible causes of negative behaviour, including:

- a real or imagined slight from you or a colleague;

- a feeling of being put upon;

- a belief that the contribution made by the person is neither appreciated nor rewarded properly in terms of pay or promotion;

- resentment at what was perceived to be unfair criticism;

- anger directed at the company or you because what the individual considered to be a reasonable request (perhaps for leave or a transfer) was turned down, or because of a perceived unfair accusation.

Dealing with the problem

It is because there can be such a variety of real or imagined causes of negative behaviour that dealing with it becomes one of the most difficult tasks you have to undertake. If the action taken is crude or insensitive, the negative behaviour will only be intensified. You might end up having to invoke the disciplinary procedure, but this should be your last resort.

In one sense, it is easier to deal with an individual clear instance of negative behaviour. This can be handled on the spot. If the problem is one of general attitude rather than specific actions, it is more difficult to cope with. Hard evidence might not be available. When individuals are accused of being generally unenthusiastic or uncooperative, for example, they can simply go into denial, and accuse you of being prejudiced. Their negative behaviour might be reinforced.

If you have to deal with this sort of problem it is best to do it informally, either when it arises or at any point during the year when you feel that something has to be done about it. An annual formal performance review or appraisal meeting is not the right time, especially if it produces ratings which are linked to a pay increase. Raising the issue then will only put individuals on the defensive, and a productive discussion will be impossible.

The discussion may be informal, but it should have three clear objectives:

1. To discuss the situation with the individual, the aim being if possible to get them to recognize for themselves that they are behaving negatively. If this cannot be achieved, then the object is to bring to the person's attention your belief that their behaviour is unacceptable in certain ways.

2. To establish the reasons for the individual's negative behaviour so far as this is feasible.

3. To discuss and agree any actions the person could take to behave more positively, or what you or the organization could do to remove the causes of the behaviour.

Discussing the problem

Start by asking generally how the person feels about their work. Do they have any problems in carrying it out? Are they happy with the support they get from you or their colleagues? Are they satisfied that they are pulling their weight to the best of their ability?

You may find that this generalized start provides the basis for the next two stages, identifying the causes and remedies. It is best if individuals are encouraged to identify for themselves that there is a problem. But in many, perhaps most, cases this is unlikely to happen. Individuals might not recognize that they are behaving negatively, or will not be prepared to admit it.

You will then have to discuss the problem. You could say truthfully that you are concerned because the person seems to be unhappy, and you wish to know whether they feel that you or the organization is treating them unfairly. If so, you want to try to put things right. Give the person time to say their piece, then provide a rational response, dealing with the specific grievances they bring up. You can indicate that if the person is not satisfied with your explanation, they can have an opportunity to discuss the problem with a more senior manager, indicating that you recognize your judgement is not final.

If the response you get to these initial points does not bring out into the open the problem as you see it, you will have to explain how the individual's behaviour gives the impression of being negative. Be as specific as possible, bringing up actual instances. For example, a discussion could be based on the questions, 'Do you recall yesterday's team meeting?' 'How did you think it went?' 'How helpful do you think you were in dealing with the problem?' 'Do you remember saying…?' 'How helpful do you think that remark was?' 'Would it surprise you to learn that I felt you were not particularly helpful in the following ways…?'

Of course, even if you adopt this careful approach, there will be occasions when individuals refuse to admit that there is anything wrong with their behaviour. If you reach this impasse, you have no alternative but to spell out to them your perception of where they have gone wrong. But do this in a positive way: 'Then I think it is only fair for me to point out that your contribution (to the meeting) would have been more helpful if you had….'

Establishing causes

If the negative behaviour is because of a real or imagined grievance against you, a colleague or the organization as a whole, try to get the person to spell out what it is as precisely as possible. At this point your job is to listen, not to judge. People can be just as angry about imaginary slights as about real ones. You have to find out how they perceive the problem before you can deal with it.

It might emerge during the discussion that the problem has nothing to do with you or the company. Perhaps the individual has family troubles, or worries about health or finance. If this is the case you can be sympathetic, and may be able to suggest remedies in the form of counselling or practical advice from within or outside the organization.

If the perceived problem is related to you, colleagues or the organization, try to get chapter and verse so that you are in a position to take remedial action or to explain the real facts of the case.

Taking remedial action

If the problem rests with the individual, the objective is, of course, to get them to recognize for themselves that corrective action is necessary and what they need to do about it – with your help as necessary. In some situations you might suggest counselling or recommend a source of advice. But be careful, since you do not want to imply that there is something wrong with the person. You should go no further than suggesting they might find your proposal helpful, hinting that they perhaps do not really need the help, but might nevertheless benefit from it. You should be careful about offering to counsel someone yourself. It is better done by professional counsellors.

If there is anything specific that the parties involved in the situation can do, the line to take is that you and the employee can tackle the problem together. Cover the issues, 'This is what I will do', 'This is what the company will do', and 'What do you think you should do?' If there is no response to the last question, this is the point where you have to spell out the action you think the person needs to take. Be as specific as possible, and try to phrase your proposals as suggestions, not commands. A joint problem-solving approach is always best.

Ten steps to managing negative behaviour

1. Define the type of negative behaviour that is being exhibited. Make notes of examples.

2. Discuss the behaviour with the individual as soon as possible, aiming to get agreement about what they are doing and the impact it makes.

3. If they do not immediately agree that there is a problem, give actual examples of their behaviour and explain why you believe it to be negative.

4. Discuss and as far as possible agree reasons for the negative behaviour, including those attributed to the individual, yourself and the organization.

5. Discuss and agree possible remedies – actions on the part of the individual, yourself or the organization.

6. Monitor the actions taken and the results obtained.

7. If improvement is not achieved and the negative behaviour is significantly affecting the performance of the individual and the team, invoke the disciplinary procedure.

8. Start with a verbal warning, indicating the ways in which the person's behaviour must improve. Give a timescale and offers of further support and help as required.

9. If there is no improvement, issue a formal warning, setting out as specifically as possible what must be achieved over a defined period of time, and indicating the disciplinary action that could be taken if this is not done.

10. If the negative behaviour persists and continues seriously to affect performance, take the threatened disciplinary action.

Poor timekeeping

If you are faced with persistent lateness and your informal warnings to the individual concerned seem to have little effect, you might be forced to invoke the disciplinary procedure. If timekeeping does not improve this could go through the successive stages of a recorded oral warning, a written warning and a final written warning. If the final warning does not work, disciplinary action will have to be taken. In serious cases this means dismissal.

Note that this raises the difficult question of time limits. When you give a final warning, it will indicate that timekeeping must improve by a certain date, the improvement period. If it does improve by that date, and the slate is wiped clean, it might be assumed that the disciplinary procedure has to start again from scratch if the person's timekeeping deteriorates again. But it is in the nature of things that some people cannot sustain efforts to get to work on time for long, and deterioration often occurs. In these circumstances, do you have to keep on going through the warning cycles time after time?

The answer should be no, if you phrase your warning correctly. It is best to avoid setting a finite end date to a final warning period, since this does imply the 'wipe the slate clean' approach. Instead, state in the warning that the individual's timekeeping will be reviewed on a fixed date. If it has not improved, further disciplinary action is likely to be taken. If it has improved, no action will be taken, but the employee should be warned that further deterioration will make them liable to a shortened disciplinary procedure, which could for example use just a final warning stage, and set a shortened period between this renewed warning and the review date. If the poor timekeeping persists, at some point you will say 'enough is enough' and initiate the disciplinary action.

Underperformance

Perhaps there is someone who is underperforming in your team. If so, what can you do about it? Essentially, you have to spot that there is a problem, understand the cause of the problem, decide on a remedy and make the remedy work.

Poor performance can be the fault of the individual, but it could also arise because of poor leadership or problems in the system of work. If the problem lies with the individual, they might:

- not be capable of doing what is required (an issue of ability);
- not know how to do it (an issue of skill);
- not be willing to do it (an issue of attitude);
- not fully understand what is expected of them.

Inadequate leadership can be a cause of individual poor performance. It is the manager's responsibility to specify the results expected and the levels of skill and competence required. As likely as not, when people do not understand what they have to do, their manager is to blame.

Performance can also be affected by the system of work. If this is badly planned and organized or does not function well, people cannot fully be blamed for their poor performance. It is the fault of management, and they must put it right.

Assuming you are confident that neither poor leadership nor the system of work are the cause of the problem, these are the seven steps you can take to deal with underperformers:

1. Identify the areas of underperformance. Be specific.
2. Establish the causes of poor performance.
3. Agree on the action required.
4. Ensure that the necessary support (such as coaching, training or extra resources) is provided to enable the action to be successful.
5. Monitor progress and provide feedback.
6. Provide additional guidance as required.
7. As a last resort, invoke the capability or disciplinary procedure, starting with an informal warning.

Appendix: Human Resource Management Research Methods

HRM specialists and those studying for HR professional qualifications may be involved in conducting or taking part in research projects. Postgraduate students may well do so. Qualified HR specialists should keep up to date as part of their continuous professional development by studying publications such as those produced by the CIPD which present research findings, or by reading articles in HR journals such as *People Management* or academic journals based on research. Students must extend their understanding of HRM through reading about research findings.

The purpose of this appendix is to explain what is involved in planning and conducting research projects. This is done against the background of a review of the nature and philosophy of research. Descriptions are given of the main approaches used by researchers, including literature reviews, quantitative and qualitative methods, and collecting and analysing data.

The nature of research

Research is concerned with establishing what is, and from this predicting what will be. It does not decide what ought to be; that is for human beings interpreting the lessons from research in their own context. Research is about the conception and testing of ideas. This is an inductive, creative and imaginative process, although new information is normally obtained within the framework of existing theory and knowledge. Logic and rational argument are methods of testing ideas after they have been created.

What emerges from research is a theory – a well-established explanatory principle which has been tested and can be used to make predictions of future developments. A theory is produced by clear, logical and linear development of argument, with a close relationship between information, hypothesis and conclusion. Quality of information is a criterion for good research, as is the use of critical evaluation techniques, as described later in this appendix.

The production of narratives which depict events (case studies) and the collection of data through surveys are elements in research programmes, but they can stand alone as useful pieces of information which illustrate practice.

Research methodology is based on research philosophy, and uses a number of approaches, described later. There is often a choice about which philosophy or approach, or which combination of them, should be used.

The characteristics of good research

The characteristics of good research as identified by Phillips and Pugh (1987) are as follows. First, it is based on an open system of thought which requires continually testing, review and criticism of other ideas and a willingness to hazard new ideas. Second, the researcher must always be prepared to examine data critically, and to request the evidence behind conclusions drawn by others. Third, the researcher should always try to generalize the research, but within stated limits. This means attempting to extract understanding from the situation and to apply it to as many other situations as possible.

Research philosophy

Research can be based on a philosophy of positivism or phenomenology.

Positivism

Positivism is the belief that researchers should focus on facts (observable reality), look for causality and fundamental laws, reduce phenomena to their simplest elements (reductionism), formulate hypotheses and then test them. Researchers are objective analysts. The emphasis in positivism is on quantifiable observations that lend themselves to statistical analysis. It tends to be deductive (the process of using logical reasoning to reach a conclusion which necessarily follows from general premises).

Phenomenology

Phenomenology focuses more on the meaning of phenomena than on the facts associated with them. Researchers adopting this philosophy try to understand what is happening. Their approach is holistic, covering the complete picture, rather than reductionist. Researchers collect and analyse evidence, but their purpose is to use this data to develop ideas that can explain the meaning of things. They believe that reality is socially constructed rather than objectively determined. Using a phenomenological approach means that the research unfolds as it proceeds – early evidence is used to indicate how to move on to the next stage of evidence collection and analysis, and so on. It tends to be inductive (the process of reaching generalized conclusions from the observation of particular instances).

Table A.1   Advantages and disadvantages of alternative research philosophies

Advantages	Disadvantages
Positivism	
Wide coverage of the range of situations	Methods tend to be flexible and artificial
Can be fast and economical	Not very effective in understanding processes or the significance people attach to actions
May be relevant to policy decisions when statistics are aggregated in large samples	Not very helpful in generating theories
	Because it focuses on what is or what has been recently, it makes it hard for policy makers to infer what actions should take place in the future
Phenomenology	
Can look at change processes over time	Data gathering can take up a great deal of time and resources
Help to understand people's meanings	The analysis and interpretation of data may be difficult
Help to adjust to new issues and ideas as they emerge	May be harder than a positivist approach to control pace, progress and end points
Contribute to the development of new theories	Policy-makers may give low credibility to a phenomenological study
Gather data which is seen as natural rather than artificial	

Source: Easterby-Smith *et al* (1991).

Approaches to research design

As Valentin (2006) has commented, 'A positivist perspective has dominated mainstream management research and theory. This assumes a broad consensus concerning the goals and practices of management. Management is seen as a purely instrumental process, objective, neutral, simply concerned with methods to ensure control and efficiency in organizations.'

Planning and conducting research programmes

Against this background, the steps required to plan and conduct a research programme are set out below.

1.   Define the research area

This should be one that interests the researcher and has a clear link to an accepted theory or an important issue which is worth exploring. The research should generate fresh insights into the topic. It is necessary to undertake background reading at this stage by means of a preliminary review of the literature (particularly academic journals but also books, especially those based on research) to identify what has already been achieved in this area and any gaps (academic articles often include proposals on further research). The context within which the research is to be carried out needs to be explained and justified.

2.   Formulate an initial research question

This provides a rationale for the research. It is in effect a statement which answers the question, 'What is this research project intended to address and what is its potential contribution to increasing knowledge?' At this stage it is based on the outcome of the initial work carried out in step 1, but it will be refined and reformulated at a later stage when more information about the research has been made available.

3.   Review the literature

A literature review will focus mainly on academic journals. The aim is to establish what is already known about the topic, identify existing theoretical frameworks and find out what other relevant research has been carried out. The conduct of literature reviews is considered in more detail later in this appendix.

4.   Develop a theoretical framework

It is necessary to conduct the research within a clear theoretical framework. This will set out the models, concepts and theories which can be drawn on and developed to provide an answer to the research question. If an appropriate framework does not exist, a grounded theory approach may be required in which the researcher uses empirical evidence directly to establish the concepts and relationships that will be contained in the theory adopted as the research framework. It is important to be clear about the assumptions, conditions and limitations within which the investigation is taking place.

5.   Finalize the research question

The initial research question needs to be finalized in the light of the outcome of the earlier steps. The final research question will identify the issues to be explored and the problems to be investigated. It will include a statement of intent which will set out what the research is to achieve. This statement leads to the formulation of the hypotheses or propositions which will be tested by survey or experiment during the research programme.

6.   Formulate hypotheses or propositions

A hypothesis provisionally states a relationship between two concepts in such a way that the consequences of the statement being true can be tested. Hypotheses (there may be more than one) indicate the form the research project will take in the shape of obtaining and analysing the evidence required to test them. Hypotheses may be attached to the statement of the research question. A proposition is a proposal put forward as an explanation of an event, a possible situation or a form of behaviour which will be tested by the research.

7.   Design the research

This means considering initially what research philosophy which will be adopted. Is it to be positivist, phenomenological, or both? It is then necessary to establish the methodology. A decision needs to be made about the extent to which the research will be quantitative, qualitative, or again a combination of the two. Methods of collecting and analysing evidence and testing hypotheses or propositions are described. The sources of evidence and how they will be accessed are identified. This includes the analysis of primary and secondary source documents, further literature reviews, surveys and field work. The design must clearly indicate how it will address the research question, and be consistent with the theoretical framework. If at a later stage this is shown not to be the case, then the design has to be amended.

8.   Draw up a research programme

This covers how the research will be conducted, the timetable and the resources (funding, people, software and so on) required. Careful project planning is essential.

9.   Prepare and submit a proposal

This justifies the research by setting out the research question and the proposed methodology. It also describes the programme and the resources required.

10.   Conduct the research project

This includes obtaining and analysing the evidence from the various sources needed to answer the research question and prove or disprove hypotheses. The significance of the findings in relation to the research question and the hypotheses is discussed, and reference is made to relevant information provided in the literature. As described later in this appendix, this involves an extended literary review, data collection, the use of logical, analytical and critical thinking processes, and the use of statistical analysis where relevant.

11.   Develop conclusions

These draw together all the evidence. They provide the answer to the research question and explain why hypotheses have been accepted or rejected. The significance of the findings is also assessed in terms of how they contribute to the development of existing knowledge and understanding. Any limitations to the study should also be mentioned.

12.   Make recommendations

These set out management guidelines emerging from the research. They may also indicate any follow-up actions required if the research has been conducted within an organization.

The ethics of research

There are a number of ethical issues that affect research. They include the need for researchers generally to act with integrity, for example in their dealings with the organization in which they are researching and the people they deal with. They must also respect the rights of participants by not publishing any information that might harm their interests, and be honest about their role when participating in research, especially when they are participating observers.

Literature reviews

Literature reviews or searches are essential preliminary steps in any research project. They often focus on articles in academic journals, although textbooks may also be consulted, especially if they are based on research. It is necessary to know what has already been covered and the theories that have been developed, to provide leads and reference points or as the basis for a grounded theory approach.

Literature searches in academic journals are much easier now because of the Business Source Corporate database made available through EBSCO. CIPD members can access this through the CIPD website, and about 350 journals are available. In most cases articles can be downloaded free of charge, although some journals restrict this service for the first 12 months after publication. Searches can be made by subject matter, but unless the research is refined a huge number of references may be turned up – searching performance management produces more than 6,000 results! The search can be extended through the references included in articles. Google Research is another useful resource. The box provides a checklist to use when evaluating an article or text.

Literature evaluation checklist

- To what extent is the article/text relevant to my research?
- What was the aim of the article/text?
- To what extent was this aim achieved?
- Are the findings supported by rigorous and convincing research?
- Does the article/text present new and interesting ideas or perspectives?
- Is the article/text clear and persuasive?
- To what extent do I agree with the views expressed?

Quantitative and qualitative methods of research

One of the key decisions to be made in planning and conducting a research programme is the extent to which quantitative methods (which broadly follow the positivist philosophy) or qualitative methods (which broadly follow the phenomenological philosophy) are used.

Quantitative research

Quantitative research is empirical – based on the collection of factual data which is measured and quantified. It answers research questions from the viewpoint of the researcher. It may involve a considerable amount of statistical analysis using methods for collecting data such as questionnaires, surveys, observation and experiment. The collection of data is distinct from its analysis.

Qualitative research

Qualitative research aims to generate insights into situations and behaviour so that the meaning of what is happening can be understood. It emphasizes the interpretation of behaviour from the viewpoint of the participants. It is based on evidence that may not be easily reduced to numbers. It makes use of interviews, case studies and observation, but it may also draw on the information obtained from surveys. It may produce narratives or 'stories' describing situations, events or processes.

Comparison and use of quantitative or qualitative research

Quantitative research measures and predicts, whereas qualitative research describes and understands.

Contrasts between quantitative and qualitative research

Quantitative research	*Qualitative research*
numbers	words
researcher distant	researcher close
macro	micro
hard data	soft data
theory testing	theory building
static	process
structured	unstructured

Source: Bryman and Bell (2007).

As Valentin (2006) notes, mainstream management journals, especially American ones, focus on empirical research using quantitative methodologies. There is a growing trend in the United Kingdom to follow suit, but in Europe there is greater preference for qualitative over quantitative methods, with case studies being a popular approach.

However, the distinction between qualitative and quantitative research is sometimes blurred. Easterby-Smith *et al* (1991) mention that increasingly, researchers argue that an attempt should be made to mix methods to some extent, because this will provide more perspectives on the phenomena to be investigated.

Methods of collecting data

The main methods of collecting data are interviews, questionnaires, surveys, case studies, observation, diaries and experimental designs.

Interviews

Interviews are an important research method. They obtain factual data and insights into attitudes and feelings and can take three forms:

- *Structured*, which means that they are entirely concerned with obtaining answers to a pre-prepared set of questions. This ensures that every topic is covered and minimizes variations between respondents. But they may be too rigid and inhibit spontaneous and revealing reactions.

- *Unstructured*, which means that no questions have been prepared in advance and the person being interviewed is left free to talk about the subject without interruption or intervention. Such 'non-directive' interviews are supposed to provide greater insight into the interviewee's perspective, avoid fitting respondents into predetermined categories and enable interviewers to explore issues as they arise. But they can be inconsequential and lead to poor data which is difficult to analyse.

- *Semi-structured*, which means that the areas of interest have been predetermined and the key questions to be asked or information to be obtained have been identified. The interviewer may have a checklist but does not follow this rigidly. This approach enables the interviewer to phrase questions and vary their order to suit the special characteristics of each interviewee. It may avoid the problems of the completely structured or unstructured interview but it does require a considerable degree of skill on the part of the interviewer.

Interviews are basically qualitative but they can become more quantitative by the use of content analysis. This records the number of times reference is made in an interview to the key issues or areas of interest it was intended to cover.

The advantages of interviews are that they obtain information directly from people involved in the area that is being researched, and can provide insights into attitudes and perspectives that questionnaires and surveys will not reveal, thus promoting in-depth understanding. They enable the interviewer to probe answers and check that questions had been understood. But the disadvantages are that:

- the construction of the interview questions may result in leading questions or bland answers;

- interviewers may influence the interviewees' reactions by imposing their own reference frame;

- respondents may tell interviewers what they want to hear;

- they are time-consuming – to set up, to conduct and to analyse;

- they require considerable interviewing skills, including the abilities to recognize what is important and relevant, to probe when necessary, to listen and to control the interview so that it covers the ground it was intended to cover.

Questionnaires

Questionnaires collect data systematically by obtaining answers on the key issues and opinions that need to be explored in a research project. They are frequently used as a means of gathering information on matters of fact or opinion. They use a variety of methods: closed questions which require a yes or no answer, ranking in order of importance or value, and Likert scales. This last method, named after Rensis Likert, the American sociologist who invented it, asks respondents to indicate the extent to which they agree or disagree with a statement. For example in response to a statements such as 'I like my job' the choice may be 1 strongly agree, 2 agree, 3 disagree, 4 strongly disagree. Alternatively an extended scale may be used and respondents are asked to ring round the number that reflects their view about the statement (the higher the number, the greater the agreement). For example:

My contribution is fully recognized 1 2 3 4 5 6 7 8 9

Extended scales facilitate the quantitative analysis of responses to questionnaires.

To construct and use a questionnaire effectively it is necessary to:

- Identify the key issues and potential questions.
- Ensure questions are clear.
- Avoid asking two questions in one item.
- Avoid leading questions which supply their own answers.
- Decide on the structure of the questionnaire, including its length (not too many items) and the choice of scale.
- Code questions for ease of analysis.
- Start with simple factual questions, moving on later to items of opinion or values.
- Add variety and the opportunity to check consistency by interspersing positive statements such as 'I like working for my boss' with occasional associated negative ones such as 'I do not get adequate support from my boss'.
- Pilot test the questionnaire.
- Code results and analyse. Where rating scales have been used the analysis can be quantified for comparison purposes. Content analysis can be used to analyse narrative answers to open-ended questions.

Questionnaires can effectively gather factual evidence but are not so useful for researchers who are investigating how or why things are happening. It is also impossible to assess the degree of subjectivity that has crept in when expressing opinions. For example, HR managers may give an opinion of the extent to which a performance-related pay scheme has in fact improved performance, but the evidence to support that opinion will be lacking. This is where interviews can be much more informative.

Surveys

Surveys obtain information from a defined population of people. Typically they are based on questionnaires, but they can provide more powerful data than other methods by using a combination of questionnaires and interviews, and possibly focus groups (groups of people gathered together to answer and discuss specific questions). When developing and administering surveys the issues are:

- The definition of the purpose of the survey and the outcomes hoped for. These must be as precise as possible.

- The population to be covered. This may involve a census of the whole population. Alternatively, if the population is large, sampling will be necessary (see below).

- The choice of methods. Relying entirely on questionnaires may limit the validity of the findings. It is better, if time and the availability of finance permit, to complement them with interviews and possibly focus groups. Consideration has to be give to the extent to which triangulation (comparing the information obtained from different sources) is desirable (it usually is) and possible.

- The questions to which answers are required, whichever method is used.

- The design of questionnaires and the ways in which interview or focus groups, if used, should be structured.

- How the outcome of the survey will be analysed and presented, including the use of case studies.

In using surveys, and possibly other methods, it may not be feasible to cover the whole population (the sampling frame) and sampling will therefore be necessary. Sampling means that a proportion of the total population is selected for study, and the aim is to see that this proportion represents the characteristics of the whole population. The sample must not be biased, and that is why in large-scale surveys use is made of random sampling. In other words, the individuals covered by a survey are not selected in accordance with any criteria except that they exist in the population and can be reached by the survey. It is the equivalent of drawing numbers out of a hat. However, if the sample frame is considered to be already arranged randomly as in the electoral roll, then structured sampling – that is, sampling at regular intervals – can be employed.

Sampling can produce varying degrees of error depending on the size of the sample. Statistical techniques can be used to establish sample errors and confidence limits. For example, they might establish that a sampling error is 3 per cent and the confidence limit is 95 per cent. This could be reasonably satisfactory, depending on the nature of the research (medical research aims to achieve 100 per cent confidence).

Case studies

A case study is a description or history of an event or sequence of events in a real-life setting. In learning and development, case studies are analysed by trainees in order to learn something by diagnosing the causes of a problem and working out how to solve it.

Case studies are used extensively in HRM research as a means of collecting empirical evidence in a real-life context. Information is collected about an event or a set of events which establishes what has happened, how it happened and why it happened. Case studies provide information which contributes to the creation of a theory as part of a grounded theory approach, or the validation of an established theory. In addition, they can take the form of stories or narratives which illuminate a decision or a set of decisions, why they were taken, how they were implemented and with what result. They can illustrate a total situation and describe the processes involved, and how individuals and groups behave in a social setting.

Case study protocol sets out the objectives of the research, how the case study will support the achievement of those objectives, including the evidence required, and how the work of producing the case study will be conducted. The methodology covers:

- sources of evidence – interviews, observation, documents and records;

- the need to use multiple sources of evidence (triangulation) so far as possible;

- the questions to which answers need to be obtained;

- how the case study should be set up, including informing those involved of what is taking place and enlisting their support;

- the schedule of interviews and other evidence-collection activities;

- how the case study database recording the evidence will be set up and maintained;

- how the case study will be presented – including the chain of evidence so that the reader can follow the argument and trace the development of events, the headings and report guidelines (these may be finalized during the course of the exercise), and whether or not the name of the organization will be revealed on publication (named case studies are more convincing than anonymous ones);

- how approval will be sought for the publication of the case study, especially if it reveals the name of the organization.

Case studies are useful ways of collecting information on the reality of organizational life and processes, but there is a danger of their being no more than a story or an anecdote which does not contribute to greater knowledge or understanding. Quite a lot of skill and persistence is required from the researcher in gaining support, ensuring that relevant and revealing information is obtained, and presenting the case study as a convincing narrative from which valid and interesting conclusions can be derived. All this must be done without taking a biased view, which can be difficult.

Observation

Observation of individuals or groups at work is a method of getting a direct and realistic impression of what is happening. It can be done by a detached or an involved observer, or by participant observation.

Detached observers simply study what is going on without getting involved with the people concerned. They may only get a superficial impression of what is happening, and may be resented by the people under observation as 'eavesdropping'.

Involved observers work closely with employees, and can move around, observe and participate as appropriate. This means that they can get closer to events and are more likely to be accepted, especially if the objectives and methods have been agreed in advance.

Participant observation in the fullest sense means that the researcher becomes an employee and experiences the work and the social processes that take place at first hand. This can provide powerful insights but is time-consuming and requires considerable skill and persistence.

The issues with any form of observation are getting close enough to events to understand their significance, then analysing the mass of information which might be produced in order to produce findings that contribute to answering the research question.

Diaries

Getting people to complete diaries of what they do is a method of building a realistic picture of how people, especially managers, spend their time.

Experimental designs

Experimental designs involve setting up an experimental group and a control group and then placing subjects at random in one of these two groups. The conditions under which the experimental group functions are then manipulated and the outcomes compared with the control group, whose conditions remain unchanged. The classic case of an experimental design was the Hawthorne experiment, the results of which had a major impact on thinking about how groups function and on the human relations movement. But this was exceptional. It is much easier to use experiments in a laboratory setting, which has been done many times with students. But there is always the feeling that such experiments do not really reflect real-life conditions.

Processes involved in research

This section describes the logical, analytical and critical thinking processes that are used in research: deduction, induction, hypothesis testing, grounded theory, paradigms and critical evaluation.

Deduction

Research involves deduction, which is the process of using logical reasoning to reach a conclusion which necessarily follows from general or universal premises. If the premises are correct so is the deduction. The conclusion is therefore contained within the evidence. It is not a creative or imaginative argument which produces new ideas.

Induction

Research can also be based on induction, which is the process of reaching generalized conclusions from the observation of particular instances. In contrast to deduction, inductive conclusions may be tentative but they contain new ideas. A creative leap may be required to reach them. Karl Popper (1972) referred to the problem of induction, which is that while science is seen as rational, deductive, logical, certain and objective, scientific progress seems to depend on processes that are imaginative, not entirely logical and tentative. But in research both deductive and inductive reasoning can be used in hypothesis testing.

Hypothesis testing

Formulating a hypothesis is an important element in a research project in that it provides a basis for the development of theory, and the collection and analysis of data. A hypothesis is a supposition – a tentative explanation of something. It is a provisional statement that is taken to be true for the purpose of argument or a study, and usually relates to an existing wider body of knowledge or theory. A hypothesis has to be tested, and should be distinguished from a theory, which by definition has already been tested. A good hypothesis contains two concepts and proposes a relationship between the two. A working hypothesis is a general hypothesis that has been operationalized so that it can be tested.

Hypothesis formulation and testing uses the strengths of both deductive and inductive argument, the former entirely conclusive but unimaginative, the latter tentative but creative. Induction produces ideas, deduction tests them.

To test a hypothesis, data has to be obtained which will demonstrate that its predicted consequences are true or false. Simply leaping to the conclusion that a hypothesis is true because a single cause of the consequence has been observed falls into a trap, which logicians call the fallacy of affirming the consequent. There might be alternative and more valid causes. The preferred method of testing is that of denying the consequent. This is 'falsification' as advocated by Popper (1959). His view was that however much data may be assembled to support a hypothesis, it is not possible to reach a conclusive proof of the truth of that hypothesis. Popper therefore proposed that it was insufficient simply to assemble confirmatory evidence. What must also be obtained is evidence that refutes the hypothesis. Only one instance of refutation is needed to falsify a theory, whereas however many confirmations of the theory exist, it will still not be proved conclusively. He illustrated his concept of falsification with swans. The hypothesis is that all swans are white, and someone who stayed in Great Britain and never visited a zoo might think this was the case. But a visit to Australia would lead to the discovery that swans can also be black. It is best, according to Popper, to take a falsification view and search for swans that are not white. This means that the original hypothesis has to be modified to state that swans can be either white or black.

Grounded theory

Grounded theory is an inductive method of developing the general features of a theory by grounding the account in empirical observations or evidence. The researcher uses empirical evidence directly to establish the concepts and relationships that will be contained in the theory. Evidence is collected from both primary sources (in other words, obtained directly by the researcher from the originator of the evidence) and secondary sources (in other words, information that is already available in the literature or on the world wide web). Use is made of triangulation, the corroboration of evidence by comparing what has emerged from different sources.

Paradigms

The term 'paradigm' has become popularized as meaning a way of looking at things. It is often used loosely, but properly it means the philosophical and theoretical framework of a scientific school or discipline within which theories, laws and generalizations and the experiments performed in support of them are formulated. In other words, it is a common perspective which underpins the work of theorists so that they use the same approach to conducting research.

Critical evaluation

Critical evaluation involves making informed judgements about the value of ideas and arguments. It uses critical thinking, which is the process of analysing and evaluating the quality of ideas, theories and concepts in order to establish the degree to which they are valid and supported by the evidence (evidence-based) and the extent to which they are biased. It means reflecting on and interpreting data, drawing warranted conclusions, and identifying faulty reasoning, assumptions and biases. It is necessary to test propositions using the boxed checklist.

Testing propositions checklist

- Was the scope of the investigation sufficiently comprehensive?
- Are the instances representative or have they been selected simply to support a point of view?
- Are there contradictory instances that have not been looked for?
- Does the proposition conflict with other propositions for which they are equally good grounds?

- If there are any conflicting beliefs or contradictory items of evidence, have they been put to the test against the original proposition?

- Could the evidence lead to other equally valid conclusions?

- Are there any other factors that have not been taken into account which may have influenced the evidence and therefore the conclusion?

- Critical evaluation requires clear thinking and the application of logical reasoning to establish the validity of a proposition, concept or idea. It is necessary to spot fallacious and misleading arguments. A fallacy is an unsound form of argument leading to an error in reasoning or a misleading impression. The most common forms of fallacy which need to be discerned in other people's arguments or avoided in your own are summarized in the next box.

Common logical fallacies

- Sweeping statements: over-simplifying the facts or selecting instances favourable to a contention while ignoring those that conflict with it.

- Potted thinking: using slogans and catchphrases to extend an assertion in an unwarrantable fashion.

- Special pleading: focusing too much on your own case and failing to see that there may be other points of view.

- Reaching false conclusions: forming the view that because some are, then all are. An assertion about several cases is twisted into an assertion about all cases. The conclusion does not follow the premise. This is what logicians call the 'undistributed middle', which occurs when a syllogism is expressed as: All A is B. All C is B. Therefore all A is C. The conclusion all A is C is false because although everything that applies to A and C also applies to B, there is nothing in their relationship to B which connects A and C together.

- Affirming the consequent: leaping to the conclusion that a hypothesis is true because a single cause of the consequence has been observed.

- Begging the question: taking for granted what has yet to be proved.

- Chop logic: 'Contrarywise', continued Tweedledee, 'if it was so, it might be, and if it were so, it would be; but as it isn't it ain't. That's logic.' Chop logic may not always be as bad as that, but it is about drawing false conclusions and using dubious methods of argument. Examples are selecting instances favourable to a contention while ignoring those that contend with it, twisting an argument used by an opponent to mean something quite different from what was intended, diverting opponents by throwing on them the burden of proof for something they have not maintained, ignoring the point in dispute, and reiterating what has been denied and ignoring what has been asserted. Politicians know all about chop logic.

The boxed checklist can be used when carrying out critical evaluation.

Critical evaluation checklist

- Is the research methodology sufficiently rigorous and appropriate?
- Are the results and conclusions consistent with the methodology used and its outcomes?
- Have hypotheses been stated clearly and tested thoroughly?
- Do there appear to be any misleading errors of omission or bias?
- Are any of the arguments tendentious?
- Are inferences, findings and conclusions derived from reliable and convincing evidence?
- Has a balanced approach been adopted?
- Is the perspective adopted by the researchers stated clearly?
- Have any underlying assumptions been identified and justified?
- Have the component parts been covered in terms of their interrelationships and their relationship with the whole?
- Have these component parts been disaggregated for close examination?
- Have they been reconstructed into a coherent whole based on underlying principles?

Statistical analysis

Whichever approach or combination of approaches is used, the results have to be analysed and presented in reports, journal articles, papers or books. Quantitative research clearly involves statistical analysis. Reports on qualitative research may be largely descriptive, but qualitative research is often supported by quantitative research and statistical analysis to illuminate and support the findings.

In general, the statistical analysis of quantified information is used to:

- identify and convey salient facts about the population under consideration;

- test hypotheses;

- make predictions on what is likely to happen;

- build a model that describes how a situation probably works;

- answer questions about the strength of evidence and how much certainty can be attached to predictions and models.

Statistics are used to describe and summarize data relating to a 'population', in other words a homogeneous set of items with variable individual values. This involves measuring frequencies, central tendencies and dispersion. They are also used to analyse the data and the sample from which the data was obtained, to measure the relationships between variables (correlation, regression and the chi-squared test), to establish the relation between cause and effect (causality) and to assess the degree of confidence that can be attached to conclusions (tests of significance). A wide variety of software is available to conduct the more sophisticated analyses.

Frequency

The number of times individual items in a population or set occur is represented in frequency distributions, expressed in tabular form or graphically. Some commonly used types of graph are illustrated in Figure A.1.

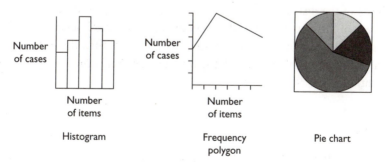

Figure A.1   Examples of charts

Measures of central tendency

Measures of central tendency identify the middle or centre of a set of data. There are three types:

- *Arithmetic average or mean* – the total of items or scores in a set divided by the number of individual items in the set. It may give a distorted picture because of large items at either end of the scale.

- *Median* – the middle item in a range of items (often used in pay surveys, when the arithmetic mean is likely to be distorted).

- *Mode* – the most commonly occurring item.

Measures of dispersion

It is often useful to measure the extent to which the items in a set are dispersed or spread over a range of data. This can be done in several ways:

- By identifying the upper quartile or lower quartile of a range of data. The strict definition of an upper quartile is the value that 25 per cent of the values in the distribution exceed, and the lower quartile is the value below which 25 per cent of the values in a distribution occur. More loosely, especially when looking at pay distributions, the upper and lower quartiles are treated as ranges rather than points in a scale, and represent the top and the bottom 25 per cent of the distribution respectively.

- By presenting the total range of values from top to bottom, which might be misleading if there are exceptional items at either end.

- By calculating the inter-quartile range, the range between the value of the upper quartile and that of the lower quartile. This can present more revealing information about the distribution than the total range.

- By calculating the standard deviation, which is used to indicate the extent to which the items or values in a distribution are grouped together or dispersed in a normal distribution (that is, one that is reasonably symmetrical around its average). As a rule of thumb, two-thirds of the distribution will be less than one standard deviation from the mean, 95 per cent of the distribution will be less than two standard deviations from the mean, and less than 1 per cent of the distribution will be more than three standard deviations from the mean. Another measure of dispersion is variance, which is the square of a standard deviation.

Correlation

Correlation represents the relationship between two variables. If they are highly correlated they are strongly connected to each other, and vice versa. In statistics, correlation is measured by the coefficient of correlation, which varies between −1 and +1 to indicate totally negative and totally positive correlations respectively. A correlation of zero means that there is no relationship between the variables. Establishing the extent to which variables are correlated is an important feature of HRM research: for example, assessing the degree to which a performance management system improves organizational performance. But correlations do not indicate causal relationships. They can only show that X is associated with Y, but this does not necessarily mean that X causes Y. Multiple correlation looks at the relationship between more than two variables.

Regression

Regression is another way of looking at the relationship between variables. Regression analysis examines how changes in levels of X relate to changes in levels of Y. A regression line (a trend line or line of best fit) can be traced on a scattergram expressing values of one variable on one axis and values of the other variable on another axis, as shown in Figure A.2.

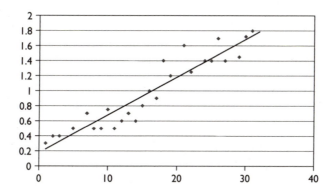

Figure A.2   A scattergram with regression (trend) line

A trend line like this can be drawn by hand as a line of best fit, but it can be calculated mathematically with greater accuracy. The distances of points from the trend line (the residuals) can be calculated as a check on the reliability of the line.

Multiple regression analysis can be conducted with the aid of a computer, which enables the values of additional variables to be predicted under various combinations of conditions.

The chi-squared test

The chi-squared test uses a statistical formula to assess the degree of agreement between the data actually obtained and that expected under a particular hypothesis.

The null hypothesis approach

A null hypothesis is a method of testing a hypothesis that is frequently used by researchers, in which it is assumed that there is no relationship between two or more variables. It asks the question 'Could the hypothetical relationship have been caused by chance?' If the answer is no, then the hypothesis is worth pursuing. However, it does not prove that the hypothesis is correct; it only indicates that something is worth pursuing. It can be associated with the chi-squared test.

Causality

Causality – determining the link between independent and dependent variables (cause and effect) – is a major issue in research, especially in the HRM field. As mentioned earlier, it may be relatively easy to establish correlations in the shape of a demonstration that X is associated with Y; it is much more difficult and sometimes impossible to prove that X *causes* Y. There are a number of reasons for this, of which the three set out below are the most important.

First, the issue is complicated because of the need to distinguish between necessary and sufficient causes.

Necessary cause: If X is a necessary cause of Y, then the presence of Y necessarily implies the presence of X. However, the presence of X does not imply that Y will occur.

Sufficient cause: If X is a sufficient cause of Y, then the presence of Y necessarily implies the presence of X. However, another cause Z might alternatively cause Y. If so, the presence of Y does not imply the presence of X.

Second, complications arise because of the phenomenon of multiple causation. There may be a number of factors contributing to a result. Researchers pursuing the holy grail of trying to establish what HRM contributes to firm performance are usually confronted with a number of reasons a firm has done well in addition to adopting 'best practice' HRM, whatever that is. Statistical methods can be used to 'control' some variables (that is, eliminate them from the analysis), but it is difficult if not impossible to ensure that HRM practices have been completely isolated and that their direct impact on firm performance has been measured. Multivariate analysis is used where there is more than one dependent variable and the dependent variables cannot be combined.

Third, there is the phenomenon of reverse causation, when a cause is predated by an effect – A might have caused B, but alternatively B may have come first and be responsible for A. For example, it is possible to demonstrate that firms with effective performance management schemes do better than those without. But it might equally be the case that it is high-performing firms that introduce effective performance management. It can be hard to be certain.

Tests of significance

Significance as a statistical concept refers to the degree to which an event could have occurred by chance. At the heart of statistical science lies a simple idea, that the chance or probability of various patterns of events can be predicted. When a particular pattern is observed it is possible to work out the chances of its occurrence, given our existing state of knowledge or by making certain assumptions. If something has been observed that is unlikely to have occurred by chance, this occurrence can be accepted as significant. The problem is that any attempt to reach general conclusions may have to rely on fragmentary data. It is usually necessary to rely on samples of the population being studied, and all sampling is subject to experimental error – the result can only be expressed in terms of probability, and confidence limits will have to be placed on it. These can be calculated in terms of the standard error that might be expected from a sample. A standard error is the estimated standard deviation of a sample mean from a true mean. This implies that on approximately 95 per cent of occasions the estimate of the mean provided by the sample will be within two standard errors of the true mean.

HRM research methods – key learning points

The nature of research
Research is concerned with establishing what is, and from this predicting what will be. It is about the conception and testing of ideas.

Research philosophy
Research design can be based on a philosophy of positivism or phenomenology.

Positivism is the belief that researchers should focus on facts (observable reality), look for causality and fundamental laws.

Phenomenology is concerned more with the meaning of phenomena than the facts associated with them.

Planning and conducting research programmes
1. Define the research area.

2. Formulate an initial research question.

3. Review the literature.

4. Assess the existing theoretical frameworks.

5. Formalize the research question.

6. Formulate hypotheses.

7. Establish the methodology.

8. Draw up a research programme.

9. Prepare and submit a proposal.

10. Collect and analyse evidence.

11. Develop conclusions.

Literature review

Literature reviews or searches are essential preliminary steps in any research project. They often focus on articles in academic journals, although textbooks may also be consulted, especially if they are based on research.

Approaches to research

Research can be quantitative or qualitative. It can use inductive or deductive methods. It involves the testing of hypotheses, and may adopt a grounded theory approach, in other words an inductive method of developing the general features of a theory by grounding the account in empirical observations or evidence. Use may be made of paradigms – common perspectives which underpin the work of theorists so that they use the same approach to conducting research. Informed judgements about the value of ideas and arguments are made through critical evaluation. This makes use of critical thinking, which is the process of analysing and evaluating the quality of ideas, theories and concepts in order to establish the degree to which they are valid and supported by the evidence.

Methods of collecting data

- Interviews obtain factual data and insights into attitudes and feelings and can be structured, unstructured or semi-structured.

- Questionnaires collect data systematically by obtaining answers on the key issues and opinions that need to be explored in a research project.

- Surveys obtain information from a defined population of people.

- Case studies collect empirical evidence in a real-life context.

The basics of statistical analysis

The statistical analysis of quantified information is used to:

- identify and convey salient facts about the population under consideration;

- test hypotheses;

- make predictions on what is likely to happen;

- build a model that describes how a situation probably works;

- answer questions about the strength of evidence and how much certainty can be attached to predictions and models.

References

Bryman, A and Bell, E (2007) *Business Research Methods*, 2nd edn, Oxford University Press, Oxford

Easterby-Smith, M, Thorpe, R and Lowe, A (1991) *Management Research: An introduction*, Sage, London

Phillips, E M and Pugh, D S (1987) *How to Get a PhD*, Open University Press, Milton Keynes

Popper, K (1959) *The Logic of Scientific Discovery*, Hutchinson, London

Popper, K (1972) *Conjectures and Refutations*, Routledge and Kegan Paul, London

Valentin, C (2006) Researching human resource development: emergence of a critical approach to HRD enquiry, *International Journal of Training and Development*, **10** (1), pp 17–29

Author Index

Subject Index